International Debt Statistics 2017

International Debt Statistics 2017

WORLD BANK GROUP

1818 H Street NW, Washington DC 20433
Telephone: 202-473-1000; Internet: www.worldbank.org

1 2 3 4 19 18 17 16

ISBN (paper): 978-1-4648-0994-1
ISBN (electronic): 978-1-4648-0995-8
DOI: 10.1596/978-1-4648-0994-1
ISSN (paper): 2310-2667
ISSN (electronic): 2310-2675

Cover design: Jomo Tariku, World Bank Group
Cover image by Jomo Tariku, World Bank Group. Permission required for reuse.

Library of Congress Cataloging-in-Publication Data has been applied for

Table of Contents

Preface

This year's edition of *International Debt Statistics*, successor to *Global Development Finance* and *World Debt Tables*, and the fourth in the series, is designed to respond to user demand for timely, comprehensive data on trends in external debt in low- and middle-income countries. It also provides summary information on the external debt of high-income countries and public (domestic and external) debt for a select group of countries.

The World Bank's Debtor Reporting System (DRS), from which the aggregate and country tables presented in this report are drawn, was established in 1951. *World Debt Tables*, the first publication that included DRS external debt data, appeared in 1973 and gained increased attention during the debt crisis of the 1980s. Since then, the publication and data have undergone numerous revisions and iterations to address the challenges and demands posed by the global economic conditions.

Presentation of and access to data have been refined to improve the user experience. The printed edition of *International Debt Statistics 2017* now provides a summary overview and a select set of indicators, while an expanded dataset is available online (datatopics.worldbank.org/debt/ids).

By providing comprehensive and timely data that reflects the latest additions and revisions, and by expanding the scope of the data available online, we aim to serve the needs of our users and to reach a wider audience. Improvements in data dissemination are matched with ongoing efforts to improve the quality and timeliness of data collection. In partnership with the major providers of debt data management systems to low- and middle-income countries, the Commonwealth Secretariat (COMSEC) and the United Nations Conference on Trade and Development (UNCTAD), we are working toward an established standard code and a set of system links that will enable countries to provide their DRS reports electronically in a seamless and automated data exchange process.

As these changes take place, we welcome your feedback and suggestions for further improvements at data@worldbank.org.

Haishan Fu
Director, Development Data Group

Acknowledgments

This volume was prepared by the Financial Data Team of the Development Data Group (DECDG), led by Evis Rucaj under the management of Grant Cameron and comprising Parul Agarwal, Karla Mirari Yee Amezaga, Peter Bourke, Cynthia Nyanchama Nyakeri, Malvina Pollock, Sun Hwa Song, Rubena Sukaj, Rasiel Vellos, and Alagiriswamy Venkatesan, who worked closely with other teams in DECDG. The team was assisted by Elysee Kiti. The overview of current developments was prepared by Malvina Pollock, Evis Rucaj, and Rasiel Vellos in consultation with the staff of DECDG; country economists reviewed the data tables. The work was carried out under the direction of Haishan Fu. Valuable input was provided by the Vice Presidency, Developmental Economics, and from the Chief Economist, Operations and Strategy department.

The online database was prepared by Shelley Fu and William Prince. International Debt Statistics electronic products were prepared by a team led by Malarvizhi Veerappan under the supervision of Soong Sup Lee and comprising Ramgopal Erabelly, Shelley Fu, Karthik Krishnamoorthy, Ugendran Machakkalai, and Nacer Megherbi. The cover was designed by Jomo Tariku. Susan Graham, Jewel McFadden, and Nora Ridolfi from the World Bank's Formal Publishing Program coordinated the publication and dissemination of the book.

User Guide to Tables

International Debt Statistics 2017 focuses on financial flows, trends in external debt, and other major financial indicators for low-, middle-, and high-income countries. The report includes more than 200 time series indicators from 1970 to 2015 for most reporting countries. This edition of *International Debt Statistics* (IDS) has been reconfigured to offer a more condensed presentation of the principal indicators, along with additional tables showcasing quarterly external debt statistics and public sector debt.

Tables

Aggregate Tables

The aggregate tables are labeled by region name. Data are shown for all low- and middle-income countries and six regional groups (East Asia and Pacific, Europe and Central Asia, Latin America and the Caribbean, Middle East and North Africa, South Asia, and Sub-Saharan Africa).

Country Tables

Country tables are labeled by country name and ordered alphabetically. Data are shown for 123 low- and middle-income countries that report public and publicly guaranteed external debt to the World Bank's Debtor Reporting System (DRS). The tables also include key debt ratios and the composition of external debt stocks and flows for each country.

Each table shows a time series with the most recent six years, as well as 2000 and 2005 as companion years. Full time series data are available for all countries in the World Bank's Open Data website (http://data.worldbank.org/data-catalog/international-debt-statistics).

Statistics

The general cutoff date for countries to report data for this publication was end-September 2016. The economic aggregates presented in the tables are prepared for the convenience of users. Although debt ratios can give useful information about developments in a debt-servicing capacity, conclusions drawn from them will not be valid unless accompanied by careful economic evaluation.

The macroeconomic data provided are collected from national statistical organizations, which in some cases may be subject to a considerable margin of error. The usual care must be taken in interpreting the ratios, particularly for the most recent years, because figures may be preliminary and subject to revision.

Notes at the bottom of each country table summarize major events that have taken place in the country in recent years; describe the sources of information for short-term and private nonguaranteed external debt if the reports were not provided by the country; and highlight main issues in the data collection process. Unless otherwise specified, data on long-term public and publicly guaranteed external debt for 2015 are based on reports provided by the country.

More detailed information on data sources, methodology, and compilation is provided in the appendix at the back of this book.

Aggregate Measures for Income Groups and Regions

Aggregate measures for income groups and regions include the 123 low- and middle-income countries that report public and publicly guaranteed external debt to the World Bank's DRS, whenever data are available. The aggregate "All low- and middle-income countries" is the sum of data for 123 countries.

Classification of Countries

For operational and analytical purposes, the World Bank's main criterion for classifying countries is gross national income (GNI) per capita (calculated by the *World Bank Atlas* method). Every country is classified as low-income, middle-income, or high-income. Low- and middle-income countries are sometimes referred to as developing countries. The term is used for convenience; it is not intended to imply that all countries in the group are experiencing similar development or that other countries have reached a preferred or final stage of development. Because GNI per capita changes over time, the country composition of income groups may change from one edition of *International Debt Statistics* to the next. Once the classification is fixed for an edition, based on GNI per capita in the most recent year for which data are available, all historical data presented are based on the same country grouping.

Symbols

0 or 0.0 means zero or small enough that the number would round to zero at the displayed number of decimal places.

.. means that data are not available or that aggregates cannot be calculated because of missing data in the years shown.

$ indicates current U.S. dollars unless otherwise specified.

User Guide to IDS Online Tables

The extended version of country tables that were previously available in the *International Debt Statistics* print edition is now available online. Using an automated query process, these reference tables will be updated based on the revisions to the International Debt Statistics database.

Users can access all the online tables, download the PDF version of the publication, and view the report as an eBook on ISSUU, as well as access the database and download the archived editions of the publication by going to http://data.worldbank.org/products/ids.

How to Access IDS Online Country Tables

To access the IDS online tables, visit http://datatopics.worldbank.org/debt/ids and select from "Country," "Region," or "Topic" options.

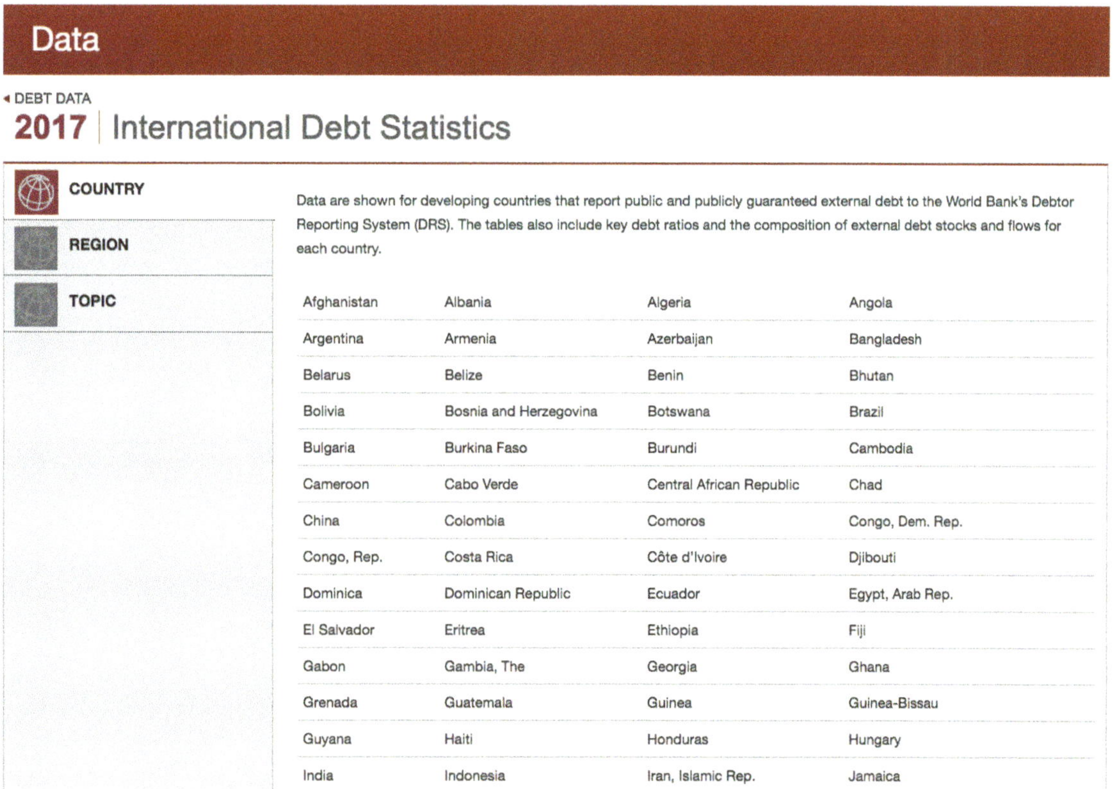

To access a specific country table directly without going through the above landing page, use the URL http://datatopics.worldbank.org/debt/ids/ and the country code (for example, http://datatopics.worldbank.org/debt/ids/country/DZA to view the table for Algeria). Similarly, to view the regional table, click on the "Region" tab and select one of the listed regions (for example http://datatopics.worldbank.org/debt/ids/region/SAS to view the table for South Asia).

2017 | International Debt Statistics

Data > Data Topics > Debt Data > Country Tables > Afghanistan

$ millions, unless otherwise indicated	2009	2010	2011	2012	2013	2014	2015
1. Summary external debt data							
External debt stocks	2,133.8	2,469.9	2,423.3	2,627.4	2,708.6	2,576.8	2,554.7
Long-term external debt	1,985.4	2,097.0	1,966.4	2,023.3	2,071.4	2,097.1	1,999.1
Public and publicly guaranteed	1,985.4	2,097.0	1,966.4	2,023.3	2,071.4	2,097.1	1,999.1
Private nonguaranteed	0.0	0.0	0.0	0.0	0.0	0.0	0.0
Use of IMF credit	131.1	352.8	355.2	372.6	387.6	375.6	334.8
Short-term external debt	17.4	20.2	101.7	231.6	249.6	104.1	220.8
of which interest arrears on long-term	17.4	20.2	66.7	209.6	218.6	85.1	187.8
Official creditors	17.3	20.2	66.7	209.6	218.6	85.1	187.8
Private creditors	0.0	0.0	0.0	0.0	0.0	0.0	0.0
Memo: principal arrears on LDOD	56.5	54.2	54.1	54.2	55.1	55.1	1.0
Official creditors	56.1	53.8	54.1	54.2	55.1	55.1	1.0
Private creditors	0.4	0.4	0.0	0.0	0.0	0.0	0.0
External debt flows							
Disbursements	132.1	126.2	84.6	81.2	70.4	35.9	31.7
Long-term external debt	96.4	108.8	76.0	62.2	52.1	35.9	31.7
IMF purchases	35.7	17.4	8.6	18.9	18.3	0.0	0.0
Principal repayments	1.3	3.1	1.0	0.9	4.7	16.8	27.9
Long-term external debt	1.3	3.1	1.0	0.9	0.9	4.2	8.4
IMF repurchases	0.0	0.0	0.0	0.0	3.7	12.6	19.5
Net flows	130.8	123.1	118.7	67.3	74.8	7.1	17.9
Long-term external debt	95.1	105.6	75.0	61.4	51.2	31.8	23.3
Short-term external debt	0.0	0.0	35.0	-13.0	9.0	-12.0	14.0
Interest payments	6.7	7.6	9.0	9.9	9.4	8.5	10.2
Long-term external debt	6.0	6.5	7.0	8.9	8.2	7.5	8.9
IMF charges	0.7	1.1	0.8	0.3	0.1	0.3	0.1
Short-term external debt	0.0	0.0	1.2	0.8	1.1	0.7	1.2
Net transfers on external debt	124.1	115.5	109.6	57.4	65.4	-1.4	7.7
Total debt service paid	8.0	10.7	10.0	10.8	14.1	25.3	38.0
Long-term external debt	7.3	9.7	8.0	9.7	9.2	11.7	17.3
IMF repurchases and charges	0.7	1.1	0.8	0.3	3.8	13.0	19.6
2. Other non-debt resource inflows							
Foreign direct investment	87.3	213.7	75.6	91.2	94.0	59.6	53.6
Portfolio equity	-1.0	0.0	-0.4	0.0	2.0	0.0	0.0
Grants (excluding technical coop.)	4,042.3	5,156.0	5,670.3	5,939.2	5,718.8	4,442.4	4,281.1
Memo: technical coop. grants	711.0	957.3	893.1	863.2	898.4	823.9	594.8

Indicators

The indicator codes for each of the indicators online and in the publication are listed below. To view a specific indicator online, go to http://data.worldbank.org/indicator/ and add the indicator code at the end of the url; for example, to view a page for total debt stocks, this line should be in your browser: http://data.worldbank.org/indicator/DT.DOD.DECT.CD.

1. SUMMARY EXTERNAL DEBT DATA

External debt stocks	DT.DOD.DECT.CD
Long-term external debt	DT.DOD.DLXF.CD
Public and publicly guaranteed	DT.DOD.DPPG.CD
Private nonguaranteed	DT.DOD.DPNG.CD
Use of IMF credit	DT.DOD.DIMF.CD
Short-term debt	DT.DOD.DSTC.CD
interest arrears on long-term	DT.IXA.DPPG.CD
Memorandum items	
Principal arrears on long-term	DT.AXA.DPPG.CD
Long-term public sector debt	DT.DOD.DPPG.CD
Long-term private sector debt	DT.DOD.PRVS.CD
Public & publicly guaranteed commitments	DT.COM.DPPG.CD

External debt flows	
Disbursements	DT.DIS.DLTF.CD
Long-term external debt	DT.DIS.DLXF.CD
IMF purchases	DT.DIS.DIMF.CD
Principal repayments	DT.AMT.DLTF.CD
Long-term external debt	DT.AMT.DLXF.CD
IMF repurchases	DT.AMT.DIMF.CD
Net flows	DT.NFL.DECT.CD
Long-term external debt	DT.NFL.DLXF.CD
Short-term external debt	DT.NFL.DSTC.CD
Interest payments (INT)	DT.INT.DECT.CD
Long-term external debt	DT.INT.DLXF.CD
IMF charges	DT.INT.DIMF.CD
Short-term external debt	DT.INT.DSTC.CD

2. OTHER NON-DEBT RESOURCE FLOWS

Foreign direct investment (net equity inflows)	BX.KLT.DINV.CD.WD
Portfolio equity flows	BX.PEF.TOTL.CD.WD

3. CURRENCY COMPOSITION OF PUBLIC AND PUBLICLY GUARANTEED DEBT (%)

Euro	DT.CUR.EURO.ZS
Japanese yen	DT.CUR.JYEN.ZS
Pound sterling	DT.CUR.UKPS.ZS
Swiss franc	DT.CUR.SWFR.ZS
U.S. dollars	DT.CUR.USDL.ZS

4. AVERAGE TERMS OF NEW COMMITMENTS

Official creditors	
Interest (%)	DT.INR.OFFT
Maturity (years)	DT.MAT.OFFT
Grace period (years)	DT.GPA.OFFT
Private creditors	
Interest (%)	DT.INR.PRVT
Maturity (years)	DT.MAT.PRVT
Grace period (years)	DT.GPA.PRVT

5. MAJOR ECONOMIC AGGREGATES

Gross national income (GNI)	NY.GNP.MKTP.CD
Exports of goods, services, and primary income	BX.GSR.TOTL.CD
Personal transfers and compensation of employees	BX.TRF.PWKR.CD.DT
Imports of goods, services, and primary income	BM.GSR.TOTL.CD
Primary income on FDI (payments)	BX.KLT.DREM.CD.DT
International reserves	FI.RES.TOTL.CD

6. RATIOS

External debt stocks to exports (%)	DT.DOD.DECT.EX.ZS
External debt stocks to GNI (%)	DT.DOD.DECT.GN.ZS
Debt service to exports (%)	DOD.DECT.GN.ZS
Short-term to external debt stocks (%)	DT.DOD.DSTC.ZS
Multilateral to external debt stocks (%)	DT.DOD.MLAT.ZS
Reserves to external debt stocks (%)	FI.RES.TOTL.DT.ZS
Current account balance	BN.CAB.XOKA.CD
Reserves to imports (months)	FI.RES.TOTL.MO

7. LONG-TERM EXTERNAL DEBT			
Debt outstanding and disbursed	DT.DOD.DLXF.CD	**Interest payments**	DT.INT.DLXF.CD
Public and publicly guaranteed	DT.DOD.DPPG.CD	**Public and publicly guaranteed**	DT.INT.DPPG.CD
Official creditors	DT.DOD.OFFT.CD	Official creditors	DT.INT.OFFT.CD
Multilateral	DT.DOD.MLAT.CD	Multilateral	DT.INT.MLAT.CD
of which: IBRD	DT.DOD.MIBR.CD	of which: IBRD	DT.INT.MIBR.CD
IDA	DT.DOD.MIDA.CD	IDA	DT.INT.MIDA.CD
Bilateral	DT.DOD.BLAT.CD	Bilateral	DT.INT.BLAT.CD
Private creditors	DT.DOD.PRVT.CD	Private creditors	DT.INT.PRVT.CD
of which: Bonds	DT.DOD.PBND.CD	of which: Bonds	DT.INT.PBND.CD
Commercial banks	DT.DOD.PCBK.CD	Commercial banks	DT.INT.PCBK.CD
Private nonguaranteed	DT.DOD.DPNG.CD	Private nonguaranteed	DT.INT.DPNG.CD
of which: Bonds	DT.DOD.PNGB.CD	of which: Bonds	DT.INT.PNGB.CD
Disbursements	DT.DIS.DLXF.CD	**Principal repayments**	DT.AMT.DLXF.CD
Public and publicly guaranteed	DT.DIS.DPPG.CD	Public and publicly guaranteed	DT.AMT.DPPG.CD
Official creditors	DT.DIS.OFFT.CD	Official creditors	DT.AMT.OFFT.CD
Multilateral	DT.DIS.MLAT.CD	Multilateral	DT.AMT.MLAT.CD
of which: IBRD	DT.DIS.MIBR.CD	of which: IBRD	DT.AMT.MIBR.CD
IDA	DT.DIS.MIDA.CD	IDA	DT.AMT.MIDA.CD
Bilateral	DT.DIS.BLAT.CD	Bilateral	DT.AMT.BLAT.CD
Private creditors	DT.DIS.PRVT.CD	Private creditors	DT.AMT.PRVT.CD
of which: Bonds	DT.DIS.PBND.CD	of which: Bonds	DT.AMT.PBND.CD
Commercial banks	DT.DIS.PCBK.CD	Commercial banks	DT.AMT.PCBK.CD
Private nonguaranteed	DT.DIS.DPNG.CD	**Private nonguaranteed**	DT.AMT.DPNG.CD
of which: Bonds	DT.DIS.PNGB.CD	of which: Bonds	DT.AMT.PNGB.CD

8. DEBT STOCK-FLOW RECONCILATION	
Total change in external debt stocks	DT.DOD.DECT.CD.CG
Net flows on external debt	DT.NFL.DECT.CD

9. DEBT STOCK-FLOW RECONCILATION	
Total amount rescheduled	DT.DXR.DPPG.CD
Total amount forgiven	DT.DFR.DPPG.CD
Debt buyback	DT.DSB.DPPG.CD

10. CONTRACTUAL OBLIGATIONS ON OUTSTANDING LONG-TERM EXTERNAL DEBT	
Official creditors	
Principal	DT.AMT.OFFT.CD
Interest	DT.INT.OFFT.CD
Private creditors	
Principal	DT.AMT.PRVT.CD
Interest	DT.INT.PRVT.CD

How to Use the DataBank

DataBank (http://databank.worldbank.org) is an online web resource that provides simple and quick access to collections of time series data. It has advanced functions for selecting and displaying data, performing customized queries, downloading data, and creating charts and maps. Users can create dynamic, custom reports based on their selection of countries, indicators, and years. All these reports can be easily edited, shared, and embedded as widgets on websites or blogs. For more information, see http://databank.worldbank.org/help.

Actions

Click to share the table using either the embed code or the URL

Click to edit and revise the table in DataBank

Click to export all metadata to Excel

Click to export the table to Excel

Click to export the table and corresponding indicator metadata to PDF

Click to print the table and corresponding indicator metadata

Click to access the IDS Online Tables Help file

PART I
Overview

Introduction

International Debt Statistics 2017 presents statistics and analysis on the external debt and financial flows (debt and equity) for the world's economies for 2015.

The primary data source for *International Debt Statistics* (IDS) is the World Bank's Debtor Reporting System (DRS) that collects debt stocks and debt-related transactions (gross disbursements, principal and interest payments) for low- and middle-income countries. But IDS also draws from the high-frequency, quarterly, external, and public debt statistics captured through the Quarterly External Debt Statistics (QEDS) and the Public Sector Debt Statistics (PSDS) databases. QEDS and PSDS both include data for high-income countries as well as low- and middle-income countries.

The main messages from International Debt Statistics 2017 are:

- ***Net debt flows (loan disbursements minus principal repayments) to low- and middle-income countries turned negative for the first time since the 2008 global financial crisis.*** Outflows in 2015 were $184 billion, a stark contrast to inflows of $542 billion in 2014. The principal driver was the contraction in short-term debt flows, which swung from a net inflow of $130 billion in 2014 to a massive $398 billion outflow in 2015. Long-term debt flows also contracted, remaining positive but falling to $214 billion—half the previous year's level.
- ***The external debt stock of low- and middle-income countries declined for the first time in more than two decades.*** External debt stocks fell 6 percent, to $6.7 trillion. The main contributors to this decline were net debt outflows in conjunction with year-on-year exchange adjustments between the currencies in which external debt is denominated and the U.S. dollar (the numeraire). Outflows were driven by an 18 percent contraction in short-term obligations compared to 2014. China, which accounts for over 21 percent of the combined external debt stock of low- and middle-income countries, drove the global trend. Excluding China, end-2015 external debt stock totaled $5.3 trillion, only marginally below the end-2014 level.
- With debt stocks in decline, external debt burdens in low- and middle-income countries remained moderate in 2015. ***The ratio of external debt to GNI averaged 26 percent for low- and middle-income countries, unchanged from 2014.*** The ratio of external debt to exports averaged 98 percent, only moderately above the prior year average of 92 percent. These ratios, calculated on the basis of the current U.S. dollar value of GNI and exports at the end of 2015, should be interpreted with care, as they mask increased debt service costs arising from the appreciation of the U.S. dollar.
- Looking beyond debt, ***net financial flows (debt and equity) dropped to $379 billion, one third the 2014 level ($1,159 billion).*** This was equivalent to 1.5 percent of low- and middle-income countries' combined GNI, down from an average of 4.9 percent in 2013–14. Equity-based foreign direct investment (FDI) proved resilient and offset the precipitous fall in debt and portfolio equity flows. FDI held steady at $543 billion in 2015, marginally higher than the previous year. Portfolio equity flows were positive in 2015 for the fourth successive year, but fell sharply to $21 billion ($81 billion in 2014). This fall reflected uncertainty over prospects for China, where portfolio equity inflows dropped to $15 billion ($52 billion in 2014).
- High-income countries reporting quarterly external debt confirm their debt levels are, on average, much higher than in low- and middle-income countries. Yet government debt-to-GDP ratios (external and domestic debt combined) moderated in 2015.

Trends in Low- and Middle-Income Country Debt Flows and Stocks, 2015

Net debt flows turn negative for the first time since the 2008 financial crisis

Net debt inflows to low- and middle-income countries registered outflows of $184 billion, in 2015 a stark contrast to the inflows of $542 billion recorded in 2014. Contributors to this reversal were the continuing economic vulnerabilities and the effect of lower commodity prices and the commensurate swing in exchange rates, which weighed heavily on medium-term investment and growth forecasts. The prospect of an imminent increase in the U.S. policy rate also affected the volume and direction of flows, particularly to the larger, more advanced emerging markets.

Negative debt flows were primarily driven by the contraction in short-term debt, which swung from a net inflow of $130 billion in 2014 to a massive, $398 billion outflow in 2015. Long-term debt flows remained positive but plummeted to $214 billion, half the previous year's level. Flows from official creditors fell 17 percent to $38 billion, and their share of total long-term debt inflows remained moderate (17 percent). Increased financing from the International Monetary Fund (IMF) and the International Bank for Reconstruction and Development (IBRD), raised multilateral creditors share of net official flows to 90 percent, (71 percent in 2014).

Changes in relative rates of return and heightened risks, as evidenced by downgrades of some low- and middle-income countries by the major rating agencies, impacted bond issuance but bonds still constituted the single most important component of net debt flows, accounting for a little over half of long-term debt flows in 2015.

External debt stock declined for the first time in more than two decades

The total external debt stock of low- and middle-income countries fell 6 percent in 2015, to $6.7 trillion. It was the first year in more than two decades where debt stocks did not rise—a marked contrast to the 10 percent increase in 2013–14.

This decline was driven by a combination of net debt outflows of $184 billion, debt forgiveness, and the downward effect of the U.S. dollar appreciation on year-on-year exchange adjustments (more than half the debt of low- and middle-income countries is denominated in currencies other than U.S. dollars). Short-term debt stocks contracted sharply, ending the year 18 percent lower than in 2014. Long-term public and publicly guaranteed debt posted a moderate 2 percent increase, pushed up by new financing from multilateral institutions, notably IBRD and the IMF, and bond issuance by sovereigns and public sector entities. Private nonguaranteed debt stocks moved in the opposite direction, falling 2 percent, as financing from both commercial banks and bond issuance contracted sharply.

Viewed from a borrower perspective, the composition of long-term debt stock, 51 percent public and publicly guaranteed debt and 49 percent private nonguaranteed debt, has remained stable over the past four years. Short-term debt, as a share of total debt outstanding, was 27 percent in 2015 (31 percent in 2014) but unchanged relative to imports.

Figure O.1 Net Debt Flows to Low- and Middle-Income Countries, 2010–15

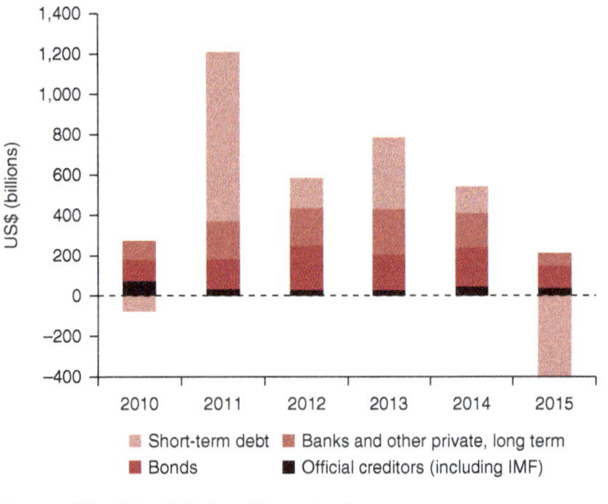

Source: World Bank Debtor Reporting System.

Figure O.2 External Debt Stock of Low- and Middle-Income Countries, 2010–15

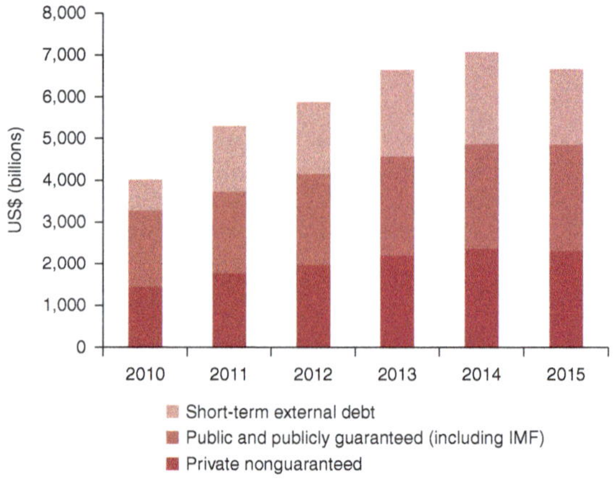

Source: World Bank Debtor Reporting System.

Aggregate Financial Flows to Low- and Middle-Income Countries, 2015

Resilient foreign direct investment kept net financial flows positive for low- and middle-income countries in 2015

Foreign direct investment (FDI) to low- and middle-income countries proved resilient in 2015 and offset the precipitous fall in debt flows and declines in portfolio equity. Net financial flows (debt and equity) plummeted to $379 billion, one third the 2014 level ($1,159 billion) but FDI flows held steady at $543 billion, marginally higher than the prior year. FDI benefited from investors responding to improvements in business and regulatory environments, medium-term growth prospects, and expanding domestic markets in many low- and middle-income countries. These positive factors served to offset concerns over fragility of the global economy, sluggish growth in commodity exporting countries, and weak aggregate demand. South Asia was the only region to see an appreciable increase in FDI flows in 2015, up 21 percent, driven largely by a positive response to changes in the regulatory framework in India. This contrasted with a more modest outcome in most other regions and the marked downturn in Europe and Central Asia where FDI flows fell, on average, 12 percent in 2015 to $55 billion ($62 billion in 2014), reflecting cutbacks in capital expenditures in the Russian Federation in response to the decline in international prices for oil and other metals and minerals, and the associated reduction in reinvested earnings as profit margins shrank. These factors also weighed on flows to oil-exporting countries in Latin America and Sub-Saharan Africa. China remained far and away the most important recipient of FDI flows to low- and middle-income countries in 2015; it accounted for 40 percent, followed by Brazil, 10 percent, and India, 7 percent.

Portfolio equity flows contract sharply but remain positive

Portfolio equity flows remained positive in 2015 for the fourth successive year. But outturns varied across the range of countries that benefited from substantial portfolio equity investments. For 2015 as a whole, they fell to $21 billion, one quarter the 2014 level. This fall reflected uncertainty over prospects for China, where net inflows dropped to $15 billion ($52 billion in 2014), and continued outflows from Thailand ($9 billion) and Russia ($6 billion). Flows to Nigeria turned negative but held up better than expected, given the fall in global oil prices and the concomitant downturn in the country's macroeconomic prospects. Conversely, investors found opportunities in South Africa and saw portfolio equity inflows jump to $7.3 billion, almost triple the 2014 level. Those to Brazil also held up well, given the ongoing political and economic turbulence, ending the year at $10 billion, down 15 percent from 2014. Portfolio equity flows still benefit only a handful of low- and middle-income countries to any significant degree. Of cumulative flows in 2013–15, around 75 percent went to just seven countries, with China absorbing the lion's share ($100 billion), followed by India and Brazil ($34 billion), respectively.

Figure O.3 Net Financial Flows to Low- and Middle-Income Countries, Debt and Equity, 2010–15

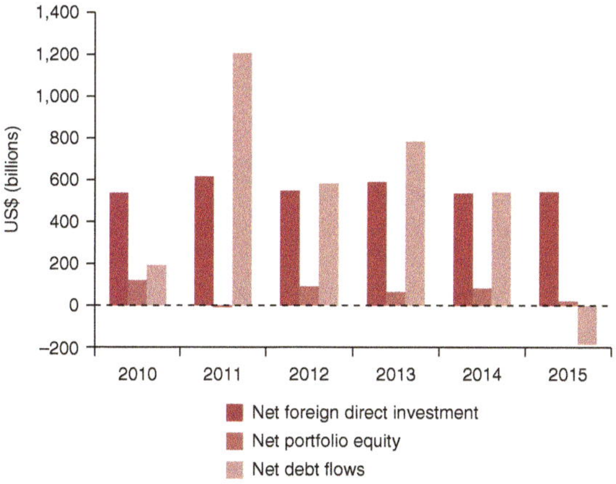

Sources: World Bank Debtor Reporting System, International Monetary Fund, and Bank for International Settlement.

Figure O.4 Net Cumulative Portfolio Equity Flows to Major Recipients, 2013–15

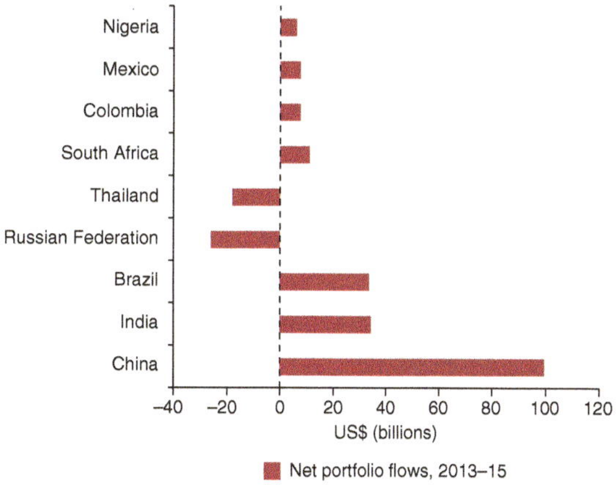

Source: International Monetary Fund.

China's domination of debt and equity flows to low- and middle-income countries softens[1]

Between 2010 and 2014, China received almost 40 percent of the $6.5 trillion in combined debt and equity flows to all low- and middle-income countries. China was also a significant provider of bilateral financing and direct investment. But China's dominance may be softening. (see box O.1).

The growth of the Chinese economy was an important contributor to the continuous upward trend in net financial flows since the global economic crisis of 2008. But this trend is reversing as a result of the 2015 economic slowdown—GDP growth slowed to 6.9 percent in 2015, compared to 7.3 percent in 2014—and China's shift from an external demand-driven economy to one focused on domestic consumption. The decline in imports saw a corresponding fall in short-term debt, which registered an outflow of $319 billion in 2015, a sharp reversal from inflows of $162 billion in 2014. Shifting investor expectations about relative near-term

Figure O.5 Net Debt and Equity Flows to Other Low- and Middle-Income countries and China, 2013–15

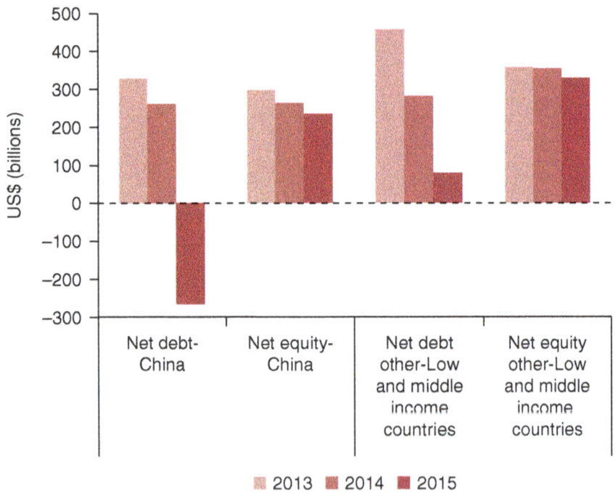

Sources: World Bank Debtor Reporting System and International Monetary Fund.

1. China has expanded its coverage of external debt statistics.

Box O.1 China Expands the Coverage of Its External Debt Statistics

China's State Administration of Foreign Exchange (SAFE) has recently improved the quality and transparency of China's external debt statistics in conformity with the internationally agreed Special Data Dissemination Standard (SDDS). This included an expansion in coverage of debt instruments and inclusion of domestic debt held by nonresidents. SAFE also disseminated a revised historical data series for International Investment Position (IIP) statistics for 2005–10 and comprehensive external debt statistics for 2015 in the Quarterly External Debt Statistics (QEDS). World Bank staff created a historical series for external debt stocks that conform to China's official and revised 2007-2015 IIP statistics. Significant changes in the revised external debt statistics include (a) government borrowing in renminbi held by nonresidents; (b) inter-company lending (formerly classified as FDI); and (c) deposits held by nonresidents in foreign and domestic currency.

The revisions are significant. Total external debt at end 2014 is now $1.8 trillion, an increase of 85 percent over the pre-revision figure of $959 billion. The short-term debt accounts for 70 percent. Concomitant with the increase in external debt stocks was deterioration in key debt indicators. The end-2014 debt-to-GNI and debt-to-export ratio rose to 17.2 percent and 64 percent, respectively; the comparable pre-revision figures were 9.3 percent and 34.8 percent, respectively.

Figure O.6 China: External Debt Statistics before and after Reporting Revisions

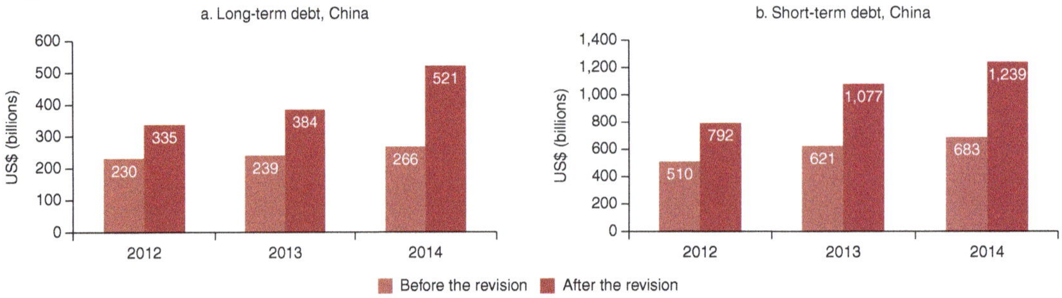

Sources: China's State Administration of Foreign Exchange (SAFE) and World Bank staff estimates.

returns on renminbi assets and concerns about near- and longer-term growth prospects dampened FDI and led to a surge in portfolio equity outflows: net portfolio equity flows fell over 70 percent in 2015.

Debt flows to the top ten middle-income country borrowers contract sharply in 2015

Net debt flows to the top ten borrowers among low- and middle-income countries, measured on the basis of end-2015 external debt stock, and excluding China and Russia, declined moderately between 2012 and 2014. In 2015 they fell sharply, to $90 billion, a third the 2014 level, driven by a contraction in long-term debt flows and a $56 billion outflow of short-term debt (compared to a small $1 billion outflow in 2014). Net long-term debt flows to public sector borrowers were down nearly 59 percent, reflecting a sharp slowdown in bond issuance by sovereigns and other public sector borrowers and retrenchment in lending by commercial bank lending. Net debt flows to non-guaranteed private sector borrowers, both bond issuance and commercial bank lending, fared better, falling less steeply, 31 percent, in 2015. The reduction in the volume of flows and their composition varied significantly at the individual country level. Brazil and Turkey together accounted for 55 percent of net long-term debt inflows to private non-guaranteed borrowers, and India and Mexico claimed close to 54 percent of the comparable flows to public sector borrowers. Most top-ten borrowers recorded an outflow of short-term debt in 2015, but the most significant were Mexico ($21 billion) and Turkey ($23 billion). Only Argentina recorded short-term inflows of any significance in 2015 ($15 billion).

In contrast to middle-income countries, financial flows to the poorest countries rose in 2015

Despite volatility in commodity prices and an uncertain outlook for the global economy financial flows (debt and equity) to the world's poorest countries, those eligible for concessional financing from the World Bank's International Development Association (IDA), and designated IDA-only, continued their upward trajectory in 2015, rising 10 percent, to $58 billion.[2] This was in marked contrast to other low- and middle-income countries, which saw comparable flows fall 67 percent over the same period. There was, however, a shift in the distribution of inflows to IDA-only countries with an increasing tilt towards equity flows—they rose 18 percent in 2015, pushing their share of net financial flows to 52 percent. Net debt flows totaled $28 billion in 2015, little changed from 2014, but registering a marked change in creditor composition. Net inflows from official creditors declined 14 percent, largely on account of the contraction in bilateral lending by China, while lending from multilateral institutions was largely static but still the largest component, 30 percent, of net long-term debt flows. Most IDA-only countries remain heavily dependent on official, concessional sources of financing, but several have gained market access in recent years, and bond issuance has accounted for an increasing share of debt flows. Rising costs reduced new bond issuance in 2015, and net inflows dropped almost 40 percent, to $3.8 billion, equivalent to 15 percent of long-term debt inflows, down from 24 percent in 2014.

2. As of July 1, 2016, there were 59 countries designated IDA-only of which 54 report to the World Bank Debtor Reporting System

Figure O.7 Top Ten Borrowers – Composition of Debt Flows, 2015

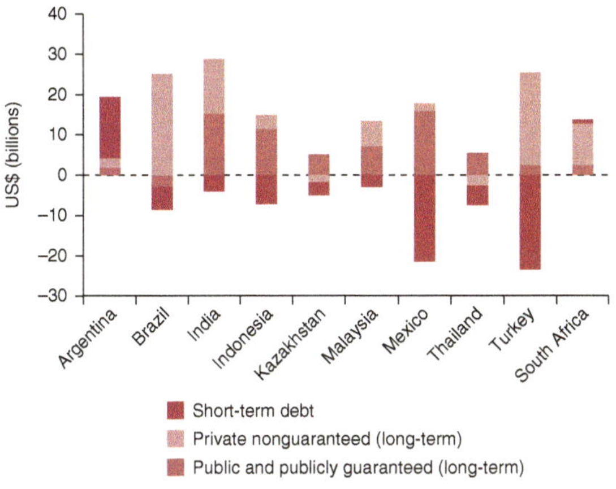

Source: World Bank Debtor Reporting System.

Figure O.8 IDA-Only Countries – Composition of Financial Flows, 2013–15

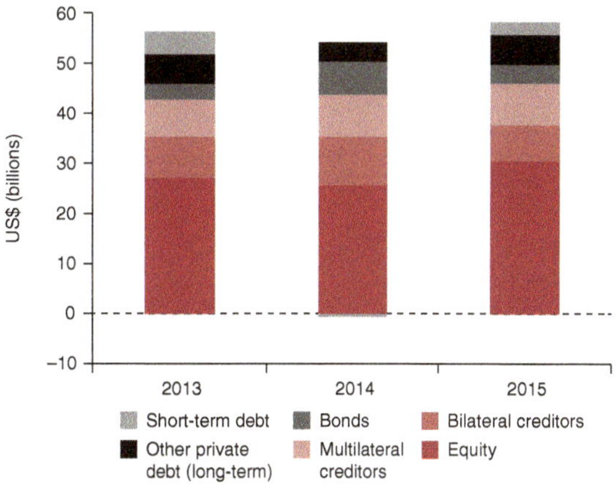

Sources: World Bank Debtor Reporting System and International Monetary Fund.

REGIONAL PERSPECTIVES, 2015

East Asia and Pacific

Net financial flows fell to $45 billion, equivalent to only 0.3 percent of GNI, driven by the sharp contraction in China's short-term debt, but other countries in the region also recorded net debt flows in 2015 that were only half of those in 2014.

Table O.1 External Debt Stock and Net Financial Flows, East Asia and Pacific, 2010–15
US$ (billion)

	2010	2011	2012	2013	2014	2015
External debt stocks	803.1	1,682.8	1,904.4	2,261.0	2,612.4	2,273.8
Net flows (debt and equity)	174.3	1,194.9	506.9	727.6	652.7	45.2
as % of GNI	2.2	12.6	4.8	6.3	5.2	0.3
Equity flows	312.9	301.3	302.5	348.4	318.7	277.4
Foreign direct investment	273.1	294.2	267.8	319.7	267.9	273.5
Portfolio equity	39.8	7.1	34.7	28.7	50.8	3.8
Net debt flows	−138.6	893.6	204.4	379.3	334.0	−232.2
Official creditors	0.6	1.7	1.8	−1.2	3.3	−5.5
Bilateral	−3.3	−0.5	−1.1	−3.1	0.6	−11.3
Multilateral	4.0	2.3	2.9	1.9	2.7	5.7
World Bank	2.7	0.9	1.4	2.4	1.7	3.3
Other multilateral	1.3	1.4	1.6	−0.4	1.1	2.4
IMF	0.0	0.0	−0.1	−0.1	−0.1	0.0
Private creditors	−139.2	891.8	202.6	380.5	330.7	−226.7
Net medium- and long-term debt flows	57.8	100.2	130.1	101.2	172.3	109.9
Public and publicly guaranteed	24.1	36.5	57.6	35.5	53.9	17.4
Private nonguaranteed	33.7	63.8	72.5	65.7	118.4	92.5
Net short-term debt flows	−196.9	791.6	72.4	279.3	158.4	−336.6
Memorandum Item						
Worker remit. & comp. of employees	56.9	62.7	67.2	73.8	88.7	106.4

Sources: World Bank Debtor Reporting System, International Monetary Fund, and Bank for International Settlement.

Figure O.9 Net Debt and Equity Flows to East Asia and Pacific excluding China, 2013–15

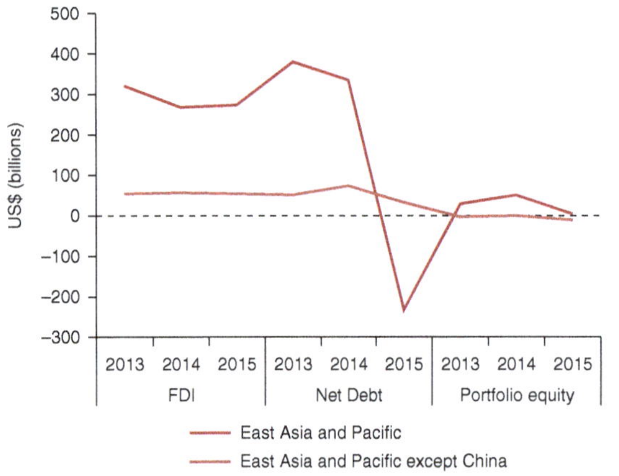

Sources: World Bank Debtor Reporting System and International Monetary Fund.

Net financial flows to the region were $45 billion in 2015, equivalent to only 7 percent of the comparable flow for 2014. A major factor behind this downturn was the sharp contraction in short-term debt flows to China ($319 billion). Net equity flows, a positive $277 billion, were 13 percent lower than the previous year, pulled down by the precipitous fall in portfolio equity flows to China, which plummeted to $15 billion, from $52 billion in 2014. Excluding China, other countries in East Asia and Pacific recorded net financial flows of $75 billion in 2015, 3.5 percent of their combined GNI, a marked decrease from the debt and equity flows of 5.8 percent of GNI realized in 2014.

Growth uncertainty about outcomes in the global economy, anticipation of a Federal Funds Rate (FFR) rate hike in the United States, and in China a slowdown in growth and the depreciation of the renminbi, affect countries across the region. Net debt flows to countries in the East Asia and Pacific region, excluding China, fell by half, and net equity inflows were down 24 percent from their 2014 level. Consistent with the trend of the past five years, Indonesia and Malaysia received more than half of net financial flows to the region (excluding China). Long-term debt inflows totaled $50 billion, divided almost evenly between public sector and nonguaranteed private sector borrowers, but with divergent trends at the individual country level. In Indonesia, for example, net debt inflows to public sector borrowers accounted for 76 percent of total long-term debt inflows. Conversely, in Thailand, public sector borrowers recorded an $970 million outflow of long-term debt in 2015. Bond issuance held up reasonably well at $27 billion, a relatively moderate decline from the $31 billion issued in 2014. Most countries recorded a contraction in short-term debt, which ended the year with an outflow of $18 billion. As in most other regions, net equity flows fared far better than debt flows in 2015, with FDI proving resilient and posting a moderate 2 percent increase. FDI into China slowed as investment in the manufacturing sector stagnated in parallel with the downturn in economic growth, investor uncertainty over future outcomes, and as a consequence of rising wage and production costs that have reduced China's advantage in labor-intensive manufacturing. However, China's potential car market, particularly in populous inland regions, propelled flows into the automotive sector, and together with investments into the service sector, kept FDI on an even keel and broadly unchanged from 2014. East Asia and Pacific countries, excluding China, received $54 billion in FDI, some 5 percent below the 2014 level, of which around 68 percent went to Indonesia, Malaysia, and Vietnam. Short-term economic uncertainties saw a decline in FDI into Indonesia in 2015. It fell 30 percent, to $15 billion, and was concentrated mainly in manufacturing, agriculture, and fisheries. Malaysia remained a destination of choice for foreign companies, and multinational corporations focused on the expansion of the production capacity, and FDI. Flows to Vietnam maintained their upward trend, rising 34 percent in 2015, thanks in large part to investment in the electronics industry and the continued expansion of production facilities, including a further $600 million plan by Samsung, the country's largest investor. Investment in Myanmar also soared to $3 billion and looks set to continue on an upward trajectory given the agreement signed with Thailand to develop the Dawei Special Economic Zone, with total investment expected to be in the region of $8.6 billion.

Figure O.10 Net Inflows to East Asia and Pacific (excluding China) and Select Countries, 2014–15

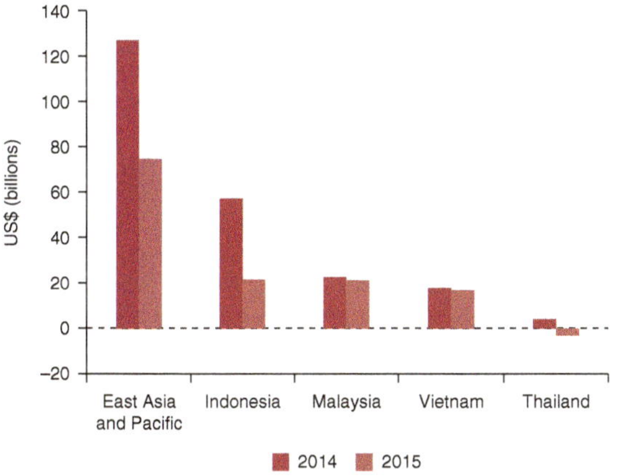

Source: World Bank Debtor Reporting System.

Figure O.11 Foreign Direct Investment Flows to Select East Asia and Pacific Countries, 2011–15

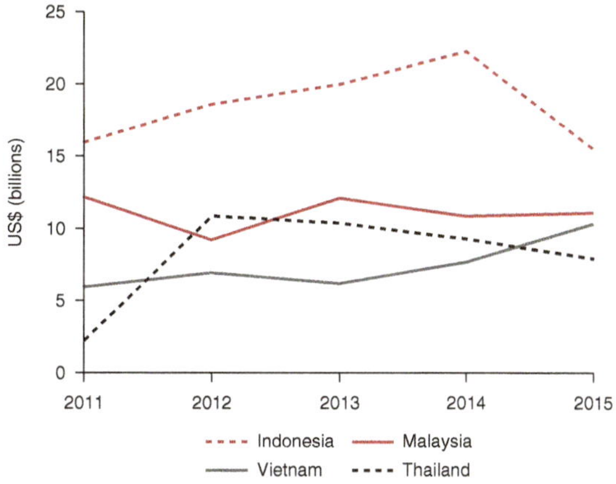

Source: International Monetary Fund.

Europe and Central Asia

Financial flows recorded an outflow of $51 billion, –1.8 percent of GNI in 2015, with net equity inflows insufficient to offset the collapse in debt where outflows surged and ended the year at $99 billion, adding to the $56 billion outflow in 2014.

Table O.2 External Debt Stock and Net Financial Flows, Europe and Central Asia, 2010–15
US$ (billion)

	2010	2011	2012	2013	2014	2015
External debt stocks	1,260.7	1,422.1	1,525.9	1,703.9	1,573.7	1,449.0
Net flows (debt and equity)	177.0	202.9	229.7	211.4	-3.5	-51.3
as % of GNI	6.0	5.6	6.0	5.3	-0.1	-1.8
Equity flows	65.1	75.9	73.7	67.5	52.7	47.7
Foreign direct investment	66.0	86.1	65.7	71.9	62.5	55.1
Portfolio equity	-0.9	-10.3	8.0	-4.5	-9.8	-7.4
Net debt flows	111.9	127.1	156.0	144.0	-56.2	-99.0
Official creditors	25.6	6.4	-5.5	-9.5	2.3	7.8
Bilateral	2.7	-0.8	-1.4	0.0	3.0	1.3
Multilateral	22.9	7.2	-4.0	-9.5	-0.7	6.5
World Bank	3.3	2.3	1.6	1.7	2.7	1.9
Other multilateral	10.6	5.9	2.4	4.6	3.9	1.5
IMF	9.0	-1.0	-8.0	-15.8	-7.3	3.1
Private creditors	86.4	120.7	161.5	153.5	-58.4	-106.7
Net medium- and long-term debt flows	42.4	98.5	131.2	117.7	-10.8	-51.8
Public and publicly guaranteed	28.9	19.6	34.3	68.3	-26.1	-27.3
Private nonguaranteed	13.5	78.9	96.9	49.3	15.2	-24.5
Net short-term debt flows	44.0	22.2	30.3	35.8	-47.6	-54.9
Memorandum Item						
Worker remit. & comp. of employees	37.3	43.8	46.4	54.6	51.6	37.3

Sources: World Bank Debtor Reporting System, International Monetary Fund, and Bank for International Settlement.

Figure O.12 Net Financial Flows to Russia and Other Europe and Central Asia Countries, 2014–15

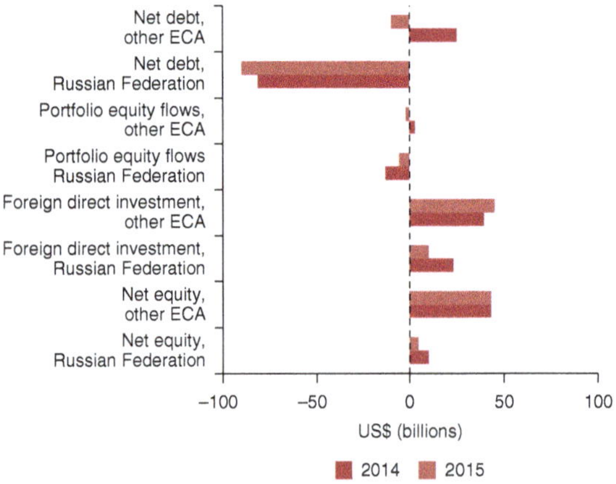

Sources: World Bank Debtor Reporting System and International Monetary Fund.

The regional trend in financial flows was dictated by Russia where falling oil prices and geopolitical tensions eroded confidence and led to a retrenchment in both debt and equity flows. Outflows widened, and an additional $84 billion left the country in 2015, on top of the $71 billion outflow of 2014. For other countries in the region, a more positive picture emerged. They too recorded debt outflows of $10 billion in 2015, principally on account of a sharp contraction in short-term debt, but net equity inflows remained moderately unchanged at $43 billion, in contrast to those to Russia, down 53 percent in the same period. Investment in Russia contracted across all sectors and was exacerbated by the disinvestment of Conoco Phillips U.S., a pioneer investor in the oil and gas sector. Comparable flows to Kazakhstan were down 56 percent, reflecting adjustment to terms-of-trade shocks and fallout from the downturn in the Russian economy, its major trading partner. Some other Central Asian countries also recorded declines as Russian investors reduced their presence in the region. In marked contrast, FDI to Ukraine surged to $4 billion

($700 million in 2014) primarily on account of a large recapitalization in the banking sector and privatization of the 3G mobile network through license sales. Similarly, inflows to Turkey, the largest recipient of FDI in the region, soared to $16 billion, boosted by a raft of mergers and acquisitions, particularly in the financial sector, including the $2.5 billion purchase of Turkiye Garanti Bankasi by Banco Vizcaya, Spain. Portfolio equity flows to Russia were negative (outflows of $5.5 billion), but most countries in the region investors found attractive opportunities.

As with other regions, the downturn in the global economic prospects and commodity prices, especially for oil and gas, had a major impact on net debt flows in 2015. They widened to an outflow of $99 billion, 76 percent increase from the outflow recorded in 2014, with Russia the dominant factor. Excluding Russia, net debt flows to other countries in the region were also negative, $9.7 billion as compared to an inflow of $25 billion in 2014. With regard to long-term debt, much of the decline resulted from the sharp reduction in new bond issuance, particularly by private sector non-guaranteed borrowers. It shrank, but amortization payments on maturing bonds rose, leading to an outflow of $1.3 billion (from an inflow of $29 billion in 2014) with the $9 billion outflow on private sector bonds offsetting the $7.7 billion net inflow on bonds issued by public sector borrowers. Short-term debt contracted sharply, leading to an outflow of $35 billion, but much of this ($23 billion) was attributable to Turkey And reflected the imposition by the Central Bank of Turkey's of new reserve requirements on maturing external debt. Long-term net debt inflows from private creditors went down by 63 percent to $17 billion. The primary recipients, Turkey and Kazakhstan, saw such flows fall 22 percent and 78 percent, respectively, in 2015. The net inflow of financing from official creditors almost tripled in 2015, to $7.8 billion from $3 billion in 2014, of which the World Bank and the IMF combined accounted for two-thirds, and with Ukraine the principal recipient.

Ukraine financial flows improved significantly in 2015

The improvement in the macroeconomic situation in Ukraine and more stable political environment led to balance-of-payments support from creditors and a positive impact on investors' risk perception. FDI inflows increased from $700 million in 2014 to $4 billion in 2015, largely on account of the recapitalization of the banking sector and launch of a plan to privatize around 300 state-owned enterprises backed by a government resolution to conduct a transparent and competitive process. The authorities also implemented measures to improve the business licensing procedures which further encouraged investment and had a spillover effect on portfolio equity investment which witnessed slow, but positive gains. They moved from an outflow of $391 million in 2014 to an inflow of $177 million in 2015. Favorable developments with regard to investment flows were complemented by measures to bring external debt down to a more sustainable level. Ukraine benefited from a $40 billion balance-of-payments support package, led by the International Monetary Fund, to stabilize the economy to which private creditors contributed through debt restructuring. Bondholders wrote down 20 percent of their claims (around $3.8 billion) and refinanced the remaining $13.3 billion at a coupon of 7.75 percent and accepted a four year extension of maturity.

Figure O.13 Net Debt Flows to Europe and Central Asia by type of creditor, excluding Russia, 2010–15

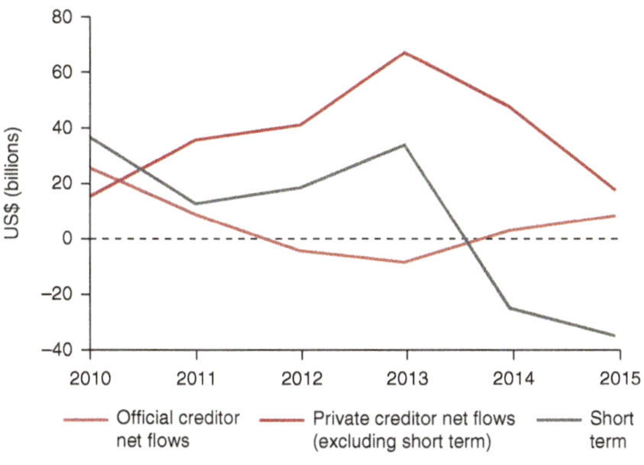

Source: World Bank Debtor Reporting System.

Figure O.14 Net Financial Flows to Ukraine, 2010–15

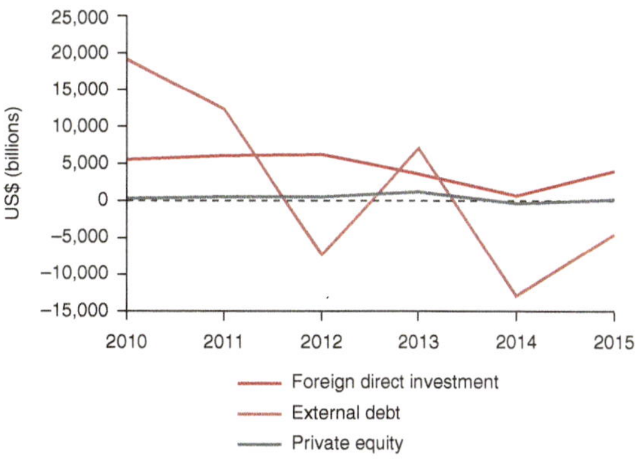

Sources: World Bank Debtor Reporting System and International Monetary Fund.

Latin America and the Caribbean

Net capital flows fell to 4.1 percent of GNI, their lowest level since 2010, as net financial flows (debt and equity) plunged to $193 billion, 37 percent below the 2014 level, and foreign direct inflows stagnated.

Table O.3 External Debt Stock and Net Financial Flows, Latin America and the Caribbean, 2010–15

	2010	2011	2012	2013	2014	2015
External debt stocks	1,098.0	1,253.9	1,387.9	1,534.9	1,688.3	1,695.7
Net flows (debt and equity)	320.9	263.8	285.3	292.4	304.7	192.7
as % of GNI	6.7	4.9	5.3	5.3	5.5	4.1
Equity flows	167.1	148.1	152.1	129.5	141.0	136.4
Foreign direct investment	127.7	145.1	133.7	115.5	120.1	120.8
Portfolio equity	39.4	2.9	18.5	14.0	20.8	15.7
Net Debt Flows	153.8	115.7	133.1	162.8	163.7	56.3
Official creditors	22.6	4.9	12.1	8.7	12.0	5.9
Bilateral	4.4	2.8	5.3	3.9	5.0	-2.6
Multilateral	18.1	2.0	6.9	4.8	7.0	8.5
World Bank	8.3	-2.9	3.6	3.2	3.0	3.3
Other multilateral	8.5	4.7	3.4	1.8	4.6	5.6
IMF	1.3	0.2	-0.1	-0.2	-0.6	-0.4
Private creditors	131.2	110.8	121.0	154.1	151.7	50.4
Net medium- and long-term debt flows	74.1	108.6	99.8	120.3	129.1	58.0
Public and publicly guaranteed	25.7	23.6	53.3	56.6	82.4	32.9
Private nonguaranteed	48.4	85.0	46.5	63.7	46.7	25.1
Net short-term debt flows	57.1	2.2	21.2	33.8	22.7	-7.6
Memorandum Item						
Worker remit. & comp. of employees	56.5	60.0	60.4	61.8	64.1	68.3

Sources: World Bank Debtor Reporting System, International Monetary Fund, and Bank for International Settlement.

Figure O.15 Foreign Direct Investment Flows to Select Latin American Countries, 2014–15

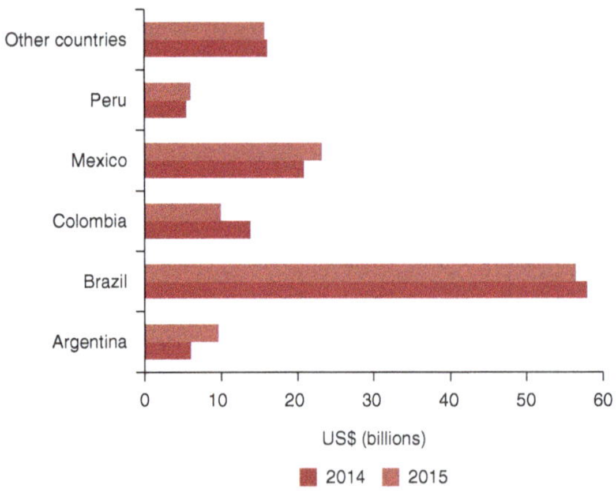

Source: International Monetary Fund.

The precipitous fall in net debt flows pulled net financial flows to the region down 37 percent with concomitant impact on their composition, raising the share of equity in net financial flows to over 71 percent, from 46 percent in 2014. Although FDI was hampered by the fall in commodity prices and slowing domestic demand, it managed to stay flat at $121 billion at the regional and, by and large, the individual country level. Argentina was the only major recipient to record any significant increase in FDI. It saw inflows jump 60 percent, but this was largely because of the low base in 2014 when the government compensated Repsol, Spain for the nationalization of its subsidiary YPF SA. Investment in Brazil kept momentum across all sectors with flows to the automotive and health sector particularly strong. With inflows of $56 billion, it was the second largest recipient, after China, of FDI into low- and middle-income countries in 2015. It also attracted $10 billion in portfolio equity inflows with the enactment of Law 13.097 in January 2015 offering new opportunities for investors, and the steep depreciation of the real offering opportunities to buy at a discount. Inflows to Mexico were bolstered by investment in the automotive industry and cross-border acquisitions, including some mega-deals like the $2.5 billion purchase of the wireless telecom company Grupo Lusacell SA de V by AT&T America.

The fall in net debt flows in 2015 is accompanied by a shift in composition

Long-term net debt inflows contracted 66 percent in 2015, to $56 billion. The decline was driven by a sharp decrease in net debt flows from commercial banks and bond issuance. In contrast to the increases of prior years, there was a parallel decline in financing from both these sources in 2015. Long-term net inflows from commercial banks dropped by 56 percent, to $29 billion, and net inflows from bond issuance were down, 54 percent, to $29 billion. The primary driver of the decline in commercial bank inflows was Brazil, which saw disbursement of new financing fall by 17 percent, while at the same time maturing obligations raised principal payments by 84 percent. Multilateral creditors were the only category of creditors to post an increase in 2015, up 21 percent over the 2014 level, but their share of net long-term debt inflows was modest, 15 percent. Most of the increase was attributable to the Inter-American Bank and other regional banks. With regard to bilateral creditors, 2015 marked a sharp reversal of the upward trajectory of flows observed in 2013 and 2014, instead registering an outflow of $2.6 billion.

As in other regions, this outcome largely reflected a slowdown in flows principally from China, Germany, and Japan. The overall contraction in growth across the region also eroded short-term debt, which registered an outflow of $7.6 billion, a significant turnaround from inflows of $22.7 billion in 2014.

Bond issuance down in 2015

Bond issuance by public and private sector borrowers in Latin America fell sharply in 2015, as the uncertain prospects for the global economy, the possibility of a rate hike by the U.S. Federal Reserve, and the downgrade in Brazil's credit rating by the major rating agencies to noninvestment grade weighed on the markets. Borrowers in the region issued bonds totaling $73 billion in 2015, a 26 percent decline over the comparable figure for 2014. New issuance by public sector borrowers was 30 percent below the prior year level, with borrowers in Brazil eschewing the markets in 2015, and issuance by public borrowers in Mexico down 41 percent. The contraction in new issuance by private nonguaranteed corporates was less pronounced; they fell only 17 percent from the prior year's level. In terms of net flows however, it was a different story. The confluence of a decline in new issuance, and a marked increase in the share of maturing bonds, reduced the net inflow to public sector borrowers by 46 percent, to $26 billion, (from $48 billion in 2014) and reduced those to private nonguaranteed corporate borrowers to $2 billion, down from a net inflow of $14 billion in the previous year.

Figure O.16 Composition of Net Debt Flows, 2013–15

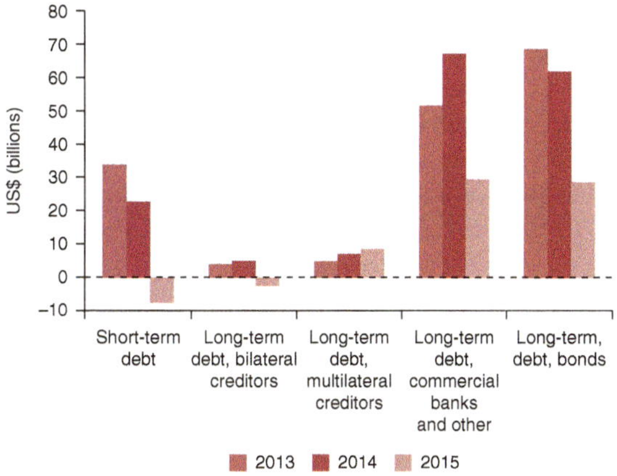

Sources: World Bank Debtor Reporting System and Bank for International Settlement.

Figure O.17 Bond Flows by Type of Borrower, 2014–15

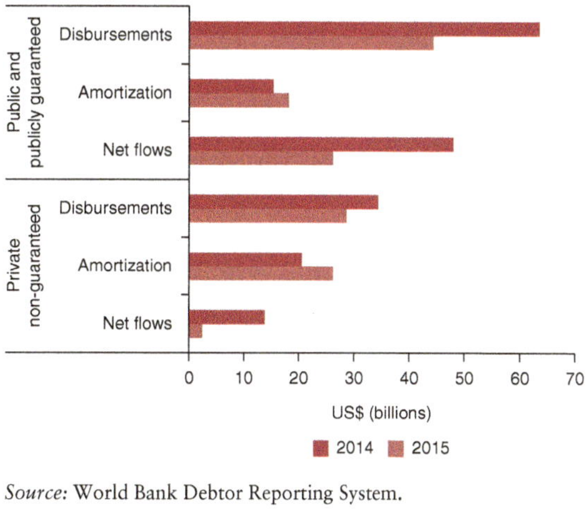

Source: World Bank Debtor Reporting System.

Middle East and North Africa

Net financial flows (debt and equity) rose 18 percent in 2015, to $28 billion, equivalent to 2.3 percent of GNI, driven by a near doubling of net debt inflows, which served to more than offset declining equity inflows.

Table O.4 External Debt Stock and Net Financial Flows, Middle East and North Africa, 2010–15
US$ (billion)

	2010	2011	2012	2013	2014	2015
External debt stocks	168.1	165.8	172.9	190.9	189.4	197.5
Net flows (debt and equity)	32.1	12.8	26.9	35.1	23.8	28.1
as % of GNI	2.8	1.0	1.9	2.6	1.9	2.3
Equity flows	24.5	14.2	19.5	17.9	16.3	14.1
Foreign direct investment	22.6	14.8	20.7	18.0	15.6	14.4
Portfolio equity	2.0	-0.6	-1.2	-0.1	0.6	-0.4
Net Debt Flows	7.6	-1.4	7.4	17.2	7.6	14.0
Official creditors	1.3	1.0	4.7	10.2	2.2	8.5
Bilateral	-1.1	-1.5	1.7	6.8	-0.6	4.9
Multilateral	2.4	2.4	3.1	3.4	2.8	3.7
World Bank	0.8	0.9	0.8	1.1	0.9	1.9
Other multilateral	1.6	1.6	1.8	1.4	0.4	0.9
IMF	0.0	-0.1	0.5	0.9	1.5	0.9
Private creditors	6.3	-2.3	2.7	7.0	5.3	5.5
Net medium- and long-term debt flows	1.4	-1.6	6.0	8.0	1.9	5.1
Public and publicly guaranteed	1.9	-1.8	5.1	7.4	1.5	4.1
Private nonguaranteed	-0.5	0.2	0.9	0.6	0.4	1.1
Net short-term debt flows	4.9	-0.7	-3.3	-1.0	3.4	0.4
Memorandum Item						
Worker remit. & comp. of employees	36.0	38.2	44.6	46.0	49.7	46.2

Sources: World Bank Debtor Reporting System, International Monetary Fund, and Bank for International Settlement.

Figure O.18 Net Debt and Foreign Direct Investment Flows, 2010–15

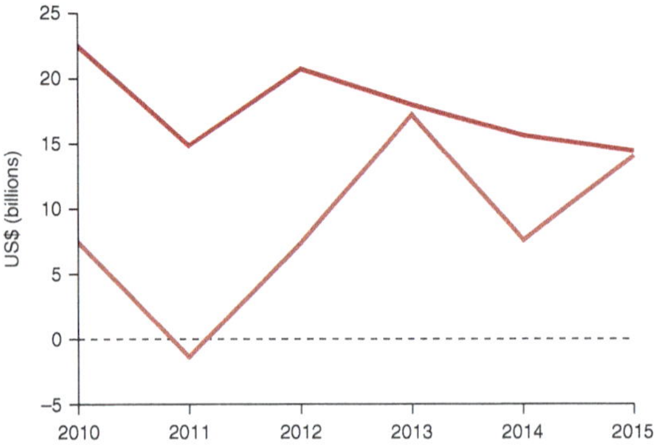

Sources: World Bank Debtor Reporting System and International Monetary Fund.

Traditionally, most countries in the region have been more reliant on equity flows than on debt, but this was not the case in 2015. FDI flows to the region fell 8 percent, to $14 billion, their lowest level since 2010, equivalent to just over half of net financial flows, down from 66 percent the previous year. Trends at the individual country level, however, were widely divergent. The Arab Republic of Egypt was dominant, absorbing 48 percent of all FDI to the region in 2015. It saw inflows surge to $6.9 billion, almost 50 percent higher than the comparable figure for 2014, as foreign affiliates expanded their activities in the financial (CIB Bank and Citadel Capital) and pharmaceutical (Pfizer) sectors. The country also benefited from significant investments in telecommunications, including Mobile Towers Services by Eaton Towers (United Kingdom) and the ongoing investment in the gas industry from Eni (Italy). In contrast, inflows to Morocco, which serves as a major manufacturing base in North Africa for European companies, fell 29 percent, although the inflows were still sizable, and the country benefited from further investment by France in the automotive industry. The downturn in oil and gas prices weighed on Algeria and led to an outflow of $0.3 billion, a marked contrast to the inflow of $1.7 billion recorded in 2013. The Islamic Republic of Iran saw FDI flows decline for the third consecutive year, to $2 billion in 2015; but lifting of sanctions is expected to provide an impetus for a rebound going forward.

The 84 percent rise in net debt flows to the region in 2015 was in stark contrast to trends in other regions, which saw marked, and in some instances, a precipitous contraction in net debt flows during the same period. As with FDI, Egypt dictated the regional trend. It recorded net debt inflows of $6 billion in 2015, 43 percent of those to the region as a whole, as compared to an outflow of $3 billion the previous year when several large debt service obligations fell due. More than two-thirds of the 2015 inflow came in the form of bilateral loans from the Gulf Cooperation Council countries, notably Kuwait, Saudi Arabia, and the United Arab Emirates. Net debt inflows to the Islamic Republic of Iran rose to $0.8 billion, more than two times the 2014 level, and Lebanon saw them jump to $1.1 billion, nearly two and a half times the 2014 level, on account of a large increase in flows from short-term debt and private creditors, respectively. Some countries within the region saw debt flows decline. In Morocco they were down by 58 percent due to a decrease in flows from short-term and private creditors, while Algeria recorded a further contraction in short-term debt leading to a net debt outflow of $0.7 billion, decreasing two and a half times from the $0.5 billion inflow in 2014. There was also a doubling of net flows from IBRD to the region, from $1 billion in 2014 to $2 billion in 2015. IBRD flows to Egypt, Morocco, and Tunisia were responsible for 94 percent of the regional total.

Debt ratios rise but remain below those of other low- and middle-income countries

Historically, the average ratio of external debt to GNI and to exports for the region have been well below those of other low- and middle-income countries, largely as a consequence of the high share of equity in net financial flows in prior years and a decade of robust export earnings. More recently, the downturn in the growth in export earnings since 2013 and the increase in net debt inflows has had an appreciable impact on both the external debt-to-GNI and debt-to-export ratios, and there has been a marked upward trajectory. By end 2015, the external debt-to-GNI ratio had risen to 16.3 percent, from 12.5 percent in 2012, and the ratio of external debt to exports climbed to 69 percent from 42 percent over the same period. But they still remain moderate relative to the average ratio of debt to GNI and debt to exports of other low- and middle-income countries, 26.2 percent and 99 percent, respectively, at end 2015. The averages, however, mask divergence across the region. In 2015, the ratio of external debt to GNI ranged from a very low 1.6 percent in the Islamic Republic of Iran to 69.5 percent in Jordan, and regarding exports, from 6.4 percent in the Islamic Republic of Iran to a high of 385.6 percent in Yemen.

Figure O.19 Net Debt Flows to Select Middle East and North Africa Countries, 2014–15

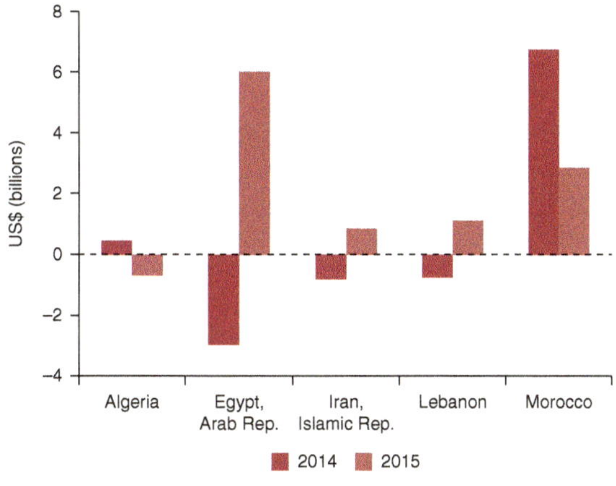

Source: World Bank Debtor Reporting System.

Figure O.20 Debt Indicators to Countries in Middle East and North Africa, 2011–15

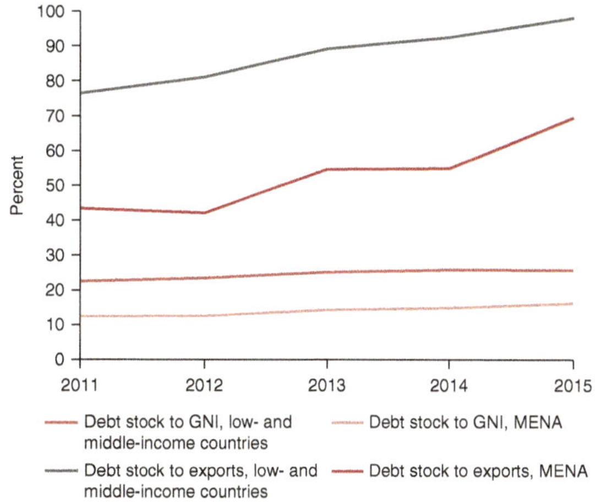

Sources: World Bank Debtor Reporting System and International Monetary Fund.

South Asia

Net financial flows fell 22 percent in 2015 to $83 billion, equivalent to 3.1 percent of GNI, the lowest level since the global and economic crisis of 2008, with the downturn impacting India and other countries in the region to a comparable degree.

Table 0.5 External Debt Stock and Net Financial Flows, South Asia, 2010–15
US$ (billion)

	2010	2011	2012	2013	2014	2015
External debt stocks	411.1	461.4	528.0	569.7	607.2	637.1
Net flows (debt and equity)	104.8	80.6	104.0	102.6	106.1	83.2
as % of GNI	5.0	3.6	4.5	4.3	4.1	3.1
Equity flows	60.7	33.6	49.5	51.6	50.3	46.8
Foreign direct investment	30.9	37.8	26.1	31.1	36.6	44.5
Portfolio equity	29.8	-4.1	23.4	20.5	13.7	2.3
Net Debt Flows	44.1	47.0	54.5	51.0	55.7	36.4
Official creditors	9.4	5.4	4.3	4.3	7.2	6.5
Bilateral	1.6	1.5	3.3	5.9	3.8	1.5
Multilateral	7.8	3.8	1.1	-1.7	3.4	5.0
World Bank	3.3	2.0	0.9	0.7	2.4	2.4
Other multilateral	2.5	1.8	1.7	0.4	1.5	1.3
IMF	2.0	0.0	-1.5	-2.8	-0.5	1.3
Private creditors	34.7	41.6	50.2	46.7	48.6	29.9
Net medium- and long-term debt flows	22.5	20.0	32.3	43.4	54.6	32.5
Public and publicly guaranteed	14.4	5.1	12.7	3.8	34.5	17.5
Private nonguaranteed	8.1	14.8	19.6	39.6	20.1	15.0
Net short-term debt flows	12.2	21.6	17.8	3.3	-6.1	-2.6
Memorandum Item						
Worker remit. & comp. of employees	82.0	96.4	108.0	110.8	115.8	117.7

Sources: World Bank Debtor Reporting System, International Monetary Fund, and Bank for International Settlement.

Figure O.21 Net Debt and Equity Flows to South Asia countries, 2010–15

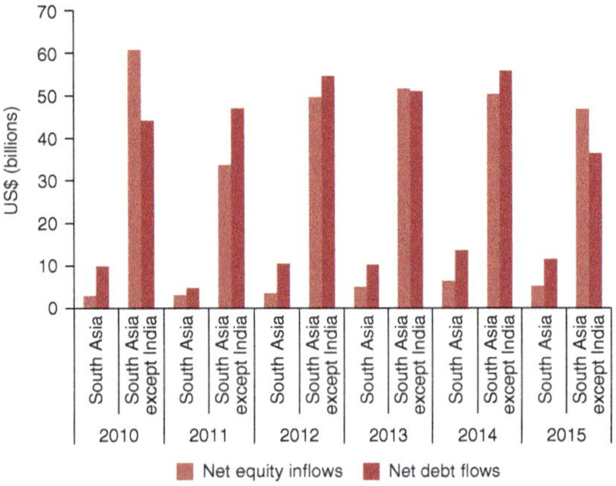

Sources: World Bank Debtor Reporting System and International Monetary Fund.

Net financial flows (debt and equity) to the region fell by 22 percent, with the 22 percent increase in FDI more than offset by the steep fall in net debt flows and portfolio equity flows down 35 percent and 84 percent, respectively, in the same period. India accounted for 99 percent of net financial flows to the region in 2015, compared to 81 percent in 2014. Excluding India, net financial flows to other South Asia countries declined 16 percent in 2015, slightly lower than similar to than the regional decline. The upswing in FDI was driven by India, which is now the third largest recipient of such flows among low- and middle-income countries, and the tenth largest recipient worldwide. The liberalization measures enacted since the current government took power have been a major factor in spurring investment from a wide range of sources, including China, Singapore, and the United States. FDI in Bangladesh hit $3 billion, a historic high, on account of investment in labor-intensive manufacturing in the textile and garment industry and for power generation and reinvested earnings. In contrast, inflows to Pakistan and Sri Lanka fell back to $884 million and $426 million, respectively, but these downturns were largely attributable to cyclical factors rather than fundamental concerns on the part of investors.

The primary factor in the downturn in net debt flows in 2015 was a marked decline in new (gross) disbursements of external financing. These fell by 46 percent in 2015 due to a combination of factors. India was the driving force, and for countries in the region other than India, the decline was more moderate, down 33 percent from the comparable flows for 2014. New bond issuance (public and private sector issuers combined) was close to one-third the level of the prior year, when issuance peaked at $37 billion. Pakistan and Sri Lanka remained active in international bond markets in 2015, but for much lower amounts. Gross disbursements from commercial banks were also down by one-third in 2015. The 14 percent fall in disbursements from official creditors was largely the consequence of a slowdown in flows from China and Japan, the region's most important bilateral creditors, and bringing overall disbursements from bilateral creditors down 33 percent in 2015. This was mitigated by increased disbursements from multilateral creditors, including a 12 percent rise in those from the World Bank (IBRD and IDA combined). IDA, the World Bank's concessional finance window to which all South Asian countries have access, remained by far the single largest multilateral creditor: disbursements in 2015 were $4 billion, with 90 percent of this going to the region's most populous countries, Bangladesh, India, and Pakistan.

Workers remittances are often overlooked in the discussion of financial flows, but they are a vital part of the development process, and particularly so in the South Asia region where they have been on a rapid upward trajectory for the past decade. In 2015, remittances to the region totaled $118 billion, equivalent to 4.4 percent of GNI. The comparable figures for 2000 were $17 billion and 2.8 percent. In 2015, the remittances received by South Asian countries were, on average, three times net debt inflows and two and a half times inflows of FDI in the same period. The worldwide growth in remittances slowed in 2015, in line with outcomes in the global economy, and this was reflected in the downturn in remittances to India, which fell 1.6 percent from the 2014 level. In contrast, those to Pakistan registered a marked 12 percent increase. India remained, however, the single largest recipient of remittances worldwide and received 59 percent of those to the region. Remittances accounted for 50 percent of net financial flows (debt, equity, and remittances combined) to India in 2015. For most other South Asian countries, remittances far surpass debt and equity inflows in importance. They accounted for 80 percent of financial flows (debt, equity, and remittances combined) to Bangladesh and Pakistan, and in Nepal, to a staggering 96 percent of combined flows.

Figure O.22 Gross Disbursements to South Asia Countries, excluding India, 2015

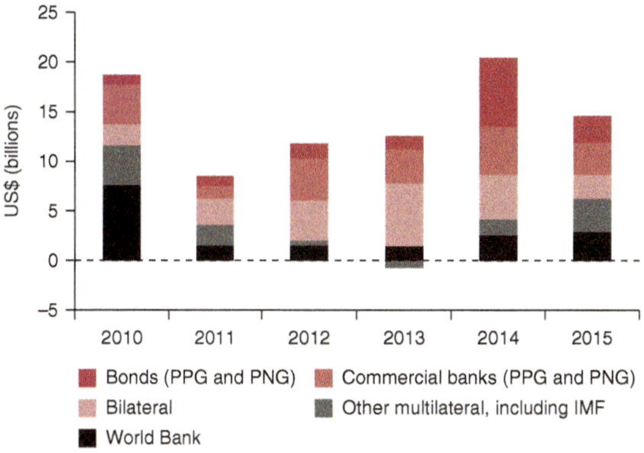

Source: World Bank Debtor Reporting System.

Figure O.23 Share of Debt, Equity, and Remittances in Flows to South Asia, 2015

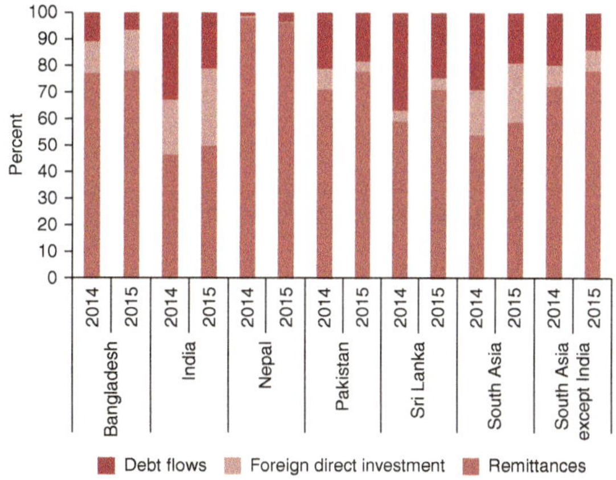

Source: World Bank Debtor Reporting System and International Monetary Fund.

Sub-Saharan Africa

Net financial flows increased 8 percent in 2015 to $82 billion, 5.5 percent of GNI, their highest level since 2008, driven upward by a continued increase in net debt flows from private creditors and a $2.9 billion inflow of short-term debt, but partially offset by a 20 percent decrease in net debt flows from official creditors.

Table O.6 External Debt Stock and Net Financial Flows, Sub-Saharan Africa, 2010–15
US$ (billion)

	2010	2011	2012	2013	2014	2015
External debt stocks	282.9	312.7	352.6	377.6	400.1	416.3
Net flows (debt and equity)	42.8	60.8	70.7	72.2	75.5	81.5
as % of GNI	3.4	4.3	4.7	4.6	4.6	5.5
Equity flows	26.7	34.9	41.1	41.2	38.0	41.5
Foreign Direct Investment	18.5	38.1	35.4	34.5	33.4	34.7
Portfolio Equity	8.1	-3.1	5.6	6.7	4.6	6.8
Net Debt Flows	16.2	25.9	29.6	30.9	37.5	40.0
Official creditors	13.8	13.3	11.8	15.3	18.2	14.5
Bilateral	6.4	6.0	4.6	7.4	8.6	5.3
Multilateral	7.5	7.3	7.3	7.9	9.6	9.2
World Bank	4.0	3.2	3.9	5.0	6.2	6.5
Other multilateral	2.3	2.7	2.5	2.7	3.7	2.8
IMF	1.2	1.4	0.9	0.2	-0.3	-0.1
Private creditors	2.4	12.6	17.8	15.6	19.3	25.5
Net medium- and long-term debt flows	2.1	12.7	8.4	14.3	19.7	22.6
Public and publicly guaranteed	0.9	5.2	5.3	7.1	11.8	9.5
Private nonguaranteed	1.3	7.4	3.1	7.1	7.9	13.1
Net short-term debt flows	0.3	-0.1	9.4	1.4	-0.4	2.9
Memorandum Item						
Worker remit. & comp. of employees	31.2	35.7	36.2	36.3	36.9	39.8

Sources: World Bank Debtor Reporting System, International Monetary Fund, and Bank for International Settlement.

Figure O. 24 Net Foreign Direct Investment Flows to Select Countries, 2015

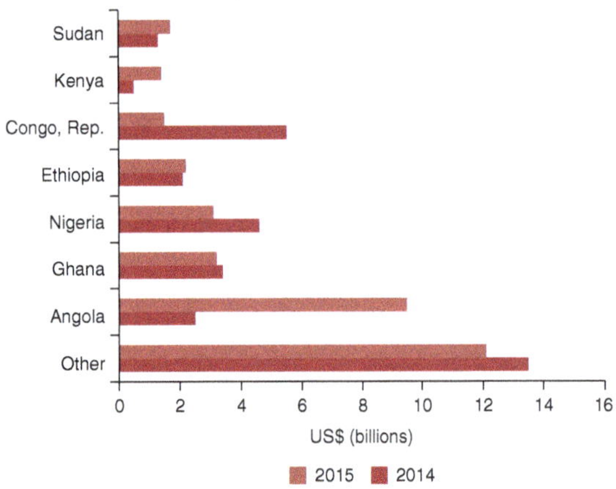

Source: International Monetary Fund.

The upward trajectory in net financial flows was a consequence of a continued increase in both debt and equity flows. Equity flows rose 9 percent in 2015 to $42 billion, maintaining their share of total financial flows at just over half. Portfolio equity flows surged 48 percent, to nearly triple the 2014 level, but were directed primarily to South Africa where investors found opportunities as stock market prices tumbled. Conversely, legislative uncertainties in the country weighed on FDI to South Africa, and flows turned negative. For Sub-Saharan Africa (excluding South Africa), FDI in 2015 was little changed from 2014, but with some important shifts across recipient countries. Angola, far and away the largest recipient, attracting $9.5 billion; local affiliates counteracted the economic downturn by borrowing from parent companies to strengthen their balance sheets. Inflows to Nigeria were dragged down by lower oil prices and delays in some major exploration projects, and those to the Republic of Congo fell sharply. High world cocoa prices keep inflows to Ghana on an even keel, and in Sudan they jumped to $1.7 billion on account of continued Chinese investment in the oil sector. Investor confidence in Kenya's business climate and booming domestic market pushed inflows to a record high of $1.4 billion, and they stayed strong in Ethiopia, which benefits from its privileged export position under the African Growth and Opportunity Act.

Net debt flows to the region, excluding South Africa, fell 16 percent in 2015, their first decline since 2012, reflected vulnerabilities to developments in the global economy, the fall in world market prices for oil and other commodities, the slowdown in China, and knock-on effects on growth prospects, with many currencies depreciating significantly against the U.S. dollar. Net debt flows to public and publicly guaranteed sector borrowers, which accounted for 82 percent of total net debt flows, decreased by 21 percent in 2015 to $22 billion, as disbursements on new financing fell sharply while amortization payments rose. However, the impact was largely concentrated in market-based borrowers like Botswana and Mauritius, and in oil exporters, notably Angola and the Republic of Congo. Net flows from bilateral creditors were hit hardest, decreasing by 38 percent, largely on account of cutbacks in financing by China or borrower cancellation of undisbursed Chinese loans (as in the case of Ghana) when Chinese lending terms tightened. Net debt flows to the private nonguaranteed sector borrowers declined almost 50 percent, to $2.9 billion, as new bond issuances decreased sharply, but these flows are concentrated in only a handful of countries. Conversely, short-term debt inflows not only remained positive, in contrast to the outflows experienced by many low- and middle-income countries, but increased to $1.9 billion, over 50 percent higher than the level of 2014.

The combined external debt stock of countries in the region (excluding South Africa) continued on an upward trajectory in 2015, rising by 7.5 percent, a marked contrast to the decline in external debt stocks reported by other low- and middle-income countries over the same period. The aggregate figure masks some wide divergence in the pace of debt accumulation at the individual level, with some countries in Sub-Saharan Africa recording the fastest rising external debt levels of any low- and middle-income countries. Between end 2013 and 2015, the external debt stock Ethiopia, Kenya, Liberia, Nigeria, and Zambia rose by over 35 percent, and that of another 16 countries in the region by more than 10 percent. In several countries, the rapid rise in outstanding external debt is attributable to large bond issuance in international capital markets. The impact of a sharp increase in external obligations at a time when global economic outcomes have heightened vulnerability to exogenous shocks is evident from the change in the debt-to-export ratio of countries in the region. This ratio rose to 116 percent at end 2015 from 87 percent at end 2014. As expected, some of the most severely affected countries were those dependent on oil or mineral exports like Nigeria and Zambia. Increased debt burdens also raise issues of debt sustainability, and as the most recent, publicly available IMF–World Bank debt sustainability analysis shows, several countries in the region, including some that benefited from the Heavily Indebted Poor Country (HIPC) initiative, have a high risk of debt distress.

Figure O.25 Net Debt Inflows to Sub-Saharan Africa, 2014–15

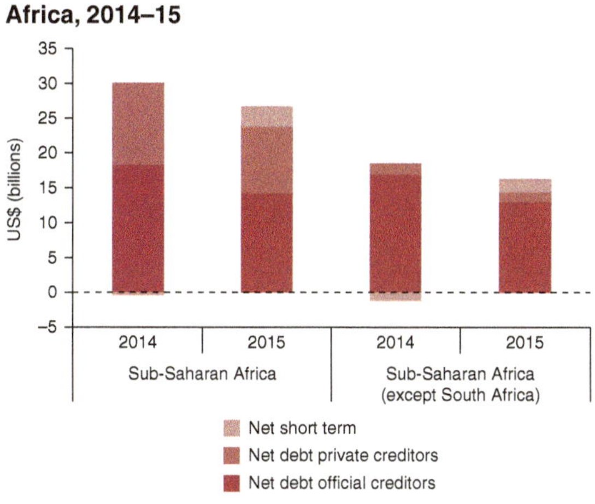

Source: World Bank Debtor Reporting System.

Figure O.26 Change in External Debt Stocks for Select African Countries, 2013–15

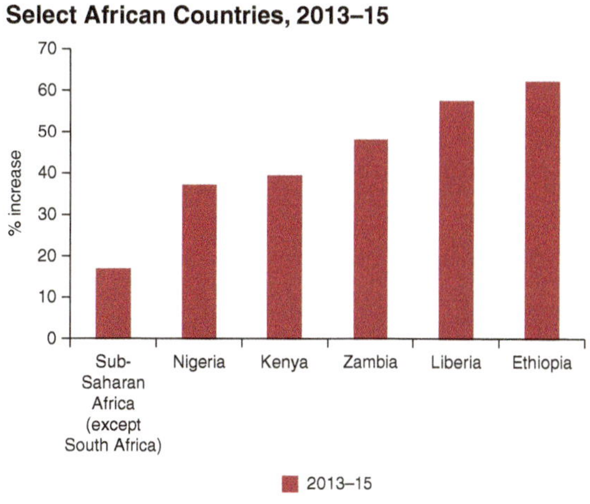

Source: World Bank Debtor Reporting System.

External Debt Trends in High-Income Economies

The combined external debt stock of high-income economies reporting to the QEDS database declined for the second consecutive year, with gross external debt stocks down an average 3.7 percent in 2015.

Figure O.27 High-Income Economies, change in external debt stock, 2015

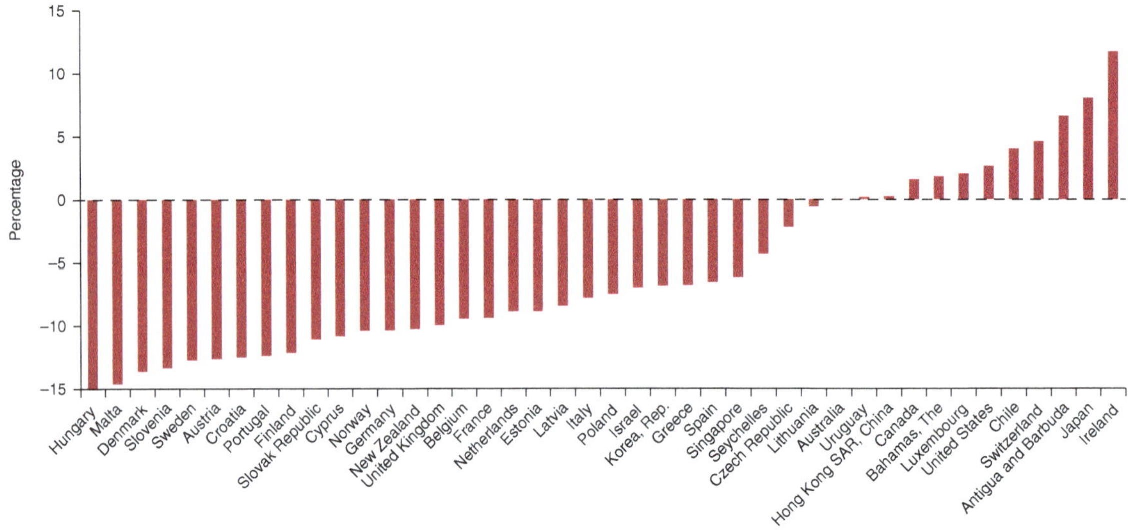

Source: Quarterly External Debt Statistics Database.

Most high-income economies saw their external debt position fall in 2015. At year end, their combined gross external debt stock stood at $67.4 trillion, down from a peak of $70.8 trillion at end 2013. At the country level, 14 of the 43 high-income economies reporting to QEDS recorded a reduction in external debt stock at end 2015, ranging from 10 percent to 15 percent, while a further 15 economies reported external debt stock reductions of between 2 percent and 9 percent. In part, lower external debt stocks reflected changes in the valuation of national currencies relative to the U.S. dollar (the QEDS reporting numeraire), but it also stemmed from a continuation of consolidated efforts to reduce public debt burdens. Iceland was in a league of its own, posting a 69 percent fall in gross external debt stock in 2015, thanks to a sizable increase in its non-borrowed foreign exchange reserves. This enabled prepayment of a bilateral loan from Poland, the Avens Bond, held by domestic pension funds, and some Eurobonds through a $500 million debt buyback operation. For 11 high-income economies, external debt stocks rose in 2015. Ireland saw the largest increase, up 12 percent, driven largely by a 73 percent rise in direct investment intercompany lending. External debt stocks rose by 8 percent in Japan, 5 percent in Switzerland, and 4 percent in Chile over the comparable figure for end 2014.

Figure O.28 External Debt Stock of G-7 and Other High-Income Economies, 2010–15

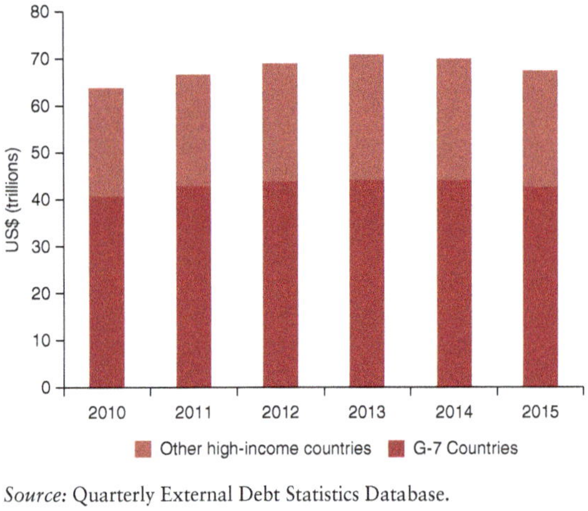

Source: Quarterly External Debt Statistics Database.

The Group of Seven (G-7) countries accounted for 63 percent of the external debt stock of all high-income countries reporting to the QEDS. At end 2015, their combined external debt stock stood at $42.6 billion, a decline of 3.4 percent from the comparable figure at end 2014. Three of the seven, France, Germany, and the United Kingdom, saw external debt stock decline by about 10 percent, while Italy's was down 7.8 percent. Conversely, Japan reported an 8.0 percent rise in external debt stock, while for the United States and Canada it rose only moderately, 2.6 percent and 1.6 percent, respectively. Other high-income economies, which together accounted for 37 percent of the external debt stock of high-income economies reporting to QEDS, fell on average by 4.2 percent in 2015.

From a borrower or sector perspective, the overall average decline in high-income economies' gross external debt position was largely the consequence of a contraction in the external debt liabilities of deposit-taking corporations (excluding central banks) and comprising primarily commercial banks. This category of external debt fell by $1.9 trillion, or 8 percent, in 2015 to $21.1 trillion at year end. Another contributing factor was the $0.7 billion (4 percent) decline in general government external debt stock, which at year's end stood at $15.3 trillion. During 2015, most high-income economies recorded reductions in their general government external debt stock, although there were a few economies where there was a marked increase in this category of debt: Norway recorded a 21 percent increase, Japan 15 percent, the Czech Republic 13 percent, and Chile 10 percent. The outlier was Hong Kong SAR, China, where the external debt of the general government was up 93 percent in 2015 on account of a doubling in debt securities. In most economies, the reduction in external debt liabilities was driven by a contraction in debt securities; they fell on average 9 percent in the case of deposit-taking corporations, and 4 percent with regard to general government.

Although external debt stocks fell in 2015, most high-income economies recorded increases in the external debt-to-GDP ratio. For all high-income economies reporting to QEDS combined, it rose to 150 percent in 2015, from 147 percent in 2014. For G-7 countries the story was mixed. In the United States, the debt-to-GDP ratio remained constant, 99 percent, despite the rise in level of external debt stocks over the past three years. The United Kingdom saw an improvement in 2015, although the debt-to-GDP ratio remains elevated at 290 percent. Other G-7 countries saw the ratio deteriorate in 2015. In Canada it rose to 100 percent, from 86 percent in 2014, and in Japan it jumped to 71 percent (59 percent in 2014). France, Germany, and Italy also saw a deterioration in the debt-to-GDP ratio in 2015.

Figure O.29 High-Income Economies, External Debt Stock by Sector, 2014–15

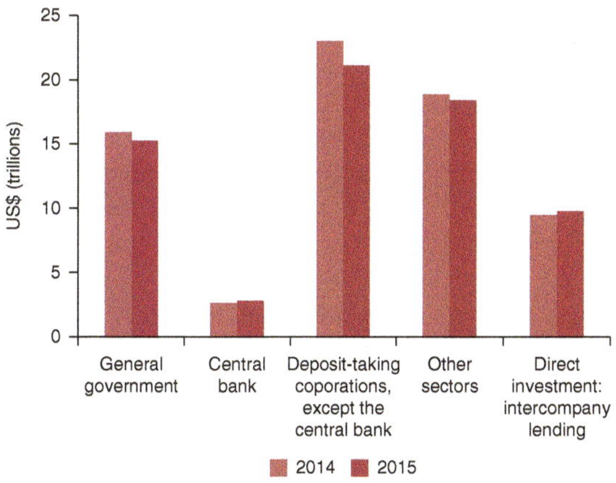

Source: Quarterly External Debt Statistics Database.

Figure O.30 G-7 Countries, External Debt-to-GDP Ratio, 2010–15

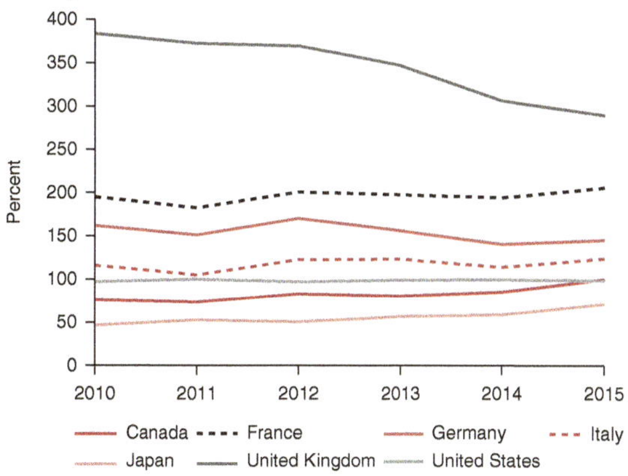

Source: Quarterly External Debt Statistics Database and International Monetary Fund.

Public Sector Debt Statistics – Trends in 2015

Government debt in OECD countries remained high but broadly unchanged in 2015.

Figure O.31 OECD Countries, Government Debt-to-GDP Ratio, 2015

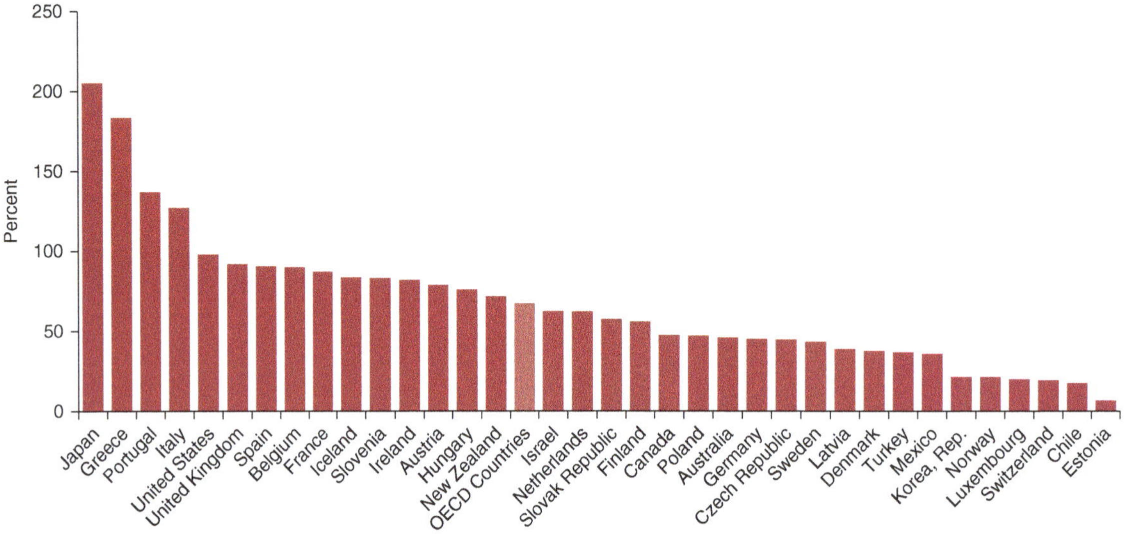

Source: World Bank, Public Sector Debt Statistics Database.

Debt-to-GDP ratios averaged 67.2 percent in OECD countries but varied widely

Countries reporting to the quarterly PSDS database indicate that government debt levels in OECD economies remained high in 2015, and broadly unchanged at $41.4 trillion, but government debt burdens, measured by the debt-to-GDP ratio varied considerably. The ratio ranged from a low of 6.7 percent for Estonia, to a high of 205 percent in the case of Japan, the highest of any advanced economy—due, in part, to higher spending on social services for an aging population coupled with slow GDP growth. Ireland saw a sharp 28 percent decrease of the government debt burden in 2015, the outcome of the 26 percent rise in GDP, resulting from a significant revision of the stock of capital assets, and an 11 percent decline in debt stock. Iceland, one of the top performers in terms of economic growth since 2008, saw its debt- to-GDP ratio drop below 100 percent. Greece remained the most indebted country in the group. Despite concerted efforts by the authorities to tighten fiscal policies and implement structural economic reforms over the past two years, the government debt-to-GDP ratio increased by a further 1.8 percentage points in 2015 to 183.1 percent. Portugal and Italy had the second and third highest debt-to-GDP ratios among OECD economies in 2015; 137 percent and 127 percent, respectively. In the United States, government debt stocks, of which 85 percent consti- tuted debt securities, rose 4.5 percent in 2015 to $17.7 trillion, equivalent to 98 percent of GDP. The United Kingdom, where 70 percent of government debt is owed to domestic creditors, had a similar debt-to-GDP ratio, 92 percent.

Figure O.32 Central Government Debt-to-GDP ratios, Select Middle-Income Countries, 2011 and 2015

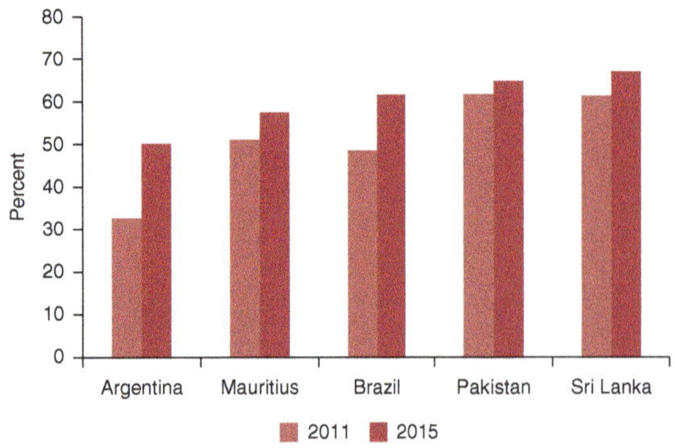

Source: World Bank, Public Sector Debt Statistics Database.

Emerging market economies debt continues to rise

Government debt levels in low- and middle-income countries were, on average, higher in 2015 than the previous year, with the ratio of central government to GDP ranging from 10.4 to 76 percent. Argentina, Brazil, Mauritius, Pakistan, and Sri Lanka had the highest ratio of central government debt to GDP among low- and middle-income countries Market risk was mitigated by increasing the domestic currency borrowing of the central government, with Brazil and China raising virtually all of government financing needs in domestic markets and domestic currency in 2015. Other countries that relied heavily on domestic markets were Mauritius, Morocco, Nigeria, and South Africa. At end 2015, the domestic currency component of government debt for countries reporting to the PSDS database, excluding Brazil and China, averaged 45 percent of the total.

Facilitating analytical use of public debt statistics and coherent cross-country comparisons

The quarterly PSDS database provides a strong methodological framework for the compilation of comprehensive statistics on public sector debt. The reporting requirement covers the public sector debt of all relevant sectors of the economy: (1) general government, (2) central government, (3) budgetary central government, (4) nonfinancial public corporations, (5) financial public corporations, and (6) the total consolidated public sector debt. Similarly the instrument coverage for each sector is both comprehensive and identical, comprised of (1) debt securities, (2) loans, (3) currency and deposits, (4) Special Drawing Rights, (5) other accounts payable, and (6) insurance, pensions, and standardized guarantee schemes. The quarterly PSD is a relatively new international reporting initiative, and countries' willingness to participate has been strong. At present, however, the vast majority of countries reporting to the quarterly PSDS database provide information for public sector debt narrowly defined as that of the central government, and in many cases for only a subset of debt instruments—typically debt securities and loans. Only 21 of the 72 countries reporting to the quarterly PSDS database on a regular basis provide reports that cover total public sector debt.

To ensure that cross-country comparisons of indicators drawn from the PSDS database are coherent, the IMF, the OECD, and the World Bank have collaborated on defining a presentation matrix that groups public sector debt into four categories or dimensions ranging from a narrow to a comprehensive coverage of instruments for each sector of the economy. The first dimension, D1, comprises debt securities and loans, typically the largest share of public debt. The second dimension, D2, comprises all D1 instruments, plus SDR holdings and currency and deposits.' The third dimension, D3, includes other accounts payable (in addition to all instruments captured by D2), and provides an important indicator of crisis in periods of financial distress. Finally, the fourth dimension, D4, includes insurance, pensions, and standardized guarantee schemes in addition to the indicators covered by D3. At present, seven countries reporting to the PSDS database provide information on public debt that covers all instruments and conforms to the D1 category; five of those are high-income OECD countries, and two are low- and middle-income countries.

Figure O.33 Status of Reporting for Public Debt of Each Sector of the Economy

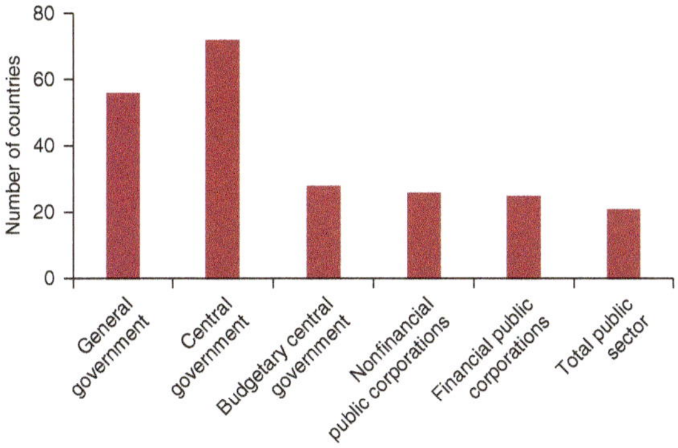

Source: World Bank, Public Sector Debt Statistics Database.

Figure O.34 Coverage of Public Sector Debt by D1-D4 Categories

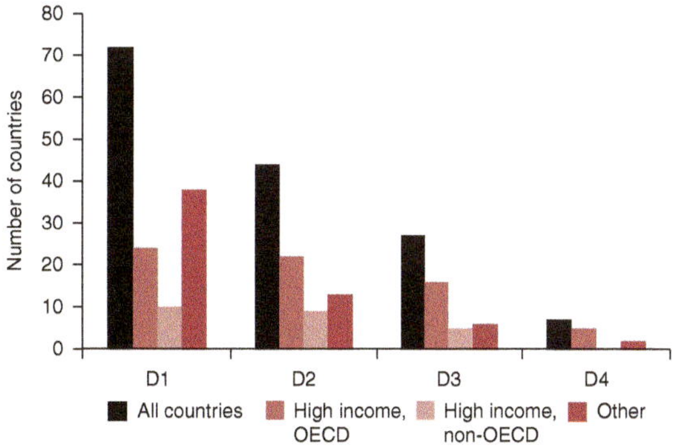

Source: Public Sector Debt Statistics Database.

PART II

Aggregate and Country Tables

ALL LOW- AND MIDDLE-INCOME COUNTRIES

(US$ billion, unless otherwise indicated)

	2000	2005	2010	2011	2012	2013	2014	2015
Summary external debt data								
External debt stocks	**2,091.2**	**2,532.3**	**4,023.8**	**5,298.6**	**5,871.8**	**6,638.1**	**7,071.2**	**6,669.4**
Long-term external debt	1,732.9	1,972.4	3,132.9	3,573.9	4,005.2	4,437.5	4,753.8	4,750.0
Public and publicly guaranteed	1,271.2	1,295.5	1,673.5	1,798.8	2,024.8	2,237.0	2,382.2	2,419.9
Official creditors	748.5	711.6	826.8	858.2	876.6	901.5	908.8	910.7
of which: IMF	78.4	69.4	154.5	154.4	146.1	128.4	113.8	113.7
Private creditors	522.7	583.9	846.8	940.6	1,148.2	1,335.5	1,473.5	1,509.2
of which: Bonds	331.2	414.9	558.5	617.8	787.9	862.9	975.4	1,028.2
Private nonguaranteed	461.7	676.9	1,459.4	1,775.1	1,980.4	2,200.6	2,371.6	2,330.1
of which: Bonds	97.5	140.5	236.5	280.1	323.5	390.3	449.9	463.3
Short-term external debt	280.0	490.6	736.4	1,570.3	1,720.5	2,072.2	2,203.6	1,805.6
interest arrears on long-term	31.8	28.7	21.0	18.0	20.3	19.4	20.4	20.9
Long-term external debt								
Disbursements	**222.4**	**366.6**	**642.2**	**770.4**	**852.3**	**929.0**	**969.0**	**803.1**
Public and publicly guaranteed	136.0	148.9	293.3	262.1	318.0	370.8	379.8	314.9
Official creditors	52.3	45.7	111.0	92.6	91.4	108.3	108.6	102.2
Private creditors	83.7	103.2	182.3	169.5	226.6	262.6	271.2	212.7
of which: Bonds	54.8	67.6	102.9	105.1	167.0	125.2	184.7	138.0
Private nonguaranteed	86.3	217.7	348.9	508.3	534.3	558.2	589.2	488.3
of which: Bonds	12.2	41.3	56.7	100.8	105.6	131.5	114.8	102.6
Principal repayments	**197.4**	**272.5**	**382.2**	**400.0**	**406.7**	**478.6**	**549.9**	**593.9**
Public and publicly guaranteed	103.2	143.5	137.7	141.7	111.9	146.5	169.5	227.8
Official creditors	46.9	69.3	51.3	60.5	53.7	62.7	56.2	69.2
Private creditors	56.3	74.2	86.5	81.2	58.2	83.8	113.2	158.6
of which: Bonds	22.0	44.0	36.8	36.4	19.0	40.8	55.8	65.7
Private nonguaranteed	94.2	129.0	244.5	258.3	294.8	332.2	380.4	366.1
of which: Bonds	16.3	17.1	17.8	18.0	33.6	36.0	47.3	61.4
Interest payments	**92.0**	**81.9**	**106.4**	**124.1**	**151.7**	**142.1**	**154.2**	**159.6**
Public and publicly guaranteed	63.2	60.3	51.0	56.3	81.1	65.4	71.2	78.4
Official creditors	25.7	23.7	15.5	16.3	17.6	17.0	17.0	17.0
Private creditors	37.5	36.6	35.5	40.0	63.4	48.4	54.2	61.4
of which: Bonds	25.4	30.3	30.2	34.6	57.5	42.2	46.5	52.7
Private nonguaranteed	28.8	21.6	55.4	67.8	70.6	76.7	83.0	81.2
of which: Bonds	8.0	8.1	12.7	18.3	16.2	21.7	24.3	25.2
Net financial flows								
Net inflows	**150.5**	**466.6**	**852.1**	**1,815.9**	**1,223.5**	**1,441.3**	**1,159.3**	**379.3**
Net debt inflows	5.2	137.5	195.0	1,207.8	585.1	785.2	542.3	-184.5
Official creditors	-5.0	-63.6	73.2	32.6	29.2	27.8	45.2	37.7
of which: World Bank	8.0	2.9	22.4	6.5	12.1	14.1	16.9	19.3
of which: IMF	-10.5	-40.0	13.4	0.5	-8.4	-17.7	-7.2	4.8
Private creditors	10.2	201.1	121.8	1,175.2	555.8	757.3	497.1	-222.2
Long-term	19.6	117.7	200.2	338.3	407.9	404.8	366.7	176.2
Bonds	28.7	47.9	105.0	151.4	220.1	179.9	196.5	113.6
Banks and other private	-9.1	69.8	95.2	186.8	187.8	224.9	170.2	62.7
Short-term	-9.3	83.4	-78.4	836.9	147.9	352.5	130.4	-398.4
Net equity inflows	145.3	329.1	657.0	608.1	638.4	656.1	616.9	563.8
Foreign direct investment	131.1	263.0	538.8	616.2	549.4	590.8	536.1	543.0
Portfolio equity	14.3	66.1	118.2	-8.1	89.0	65.3	80.8	20.8
Major economic aggregates								
Gross national income (GNI)	5,701.6	9,416.2	20,022.7	23,544.4	24,991.9	26,363.2	27,360.3	25,892.2
Exports of goods, services & prim. income	1,499.1	3,128.6	5,634.5	6,937.3	7,250.8	7,463.6	7,658.8	6,819.9
Imports of goods, services & prim. income	1,544.5	3,077.0	5,814.3	7,243.5	7,568.1	7,948.3	7,988.4	7,080.0
Primary income on FDI	64.7	184.6	496.4	594.8	543.9	578.6	361.7	272.7
Personal transfers & comp. of employees	73.0	170.8	300.0	336.8	362.8	383.3	406.9	415.7
International reserves	592.3	1,894.5	5,350.1	5,832.0	6,122.9	6,613.4	6,497.9	5,861.5
Ratios								
External debt stocks to exports (%)	139.5	80.9	71.4	76.4	81.0	88.9	92.3	97.8
External debt stocks to GNI (%)	36.7	26.9	20.1	22.5	23.5	25.2	25.8	25.8
Debt service to exports (%)	22.0	13.4	9.5	8.3	8.6	9.3	10.1	11.9
Short-term to external debt stocks (%)	13.4	19.4	18.3	29.6	29.3	31.2	31.2	27.1
Multilateral to external debt stocks (%)	15.5	14.6	12.0	9.5	9.0	8.3	7.9	8.6
Reserves to external debt stocks (%)	28.3	74.8	133.0	110.1	104.3	99.6	91.9	87.9

EAST ASIA AND PACIFIC

(US$ billion, unless otherwise indicated)

	2000	2005	2010	2011	2012	2013	2014	2015
Summary external debt data								
External debt stocks	**497.0**	**642.8**	**803.1**	**1,682.8**	**1,904.4**	**2,261.0**	**2,612.4**	**2,273.8**
Long-term external debt	418.1	434.7	627.2	715.3	864.9	942.2	1,136.7	1,135.4
Public and publicly guaranteed	270.9	279.4	375.4	400.4	462.7	478.6	519.7	521.8
Official creditors	171.4	172.5	211.3	216.4	211.0	195.7	188.7	180.7
of which: IMF	17.8	10.0	20.5	20.4	20.3	20.3	19.0	18.2
Private creditors	99.5	106.9	164.1	183.9	251.7	282.9	331.0	341.1
of which: Bonds	35.8	67.4	124.1	136.5	198.0	213.9	247.8	267.8
Private nonguaranteed	147.2	155.4	251.7	315.0	402.2	463.6	617.0	613.6
of which: Bonds	36.7	36.2	37.9	60.5	93.3	113.8	161.4	203.7
Short-term external debt	61.1	198.1	155.5	947.1	1,019.3	1,298.5	1,456.7	1,120.1
interest arrears on long-term	5.2	0.9	1.2	1.2	1.0	0.9	0.8	0.8
Long-term external debt								
Disbursements	**42.6**	**79.3**	**124.6**	**176.7**	**217.6**	**197.6**	**285.1**	**270.2**
Public and publicly guaranteed	29.2	30.0	53.4	67.9	83.3	58.3	87.2	73.4
Official creditors	16.1	9.1	17.0	16.8	16.6	15.8	17.5	16.3
Private creditors	13.1	20.9	36.3	51.2	66.7	42.5	69.7	57.1
of which: Bonds	4.5	15.5	20.7	30.9	52.9	22.7	50.3	39.9
Private nonguaranteed	13.4	49.3	71.3	108.8	134.3	139.3	197.9	196.8
of which: Bonds	3.2	7.8	4.1	25.4	39.9	41.8	56.3	61.7
Principal repayments	**47.0**	**66.9**	**66.3**	**74.7**	**85.6**	**97.6**	**109.5**	**165.9**
Public and publicly guaranteed	22.8	24.4	28.6	29.7	23.8	23.9	29.9	61.5
Official creditors	10.3	10.8	16.4	15.0	14.7	16.9	14.1	21.8
Private creditors	12.6	13.6	12.2	14.7	9.1	7.0	15.8	39.7
of which: Bonds	1.2	4.3	5.1	5.7	1.6	0.4	11.2	11.7
Private nonguaranteed	24.2	42.5	37.6	45.0	61.7	73.7	79.5	104.3
of which: Bonds	6.6	4.3	4.2	4.1	4.3	9.1	11.0	18.3
Interest payments	**20.5**	**12.7**	**17.2**	**19.7**	**21.8**	**24.1**	**26.9**	**30.3**
Public and publicly guaranteed	12.9	8.6	9.7	10.3	11.3	11.2	11.4	12.5
Official creditors	7.3	4.0	3.7	3.9	4.7	3.9	3.6	3.5
Private creditors	5.7	4.6	5.9	6.4	6.6	7.3	7.8	9.0
of which: Bonds	2.3	3.2	5.0	5.4	5.7	6.5	7.1	7.9
Private nonguaranteed	7.5	4.1	7.5	9.4	10.5	12.9	15.5	17.8
of which: Bonds	2.6	1.6	1.7	4.1	4.9	6.6	8.7	10.0
Net financial flows								
Net inflows	**41.2**	**188.0**	**174.3**	**1,194.9**	**506.9**	**727.6**	**652.7**	**45.2**
Net debt inflows	-14.2	47.7	-138.6	893.6	204.4	379.3	334.0	-232.2
Official creditors	7.0	-3.2	0.6	1.7	1.8	-1.2	3.3	-5.5
of which: World Bank	1.8	-0.6	2.7	0.9	1.4	2.4	1.7	3.3
of which: IMF	1.2	-1.6	0.0	0.0	-0.1	-0.1	-0.1	0.0
Private creditors	-21.2	51.0	-139.2	891.8	202.6	380.5	330.7	-226.7
Long-term	-10.2	14.1	57.8	100.2	130.1	101.2	172.3	109.9
Bonds	0.0	14.7	15.6	46.5	86.9	54.8	84.4	71.6
Banks and other private	-10.2	-0.7	42.1	53.7	43.3	46.4	87.9	38.3
Short-term	-11.0	36.9	-196.9	791.6	72.4	279.3	158.4	-336.6
Net equity inflows	55.3	140.2	312.9	301.3	302.5	348.4	318.7	277.4
Foreign direct investment	48.7	114.3	273.1	294.2	267.8	319.7	267.9	273.5
Portfolio equity	6.6	26.0	39.8	7.1	34.7	28.7	50.8	3.8
Major economic aggregates								
Gross national income (GNI)	1,703.9	3,071.2	7,792.8	9,456.3	10,599.2	11,621.4	12,540.3	12,964.9
Exports of goods, services & prim. income	533.2	1,299.7	2,551.8	3,115.8	3,341.8	3,559.6	3,813.0	3,638.9
Imports of goods, services & prim. income	503.4	1,197.9	2,341.7	2,998.1	3,172.2	3,458.3	3,564.3	3,312.8
Primary income on FDI	31.7	73.7	206.5	256.9	232.8	268.7	64.6	55.6
Personal transfers & comp. of employees	12.6	28.8	56.9	62.7	67.2	73.8	88.7	106.4
International reserves	275.5	1,003.8	3,315.6	3,708.8	3,871.9	4,344.3	4,352.2	3,808.8
Ratios								
External debt stocks to exports (%)	93.2	49.5	31.5	54.0	57.0	63.5	68.5	62.5
External debt stocks to GNI (%)	29.2	20.9	10.3	17.8	18.0	19.5	20.8	17.5
Debt service to exports (%)	13.6	6.6	4.4	4.1	4.3	4.4	4.5	6.4
Short-term to external debt stocks (%)	12.3	30.8	19.4	56.3	53.5	57.4	55.8	49.3
Multilateral to external debt stocks (%)	13.2	10.0	10.8	5.3	4.8	4.1	3.6	4.3
Reserves to external debt stocks (%)	55.4	156.1	412.9	220.4	203.3	192.1	166.6	167.5

EUROPE AND CENTRAL ASIA

(US$ billion, unless otherwise indicated)

	2000	2005	2010	2011	2012	2013	2014	2015
Summary external debt data								
External debt stocks	**350.1**	**611.6**	**1,260.7**	**1,422.1**	**1,525.9**	**1,703.9**	**1,573.7**	**1,449.0**
Long-term external debt	260.4	471.7	968.9	1,110.8	1,190.5	1,350.1	1,274.1	1,202.2
Public and publicly guaranteed	194.6	197.7	360.5	403.9	440.9	534.0	500.3	466.6
Official creditors	114.0	85.8	108.1	114.1	117.0	124.2	124.3	121.6
of which: IMF	34.2	32.7	62.3	61.1	53.1	37.2	28.1	29.9
Private creditors	80.6	111.9	252.4	289.8	323.9	409.7	376.0	344.9
of which: Bonds	45.1	66.0	88.2	102.0	142.3	172.3	168.5	164.8
Private nonguaranteed	65.8	274.1	608.4	706.9	749.5	816.1	773.8	735.6
of which: Bonds	3.3	25.6	34.0	41.0	45.9	64.5	64.9	55.9
Short-term external debt	55.5	107.2	229.6	250.2	282.4	316.6	271.6	216.9
interest arrears on long-term	8.5	4.1	2.3	0.7	2.5	0.9	3.5	3.8
Long-term external debt								
Disbursements	**35.6**	**140.0**	**234.8**	**260.9**	**282.1**	**300.7**	**184.9**	**146.3**
Public and publicly guaranteed	20.7	26.6	88.0	63.1	66.1	113.6	44.5	52.1
Official creditors	6.7	5.1	22.6	17.1	12.1	17.0	18.1	14.8
Private creditors	14.0	21.5	65.4	46.0	54.0	96.6	26.4	37.3
of which: Bonds	7.5	8.3	23.3	22.6	43.8	43.2	23.7	29.7
Private nonguaranteed	14.8	113.4	146.8	197.8	216.0	187.1	140.4	94.2
of which: Bonds	0.5	14.1	2.8	15.2	12.0	24.5	17.3	6.9
Principal repayments	**25.2**	**80.6**	**175.8**	**155.0**	**148.3**	**176.8**	**186.2**	**193.4**
Public and publicly guaranteed	12.3	38.2	42.5	36.1	29.2	39.0	61.0	74.7
Official creditors	5.7	23.6	6.0	9.8	9.5	10.7	8.6	10.1
Private creditors	6.7	14.6	36.5	26.3	19.7	28.3	52.5	64.5
of which: Bonds	2.2	10.2	10.0	8.8	3.5	13.8	23.4	31.3
Private nonguaranteed	12.9	42.4	133.3	118.9	119.1	137.8	125.2	118.7
of which: Bonds	0.9	2.0	2.9	4.4	9.1	8.8	11.3	15.7
Interest payments	**11.9**	**18.8**	**34.1**	**40.4**	**40.8**	**40.3**	**44.2**	**40.7**
Public and publicly guaranteed	8.3	11.5	8.8	11.1	11.8	12.4	13.7	12.9
Official creditors	2.9	4.0	1.9	2.5	2.7	2.4	2.6	2.3
Private creditors	5.4	7.5	6.9	8.6	9.1	10.0	11.2	10.6
of which: Bonds	3.6	5.6	4.8	6.5	6.8	8.3	9.1	8.8
Private nonguaranteed	3.5	7.3	25.3	29.3	29.0	27.9	30.4	27.8
of which: Bonds	0.3	1.9	2.2	2.3	2.2	2.6	3.6	4.4
Net financial flows								
Net inflows	**26.3**	**120.6**	**177.0**	**202.9**	**229.7**	**211.4**	**-3.5**	**-51.3**
Net debt inflows	18.3	69.4	111.9	127.1	156.0	144.0	-56.2	-99.0
Official creditors	0.6	-28.2	25.6	6.4	-5.5	-9.5	2.3	7.8
of which: World Bank	1.9	-0.6	3.3	2.3	1.6	1.7	2.7	1.9
of which: IMF	-0.5	-9.8	9.0	-1.0	-8.0	-15.8	-7.3	3.1
Private creditors	17.8	97.7	86.4	120.7	161.5	153.5	-58.4	-106.7
Long-term	9.2	77.8	42.4	98.5	131.2	117.7	-10.8	-51.8
Bonds	4.9	10.2	13.1	24.6	43.2	45.2	6.3	-10.4
Banks and other private	4.3	67.5	29.3	73.9	88.0	72.5	-17.2	-41.4
Short-term	8.5	19.9	44.0	22.2	30.3	35.8	-47.6	-54.9
Net equity inflows	7.9	51.1	65.1	75.9	73.7	67.5	52.7	47.7
Foreign direct investment	7.1	44.7	66.0	86.1	65.7	71.9	62.5	55.1
Portfolio equity	0.9	6.5	-0.9	-10.3	8.0	-4.5	-9.8	-7.4
Major economic aggregates								
Gross national income (GNI)	677.9	1,627.8	2,968.7	3,644.5	3,813.7	3,987.5	3,747.1	2,818.4
Exports of goods, services & prim. income	243.6	580.2	988.8	1,260.5	1,312.8	1,323.6	1,290.2	982.3
Imports of goods, services & prim. income	223.2	550.8	998.7	1,267.5	1,326.6	1,388.7	1,292.6	978.2
Primary income on FDI	2.9	31.8	81.2	107.8	112.0	117.4	106.3	67.9
Personal transfers & comp. of employees	8.3	18.0	37.3	43.8	46.4	54.6	51.6	37.3
International reserves	59.3	295.3	682.2	695.9	741.8	737.9	581.8	540.6
Ratios								
External debt stocks to exports (%)	143.7	105.4	127.5	112.8	116.2	128.7	122.0	147.5
External debt stocks to GNI (%)	51.6	37.6	42.5	39.0	40.0	42.7	42.0	51.4
Debt service to exports (%)	19.0	20.2	22.0	16.2	15.5	18.2	19.3	24.8
Short-term to external debt stocks (%)	15.9	17.5	18.2	17.6	18.5	18.6	17.3	15.0
Multilateral to external debt stocks (%)	8.1	6.1	5.9	5.7	5.7	5.6	5.9	6.2
Reserves to external debt stocks (%)	16.9	48.3	54.1	48.9	48.6	43.3	37.0	37.3

LATIN AMERICA AND THE CARIBBEAN

(US$ billion, unless otherwise indicated)

	2000	2005	2010	2011	2012	2013	2014	2015
Summary external debt data								
External debt stocks	**725.3**	**703.8**	**1,098.0**	**1,253.9**	**1,387.9**	**1,534.9**	**1,688.3**	**1,695.7**
Long-term external debt	611.9	577.0	870.6	1,023.5	1,136.2	1,249.4	1,383.1	1,399.2
Public and publicly guaranteed	396.4	412.0	475.0	503.1	567.3	626.2	716.0	744.1
Official creditors	137.3	131.1	166.8	170.3	182.0	189.5	200.5	201.4
of which: IMF	11.1	13.4	23.6	23.8	23.7	23.5	21.5	20.2
Private creditors	259.1	280.9	308.2	332.8	385.4	436.7	515.6	542.7
of which: Bonds	222.9	240.9	266.5	290.6	328.5	349.3	391.1	408.2
Private nonguaranteed	215.5	165.0	395.6	520.3	568.9	623.2	667.1	655.1
of which: Bonds	53.7	67.9	142.0	153.8	160.6	188.5	199.2	177.1
Short-term external debt	102.4	113.4	203.8	206.7	228.0	262.0	283.7	276.2
interest arrears on long-term	1.7	9.1	5.8	6.4	6.6	6.8	5.8	5.9
Long-term external debt								
Disbursements	**110.5**	**93.1**	**188.9**	**229.2**	**230.6**	**265.0**	**269.9**	**226.1**
Public and publicly guaranteed	57.3	55.8	87.4	73.4	95.1	110.8	129.6	93.3
Official creditors	15.8	12.3	35.1	22.9	24.7	25.0	26.0	22.8
Private creditors	41.4	43.5	52.3	50.5	70.5	85.8	103.6	70.5
of which: Bonds	34.5	37.4	39.4	40.1	48.8	39.3	63.4	44.3
Private nonguaranteed	53.3	37.2	101.5	155.8	135.4	154.2	140.3	132.7
of which: Bonds	7.6	15.3	47.4	55.1	49.4	59.1	34.5	28.6
Principal repayments	**96.9**	**76.8**	**93.5**	**116.0**	**118.5**	**135.7**	**128.2**	**161.8**
Public and publicly guaranteed	42.1	41.2	40.4	45.2	29.5	45.3	34.6	54.2
Official creditors	16.5	16.0	13.8	18.3	12.4	16.0	13.4	16.5
Private creditors	25.6	25.2	26.6	26.9	17.1	29.2	21.2	37.7
of which: Bonds	17.2	17.9	18.7	16.8	9.0	14.9	15.4	18.2
Private nonguaranteed	54.8	35.6	53.1	70.8	89.0	90.4	93.6	107.6
of which: Bonds	8.8	10.4	7.3	6.6	14.9	14.9	20.6	26.2
Interest payments	**46.2**	**32.6**	**40.6**	**47.2**	**69.3**	**56.2**	**58.1**	**63.1**
Public and publicly guaranteed	29.9	24.4	22.7	24.7	46.5	29.3	32.5	38.1
Official creditors	8.3	5.4	4.5	4.7	4.7	5.0	5.2	5.2
Private creditors	21.6	18.9	18.2	20.0	41.8	24.3	27.3	32.8
of which: Bonds	18.3	17.3	16.9	18.6	40.1	22.1	24.4	29.2
Private nonguaranteed	16.3	8.3	17.9	22.5	22.9	26.9	25.6	25.0
of which: Bonds	4.7	4.2	7.9	10.3	7.7	11.3	10.4	9.4
Net financial flows								
Net inflows	**59.0**	**80.7**	**320.9**	**263.8**	**285.3**	**292.4**	**304.7**	**192.7**
Net debt inflows	-2.0	9.4	153.8	115.7	133.1	162.8	163.7	56.3
Official creditors	-11.4	-31.1	22.6	4.9	12.1	8.7	12.0	5.9
of which: World Bank	2.0	-0.6	8.3	-2.9	3.6	3.2	3.0	3.3
of which: IMF	-10.7	-27.4	1.3	0.2	-0.1	-0.2	-0.6	-0.4
Private creditors	9.4	40.5	131.2	110.8	121.0	154.1	151.7	50.4
Long-term	14.3	20.0	74.1	108.6	99.8	120.3	129.1	58.0
Bonds	16.1	24.4	60.8	71.7	74.3	68.6	61.9	28.5
Banks and other private	-1.8	-4.4	13.3	36.8	25.5	51.7	67.2	29.5
Short-term	-5.0	20.5	57.1	2.2	21.2	33.8	22.7	-7.6
Net equity inflows	61.0	71.3	167.1	148.1	152.1	129.5	141.0	136.4
Foreign direct investment	61.2	60.6	127.7	145.1	133.7	115.5	120.1	120.8
Portfolio equity	-0.1	10.6	39.4	2.9	18.5	14.0	20.8	15.7
Major economic aggregates								
Gross national income (GNI)	1,976.0	2,455.2	4,777.4	5,427.5	5,412.7	5,490.7	5,552.7	4,692.7
Exports of goods, services & prim. income	406.3	601.6	936.1	1,153.1	1,170.0	1,170.5	1,148.0	1,000.8
Imports of goods, services & prim. income	473.8	624.1	1,096.2	1,325.0	1,353.7	1,382.4	1,392.2	1,238.5
Primary income on FDI	19.7	43.4	118.8	133.5	110.0	97.2	101.3	81.7
Personal transfers & comp. of employees	19.6	48.7	56.5	60.0	60.4	61.8	64.1	68.3
International reserves	136.0	228.0	584.1	672.1	728.1	730.0	757.2	722.8
Ratios								
External debt stocks to exports (%)	178.5	117.0	117.3	108.7	118.6	131.1	147.1	169.4
External debt stocks to GNI (%)	36.7	28.7	23.0	23.1	25.6	28.0	30.4	36.1
Debt service to exports (%)	40.5	24.0	14.9	14.6	16.6	17.1	17.0	23.3
Short-term to external debt stocks (%)	14.1	16.1	18.6	16.5	16.4	17.1	16.8	16.3
Multilateral to external debt stocks (%)	12.5	14.3	11.7	10.3	9.8	9.2	8.7	9.1
Reserves to external debt stocks (%)	18.7	32.4	53.2	53.6	52.5	47.6	44.8	42.6

MIDDLE EAST AND NORTH AFRICA

(US$ billion, unless otherwise indicated)

	2000	2005	2010	2011	2012	2013	2014	2015
Summary external debt data								
External debt stocks	**143.7**	**150.5**	**168.1**	**165.8**	**172.9**	**190.9**	**189.4**	**197.5**
Long-term external debt	116.5	122.8	122.0	120.6	130.4	148.5	142.8	149.9
Public and publicly guaranteed	112.5	116.0	114.3	112.6	121.3	138.6	133.2	140.0
Official creditors	88.2	77.8	78.2	78.6	82.5	92.3	86.8	90.2
of which: IMF	3.5	1.6	8.3	8.2	8.6	9.5	10.2	10.7
Private creditors	24.4	38.2	36.1	34.0	38.8	46.4	46.4	49.8
of which: Bonds	7.3	22.1	26.8	25.9	31.5	39.1	39.1	41.7
Private nonguaranteed	4.0	6.8	7.8	8.0	9.1	9.9	9.6	9.9
of which: Bonds	0.8	1.0	0.5	0.5	0.7	0.7	0.7	0.7
Short-term external debt	23.7	26.2	37.7	37.0	33.8	32.9	36.4	36.8
interest arrears on long-term	2.6	0.3	0.3	0.4	0.5	0.6	0.6	0.6
Long-term external debt								
Disbursements	**9.2**	**14.9**	**14.8**	**13.5**	**21.8**	**29.3**	**16.9**	**26.5**
Public and publicly guaranteed	7.9	13.0	13.5	12.1	18.9	25.8	14.5	23.8
Official creditors	3.4	5.5	7.2	7.6	10.4	15.8	7.8	14.9
Private creditors	4.5	7.4	6.2	4.5	8.5	10.0	6.7	9.0
of which: Bonds	2.0	4.1	5.5	4.0	8.3	9.5	4.9	6.8
Private nonguaranteed	1.3	1.9	1.4	1.5	2.9	3.5	2.4	2.7
of which: Bonds	0.1	0.5	0.0	0.0	0.5	0.0	0.0	0.0
Principal repayments	**10.6**	**14.2**	**12.2**	**14.2**	**11.6**	**11.9**	**14.3**	**13.7**
Public and publicly guaranteed	10.4	13.3	10.3	12.8	9.6	9.0	12.3	12.1
Official creditors	5.9	7.9	6.0	6.5	6.2	6.4	7.1	7.2
Private creditors	4.5	5.5	4.4	6.3	3.4	2.6	5.2	4.9
of which: Bonds	0.8	1.9	2.2	4.8	2.6	1.7	4.5	4.0
Private nonguaranteed	0.2	0.8	1.8	1.3	2.0	2.9	2.0	1.6
of which: Bonds	0.1	0.3	0.2	0.0	0.3	0.0	0.0	0.0
Interest payments	**4.9**	**4.8**	**4.3**	**4.2**	**4.0**	**4.2**	**4.2**	**4.3**
Public and publicly guaranteed	4.7	4.5	4.0	4.0	3.7	4.0	4.1	4.1
Official creditors	3.1	2.5	2.1	1.9	1.9	1.8	1.7	1.6
Private creditors	1.6	2.0	1.9	2.0	1.9	2.1	2.4	2.5
of which: Bonds	0.5	1.4	1.6	1.8	1.7	1.9	2.2	2.3
Private nonguaranteed	0.2	0.3	0.3	0.2	0.2	0.3	0.1	0.2
of which: Bonds	0.1	0.1	0.1	0.0	0.0	0.0	0.0	0.0
Net financial flows								
Net inflows	**4.6**	**18.6**	**32.1**	**12.8**	**26.9**	**35.1**	**23.8**	**28.1**
Net debt inflows	0.6	0.3	7.6	-1.4	7.4	17.2	7.6	14.0
Official creditors	-2.7	-3.1	1.3	1.0	4.7	10.2	2.2	8.5
of which: World Bank	-0.3	0.0	0.8	0.9	0.8	1.1	0.9	1.9
of which: IMF	-0.2	-0.7	0.0	-0.1	0.5	0.9	1.5	0.9
Private creditors	3.3	3.4	6.3	-2.3	2.7	7.0	5.3	5.5
Long-term	1.1	3.1	1.4	-1.6	6.0	8.0	1.9	5.1
Bonds	1.3	2.5	3.2	-0.8	5.8	7.8	0.5	2.8
Banks and other private	-0.2	0.5	-1.8	-0.8	0.2	0.2	1.4	2.3
Short-term	2.2	0.3	4.9	-0.7	-3.3	-1.0	3.4	0.4
Net equity inflows	4.0	18.3	24.5	14.2	19.5	17.9	16.3	14.1
Foreign direct investment	3.7	15.9	22.6	14.8	20.7	18.0	15.6	14.4
Portfolio equity	0.3	2.4	2.0	-0.6	-1.2	-0.1	0.6	-0.4
Major economic aggregates								
Gross national income (GNI)	376.5	580.4	1,130.3	1,331.9	1,383.1	1,329.9	1,264.4	1,208.6
Exports of goods, services & prim. income	116.9	206.9	328.7	382.6	411.5	349.9	345.5	284.3
Imports of goods, services & prim. income	108.4	206.7	362.2	400.9	420.2	410.5	424.7	382.0
Primary income on FDI	1.7	10.7	17.5	18.1	19.0	20.1	20.3	14.6
Personal transfers & comp. of employees	10.5	21.7	36.0	38.2	44.6	46.0	49.7	46.2
International reserves	44.0	138.2	298.8	274.4	279.1	289.5	273.8	0.0
Ratios								
External debt stocks to exports (%)	122.9	72.8	51.1	43.3	42.0	54.6	54.8	69.5
External debt stocks to GNI (%)	38.2	25.9	14.9	12.4	12.5	14.4	15.0	16.3
Debt service to exports (%)	14.5	10.2	5.2	5.0	4.0	4.8	5.5	6.6
Short-term to external debt stocks (%)	16.5	17.4	22.4	22.3	19.6	17.2	19.2	18.7
Multilateral to external debt stocks (%)	16.1	17.3	21.6	23.1	23.7	23.4	22.6	21.7
Reserves to external debt stocks (%)	30.6	91.8	177.8	165.5	161.4	151.6	144.5	0.0

SOUTH ASIA

(US$ billion, unless otherwise indicated)

	2000	2005	2010	2011	2012	2013	2014	2015
Summary external debt data								
External debt stocks	**162.3**	**189.2**	**411.1**	**461.4**	**528.0**	**569.7**	**607.2**	**637.1**
Long-term external debt	153.1	174.0	324.3	352.9	403.1	444.5	489.3	521.3
Public and publicly guaranteed	134.5	116.0	188.9	201.5	232.2	236.7	268.6	286.6
Official creditors	101.8	109.2	156.0	163.3	165.4	166.4	164.1	164.9
of which: IMF	3.2	3.7	20.3	20.3	18.8	16.0	14.6	15.2
Private creditors	32.7	6.8	32.8	38.1	66.8	70.3	104.5	121.8
of which: Bonds	10.9	2.5	18.3	21.1	29.6	28.7	62.4	73.2
Private nonguaranteed	18.5	58.0	135.4	151.4	170.9	207.8	220.8	234.6
of which: Bonds	1.6	6.5	13.5	11.1	8.1	8.4	8.5	10.1
Short-term external debt	6.0	11.6	66.5	88.2	106.1	109.2	103.3	100.6
interest arrears on long-term	0.1	0.0	0.1	0.2	0.2	0.1	0.3	0.2
Long-term external debt								
Disbursements	**14.0**	**24.3**	**53.8**	**51.4**	**63.7**	**85.3**	**152.3**	**80.6**
Public and publicly guaranteed	13.4	10.9	30.7	20.7	28.7	25.7	62.4	39.4
Official creditors	6.1	7.3	13.5	12.4	12.8	14.9	15.8	13.6
Private creditors	7.3	3.6	17.2	8.2	15.9	10.7	46.7	25.8
of which: Bonds	5.5	2.3	12.1	3.0	9.0	3.3	33.9	11.4
Private nonguaranteed	0.6	13.5	23.1	30.8	35.0	59.6	89.9	41.2
of which: Bonds	0.0	3.5	1.3	0.7	0.7	1.3	3.0	2.8
Principal repayments	**9.0**	**21.8**	**23.8**	**26.1**	**25.5**	**34.8**	**90.0**	**42.9**
Public and publicly guaranteed	8.3	14.5	8.9	10.2	10.1	14.8	20.2	16.7
Official creditors	5.1	4.5	6.0	7.1	6.9	7.9	8.1	8.4
Private creditors	3.3	10.0	2.8	3.1	3.2	7.0	12.1	8.3
of which: Bonds	0.1	8.6	0.7	0.2	0.5	4.2	0.2	0.5
Private nonguaranteed	0.7	7.3	15.0	15.9	15.4	20.0	69.8	26.2
of which: Bonds	0.0	0.1	2.5	2.8	3.7	1.1	2.3	0.9
Interest payments	**5.3**	**5.2**	**6.4**	**7.8**	**9.5**	**10.5**	**13.0**	**12.0**
Public and publicly guaranteed	4.4	3.9	2.7	2.7	3.0	3.0	3.5	3.8
Official creditors	2.3	1.9	2.0	2.1	2.1	2.0	1.9	1.9
Private creditors	2.1	2.0	0.7	0.6	0.8	1.0	1.6	1.8
of which: Bonds	0.2	1.8	0.2	0.3	0.4	0.5	0.7	0.9
Private nonguaranteed	0.9	1.3	3.7	5.1	6.5	7.5	9.5	8.2
of which: Bonds	0.2	0.2	0.5	0.9	0.5	0.5	0.4	0.4
Net financial flows								
Net inflows	**10.6**	**27.3**	**104.8**	**80.6**	**104.0**	**102.6**	**106.1**	**83.2**
Net debt inflows	3.8	4.2	44.1	47.0	54.5	51.0	55.7	36.4
Official creditors	0.8	2.8	9.4	5.4	4.3	4.3	7.2	6.5
of which: World Bank	1.0	2.3	3.3	2.0	0.9	0.7	2.4	2.4
of which: IMF	-0.3	0.0	2.0	0.0	-1.5	-2.8	-0.5	1.3
Private creditors	3.0	1.4	34.7	41.6	50.2	46.7	48.6	29.9
Long-term	3.9	-0.3	22.5	20.0	32.3	43.4	54.6	32.5
Bonds	5.4	-2.8	10.1	0.7	5.5	-0.6	34.4	12.7
Banks and other private	-1.5	2.6	12.4	19.2	26.9	44.0	20.3	19.8
Short-term	-0.9	1.7	12.2	21.6	17.8	3.3	-6.1	-2.6
Net equity inflows	6.9	23.1	60.7	33.6	49.5	51.6	50.3	46.8
Foreign direct investment	4.4	10.7	30.9	37.8	26.1	31.1	36.6	44.5
Portfolio equity	2.5	12.4	29.8	-4.1	23.4	20.5	13.7	2.3
Major economic aggregates								
Gross national income (GNI)	624.7	1,053.0	2,091.0	2,267.6	2,296.2	2,362.9	2,583.4	2,669.9
Exports of goods, services & prim. income	88.8	202.5	427.0	538.8	534.8	564.9	588.3	532.4
Imports of goods, services & prim. income	117.5	260.7	570.9	711.8	747.5	736.0	742.1	676.9
Primary income on FDI	0.7	8.0	25.7	27.9	21.1	18.7	20.5	20.5
Personal transfers & comp. of employees	17.2	34.2	82.0	96.4	108.0	110.8	115.8	117.7
International reserves	43.3	149.5	315.4	310.6	310.8	318.9	358.9	401.6
Ratios								
External debt stocks to exports (%)	182.8	93.4	96.3	85.6	98.7	100.9	103.2	119.7
External debt stocks to GNI (%)	26.0	18.0	19.7	20.3	23.0	24.1	23.5	23.9
Debt service to exports (%)	17.2	13.7	7.4	6.6	7.3	9.0	18.1	10.8
Short-term to external debt stocks (%)	3.7	6.1	16.2	19.1	20.1	19.2	17.0	15.8
Multilateral to external debt stocks (%)	37.6	36.5	24.4	22.6	20.2	18.8	17.5	16.7
Reserves to external debt stocks (%)	26.7	79.0	76.7	67.3	58.9	56.0	59.1	63.0

SUB-SAHARAN AFRICA

(US$ billion, unless otherwise indicated)

	2000	2005	2010	2011	2012	2013	2014	2015
Summary external debt data								
External debt stocks	**212.8**	**234.7**	**282.9**	**312.7**	**352.6**	**377.6**	**400.1**	**416.3**
Long-term external debt	172.9	192.5	220.0	250.8	280.0	302.8	327.9	342.0
Public and publicly guaranteed	162.2	174.9	159.5	177.3	200.3	222.8	244.5	260.8
Official creditors	135.9	135.6	106.4	115.4	118.7	133.4	144.5	151.9
of which: IMF	8.7	8.1	19.5	20.7	21.6	21.9	20.4	19.4
Private creditors	26.3	39.4	53.1	61.9	81.6	89.4	100.0	108.9
of which: Bonds	9.1	16.0	34.7	41.7	58.0	59.5	66.7	72.5
Private nonguaranteed	10.7	17.6	60.5	73.5	79.7	79.9	83.4	81.2
of which: Bonds	1.4	3.2	8.8	13.1	15.0	14.4	15.2	15.8
Short-term external debt	31.2	34.0	43.4	41.1	51.0	52.9	51.9	54.9
interest arrears on long-term	13.6	14.3	11.3	9.1	9.6	10.1	9.5	9.6
Long-term external debt								
Disbursements	**10.4**	**15.0**	**25.3**	**38.6**	**36.5**	**51.1**	**59.8**	**53.4**
Public and publicly guaranteed	7.5	12.7	20.4	24.9	25.8	36.6	41.6	32.8
Official creditors	4.1	6.3	15.6	15.8	14.9	19.8	23.5	19.8
Private creditors	3.4	6.4	4.8	9.1	10.9	16.8	18.2	13.0
of which: Bonds	0.8	0.0	2.0	4.5	4.3	7.3	8.4	6.0
Private nonguaranteed	2.9	2.4	4.9	13.7	10.7	14.6	18.2	20.6
of which: Bonds	0.7	0.0	1.1	4.4	3.2	4.8	3.8	2.6
Principal repayments	**8.6**	**12.2**	**10.5**	**14.0**	**17.2**	**21.8**	**21.7**	**16.3**
Public and publicly guaranteed	7.2	11.8	6.9	7.7	9.6	14.4	11.4	8.7
Official creditors	3.5	6.6	3.0	3.8	4.0	4.7	5.0	5.2
Private creditors	3.8	5.2	3.9	3.9	5.7	9.7	6.4	3.5
of which: Bonds	0.5	1.1	0.0	0.1	1.8	5.9	1.1	0.0
Private nonguaranteed	1.4	0.4	3.6	6.3	7.6	7.4	10.3	7.6
of which: Bonds	0.0	0.0	0.8	0.0	1.3	2.1	2.1	0.3
Interest payments	**3.3**	**7.8**	**3.8**	**4.8**	**6.3**	**6.9**	**7.9**	**9.3**
Public and publicly guaranteed	2.9	7.4	3.0	3.6	4.8	5.6	6.0	7.0
Official creditors	1.8	5.9	1.1	1.2	1.6	1.9	2.1	2.4
Private creditors	1.1	1.5	1.9	2.4	3.2	3.6	3.9	4.6
of which: Bonds	0.6	0.9	1.7	2.1	2.7	2.8	2.9	3.6
Private nonguaranteed	0.4	0.4	0.8	1.2	1.5	1.3	1.9	2.2
of which: Bonds	0.0	0.2	0.5	0.7	0.8	0.7	1.1	1.1
Net financial flows								
Net inflows	**8.9**	**31.6**	**42.8**	**60.8**	**70.7**	**72.2**	**75.5**	**81.5**
Net debt inflows	-1.3	6.5	16.2	25.9	29.6	30.9	37.5	40.0
Official creditors	0.7	-0.7	13.8	13.3	11.8	15.3	18.2	14.5
of which: World Bank	1.5	2.4	4.0	3.2	3.9	5.0	6.2	6.5
of which: IMF	0.1	-0.4	1.2	1.4	0.9	0.2	-0.3	-0.1
Private creditors	-2.0	7.2	2.4	12.6	17.8	15.6	19.3	25.5
Long-term	1.2	3.1	2.1	12.7	8.4	14.3	19.7	22.6
Bonds	1.0	-1.1	2.3	8.7	4.4	4.1	9.1	8.3
Banks and other private	0.2	4.2	-0.1	3.9	4.0	10.1	10.6	14.3
Short-term	-3.2	4.1	0.3	-0.1	9.4	1.4	-0.4	2.9
Net equity inflows	10.2	25.1	26.7	34.9	41.1	41.2	38.0	41.5
Foreign direct investment	6.0	16.9	18.5	38.1	35.4	34.5	33.4	34.7
Portfolio equity	4.2	8.2	8.1	-3.1	5.6	6.7	4.6	6.8
Major economic aggregates								
Gross national income (GNI)	339.3	625.2	1,260.7	1,416.7	1,489.5	1,566.7	1,649.3	1,487.0
Exports of goods, services & prim. income	114.3	239.4	403.1	486.6	478.8	488.4	460.8	358.9
Imports of goods, services & prim. income	115.2	236.1	448.5	542.1	549.5	571.8	570.1	484.5
Primary income on FDI	8.0	17.0	46.7	50.5	49.1	56.6	48.7	32.4
Personal transfers & comp. of employees	4.8	20.1	31.2	35.7	36.2	36.3	36.9	39.8
International reserves	34.2	79.8	154.1	170.1	191.2	192.8	174.0	153.3
Ratios								
External debt stocks to exports (%)	186.2	98.0	70.2	64.2	73.6	77.3	86.8	116.0
External debt stocks to GNI (%)	62.7	37.5	22.4	22.1	23.7	24.1	24.3	28.0
Debt service to exports (%)	11.9	9.0	3.8	4.0	5.2	6.2	6.8	7.7
Short-term to external debt stocks (%)	14.7	14.5	15.3	13.1	14.5	14.0	13.0	13.2
Multilateral to external debt stocks (%)	25.6	30.9	20.7	20.1	18.9	19.6	19.7	19.9
Reserves to external debt stocks (%)	16.1	34.0	54.5	54.4	54.2	51.1	43.5	36.8

AFGHANISTAN

(US$ million, unless otherwise indicated)

	2000	2005	2010	2011	2012	2013	2014	2015
Summary external debt data								
External debt stocks	..	..	**2,425**	**2,617**	**2,719**	**2,577**	**2,580**	**2,489**
Long-term external debt	..	..	1,966	2,023	2,071	2,097	1,999	1,959
Public and publicly guaranteed	..	..	1,966	2,023	2,071	2,097	1,999	1,959
Official creditors	..	..	1,966	2,023	2,071	2,097	1,999	1,959
of which: IMF	..	..	355	373	388	376	335	300
Private creditors	..	..	0	0	0	0	0	0
of which: Bonds	..	..	0	0	0	0	0	0
Private nonguaranteed	..	..	..	..	..	..	..	..
of which: Bonds	..	..	..	..	..	..	..	..
Short-term external debt	..	..	104	222	261	104	246	229
interest arrears on long-term	..	..	67	210	219	85	195	188
Long-term external debt								
Disbursements	..	..	**76**	**62**	**52**	**37**	**32**	**26**
Public and publicly guaranteed	..	..	76	62	52	37	32	26
Official creditors	..	..	76	62	52	37	32	26
Private creditors	..	..	0	0	0	0	0	0
of which: Bonds	..	..	0	0	0	0	0	0
Private nonguaranteed	..	..	..	..	..	..	..	..
of which: Bonds	..	..	..	..	..	..	..	..
Principal repayments	..	..	**1**	**1**	**2**	**4**	**8**	**13**
Public and publicly guaranteed	..	..	1	1	2	4	8	13
Official creditors	..	..	1	1	2	4	8	13
Private creditors	..	..	0	0	0	0	0	0
of which: Bonds	..	..	0	0	0	0	0	0
Private nonguaranteed	..	..	..	..	..	..	..	..
of which: Bonds	..	..	..	..	..	..	..	..
Interest payments	..	..	**7**	**9**	**8**	**8**	**9**	**9**
Public and publicly guaranteed	..	..	7	9	8	8	9	9
Official creditors	..	..	7	9	8	8	9	9
Private creditors	..	..	0	0	0	0	0	0
of which: Bonds	..	..	0	0	0	0	0	0
Private nonguaranteed	..	..	..	..	..	..	..	..
of which: Bonds	..	..	..	..	..	..	..	..
Net financial flows								
Net inflows	..	..	**174**	**113**	**159**	**36**	**85**	**151**
Net debt inflows	..	..	121	55	95	-3	37	-18
Official creditors	..	..	84	80	65	20	4	-8
of which: World Bank	..	..	8	8	9	4	-2	-3
of which: IMF	..	..	9	19	15	-13	-19	-20
Private creditors	..	..	37	-25	30	-23	33	-10
Long-term	..	..	..	..	..	..	..	..
Bonds	..	..	..	..	..	..	..	..
Banks and other private	..	..	..	..	..	..	..	..
Short-term	..	..	37	-25	30	-23	33	-10
Net equity inflows	..	..	54	58	64	40	49	169
Foreign direct investment	..	..	54	58	62	40	49	169
Portfolio equity	..	..	0	0	2	0	..	..
Major economic aggregates								
Gross national income (GNI)	..	..	15,999	18,013	21,572	21,517	20,722	19,786
Exports of goods, services & prim. income	..	..	2,681	3,337	2,162	1,741	2,094	1,513
Imports of goods, services & prim. income	..	..	6,198	7,928	10,366	9,651	8,733	8,661
Primary income on FDI	..	..	0	0	1	0	0	0
Personal transfers & comp. of employees	..	..	342	185	252	314	268	301
International reserves	..	..	4,174	5,268	5,983	6,442	6,681	6,232
Ratios								
External debt stocks to exports (%)	..	..	90.5	78.4	125.8	148.0	123.2	164.4
External debt stocks to GNI (%)	..	..	15.2	14.5	12.6	12.0	12.5	12.6
Debt service to exports (%)	..	..	0.4	0.3	0.7	1.4	1.8	2.9
Short-term to external debt stocks (%)	..	..	4.3	8.5	9.6	4.0	9.6	9.2
Multilateral to external debt stocks (%)	..	..	41.9	41.0	41.2	44.5	42.1	41.4
Reserves to external debt stocks (%)	..	..	172.1	201.3	220.0	250.0	258.9	250.4

Notes: Short-term debt is based on data from the BIS. Data include the effects of Paris Club debt restructuring agreements signed in 2010 and HIPC and MDRI debt relief.

ALBANIA

(US$ million, unless otherwise indicated)

	2000	2005	2010	2011	2012	2013	2014	2015
Summary external debt data								
External debt stocks	**1,122**	**2,104**	**5,376**	**6,314**	**7,160**	**8,806**	**8,399**	**8,269**
Long-term external debt	937	1,791	4,504	5,105	5,583	6,706	6,373	6,268
Public and publicly guaranteed	921	1,377	3,219	3,373	3,556	3,763	3,668	3,660
Official creditors	895	1,350	2,177	2,315	2,543	2,696	2,747	2,677
of which: IMF	148	158	129	117	107	97	151	244
Private creditors	26	28	1,041	1,058	1,013	1,067	921	983
of which: Bonds	0	0	477	556	567	593	522	631
Private nonguaranteed	16	413	1,285	1,732	2,027	2,943	2,705	2,607
of which: Bonds	..	..	..	..	..	..	..	..
Short-term external debt	37	155	743	1,092	1,470	2,003	1,875	1,758
interest arrears on long-term	3	1	0	0	0	0	0	0
Long-term external debt								
Disbursements	**119**	**490**	**820**	**755**	**683**	**751**	**723**	**1,181**
Public and publicly guaranteed	119	120	631	418	336	260	439	795
Official creditors	119	119	198	274	315	251	424	273
Private creditors	0	0	433	144	21	9	14	523
of which: Bonds	0	0	398	101	0	0	0	499
Private nonguaranteed	0	370	189	336	347	491	285	385
of which: Bonds	..	..	..	..	..	..	..	..
Principal repayments	**9**	**53**	**250**	**302**	**350**	**348**	**490**	**831**
Public and publicly guaranteed	9	40	174	191	190	126	176	531
Official creditors	8	39	87	99	106	124	143	169
Private creditors	1	1	87	91	84	2	33	363
of which: Bonds	0	0	0	0	0	0	0	333
Private nonguaranteed	0	13	76	112	160	222	314	299
of which: Bonds	..	..	..	..	..	..	..	..
Interest payments	**8**	**36**	**109**	**164**	**178**	**193**	**181**	**73**
Public and publicly guaranteed	7	23	66	106	101	72	77	70
Official creditors	7	23	32	36	37	36	43	42
Private creditors	0	0	35	70	64	36	34	29
of which: Bonds	0	0	1	32	30	31	29	25
Private nonguaranteed	1	12	43	59	77	120	104	3
of which: Bonds	..	..	..	..	..	..	..	..
Net financial flows								
Net inflows	**273**	**856**	**1,679**	**1,626**	**1,433**	**1,774**	**1,134**	**1,275**
Net debt inflows	130	594	620	789	700	926	168	333
Official creditors	122	83	99	163	199	116	344	205
of which: World Bank	64	30	18	40	22	0	227	-3
of which: IMF	12	3	-12	-12	-10	-10	63	100
Private creditors	7	511	521	627	501	810	-176	128
Long-term	-1	357	459	278	123	277	-48	246
Bonds	..	..	398	101	0	0	0	166
Banks and other private	-1	357	61	177	123	277	-48	79
Short-term	8	154	63	349	378	533	-128	-117
Net equity inflows	143	262	1,058	837	732	848	966	942
Foreign direct investment	143	262	1,052	813	714	846	932	879
Portfolio equity	..	..	7	23	18	2	34	63
Major economic aggregates								
Gross national income (GNI)	3,739	8,322	11,808	12,855	12,228	12,809	13,120	11,290
Exports of goods, services & prim. income	670	1,687	3,704	4,078	3,800	3,859	3,900	3,277
Imports of goods, services & prim. income	1,360	3,553	6,280	7,010	6,189	6,158	6,562	5,351
Primary income on FDI	0	2	381	140	169	29	192	170
Personal transfers & comp. of employees	598	1,290	1,156	1,126	1,027	1,094	1,142	1,047
International reserves	616	1,404	2,470	2,394	2,516	2,712	2,604	3,085
Ratios								
External debt stocks to exports (%)	167.4	124.7	145.1	154.8	188.4	228.2	215.3	252.4
External debt stocks to GNI (%)	30.0	25.3	45.5	49.1	58.6	68.7	64.0	73.2
Debt service to exports (%)	4.5	6.2	10.3	11.8	14.2	14.3	17.5	27.9
Short-term to external debt stocks (%)	3.3	7.4	13.8	17.3	20.5	22.7	22.3	21.3
Multilateral to external debt stocks (%)	38.0	41.3	28.3	26.4	26.1	22.8	24.9	24.6
Reserves to external debt stocks (%)	54.9	66.7	45.9	37.9	35.1	30.8	31.0	37.3

ALGERIA

(US$ million, unless otherwise indicated)

	2000	2005	2010	2011	2012	2013	2014	2015
Summary external debt data								
External debt stocks	**25,477**	**17,092**	**7,260**	**6,065**	**5,516**	**5,246**	**5,521**	**4,677**
Long-term external debt	23,369	16,393	3,637	3,084	2,469	2,072	1,810	1,194
Public and publicly guaranteed	23,369	15,527	2,669	2,266	1,647	1,452	1,125	870
Official creditors	17,518	12,500	1,903	1,663	1,218	1,131	895	708
of which: IMF	1,886	184	1,845	1,840	1,842	1,845	1,736	1,660
Private creditors	5,851	3,027	766	603	429	321	230	162
of which: Bonds	0	0	0	0	0	0	0	0
Private nonguaranteed	..	866	968	818	822	620	685	323
of which: Bonds	..	..	..	..	..	..	..	..
Short-term external debt	222	516	1,778	1,142	1,205	1,328	1,975	1,823
interest arrears on long-term	0	0	0	0	0	0	0	0
Long-term external debt								
Disbursements	**1,219**	**1,240**	**43**	**36**	**29**	**22**	**43**	**58**
Public and publicly guaranteed	1,219	777	41	36	28	22	4	0
Official creditors	799	446	40	32	28	22	4	0
Private creditors	420	331	1	4	0	0	0	0
of which: Bonds	0	0	0	0	0	0	0	0
Private nonguaranteed	..	463	2	0	0	..	39	58
of which: Bonds	..	..	..	..	..	..	..	..
Principal repayments	**2,721**	**4,448**	**557**	**536**	**742**	**466**	**231**	**582**
Public and publicly guaranteed	2,721	4,219	324	415	589	263	207	167
Official creditors	1,055	3,014	167	255	488	146	135	111
Private creditors	1,666	1,205	157	160	101	117	71	56
of which: Bonds	0	0	0	0	0	0	0	0
Private nonguaranteed	..	229	234	121	153	203	24	415
of which: Bonds	..	..	..	..	..	..	..	..
Interest payments	**1,552**	**889**	**95**	**80**	**103**	**51**	**37**	**79**
Public and publicly guaranteed	1,552	864	64	58	85	38	27	21
Official creditors	1,132	719	35	32	67	20	16	13
Private creditors	421	145	29	26	18	18	11	8
of which: Bonds	0	0	0	0	0	0	0	0
Private nonguaranteed	..	25	31	22	18	13	9	59
of which: Bonds	..	..	..	..	..	..	..	..
Net financial flows								
Net inflows	**-1,288**	**-2,578**	**2,087**	**1,493**	**916**	**1,399**	**1,926**	**-932**
Net debt inflows	-1,568	-3,734	-229	-1,136	-650	-321	459	-676
Official creditors	-349	-3,180	-127	-222	-460	-124	-131	-111
of which: World Bank	-114	-125	-1	-1	-1	-5	0	0
of which: IMF	-93	-612	0	0	0	0	0	0
Private creditors	-1,219	-555	-101	-914	-190	-197	590	-565
Long-term	-1,246	-640	-387	-277	-253	-320	-57	-413
Bonds	..	..	..	..	..	..	..	..
Banks and other private	-1,246	-640	-387	-277	-253	-320	-57	-413
Short-term	27	85	286	-637	63	123	647	-152
Net equity inflows	280	1,156	2,315	2,628	1,565	1,720	1,467	-256
Foreign direct investment	280	1,156	2,315	2,628	1,565	1,720	1,467	-256
Portfolio equity	..	..	..	..	..	..	..	..
Major economic aggregates								
Gross national income (GNI)	52,080	98,611	160,996	198,125	206,733	205,788	208,831	162,254
Exports of goods, services & prim. income	..	50,268	65,168	80,831	79,095	72,135	66,575	39,943
Imports of goods, services & prim. income	..	31,155	55,612	65,944	70,161	73,738	79,302	69,719
Primary income on FDI	..	5,485	4,858	6,313	7,453	8,005	8,010	6,364
Personal transfers & comp. of employees	790	170	197	203	215	210	304	275
International reserves	12,024	56,303	162,614	182,822	191,297	194,712	179,618	144,677
Ratios								
External debt stocks to exports (%)	..	34.0	11.1	7.5	7.0	7.3	8.3	11.7
External debt stocks to GNI (%)	48.9	17.3	4.5	3.1	2.7	2.5	2.6	2.9
Debt service to exports (%)	..	11.9	1.0	0.8	1.1	0.7	0.4	1.7
Short-term to external debt stocks (%)	0.9	3.0	24.5	18.8	21.8	25.3	35.8	39.0
Multilateral to external debt stocks (%)	16.2	14.3	0.1	0.1	0.1	0.0	0.0	0.0
Reserves to external debt stocks (%)	47.2	329.4	2,239.8	3,014.5	3,468.3	3,711.9	3,253.2	3,093.4

ANGOLA

(US$ million, unless otherwise indicated)

	2000	2005	2010	2011	2012	2013	2014	2015
Summary external debt data								
External debt stocks	**9,763**	**12,224**	**16,949**	**19,298**	**21,106**	**25,004**	**28,903**	**27,991**
Long-term external debt	8,085	9,518	15,466	17,525	19,203	23,349	27,826	27,304
Public and publicly guaranteed	8,085	9,518	15,466	17,525	19,203	23,349	27,826	27,304
Official creditors	2,703	3,174	8,161	9,687	9,615	11,825	13,726	13,405
of which: IMF	356	390	1,302	1,606	1,740	1,479	914	532
Private creditors	5,382	6,344	7,305	7,837	9,588	11,525	14,101	13,899
of which: Bonds	0	0	0	10	1,000	1,000	1,000	2,500
Private nonguaranteed	..	..	..	..	..	..	..	..
of which: Bonds	..	..	..	..	..	..	..	..
Short-term external debt	1,323	2,316	181	168	164	176	162	155
interest arrears on long-term	874	577	68	62	58	70	58	51
Long-term external debt								
Disbursements	**1,045**	**3,676**	**3,951**	**4,793**	**5,215**	**7,825**	**9,647**	**3,592**
Public and publicly guaranteed	1,045	3,676	3,951	4,793	5,215	7,825	9,647	3,592
Official creditors	34	321	3,658	2,353	1,103	3,612	3,664	1,540
Private creditors	1,011	3,355	293	2,440	4,112	4,213	5,983	2,051
of which: Bonds	0	0	0	10	1,051	0	0	1,500
Private nonguaranteed	..	..	..	..	..	..	..	..
of which: Bonds	..	..	..	..	..	..	..	..
Principal repayments	**1,530**	**2,289**	**2,110**	**2,681**	**3,554**	**3,723**	**4,883**	**3,964**
Public and publicly guaranteed	1,530	2,289	2,110	2,681	3,554	3,723	4,883	3,964
Official creditors	268	505	283	820	1,164	1,380	1,648	1,826
Private creditors	1,262	1,784	1,827	1,862	2,390	2,344	3,234	2,138
of which: Bonds	0	0	0	0	61	0	0	0
Private nonguaranteed	..	..	..	..	..	..	..	..
of which: Bonds	..	..	..	..	..	..	..	..
Interest payments	**149**	**257**	**176**	**154**	**640**	**919**	**1,020**	**1,078**
Public and publicly guaranteed	149	257	176	154	640	919	1,020	1,078
Official creditors	36	61	114	79	321	414	444	447
Private creditors	113	195	63	75	319	505	576	631
of which: Bonds	0	0	0	0	1	47	70	70
Private nonguaranteed	..	..	..	..	..	..	..	..
of which: Bonds	..	..	..	..	..	..	..	..
Net financial flows								
Net inflows	**145**	**3,743**	**3,296**	**6,491**	**6,148**	**8,024**	**6,793**	**8,736**
Net debt inflows	-733	2,603	-29	2,421	1,791	3,840	4,263	-717
Official creditors	-234	-185	3,900	1,849	70	1,970	1,516	-631
of which: World Bank	24	25	-1	7	36	47	40	472
of which: IMF	0	0	524	316	131	-262	-500	-345
Private creditors	-499	2,788	-3,929	572	1,722	1,870	2,747	-87
Long-term	-251	1,572	-1,534	579	1,722	1,870	2,748	-87
Bonds	..	..	..	10	990	..	..	1,500
Banks and other private	-251	1,572	-1,534	569	732	1,870	2,748	-1,587
Short-term	-248	1,216	-2,395	-7	0	0	-2	0
Net equity inflows	879	1,140	3,326	4,070	4,357	4,184	2,530	9,453
Foreign direct investment	879	1,140	3,326	4,070	4,357	4,184	2,530	9,453
Portfolio equity	..	..	..	..	..	..	..	..
Major economic aggregates								
Gross national income (GNI)	7,449	24,203	74,384	94,419	102,815	112,444	114,067	89,886
Exports of goods, services & prim. income	8,222	24,312	51,586	68,252	72,133	70,381	61,497	34,604
Imports of goods, services & prim. income	7,454	19,201	43,642	53,805	56,518	59,909	63,033	44,043
Primary income on FDI	929	3,406	7,526	9,040	9,722	9,331	7,850	4,292
Personal transfers & comp. of employees	..	..	18	0	0	11	31	11
International reserves	1,198	3,197	19,749	28,786	33,415	32,780	28,130	23,791
Ratios								
External debt stocks to exports (%)	118.7	50.3	32.9	28.3	29.3	35.5	47.0	80.9
External debt stocks to GNI (%)	131.1	50.5	22.8	20.4	20.5	22.2	25.3	31.1
Debt service to exports (%)	20.9	10.8	4.5	4.2	5.8	7.0	10.4	15.6
Short-term to external debt stocks (%)	13.5	18.9	1.1	0.9	0.8	0.7	0.6	0.6
Multilateral to external debt stocks (%)	3.0	3.0	2.6	2.4	2.3	2.2	4.0	5.7
Reserves to external debt stocks (%)	12.3	26.2	116.5	149.2	158.3	131.1	97.3	85.0

Notes: Short-term debt before 2009 is based on data from the BIS.

ARGENTINA

(US$ million, unless otherwise indicated)

	2000	2005	2010	2011	2012	2013	2014	2015
Summary external debt data								
External debt stocks	**150,063**	**130,788**	**126,641**	**139,509**	**136,543**	**146,569**	**144,972**	**159,694**
Long-term external debt	116,267	85,780	107,117	110,662	108,186	106,766	113,712	113,113
Public and publicly guaranteed	90,358	59,419	69,183	68,163	67,243	66,230	73,008	72,246
Official creditors	20,822	20,564	23,109	23,804	23,700	24,505	28,989	28,175
of which: IMF	5,470	9,968	3,111	3,101	3,105	3,111	2,927	2,799
Private creditors	69,536	38,856	46,074	44,359	43,543	41,725	44,019	44,072
of which: Bonds	69,009	38,347	44,342	42,949	42,174	40,471	43,386	43,606
Private nonguaranteed	25,909	26,361	37,934	42,499	40,943	40,536	40,703	40,867
of which: Bonds	11,138	8,772	7,855	9,129	6,536	6,579	7,199	8,516
Short-term external debt	28,325	35,041	16,413	25,746	25,252	36,692	28,334	43,781
interest arrears on long-term	10	7,935	4,878	5,528	5,712	6,001	4,950	5,151
Long-term external debt								
Disbursements	**18,794**	**4,727**	**6,922**	**10,777**	**7,620**	**10,877**	**19,636**	**15,124**
Public and publicly guaranteed	14,312	3,219	2,622	2,614	2,330	3,895	13,961	8,259
Official creditors	1,971	993	2,455	2,588	2,124	2,935	6,253	2,274
Private creditors	12,341	2,227	167	26	206	960	7,708	5,985
of which: Bonds	12,339	2,227	90	0	171	948	7,090	5,985
Private nonguaranteed	4,482	1,507	4,300	8,163	5,290	6,982	5,675	6,865
of which: Bonds	1,408	540	2,037	1,320	211	375	200	258
Principal repayments	**11,689**	**3,491**	**11,690**	**12,076**	**9,785**	**11,761**	**9,743**	**10,858**
Public and publicly guaranteed	6,185	1,724	6,035	5,365	3,478	4,768	4,736	6,414
Official creditors	1,871	1,501	1,923	1,907	2,085	1,946	2,720	2,647
Private creditors	4,314	224	4,111	3,457	1,393	2,821	2,015	3,767
of which: Bonds	4,097	222	3,824	3,124	1,307	2,676	1,918	3,602
Private nonguaranteed	5,503	1,766	5,655	6,712	6,307	6,994	5,008	4,444
of which: Bonds	2,309	680	969	26	785	999	..	..
Interest payments	**9,936**	**2,170**	**3,789**	**3,394**	**3,234**	**3,194**	**6,469**	**5,997**
Public and publicly guaranteed	7,896	1,454	2,700	2,456	2,327	2,363	5,073	5,068
Official creditors	1,600	756	614	571	534	604	1,006	933
Private creditors	6,295	698	2,086	1,884	1,793	1,759	4,067	4,135
of which: Bonds	6,154	697	2,023	1,832	1,750	1,719	4,033	4,110
Private nonguaranteed	2,041	716	1,089	938	907	831	1,396	930
of which: Bonds	1,109	585	567	717	757	725	705	312
Net financial flows								
Net inflows	**12,923**	**20,469**	**5,452**	**15,415**	**9,226**	**21,212**	**8,814**	**29,348**
Net debt inflows	6,820	14,771	-2,303	7,383	-2,843	10,266	2,586	19,512
Official creditors	915	-4,079	532	681	39	989	3,533	-373
of which: World Bank	481	-566	46	211	68	491	-71	-141
of which: IMF	815	-3,571	..	..	..	..	..	..
Private creditors	5,905	18,850	-2,835	6,702	-2,882	9,277	-947	19,885
Long-term	7,005	1,744	-5,300	-1,980	-2,204	-1,873	6,360	4,639
Bonds	7,340	1,864	-2,667	-1,829	-1,711	-2,352	5,372	2,641
Banks and other private	-335	-120	-2,633	-151	-492	479	988	1,998
Short-term	-1,100	17,106	2,465	8,683	-678	11,150	-7,306	15,246
Net equity inflows	6,103	5,698	7,755	8,032	12,069	10,947	6,228	9,835
Foreign direct investment	9,331	5,747	7,826	8,240	12,204	10,605	6,010	9,596
Portfolio equity	-3,227	-48	-71	-208	-135	342	218	239
Major economic aggregates								
Gross national income (GNI)	276,656	191,972	412,026	519,318	536,864	543,104	519,702	572,913
Exports of goods, services & prim. income	38,657	51,204	84,319	101,451	97,243	92,962	84,706	73,048
Imports of goods, services & prim. income	48,037	46,414	85,428	105,356	98,143	104,279	92,579	88,620
Primary income on FDI	3,086	5,456	12,101	12,361	10,236	9,796	8,114	8,793
Personal transfers & comp. of employees	86	432	644	697	576	534	504	483
International reserves	25,147	27,179	49,734	43,227	39,920	28,143	29,017	23,417
Ratios								
External debt stocks to exports (%)	388.2	255.4	150.2	137.5	140.4	157.7	171.1	218.6
External debt stocks to GNI (%)	54.2	68.1	30.7	26.9	25.4	27.0	27.9	27.9
Debt service to exports (%)	64.3	19.7	18.5	15.6	13.7	16.7	19.6	24.1
Short-term to external debt stocks (%)	18.9	26.8	13.0	18.5	18.5	25.0	19.5	27.4
Multilateral to external debt stocks (%)	11.0	12.0	13.4	12.9	13.4	13.3	13.7	12.4
Reserves to external debt stocks (%)	16.8	20.8	39.3	31.0	29.2	19.2	20.0	14.7

Notes: Long-term private nonguaranteed debt data before 2008 are World Bank staff estimates. Long-term provincial debt data are World Bank staff estimates. Short-term debt before 2010 is based on data from the BIS.

ARMENIA

(US$ million, unless otherwise indicated)

	2000	2005	2010	2011	2012	2013	2014	2015
Summary external debt data								
External debt stocks	**1,010**	**1,968**	**6,304**	**7,407**	**7,637**	**8,678**	**8,551**	**8,925**
Long-term external debt	675	1,368	4,772	5,541	5,884	6,807	7,073	7,725
Public and publicly guaranteed	675	923	2,557	2,736	2,956	3,312	3,376	3,992
Official creditors	658	921	2,556	2,733	2,942	2,594	2,658	2,968
of which: IMF	290	302	876	963	911	720	570	536
Private creditors	17	1	1	4	14	718	718	1,024
of which: Bonds	0	0	0	0	0	700	700	1,000
Private nonguaranteed	..	446	2,216	2,805	2,928	3,495	3,698	3,733
of which: Bonds	..	..	..	..	..	..	..	100
Short-term external debt	44	298	656	904	842	1,150	908	664
interest arrears on long-term	6	0	0	0	0	0	0	0
Long-term external debt								
Disbursements	**63**	**168**	**1,734**	**1,490**	**1,633**	**2,817**	**2,079**	**2,055**
Public and publicly guaranteed	63	50	198	206	280	937	282	971
Official creditors	62	50	198	203	270	234	280	474
Private creditors	1	0	0	2	10	703	2	497
of which: Bonds	0	0	0	0	0	700	0	488
Private nonguaranteed	..	117	1,536	1,285	1,353	1,880	1,797	1,084
of which: Bonds	..	..	..	..	..	..	..	100
Principal repayments	**15**	**69**	**857**	**742**	**854**	**1,599**	**1,077**	**1,308**
Public and publicly guaranteed	15	16	24	28	30	537	41	260
Official creditors	13	16	24	28	30	537	41	59
Private creditors	2	0	0	0	0	0	0	200
of which: Bonds	0	0	0	0	0	0	0	200
Private nonguaranteed	..	53	833	714	824	1,063	1,035	1,048
of which: Bonds	..	..	..	..	..	..	..	..
Interest payments	**9**	**23**	**60**	**128**	**128**	**126**	**176**	**199**
Public and publicly guaranteed	9	9	35	38	43	42	71	100
Official creditors	9	9	35	38	43	42	29	46
Private creditors	0	0	0	0	0	0	42	54
of which: Bonds	0	0	0	0	0	0	42	54
Private nonguaranteed	..	14	25	91	84	84	105	99
of which: Bonds	..	..	..	..	..	..	..	..
Net financial flows								
Net inflows	**112**	**240**	**1,535**	**1,476**	**1,257**	**1,662**	**979**	**646**
Net debt inflows	21	-38	1,167	1,087	665	1,335	647	494
Official creditors	34	10	337	266	188	-494	125	406
of which: World Bank	54	31	73	76	132	112	96	93
of which: IMF	-16	-25	163	91	-52	-191	-113	-9
Private creditors	-13	-48	829	821	478	1,828	522	88
Long-term	-2	64	703	573	539	1,521	764	332
Bonds	..	..	..	..	..	700	0	388
Banks and other private	-2	64	703	573	539	821	764	-56
Short-term	-11	-112	127	248	-62	308	-242	-245
Net equity inflows	91	279	368	389	591	328	332	153
Foreign direct investment	90	278	361	386	589	329	332	149
Portfolio equity	0	0	7	3	2	-2	1	4
Major economic aggregates								
Gross national income (GNI)	1,964	5,106	9,719	10,502	11,042	11,661	12,200	10,975
Exports of goods, services & prim. income	558	1,944	3,260	3,808	4,033	4,415	4,532	4,023
Imports of goods, services & prim. income	1,031	2,520	5,128	5,623	5,824	6,053	6,159	4,868
Primary income on FDI	22	170	362	379	335	181	184	-33
Personal transfers & comp. of employees	182	915	1,669	1,799	1,915	2,192	2,079	1,491
International reserves	302	669	1,866	1,932	1,799	2,252	1,489	1,775
Ratios								
External debt stocks to exports (%)	181.0	101.3	193.4	194.5	189.4	196.5	188.7	221.9
External debt stocks to GNI (%)	51.4	38.5	64.9	70.5	69.2	74.4	70.1	81.3
Debt service to exports (%)	9.1	7.3	29.7	24.6	29.1	46.4	31.7	38.7
Short-term to external debt stocks (%)	4.4	15.1	10.4	12.2	11.0	13.3	10.6	7.4
Multilateral to external debt stocks (%)	48.0	41.1	24.0	22.2	24.4	23.6	25.2	27.6
Reserves to external debt stocks (%)	29.9	34.0	29.6	26.1	23.6	25.9	17.4	19.9

Notes: Long-term private nonguaranteed debt data from 2011 are World Bank staff estimates based on reports provided by the country.

AZERBAIJAN

(US$ million, unless otherwise indicated)

	2000	2005	2010	2011	2012	2013	2014	2015
Summary external debt data								
External debt stocks	**1,585**	**2,247**	**7,159**	**7,289**	**10,331**	**10,065**	**11,788**	**13,215**
Long-term external debt	893	1,678	5,878	6,933	8,448	8,218	9,543	11,352
Public and publicly guaranteed	794	1,491	3,720	4,317	5,695	6,075	8,094	8,505
Official creditors	656	1,216	2,565	3,145	4,033	4,192	4,464	4,715
of which: IMF	536	383	282	265	252	242	224	213
Private creditors	138	274	1,155	1,171	1,662	1,884	3,630	3,790
of which: Bonds	0	0	0	0	500	500	2,250	2,250
Private nonguaranteed	99	187	2,158	2,616	2,752	2,142	1,448	2,847
of which: Bonds	..	..	..	..	..	..	..	..
Short-term external debt	156	186	999	91	1,631	1,605	2,021	1,651
interest arrears on long-term	0	0	0	0	0	0	0	0
Long-term external debt								
Disbursements	**306**	**432**	**2,547**	**1,941**	**2,477**	**1,327**	**3,178**	**3,556**
Public and publicly guaranteed	301	307	633	878	1,659	1,073	2,868	1,144
Official creditors	213	72	453	698	1,069	741	759	646
Private creditors	88	236	180	180	590	333	2,108	497
of which: Bonds	0	0	0	0	500	0	1,750	0
Private nonguaranteed	6	124	1,914	1,063	818	253	310	2,412
of which: Bonds	..	..	..	..	..	..	..	..
Principal repayments	**22**	**152**	**321**	**862**	**927**	**1,511**	**1,491**	**919**
Public and publicly guaranteed	14	55	249	254	243	646	499	525
Official creditors	12	38	112	118	128	494	257	284
Private creditors	2	16	136	136	114	152	242	242
of which: Bonds	0	0	0	0	0	0	0	0
Private nonguaranteed	7	97	72	608	684	866	992	393
of which: Bonds	..	..	..	..	..	..	..	..
Interest payments	**37**	**27**	**81**	**948**	**945**	**930**	**258**	**161**
Public and publicly guaranteed	32	20	68	77	97	104	105	105
Official creditors	31	16	33	42	43	52	44	52
Private creditors	1	4	35	35	54	52	60	53
of which: Bonds	0	0	0	0	14	27	27	27
Private nonguaranteed	5	7	13	871	848	826	154	56
of which: Bonds	..	..	..	..	..	..	..	..
Net financial flows								
Net inflows	**490**	**4,775**	**5,969**	**4,639**	**8,371**	**2,429**	**6,540**	**6,338**
Net debt inflows	360	299	2,616	153	3,077	-221	2,099	2,266
Official creditors	149	4	326	563	927	237	498	361
of which: World Bank	27	46	137	215	366	3	314	204
of which: IMF	-51	-29	-15	-17	-13	-10	-4	-2
Private creditors	211	295	2,290	-409	2,150	-457	1,601	1,905
Long-term	84	247	1,886	499	610	-431	1,185	2,275
Bonds	..	..	..	..	500	0	1,750	0
Banks and other private	84	247	1,886	499	110	-431	-565	2,275
Short-term	127	48	404	-908	1,540	-26	416	-370
Net equity inflows	130	4,476	3,354	4,485	5,293	2,649	4,441	4,072
Foreign direct investment	130	4,476	3,353	4,485	5,293	2,619	4,430	4,048
Portfolio equity	..	..	1	0	0	30	10	24
Major economic aggregates								
Gross national income (GNI)	4,987	11,599	49,436	61,092	63,181	69,440	72,617	51,241
Exports of goods, services & prim. income	2,174	8,341	28,910	38,058	37,837	36,941	34,231	21,288
Imports of goods, services & prim. income	2,415	8,658	14,379	21,586	22,811	24,650	23,974	21,733
Primary income on FDI	317	1,582	3,815	5,488	4,906	4,507	3,359	2,275
Personal transfers & comp. of employees	57	623	1,410	1,893	1,990	1,733	1,846	1,270
International reserves	680	1,178	6,409	10,274	11,277	14,401	14,647	6,291
Ratios								
External debt stocks to exports (%)	72.9	26.9	24.8	19.2	27.3	27.2	34.4	62.1
External debt stocks to GNI (%)	31.8	19.4	14.5	11.9	16.4	14.5	16.2	25.8
Debt service to exports (%)	6.4	2.9	1.5	4.8	5.1	6.7	5.2	5.2
Short-term to external debt stocks (%)	9.9	8.3	14.0	1.2	15.8	15.9	17.1	12.5
Multilateral to external debt stocks (%)	20.4	28.0	24.5	29.4	27.5	29.8	28.3	27.3
Reserves to external debt stocks (%)	42.9	52.4	89.5	141.0	109.2	143.1	124.3	47.6

Notes: Long-term private nonguaranteed debt data are World Bank staff estimates based on the market data. Short-term debt is based on data from the BIS.

BANGLADESH

(US$ million, unless otherwise indicated)

	2000	2005	2010	2011	2012	2013	2014	2015
Summary external debt data								
External debt stocks	**15,603**	**18,506**	**26,881**	**27,277**	**28,559**	**33,997**	**35,665**	**38,640**
Long-term external debt	14,992	17,441	22,529	23,901	25,387	28,765	30,042	30,394
Public and publicly guaranteed	14,992	17,441	21,453	22,447	23,598	26,574	26,934	27,101
Official creditors	14,815	17,265	21,420	22,425	23,584	26,563	26,924	27,092
of which: IMF	277	376	1,403	1,271	1,213	1,496	1,470	1,613
Private creditors	176	176	33	22	13	12	10	8
of which: Bonds	0	0	0	0	0	0	0	0
Private nonguaranteed	0	0	1,076	1,454	1,789	2,191	3,109	3,294
of which: Bonds	..	..	..	..	..	..	..	..
Short-term external debt	334	688	2,949	2,105	1,959	3,735	4,153	6,633
interest arrears on long-term	0	16	2	2	2	2	2	2
Long-term external debt								
Disbursements	**863**	**880**	**1,269**	**1,529**	**2,772**	**5,019**	**4,408**	**2,520**
Public and publicly guaranteed	863	880	978	1,078	2,347	4,530	3,397	2,269
Official creditors	796	880	978	1,078	2,347	4,530	3,397	2,269
Private creditors	67	0	0	0	0	0	0	0
of which: Bonds	0	0	0	0	0	0	0	0
Private nonguaranteed	0	0	291	451	425	489	1,011	251
of which: Bonds	..	..	..	..	..	..	..	..
Principal repayments	**489**	**575**	**816**	**1,144**	**1,084**	**1,350**	**1,385**	**1,054**
Public and publicly guaranteed	489	575	741	1,057	995	1,262	1,291	989
Official creditors	467	559	730	1,045	986	1,261	1,290	987
Private creditors	22	16	11	11	9	2	2	2
of which: Bonds	0	0	0	0	0	0	0	0
Private nonguaranteed	0	0	75	87	89	88	93	66
of which: Bonds	..	..	..	..	..	..	..	..
Interest payments	**165**	**199**	**208**	**273**	**257**	**262**	**279**	**242**
Public and publicly guaranteed	165	199	200	259	243	249	262	212
Official creditors	156	197	199	258	242	249	261	212
Private creditors	9	2	2	1	1	1	1	0
of which: Bonds	0	0	0	0	0	0	0	0
Private nonguaranteed	0	0	8	15	14	13	18	30
of which: Bonds	..	..	..	..	..	..	..	..
Net financial flows								
Net inflows	**647**	**1,010**	**2,252**	**382**	**2,701**	**7,921**	**6,122**	**7,023**
Net debt inflows	367	365	1,421	-590	1,483	5,724	3,507	4,154
Official creditors	242	421	203	-98	1,302	3,548	2,173	1,491
of which: World Bank	270	394	83	93	434	397	524	601
of which: IMF	-87	99	-45	-131	-59	278	65	209
Private creditors	125	-56	1,219	-492	180	2,176	1,334	2,664
Long-term	46	-16	205	352	327	400	916	183
Bonds	..	..	..	..	..	..	..	..
Banks and other private	46	-16	205	352	327	400	916	183
Short-term	80	-40	1,014	-844	-146	1,776	418	2,480
Net equity inflows	280	646	831	972	1,218	2,197	2,615	2,869
Foreign direct investment	279	626	885	922	1,085	1,935	2,257	2,986
Portfolio equity	1	20	-54	50	134	262	358	-118
Major economic aggregates								
Gross national income (GNI)	55,102	72,521	124,617	138,823	144,642	162,054	184,407	207,743
Exports of goods, services & prim. income	7,293	11,322	21,764	27,148	27,768	31,768	33,138	34,929
Imports of goods, services & prim. income	10,018	15,970	31,035	39,553	39,740	44,208	47,985	48,113
Primary income on FDI	149	669	1,210	1,298	1,622	2,104	2,303	2,255
Personal transfers & comp. of employees	1,968	4,642	10,850	12,071	14,120	13,867	14,988	15,388
International reserves	1,486	2,767	10,564	8,510	12,031	17,564	21,785	27,023
Ratios								
External debt stocks to exports (%)	214.0	163.4	123.5	100.5	102.8	107.0	107.6	110.6
External debt stocks to GNI (%)	28.3	25.5	21.6	19.6	19.7	21.0	19.3	18.6
Debt service to exports (%)	10.6	7.2	5.1	5.9	5.6	5.7	5.4	4.1
Short-term to external debt stocks (%)	2.1	3.7	11.0	7.7	6.9	11.0	11.6	17.2
Multilateral to external debt stocks (%)	70.5	75.9	68.7	68.5	68.4	59.2	55.4	51.8
Reserves to external debt stocks (%)	9.5	15.0	39.3	31.2	42.1	51.7	61.1	69.9

Notes: Short-term debt before 2012 is based on data from the BIS. Long-term private nonguaranteed debt data from 2007 are World Bank staff estimates based on reports provided by the country and are not available prior to 2007.

BELARUS

(US$ million, unless otherwise indicated)

	2000	2005	2010	2011	2012	2013	2014	2015
Summary external debt data								
External debt stocks	**2,620**	**5,300**	**28,412**	**33,933**	**33,756**	**39,573**	**40,014**	**37,876**
Long-term external debt	787	1,270	12,486	16,437	18,532	23,579	26,573	25,890
Public and publicly guaranteed	689	786	8,014	10,616	12,559	14,622	15,628	15,410
Official creditors	400	566	5,729	8,382	7,303	8,540	10,114	10,563
of which: IMF	594	527	4,063	4,050	3,588	1,932	613	511
Private creditors	289	219	2,286	2,234	5,256	6,082	5,514	4,847
of which: Bonds	0	0	1,019	1,800	1,800	1,800	1,800	800
Private nonguaranteed	98	485	4,471	5,821	5,973	8,957	10,945	10,481
of which: Bonds	..	..	..	..	..	..	..	..
Short-term external debt	1,239	3,503	11,864	13,446	11,635	14,062	12,827	11,474
interest arrears on long-term	14	1	4	4	4	4	5	5
Long-term external debt								
Disbursements	**249**	**648**	**3,810**	**5,406**	**3,542**	**4,675**	**5,273**	**3,711**
Public and publicly guaranteed	143	254	2,679	3,926	2,223	3,108	3,693	2,887
Official creditors	25	188	1,580	2,826	1,050	1,603	3,044	1,720
Private creditors	118	66	1,099	1,100	1,173	1,505	650	1,166
of which: Bonds	0	0	1,000	800	0	0	0	0
Private nonguaranteed	106	395	1,132	1,479	1,320	1,567	1,580	825
of which: Bonds	..	..	..	..	..	..	..	..
Principal repayments	**206**	**511**	**1,265**	**2,347**	**3,419**	**1,938**	**2,974**	**4,034**
Public and publicly guaranteed	134	177	463	1,318	2,656	1,064	2,097	2,806
Official creditors	52	94	110	170	2,553	379	893	985
Private creditors	82	83	353	1,149	103	685	1,204	1,822
of which: Bonds	0	0	0	19	0	0	0	1,000
Private nonguaranteed	71	333	802	1,029	763	874	877	1,228
of which: Bonds	..	..	..	..	..	..	..	..
Interest payments	**39**	**54**	**208**	**572**	**851**	**783**	**884**	**1,024**
Public and publicly guaranteed	38	39	128	460	730	603	691	824
Official creditors	18	17	114	312	431	267	312	431
Private creditors	19	22	14	148	298	336	379	393
of which: Bonds	0	0	4	129	159	159	159	158
Private nonguaranteed	1	15	80	112	121	181	193	200
of which: Bonds	..	..	..	..	..	..	..	..
Net financial flows								
Net inflows	**27**	**1,009**	**7,348**	**8,413**	**-903**	**5,290**	**1,352**	**-313**
Net debt inflows	-89	695	6,000	4,640	-2,150	3,515	-199	-1,752
Official creditors	-83	85	2,138	2,657	-1,967	-423	888	659
of which: World Bank	-9	-9	36	26	107	132	37	56
of which: IMF	-56	-9	668	..	-464	-1,648	-1,263	-77
Private creditors	-6	610	3,861	1,983	-183	3,939	-1,087	-2,411
Long-term	70	44	1,075	402	1,626	1,512	148	-1,058
Bonds	..	..	1,000	781	0	0	0	-1,000
Banks and other private	70	44	75	-379	1,626	1,512	148	-58
Short-term	-76	566	2,786	1,582	-1,810	2,426	-1,236	-1,353
Net equity inflows	116	314	1,348	3,773	1,247	1,774	1,551	1,438
Foreign direct investment	116	314	1,348	3,773	1,251	1,772	1,546	1,434
Portfolio equity	1	1	1	0	-4	2	5	5
Major economic aggregates								
Gross national income (GNI)	12,690	30,266	54,058	59,052	62,145	70,445	73,740	52,072
Exports of goods, services & prim. income	7,074	17,705	29,805	47,242	52,803	44,905	44,203	33,413
Imports of goods, services & prim. income	7,687	17,411	38,402	49,812	51,442	49,930	47,107	35,750
Primary income on FDI	4	135	1,039	1,186	1,258	2,373	2,043	1,789
Personal transfers & comp. of employees	114	199	575	891	1,053	1,214	1,231	767
International reserves	350	1,137	3,431	6,011	5,809	4,938	3,422	2,744
Ratios								
External debt stocks to exports (%)	37.0	29.9	95.3	71.8	63.9	88.1	90.5	113.4
External debt stocks to GNI (%)	20.6	17.5	52.6	57.5	54.3	56.2	54.3	72.7
Debt service to exports (%)	5.5	4.0	5.8	6.8	9.4	10.3	12.1	15.9
Short-term to external debt stocks (%)	47.3	66.1	41.8	39.6	34.5	35.5	32.1	30.3
Multilateral to external debt stocks (%)	8.3	1.5	1.0	7.8	6.5	8.3	7.9	7.5
Reserves to external debt stocks (%)	13.4	21.4	12.1	17.7	17.2	12.5	8.6	7.2

Notes: Long-term private nonguaranteed debt data from 2014 are World Bank staff estimates based on reports provided by the country.

BELIZE

(US$ million, unless otherwise indicated)

	2000	2005	2010	2011	2012	2013	2014	2015
Summary external debt data								
External debt stocks	**630**	**1,022**	**1,303**	**1,274**	**1,196**	**1,248**	**1,286**	**1,330**
Long-term external debt	557	989	1,261	1,232	1,158	1,214	1,255	1,298
Public and publicly guaranteed	557	989	1,018	1,014	984	1,052	1,101	1,153
Official creditors	252	402	436	435	437	526	575	627
of which: IMF	23	26	35	35	32	28	26	25
Private creditors	305	588	582	578	547	527	527	527
of which: Bonds	75	482	21	21	3	527	527	527
Private nonguaranteed	..	..	243	218	173	162	154	145
of which: Bonds	..	..	..	..	..	..	..	..
Short-term external debt	50	7	7	8	6	6	5	7
interest arrears on long-term	0	7	7	8	6	6	5	7
Long-term external debt								
Disbursements	**218**	**213**	**39**	**53**	**41**	**166**	**90**	**96**
Public and publicly guaranteed	218	213	32	36	37	164	87	95
Official creditors	39	48	32	36	37	123	87	95
Private creditors	179	165	0	0	0	41	0	0
of which: Bonds	86	143	0	0	0	41	0	0
Private nonguaranteed	..	..	7	18	4	2	3	1
of which: Bonds	..	..	..	..	..	..	..	..
Principal repayments	**41**	**155**	**69**	**72**	**103**	**102**	**47**	**46**
Public and publicly guaranteed	41	155	49	40	54	89	37	39
Official creditors	20	25	45	36	35	35	37	39
Private creditors	22	131	4	4	18	54	0	0
of which: Bonds	11	36	0	0	18	54	0	0
Private nonguaranteed	..	..	20	32	49	13	10	7
of which: Bonds	..	..	..	..	..	..	..	..
Interest payments	**32**	**73**	**58**	**59**	**49**	**30**	**44**	**42**
Public and publicly guaranteed	32	73	47	48	40	22	37	37
Official creditors	12	18	15	11	11	11	11	11
Private creditors	19	55	32	37	29	11	26	26
of which: Bonds	1	41	2	2	1	11	26	26
Private nonguaranteed	..	..	11	11	9	8	7	4
of which: Bonds	..	..	..	..	..	..	..	..
Net financial flows								
Net inflows	**200**	**163**	**65**	**76**	**130**	**153**	**183**	**109**
Net debt inflows	176	57	-30	-19	-64	61	42	50
Official creditors	19	23	-13	-1	-1	85	49	56
of which: World Bank	-1	-4	-4	-2	1	1	0	4
of which: IMF	0	0	0	0	-3	-4	-1	0
Private creditors	157	34	-17	-18	-63	-24	-7	-6
Long-term	158	34	-17	-18	-63	-24	-7	-6
Bonds	75	107	..	..	-18	-13	..	..
Banks and other private	83	-73	-17	-18	-45	-11	-7	-6
Short-term	-1	..	..	..	..	..	..	..
Net equity inflows	25	106	94	94	194	92	141	59
Foreign direct investment	25	106	94	94	194	92	141	59
Portfolio equity	..	..	..	..	..	..	..	..
Major economic aggregates								
Gross national income (GNI)	779	1,000	1,259	1,389	1,453	1,508	1,580	1,628
Exports of goods, services & prim. income	431	622	834	949	1,040	1,062	1,091	1,041
Imports of goods, services & prim. income	650	824	972	1,052	1,148	1,208	1,301	1,285
Primary income on FDI	31	35	102	40	68	85	98	51
Personal transfers & comp. of employees	25	45	78	75	76	74	80	85
International reserves	123	71	218	237	289	403	487	437
Ratios								
External debt stocks to exports (%)	146.3	164.4	156.2	134.3	115.0	117.5	117.8	127.8
External debt stocks to GNI (%)	80.9	102.2	103.5	91.8	82.3	82.8	81.4	81.7
Debt service to exports (%)	17.9	36.8	15.2	13.8	14.9	12.7	8.4	8.4
Short-term to external debt stocks (%)	7.9	0.7	0.5	0.6	0.5	0.5	0.4	0.5
Multilateral to external debt stocks (%)	22.1	22.0	19.4	20.3	22.3	22.8	22.6	23.0
Reserves to external debt stocks (%)	19.5	7.0	16.7	18.6	24.2	32.3	37.9	32.9

Notes: Long-term private nonguaranteed debt data from 2008 are based on Central Bank data.

BENIN

(US$ million, unless otherwise indicated)

	2000	2005	2010	2011	2012	2013	2014	2015
Summary external debt data								
External debt stocks	**1,400**	**1,552**	**1,599**	**1,869**	**2,060**	**2,014**	**2,045**	**2,179**
Long-term external debt	1,237	1,445	1,113	1,194	1,308	1,599	1,766	1,898
Public and publicly guaranteed	1,237	1,445	1,113	1,194	1,308	1,599	1,766	1,898
Official creditors	1,234	1,445	1,113	1,194	1,308	1,599	1,766	1,898
of which: IMF	96	66	146	177	210	225	220	202
Private creditors	3	0	0	0	0	0	0	0
of which: Bonds	0	0	0	0	0	0	0	0
Private nonguaranteed	..	..	..	..	..	..	..	..
of which: Bonds	..	..	..	..	..	..	..	..
Short-term external debt	66	41	341	497	542	189	59	78
interest arrears on long-term	1	2	25	28	47	54	24	49
Long-term external debt								
Disbursements	**39**	**97**	**184**	**116**	**122**	**337**	**330**	**275**
Public and publicly guaranteed	39	97	184	116	122	337	330	275
Official creditors	39	97	184	116	122	337	330	275
Private creditors	0	0	0	0	0	0	0	0
of which: Bonds	0	0	0	0	0	0	0	0
Private nonguaranteed	..	..	..	..	..	..	..	..
of which: Bonds	..	..	..	..	..	..	..	..
Principal repayments	**43**	**24**	**25**	**29**	**39**	**68**	**51**	**43**
Public and publicly guaranteed	43	24	25	29	39	68	51	43
Official creditors	43	20	25	29	39	68	51	43
Private creditors	0	4	0	0	0	0	0	0
of which: Bonds	0	0	0	0	0	0	0	0
Private nonguaranteed	..	..	..	..	..	..	..	..
of which: Bonds	..	..	..	..	..	..	..	..
Interest payments	**16**	**14**	**13**	**13**	**16**	**18**	**25**	**24**
Public and publicly guaranteed	16	14	13	13	16	18	25	24
Official creditors	16	14	13	13	16	18	24	24
Private creditors	0	0	0	0	0	0	0	0
of which: Bonds	0	0	0	0	0	0	0	0
Private nonguaranteed	..	..	..	..	..	..	..	..
of which: Bonds	..	..	..	..	..	..	..	..
Net financial flows								
Net inflows	**-55**	**54**	**288**	**424**	**340**	**107**	**368**	**448**
Net debt inflows	-54	82	309	274	141	-75	186	219
Official creditors	-6	71	175	120	115	284	287	223
of which: World Bank	33	43	78	21	33	120	102	87
of which: IMF	-2	-6	16	33	32	15	9	-8
Private creditors	-48	11	134	154	26	-360	-101	-5
Long-term	..	-4	..	..	..	..	..	..
Bonds	..	..	..	..	..	..	..	..
Banks and other private	..	-4	..	..	..	..	..	..
Short-term	-48	15	134	154	26	-360	-101	-5
Net equity inflows	-1	-28	-21	150	199	182	182	229
Foreign direct investment	-1	-31	-26	149	198	178	176	229
Portfolio equity	0	2	5	1	1	4	6	..
Major economic aggregates								
Gross national income (GNI)	2,557	4,786	6,917	7,760	8,050	9,042	9,516	8,449
Exports of goods, services & prim. income	552	797	1,707	1,765	1,969	2,651	3,197	2,116
Imports of goods, services & prim. income	743	1,188	2,393	2,423	2,746	3,578	4,376	3,012
Primary income on FDI	-1	9	55	66	91	128	144	..
Personal transfers & comp. of employees	86	147	139	172	208	249	304	304
International reserves	459	655	1,200	887	713	695	726	732
Ratios								
External debt stocks to exports (%)	253.6	194.6	93.7	105.8	104.6	76.0	64.0	103.0
External debt stocks to GNI (%)	54.7	32.4	23.1	24.1	25.6	22.3	21.5	25.8
Debt service to exports (%)	13.6	6.0	3.3	4.0	4.3	3.4	2.6	3.6
Short-term to external debt stocks (%)	4.7	2.6	21.3	26.6	26.3	9.4	2.9	3.6
Multilateral to external debt stocks (%)	69.2	87.4	58.3	53.4	53.2	68.3	71.1	70.2
Reserves to external debt stocks (%)	32.8	42.2	75.0	47.5	34.6	34.5	35.5	33.6

Notes: Short-term debt is based on data from the BIS. Data include the effects of Paris Club debt restructuring agreement and HIPC and MDRI debt relief.

BHUTAN

(US$ million, unless otherwise indicated)

	2000	2005	2010	2011	2012	2013	2014	2015
Summary external debt data								
External debt stocks	**212**	**657**	**935**	**1,072**	**1,450**	**1,603**	**1,836**	**1,956**
Long-term external debt	202	636	919	1,054	1,365	1,519	1,821	1,945
Public and publicly guaranteed	202	636	919	1,045	1,358	1,514	1,820	1,945
Official creditors	202	636	899	1,016	1,320	1,464	1,769	1,898
of which: IMF	8	9	9	9	9	9	9	8
Private creditors	0	0	21	29	38	49	50	47
of which: Bonds	0	0	0	0	0	0	0	0
Private nonguaranteed	..	..	..	10	8	5	2	0
of which: Bonds	..	..	..	..	..	..	..	..
Short-term external debt	2	12	6	8	75	75	6	2
interest arrears on long-term	0	4	0	0	0	0	0	0
Long-term external debt								
Disbursements	**35**	**82**	**178**	**270**	**409**	**293**	**424**	**304**
Public and publicly guaranteed	35	82	178	260	409	293	424	304
Official creditors	35	82	162	251	400	283	417	297
Private creditors	0	0	16	9	9	9	7	7
of which: Bonds	0	0	0	0	0	0	0	0
Private nonguaranteed	..	..	..	10	0	0	0	0
of which: Bonds	..	..	..	..	..	..	..	..
Principal repayments	**5**	**5**	**47**	**45**	**69**	**39**	**42**	**92**
Public and publicly guaranteed	5	5	47	45	67	37	40	90
Official creditors	5	5	47	45	67	37	40	86
Private creditors	0	0	0	0	0	0	0	4
of which: Bonds	0	0	0	0	0	0	0	0
Private nonguaranteed	..	..	..	..	2	2	2	1
of which: Bonds	..	..	..	..	..	..	..	..
Interest payments	**2**	**2**	**41**	**40**	**60**	**38**	**40**	**37**
Public and publicly guaranteed	2	2	41	40	60	38	40	37
Official creditors	2	2	40	38	58	35	37	34
Private creditors	0	0	1	2	2	2	3	3
of which: Bonds	0	0	0	0	0	0	0	0
Private nonguaranteed	..	..	..	..	0	0	0	0
of which: Bonds	..	..	..	..	..	..	..	..
Net financial flows								
Net inflows	**30**	**92**	**152**	**247**	**418**	**302**	**323**	**241**
Net debt inflows	30	85	132	227	407	253	313	208
Official creditors	30	77	115	206	334	246	377	211
of which: World Bank	3	8	0	27	36	2	5	21
of which: IMF	0	0	0	0	0	0	0	0
Private creditors	0	8	17	21	73	7	-64	-3
Long-term	..	..	16	19	6	7	5	1
Bonds	..	..	..	..	..	..	..	..
Banks and other private	..	..	16	19	6	7	5	1
Short-term	0	8	1	2	67	..	-69	-4
Net equity inflows	..	6	20	20	11	49	10	33
Foreign direct investment	..	6	20	20	11	49	10	33
Portfolio equity	..	..	..	..	..	..	..	..
Major economic aggregates								
Gross national income (GNI)	439	807	1,497	1,706	1,682	1,682	1,824	1,848
Exports of goods, services & prim. income	..	..	607	762	746	685	679	727
Imports of goods, services & prim. income	..	..	1,024	1,425	1,340	1,284	1,259	1,386
Primary income on FDI	..	..	4	5	2	20	2	27
Personal transfers & comp. of employees	..	..	8	10	18	12	14	20
International reserves	318	467	1,002	790	955	991	1,245	1,103
Ratios								
External debt stocks to exports (%)	..	..	154.0	140.6	194.2	233.9	270.6	269.1
External debt stocks to GNI (%)	48.2	81.3	62.4	62.8	86.2	95.3	100.7	105.8
Debt service to exports (%)	..	..	14.4	11.2	17.4	11.3	12.2	17.8
Short-term to external debt stocks (%)	0.7	1.9	0.6	0.7	5.2	4.7	0.3	0.1
Multilateral to external debt stocks (%)	47.6	26.8	35.3	35.8	29.8	28.0	25.6	24.0
Reserves to external debt stocks (%)	150.1	71.2	107.2	73.7	65.9	61.8	67.8	56.4

Notes: Short-term debt is based on data from the BIS.

BOLIVIA, PLURINATIONAL STATE OF

(US$ million, unless otherwise indicated)

	2000	2005	2010	2011	2012	2013	2014	2015
Summary external debt data								
External debt stocks	**5,887**	**6,961**	**5,745**	**6,149**	**6,574**	**8,051**	**8,780**	**9,849**
Long-term external debt	5,230	6,497	5,156	5,574	5,991	7,548	8,253	9,235
Public and publicly guaranteed	4,204	4,583	2,798	3,401	4,146	5,191	5,641	6,329
Official creditors	4,171	4,556	2,774	3,312	3,625	4,172	4,625	5,316
of which: IMF	255	282	253	252	252	253	238	227
Private creditors	33	27	24	89	520	1,019	1,015	1,013
of which: Bonds	0	0	0	0	500	1,000	1,000	1,000
Private nonguaranteed	1,026	1,914	2,358	2,173	1,846	2,357	2,612	2,906
of which: Bonds	..	..	..	..	..	..	..	..
Short-term external debt	402	182	336	324	330	250	289	387
interest arrears on long-term	2	0	0	0	0	0	0	0
Long-term external debt								
Disbursements	**745**	**880**	**538**	**776**	**1,251**	**1,445**	**1,551**	**1,375**
Public and publicly guaranteed	277	434	509	776	1,251	1,220	709	983
Official creditors	264	429	506	709	684	720	709	983
Private creditors	13	4	3	67	567	500	0	0
of which: Bonds	0	0	0	0	500	500	0	0
Private nonguaranteed	468	447	30	..	..	225	842	392
of which: Bonds	..	..	..	..	..	..	..	..
Principal repayments	**438**	**316**	**568**	**358**	**558**	**428**	**796**	**684**
Public and publicly guaranteed	157	185	247	173	375	189	210	246
Official creditors	153	183	177	171	373	186	207	244
Private creditors	4	2	70	2	2	2	2	2
of which: Bonds	0	0	0	0	0	0	0	0
Private nonguaranteed	281	131	322	185	183	240	586	438
of which: Bonds	..	..	..	..	..	..	..	..
Interest payments	**160**	**159**	**76**	**78**	**80**	**114**	**155**	**167**
Public and publicly guaranteed	113	100	54	57	65	96	137	150
Official creditors	112	100	50	54	65	71	82	96
Private creditors	1	0	4	4	0	25	54	54
of which: Bonds	0	0	0	0	0	24	54	54
Private nonguaranteed	47	59	22	20	14	18	18	17
of which: Bonds	..	..	..	..	..	..	..	..
Net financial flows								
Net inflows	**707**	**356**	**776**	**1,307**	**1,922**	**2,637**	**1,442**	**1,292**
Net debt inflows	291	448	2	406	699	937	794	788
Official creditors	105	220	329	538	311	533	502	738
of which: World Bank	49	62	44	42	47	54	31	261
of which: IMF	-5	-26	..	..	..	..	..	..
Private creditors	186	227	-327	-133	387	404	292	50
Long-term	196	318	-359	-120	381	483	254	-48
Bonds	..	..	..	..	500	500	0	0
Banks and other private	196	318	-359	-120	-119	-17	254	-48
Short-term	-10	-91	32	-13	6	-79	39	98
Net equity inflows	416	-91	774	902	1,224	1,699	648	503
Foreign direct investment	416	-91	774	902	1,224	1,699	648	503
Portfolio equity	..	..	..	..	..	..	..	..
Major economic aggregates								
Gross national income (GNI)	8,172	9,173	18,786	22,802	25,455	28,752	31,289	33,010
Exports of goods, services & prim. income	1,610	3,401	6,919	9,260	12,399	12,923	13,663	9,614
Imports of goods, services & prim. income	2,443	3,362	7,126	9,900	11,690	13,139	14,864	12,689
Primary income on FDI	148	271	863	977	1,649	1,916	1,690	1,690
Personal transfers & comp. of employees	127	337	960	1,043	1,111	1,201	1,184	1,210
International reserves	926	1,328	8,134	9,911	11,659	12,783	13,481	11,601
Ratios								
External debt stocks to exports (%)	365.7	204.7	83.0	66.4	53.0	62.3	64.3	102.4
External debt stocks to GNI (%)	72.0	75.9	30.6	27.0	25.8	28.0	28.1	29.8
Debt service to exports (%)	39.8	15.7	9.5	4.8	5.2	4.3	7.0	8.9
Short-term to external debt stocks (%)	6.8	2.6	5.9	5.3	5.0	3.1	3.3	3.9
Multilateral to external debt stocks (%)	48.8	60.6	39.4	42.2	45.9	42.4	43.6	46.4
Reserves to external debt stocks (%)	15.7	19.1	141.6	161.2	177.4	158.8	153.5	117.8

BOSNIA AND HERZEGOVINA

(US$ million, unless otherwise indicated)

	2000	2005	2010	2011	2012	2013	2014	2015
Summary external debt data								
External debt stocks	**2,791**	**7,008**	**14,032**	**14,126**	**14,557**	**15,192**	**14,115**	**12,887**
Long-term external debt	2,622	6,095	12,115	12,032	12,537	13,324	12,442	11,443
Public and publicly guaranteed	1,959	2,563	3,733	3,874	4,201	4,748	4,634	4,229
Official creditors	1,834	2,408	3,267	3,451	3,797	4,355	4,309	3,962
of which: IMF	131	91	769	766	888	848	892	800
Private creditors	125	155	466	423	404	394	325	267
of which: Bonds	0	0	273	241	221	205	158	121
Private nonguaranteed	663	3,532	8,381	8,158	8,336	8,576	7,808	7,214
of which: Bonds	..	..	..	..	..	..	..	..
Short-term external debt	38	821	1,149	1,328	1,132	1,020	781	644
interest arrears on long-term	1	0	0	0	0	0	0	0
Long-term external debt								
Disbursements	**103**	**1,292**	**441**	**582**	**1,268**	**1,351**	**561**	**849**
Public and publicly guaranteed	98	153	441	382	448	643	561	290
Official creditors	98	153	427	370	431	625	535	271
Private creditors	0	0	14	12	17	18	25	19
of which: Bonds	0	0	0	0	0	0	0	0
Private nonguaranteed	5	1,138	0	199	820	708	0	559
of which: Bonds	..	..	..	..	..	..	..	..
Principal repayments	**171**	**95**	**1,293**	**594**	**810**	**669**	**989**	**1,495**
Public and publicly guaranteed	170	55	145	171	167	200	222	342
Official creditors	170	51	108	129	124	155	174	298
Private creditors	0	3	37	43	43	46	48	44
of which: Bonds	0	0	25	26	24	25	24	21
Private nonguaranteed	1	41	1,147	423	642	468	768	1,153
of which: Bonds	..	..	..	..	..	..	..	..
Interest payments	**119**	**136**	**177**	**186**	**183**	**178**	**247**	**191**
Public and publicly guaranteed	89	53	55	66	65	58	80	56
Official creditors	86	48	47	55	56	53	75	53
Private creditors	2	6	9	11	9	5	4	3
of which: Bonds	0	0	5	6	5	2	2	1
Private nonguaranteed	30	83	121	120	118	120	168	135
of which: Bonds	..	..	..	..	..	..	..	..
Net financial flows								
Net inflows	**94**	**2,040**	**-774**	**510**	**545**	**747**	**-337**	**-598**
Net debt inflows	-53	1,726	-923	167	383	529	-569	-837
Official creditors	-56	63	556	241	427	429	461	-81
of which: World Bank	44	32	123	32	0	-16	27	17
of which: IMF	16	-39	237	..	120	-41	99	-54
Private creditors	3	1,663	-1,479	-75	-44	100	-1,029	-756
Long-term	4	1,094	-1,171	-254	152	212	-790	-619
Bonds	..	..	-25	-26	-24	-25	-24	-21
Banks and other private	4	1,094	-1,146	-228	176	237	-766	-598
Short-term	0	569	-308	179	-196	-112	-239	-137
Net equity inflows	146	314	149	343	162	218	232	239
Foreign direct investment	146	314	149	343	162	219	237	236
Portfolio equity	..	..	..	..	0	-1	-6	2
Major economic aggregates								
Gross national income (GNI)	6,096	11,693	17,442	18,778	17,341	18,386	18,644	16,149
Exports of goods, services & prim. income	2,247	4,227	5,691	6,646	6,138	6,719	6,949	6,124
Imports of goods, services & prim. income	4,234	8,103	9,111	10,931	10,043	10,191	11,008	9,077
Primary income on FDI	..	97	79	276	228	182	331	312
Personal transfers & comp. of employees	1,581	2,038	1,822	1,958	1,846	1,958	2,107	1,801
International reserves	497	2,548	4,366	4,150	4,283	4,868	4,744	4,689
Ratios								
External debt stocks to exports (%)	124.2	165.8	246.6	212.6	237.2	226.1	203.1	210.4
External debt stocks to GNI (%)	45.8	59.9	80.4	75.2	83.9	82.6	75.7	79.8
Debt service to exports (%)	14.2	7.3	27.4	13.1	18.1	16.7	22.1	29.7
Short-term to external debt stocks (%)	1.4	11.7	8.2	9.4	7.8	6.7	5.5	5.0
Multilateral to external debt stocks (%)	45.4	24.4	17.2	18.1	19.8	22.2	24.0	24.4
Reserves to external debt stocks (%)	17.8	36.4	31.1	29.4	29.4	32.0	33.6	36.4

Notes: Long-term private nonguaranteed debt data from 2005 are World Bank staff estimates. Short-term debt is based on data from the BIS.

BOTSWANA

(US$ million, unless otherwise indicated)

	2000	2005	2010	2011	2012	2013	2014	2015
Summary external debt data								
External debt stocks	**452**	**461**	**1,795**	**2,389**	**2,477**	**2,418**	**2,407**	**2,147**
Long-term external debt	438	412	1,349	1,890	2,003	1,883	1,907	1,687
Public and publicly guaranteed	438	412	1,349	1,890	1,924	1,804	1,827	1,687
Official creditors	410	401	1,348	1,889	1,924	1,804	1,787	1,656
of which: IMF	6	6	88	88	88	88	83	80
Private creditors	28	12	1	1	0	0	40	31
of which: Bonds	0	0	0	0	0	0	0	0
Private nonguaranteed	0	0	0	0	80	80	80	0
of which: Bonds	0	0	0	0	80	80	80	0
Short-term external debt	9	42	357	411	385	446	417	380
interest arrears on long-term	0	0	0	0	0	0	0	0
Long-term external debt								
Disbursements	**28**	**11**	**17**	**595**	**149**	**29**	**77**	**8**
Public and publicly guaranteed	28	11	17	595	69	29	77	8
Official creditors	24	11	17	595	69	29	37	8
Private creditors	4	0	0	0	0	0	40	0
of which: Bonds	0	0	0	0	0	0	0	0
Private nonguaranteed	0	0	0	0	80	0	0	0
of which: Bonds	0	0	0	0	80	0	0	0
Principal repayments	**52**	**40**	**58**	**55**	**33**	**154**	**32**	**211**
Public and publicly guaranteed	52	40	58	55	33	154	32	132
Official creditors	45	38	57	55	32	154	32	123
Private creditors	7	2	1	0	1	0	0	9
of which: Bonds	0	0	0	0	0	0	0	0
Private nonguaranteed	0	0	0	0	0	0	0	80
of which: Bonds	0	0	0	0	0	0	0	80
Interest payments	**15**	**12**	**17**	**18**	**21**	**33**	**19**	**19**
Public and publicly guaranteed	15	12	17	18	21	28	16	14
Official creditors	14	11	17	18	21	28	16	14
Private creditors	1	0	0	0	0	0	0	0
of which: Bonds	0	0	0	0	0	0	0	0
Private nonguaranteed	0	0	0	0	0	5	2	5
of which: Bonds	0	0	0	0	0	5	2	5
Net financial flows								
Net inflows	**-30**	**229**	**391**	**1,988**	**753**	**577**	**432**	**209**
Net debt inflows	-35	-9	158	593	90	-64	16	-240
Official creditors	-21	-27	-41	539	37	-125	5	-115
of which: World Bank	-8	-2	6	52	38	12	23	-1
of which: IMF	..	..	..	..	..	..	..	..
Private creditors	-14	19	199	54	53	61	11	-125
Long-term	-3	-2	-1	0	79	..	40	-89
Bonds	..	..	..	..	80	..	..	-80
Banks and other private	-3	-2	-1	0	-1	..	40	-9
Short-term	-11	21	199	54	-26	61	-29	-37
Net equity inflows	4	238	233	1,395	663	641	416	450
Foreign direct investment	10	211	222	1,413	671	640	416	450
Portfolio equity	-6	27	11	-17	-9	2	0	0
Major economic aggregates								
Gross national income (GNI)	5,436	9,096	12,237	15,571	14,730	14,439	15,534	14,203
Exports of goods, services & prim. income	3,378	5,739	5,835	7,918	7,115	9,376	10,097	7,744
Imports of goods, services & prim. income	3,050	4,737	7,360	8,590	9,024	9,677	9,341	8,232
Primary income on FDI	658	1,066	731	285	116	536	512	449
Personal transfers & comp. of employees	19	118	22	20	18	36	46	31
International reserves	6,318	6,309	7,885	8,082	7,628	7,726	8,323	7,546
Ratios								
External debt stocks to exports (%)	13.4	8.0	30.8	30.2	34.8	25.8	23.8	27.7
External debt stocks to GNI (%)	8.3	5.1	14.7	15.3	16.8	16.7	15.5	15.1
Debt service to exports (%)	2.0	0.9	1.4	1.0	0.8	2.1	0.6	3.1
Short-term to external debt stocks (%)	2.0	9.1	19.9	17.2	15.5	18.4	17.3	17.7
Multilateral to external debt stocks (%)	65.7	56.9	67.9	74.8	74.1	71.7	72.0	75.2
Reserves to external debt stocks (%)	1,396.5	1,369.9	439.4	338.3	308.0	319.6	345.8	351.4

Notes: Short-term debt is based on data from the BIS.

BRAZIL

(US$ million, unless otherwise indicated)

	2000	2005	2010	2011	2012	2013	2014	2015
Summary external debt data								
External debt stocks	**242,512**	**188,365**	**352,364**	**404,046**	**440,515**	**483,766**	**556,921**	**543,399**
Long-term external debt	209,303	163,859	282,426	357,473	403,494	445,813	494,562	487,057
Public and publicly guaranteed	96,622	94,354	97,486	94,712	116,664	136,555	174,323	172,274
Official creditors	29,845	26,160	41,517	36,568	39,007	39,325	42,116	41,750
of which: IMF	2,235	513	4,446	4,432	4,437	4,446	4,183	4,001
Private creditors	66,776	68,194	55,968	58,144	77,658	97,230	132,207	130,525
of which: Bonds	54,096	59,077	46,806	45,408	48,471	52,125	53,855	46,629
Private nonguaranteed	112,682	69,505	184,940	262,761	286,830	309,258	320,239	314,783
of which: Bonds	16,846	35,969	83,032	79,363	69,053	61,384	55,073	51,276
Short-term external debt	30,973	23,993	65,492	42,140	32,583	33,507	58,177	52,341
interest arrears on long-term	176	0	0	0	0	27	17	0
Long-term external debt								
Disbursements	**44,079**	**27,414**	**85,379**	**111,458**	**79,639**	**107,805**	**115,767**	**93,972**
Public and publicly guaranteed	19,664	13,207	19,957	13,655	27,987	36,911	41,796	19,999
Official creditors	5,272	3,327	11,317	3,250	4,985	5,179	5,296	3,568
Private creditors	14,391	9,880	8,640	10,405	23,002	31,732	36,499	16,432
of which: Bonds	10,836	8,252	5,433	3,631	6,587	8,680	6,287	852
Private nonguaranteed	24,415	14,207	65,422	97,803	51,652	70,894	73,971	73,972
of which: Bonds	2,886	6,579	32,384	30,765	8,822	4,780	8,163	9,678
Principal repayments	**34,746**	**25,788**	**32,026**	**41,778**	**30,590**	**63,750**	**44,956**	**71,341**
Public and publicly guaranteed	10,932	9,481	9,628	15,852	6,689	14,897	9,071	22,689
Official creditors	7,093	3,334	2,665	8,355	2,321	4,455	1,949	3,656
Private creditors	3,839	6,147	6,963	7,498	4,369	10,442	7,122	19,033
of which: Bonds	2,056	4,187	5,770	4,281	3,269	4,325	5,254	5,232
Private nonguaranteed	23,813	16,306	22,398	25,925	23,901	48,853	35,885	48,652
of which: Bonds	2,775	7,063	2,656	3,666	7,154	11,459	9,588	10,741
Interest payments	**15,297**	**10,314**	**13,157**	**16,615**	**14,259**	**17,830**	**16,438**	**17,723**
Public and publicly guaranteed	6,943	6,700	5,172	5,446	5,019	6,007	5,706	5,875
Official creditors	1,932	1,058	968	1,013	963	918	798	810
Private creditors	5,010	5,642	4,204	4,433	4,057	5,089	4,908	5,066
of which: Bonds	4,212	5,033	3,864	3,902	3,392	3,805	3,658	3,313
Private nonguaranteed	8,355	3,614	7,985	11,169	9,240	11,823	10,731	11,848
of which: Bonds	1,562	2,161	4,207	5,859	3,107	3,722	3,354	3,334
Net financial flows								
Net inflows	**37,563**	**-1,961**	**191,712**	**138,210**	**109,158**	**87,423**	**165,182**	**83,264**
Net debt inflows	4,471	-23,457	79,059	46,329	39,491	44,951	95,491	16,812
Official creditors	-8,514	-23,817	8,652	-5,104	2,664	724	3,347	-88
of which: World Bank	805	-255	3,512	-4,553	2,409	2,259	1,998	660
of which: IMF	-6,693	-23,810	0	0	0	0	0	0
Private creditors	12,985	360	70,407	51,433	36,827	44,227	92,144	16,900
Long-term	11,154	1,634	44,700	74,785	46,384	43,331	67,463	22,718
Bonds	8,892	3,580	29,391	26,449	4,986	-2,324	-391	-5,442
Banks and other private	2,262	-1,947	15,309	48,336	41,398	45,655	67,855	28,161
Short-term	1,831	-1,274	25,706	-23,352	-9,557	897	24,680	-5,818
Net equity inflows	33,092	21,496	112,653	91,881	69,667	42,472	69,691	66,452
Foreign direct investment	30,016	15,045	74,982	84,707	64,066	30,835	57,918	56,421
Portfolio equity	3,076	6,451	37,671	7,174	5,602	11,636	11,773	10,030
Major economic aggregates								
Gross national income (GNI)	626,889	856,743	2,172,767	2,571,003	2,380,537	2,356,028	2,368,460	1,735,974
Exports of goods, services & prim. income	67,337	136,200	249,757	315,431	289,877	291,769	276,912	235,800
Imports of goods, services & prim. income	93,083	125,773	328,412	395,386	366,774	370,240	383,819	297,406
Primary income on FDI	4,238	11,035	62,183	63,171	36,108	17,445	35,803	28,544
Personal transfers & comp. of employees	1,350	2,805	3,083	3,215	2,784	2,718	2,648	2,897
International reserves	32,434	53,245	287,056	350,356	369,566	356,214	360,965	354,175
Ratios								
External debt stocks to exports (%)	360.1	138.3	141.1	128.1	152.0	165.8	201.1	230.4
External debt stocks to GNI (%)	38.7	22.0	16.2	15.7	18.5	20.5	23.5	31.3
Debt service to exports (%)	87.0	46.2	18.4	18.7	15.7	28.1	22.5	38.1
Short-term to external debt stocks (%)	12.8	12.7	18.6	10.4	7.4	6.9	10.4	9.6
Multilateral to external debt stocks (%)	7.8	10.4	8.5	6.2	6.3	5.9	5.6	5.8
Reserves to external debt stocks (%)	13.4	28.3	81.5	86.7	83.9	73.6	64.8	65.2

BULGARIA

(US$ million, unless otherwise indicated)

	2000	2005	2010	2011	2012	2013	2014	2015
Summary external debt data								
External debt stocks	**12,009**	**18,507**	**50,635**	**47,642**	**51,289**	**51,307**	**47,834**	**37,492**
Long-term external debt	8,440	12,532	34,551	33,857	36,570	37,198	34,845	28,064
Public and publicly guaranteed	7,671	5,075	4,782	4,579	5,718	4,536	5,706	6,139
Official creditors	2,603	3,045	3,151	3,140	3,094	3,231	2,744	2,477
of which: IMF	2,118	1,533	941	938	939	941	885	847
Private creditors	5,068	2,030	1,631	1,440	2,624	1,305	2,962	3,662
of which: Bonds	4,982	1,920	1,618	1,434	2,618	1,299	2,957	3,657
Private nonguaranteed	769	7,457	29,768	29,277	30,852	32,662	29,139	21,925
of which: Bonds	0	526	134	24	274	1,594	1,444	1,444
Short-term external debt	1,451	4,442	15,143	12,848	13,780	13,168	12,103	8,582
interest arrears on long-term	1	0	0	0	0	0	0	0
Long-term external debt								
Disbursements	**719**	**4,895**	**1,569**	**10,803**	**6,171**	**6,460**	**5,468**	**5,712**
Public and publicly guaranteed	405	402	199	292	1,429	380	2,078	2,281
Official creditors	381	383	199	292	228	380	174	210
Private creditors	24	19	0	0	1,201	0	1,904	2,070
of which: Bonds	0	0	0	0	1,201	0	1,904	2,070
Private nonguaranteed	313	4,493	1,370	10,511	4,743	6,081	3,389	3,431
of which: Bonds	0	249	0	0	340	1,320	0	0
Principal repayments	**527**	**3,349**	**3,550**	**3,567**	**3,777**	**5,201**	**4,434**	**8,218**
Public and publicly guaranteed	298	1,761	268	258	263	1,650	293	1,273
Official creditors	297	255	261	251	263	269	293	228
Private creditors	2	1,507	7	7	0	1,380	0	1,045
of which: Bonds	0	1,496	0	0	0	1,380	0	1,045
Private nonguaranteed	229	1,588	3,282	3,308	3,514	3,551	4,142	6,945
of which: Bonds	0	10	0	109	57	0	150	0
Interest payments	**453**	**479**	**607**	**785**	**749**	**863**	**718**	**2,099**
Public and publicly guaranteed	420	327	177	188	161	235	121	162
Official creditors	139	93	71	83	82	69	68	58
Private creditors	282	234	106	105	79	166	53	104
of which: Bonds	281	229	106	105	79	166	53	104
Private nonguaranteed	32	152	430	598	588	628	598	1,936
of which: Bonds	0	30	11	6	0	12	42	36
Net financial flows								
Net inflows	**1,329**	**4,774**	**-2,994**	**6,196**	**4,259**	**2,434**	**871**	**-4,078**
Net debt inflows	511	2,308	-4,635	4,941	3,326	648	-32	-6,028
Official creditors	221	-315	-62	41	-35	111	-118	-17
of which: World Bank	44	115	-70	-56	-56	-59	-103	-87
of which: IMF	137	-443	0	0	0	0	0	0
Private creditors	290	2,623	-4,573	4,901	3,362	537	87	-6,011
Long-term	107	1,418	-1,919	7,196	2,429	1,149	1,152	-2,489
Bonds	..	-1,257	..	-109	1,483	-60	1,754	1,025
Banks and other private	107	2,675	-1,919	7,305	946	1,209	-602	-3,514
Short-term	183	1,206	-2,654	-2,296	932	-611	-1,065	-3,522
Net equity inflows	818	2,466	1,641	1,254	933	1,786	903	1,950
Foreign direct investment	813	2,017	1,642	1,301	928	1,805	979	1,959
Portfolio equity	5	449	-1	-46	4	-19	-77	-9
Major economic aggregates								
Gross national income (GNI)	12,825	29,905	48,581	54,729	52,223	53,528	55,405	46,938
Exports of goods, services & prim. income	7,321	17,674	26,144	34,902	33,593	37,139	38,088	33,220
Imports of goods, services & prim. income	8,314	22,034	29,108	36,961	36,831	39,619	40,167	34,830
Primary income on FDI	107	912	1,284	2,074	1,414	2,366	2,122	2,366
Personal transfers & comp. of employees	58	1,613	1,333	1,483	1,449	1,667	1,685	1,495
International reserves	3,155	8,041	15,421	15,252	18,371	18,335	18,576	20,783
Ratios								
External debt stocks to exports (%)	164.0	104.7	193.7	136.5	152.7	138.1	125.6	112.9
External debt stocks to GNI (%)	93.6	61.9	104.2	87.1	98.2	95.9	86.3	79.9
Debt service to exports (%)	17.5	25.3	16.1	12.8	13.9	16.7	14.0	31.6
Short-term to external debt stocks (%)	12.1	24.0	29.9	27.0	26.9	25.7	25.3	22.9
Multilateral to external debt stocks (%)	12.8	13.3	4.6	5.0	4.8	5.3	5.0	5.8
Reserves to external debt stocks (%)	26.3	43.4	30.5	32.0	35.8	35.7	38.8	55.4

Notes: Long-term private nonguaranteed debt data from 2008 are World Bank staff estimates based on reports provided by the country. Short-term debt before 2009 is World Bank staff estimates based on Central Bank data. The data may include long-term public and publicly guaranteed debt owed by the state-owned railway.

BURKINA FASO

(US$ million, unless otherwise indicated)

	2000	2005	2010	2011	2012	2013	2014	2015
Summary external debt data								
External debt stocks	**1,438**	**2,001**	**2,148**	**2,290**	**2,519**	**2,565**	**2,544**	**2,627**
Long-term external debt	1,229	1,861	1,931	2,057	2,218	2,261	2,261	2,344
Public and publicly guaranteed	1,229	1,861	1,931	2,057	2,218	2,261	2,261	2,344
Official creditors	1,226	1,861	1,913	2,043	2,205	2,250	2,253	2,341
of which: IMF	124	117	217	233	301	304	283	283
Private creditors	3	0	18	15	13	11	7	3
of which: Bonds	0	0	0	0	0	0	0	0
Private nonguaranteed	..	..	..	..	..	..	..	..
of which: Bonds	..	..	..	..	..	..	..	..
Short-term external debt	84	22	0	0	0	0	0	0
interest arrears on long-term	5	0	0	0	0	0	0	0
Long-term external debt								
Disbursements	**91**	**208**	**276**	**171**	**159**	**60**	**217**	**274**
Public and publicly guaranteed	91	208	276	171	159	60	217	274
Official creditors	91	208	276	171	159	60	217	274
Private creditors	0	0	0	0	0	0	0	0
of which: Bonds	0	0	0	0	0	0	0	0
Private nonguaranteed	..	..	..	..	..	..	..	..
of which: Bonds	..	..	..	..	..	..	..	..
Principal repayments	**26**	**25**	**30**	**43**	**43**	**48**	**57**	**70**
Public and publicly guaranteed	26	25	30	43	43	48	57	70
Official creditors	26	25	27	40	41	46	55	66
Private creditors	0	0	2	3	2	2	2	4
of which: Bonds	0	0	0	0	0	0	0	0
Private nonguaranteed	..	..	..	..	..	..	..	..
of which: Bonds	..	..	..	..	..	..	..	..
Interest payments	**12**	**16**	**18**	**21**	**21**	**22**	**23**	**22**
Public and publicly guaranteed	12	16	18	21	21	22	23	22
Official creditors	12	16	18	21	21	22	23	22
Private creditors	0	0	0	0	0	0	0	0
of which: Bonds	0	0	0	0	0	0	0	0
Private nonguaranteed	..	..	..	..	..	..	..	..
of which: Bonds	..	..	..	..	..	..	..	..
Net financial flows								
Net inflows	**67**	**210**	**236**	**273**	**114**	**87**	**464**	**383**
Net debt inflows	47	193	266	145	184	14	157	216
Official creditors	66	195	269	147	186	17	159	219
of which: World Bank	36	102	67	64	60	24	85	130
of which: IMF	0	12	20	17	68	2	-3	12
Private creditors	-19	-2	-2	-3	-2	-2	-2	-4
Long-term	0	0	-2	-3	-2	-2	-2	-4
Bonds	..	..	..	..	..	..	..	..
Banks and other private	0	0	-2	-3	-2	-2	-2	-4
Short-term	-19	-2	..	..	..	..	..	..
Net equity inflows	21	17	-30	128	-70	73	307	167
Foreign direct investment	23	21	-32	132	118	266	241	167
Portfolio equity	-3	-4	3	-4	-188	-194	66	..
Major economic aggregates								
Gross national income (GNI)	2,606	5,442	9,203	10,392	10,721	11,926	12,190	10,941
Exports of goods, services & prim. income	251	583	1,981	2,913	3,393	3,280	3,366	2,556
Imports of goods, services & prim. income	691	1,452	2,655	3,618	4,056	5,065	4,842	3,996
Primary income on FDI	3	7	26	60	82	178	384	..
Personal transfers & comp. of employees	67	57	120	221	210	308	396	396
International reserves	243	438	1,068	957	1,025	628	297	260
Ratios								
External debt stocks to exports (%)	573.9	343.0	108.5	78.6	74.2	78.2	75.6	102.8
External debt stocks to GNI (%)	55.2	36.8	23.3	22.0	23.5	21.5	20.9	24.0
Debt service to exports (%)	19.0	7.9	2.5	2.3	2.1	2.4	2.7	4.4
Short-term to external debt stocks (%)	5.9	1.1	0.0	0.0	0.0	0.0	0.0	0.0
Multilateral to external debt stocks (%)	71.5	84.6	75.0	76.3	75.8	76.5	78.1	77.8
Reserves to external debt stocks (%)	16.9	21.9	49.7	41.8	40.7	24.5	11.7	9.9

Notes: Short-term debt before 2009 is based on data from the BIS. Data include HIPC and MDRI debt relief.

BURUNDI

(US$ million, unless otherwise indicated)

	2000	2005	2010	2011	2012	2013	2014	2015
Summary external debt data								
External debt stocks	**1,125.9**	**1,287.9**	**620.9**	**604.4**	**667.3**	**683.6**	**690.2**	**626.0**
Long-term external debt	1,036.0	1,176.1	381.8	363.2	411.4	398.1	403.6	408.1
Public and publicly guaranteed	1,036.0	1,176.1	381.8	363.2	411.4	398.1	403.6	408.1
Official creditors	1,032.0	1,174.0	376.8	358.2	407.0	393.8	399.2	403.7
of which: IMF	24.9	77.7	223.4	240.7	248.7	254.2	238.3	217.6
Private creditors	4.0	2.1	5.0	5.0	4.4	4.4	4.4	4.4
of which: Bonds	0.0	0.0	0.0	0.0	0.0	0.0	0.0	0.0
Private nonguaranteed	..	..	..	..	..	..	..	..
of which: Bonds	..	..	..	..	..	..	..	..
Short-term external debt	65.0	34.1	15.7	0.4	7.3	31.3	48.3	0.3
interest arrears on long-term	19.7	33.1	0.7	0.4	0.3	0.3	0.3	0.3
Long-term external debt								
Disbursements	**41.3**	**42.1**	**31.6**	**28.0**	**60.2**	**6.9**	**39.9**	**21.0**
Public and publicly guaranteed	41.3	42.1	31.6	28.0	60.2	6.9	39.9	21.0
Official creditors	38.2	42.1	31.6	28.0	60.2	6.9	39.9	21.0
Private creditors	3.0	0.0	0.0	0.0	0.0	0.0	0.0	0.0
of which: Bonds	0.0	0.0	0.0	0.0	0.0	0.0	0.0	0.0
Private nonguaranteed	..	..	..	..	..	..	..	..
of which: Bonds	..	..	..	..	..	..	..	..
Principal repayments	**9.4**	**27.2**	**2.4**	**5.8**	**10.2**	**18.3**	**8.7**	**4.8**
Public and publicly guaranteed	9.4	27.2	2.4	5.8	10.2	18.3	8.7	4.8
Official creditors	9.4	22.6	2.4	5.8	9.6	18.3	8.7	4.8
Private creditors	0.0	4.6	0.0	0.0	0.6	0.0	0.0	0.0
of which: Bonds	0.0	0.0	0.0	0.0	0.0	0.0	0.0	0.0
Private nonguaranteed	..	..	..	..	..	..	..	..
of which: Bonds	..	..	..	..	..	..	..	..
Interest payments	**4.5**	**11.9**	**1.4**	**2.0**	**3.0**	**3.2**	**3.7**	**3.7**
Public and publicly guaranteed	4.5	11.9	1.4	2.0	3.0	3.2	3.7	3.7
Official creditors	4.5	11.9	1.4	2.0	3.0	3.2	3.7	3.7
Private creditors	0.0	0.0	0.0	0.0	0.0	0.0	0.0	0.0
of which: Bonds	0.0	0.0	0.0	0.0	0.0	0.0	0.0	0.0
Private nonguaranteed	..	..	..	..	..	..	..	..
of which: Bonds	..	..	..	..	..	..	..	..
Net financial flows								
Net inflows	**30.1**	**34.7**	**58.1**	**29.1**	**65.2**	**24.5**	**94.4**	**-34.9**
Net debt inflows	18.4	34.1	57.3	25.8	64.6	17.6	47.4	-42.2
Official creditors	24.3	40.7	49.3	40.8	58.2	-6.4	30.4	5.8
of which: World Bank	27.6	18.9	17.8	8.6	5.0	-0.9	-1.6	-2.2
of which: IMF	-4.5	21.1	20.1	18.6	7.6	5.0	-0.9	-10.5
Private creditors	-5.9	-6.6	8.0	-15.0	6.4	24.0	17.0	-48.0
Long-term	3.0	-4.6	0.0	0.0	-0.6	0.0	0.0	0.0
Bonds	..	..	..	..	..	..	..	..
Banks and other private	3.0	-4.6	0.0	0.0	-0.6	0.0	0.0	0.0
Short-term	-8.9	-2.0	8.0	-15.0	7.0	24.0	17.0	-48.0
Net equity inflows	11.7	0.6	0.8	3.4	0.6	6.9	47.1	7.4
Foreign direct investment	11.7	0.6	0.8	3.4	0.6	6.9	47.1	7.4
Portfolio equity	..	..	..	..	..	..	..	..
Major economic aggregates								
Gross national income (GNI)	884.8	1,099.6	2,014.8	2,338.2	2,463.3	2,713.1	3,093.7	3,077.9
Exports of goods, services & prim. income	55.4	98.7	181.9	243.1	235.6	235.0	220.0	192.4
Imports of goods, services & prim. income	164.9	343.9	618.7	790.3	943.3	925.9	945.2	844.9
Primary income on FDI	0.4	2.1	..	..	8.5	4.8	12.9	5.8
Personal transfers & comp. of employees	..	0.1	34.5	45.5	46.4	48.6	56.3	51.0
International reserves	32.9	100.1	330.7	294.0	307.2	328.2	316.0	135.1
Ratios								
External debt stocks to exports (%)	2031.9	1304.3	341.4	248.6	283.3	290.9	313.7	325.3
External debt stocks to GNI (%)	127.2	117.1	30.8	25.8	27.1	25.2	22.3	20.3
Debt service to exports (%)	40.9	40.5	2.4	4.2	8.9	13.8	13.3	13.5
Short-term to external debt stocks (%)	5.8	2.6	2.5	0.1	1.1	4.6	7.0	0.0
Multilateral to external debt stocks (%)	79.1	81.9	52.4	51.1	50.4	47.2	45.5	49.1
Reserves to external debt stocks (%)	2.9	7.8	53.3	48.6	46.0	48.0	45.8	21.6

Notes: Data include the effects of Paris Club debt restructuring agreement and HIPC and MDRI debt relief.

CABO VERDE

(US$ million, unless otherwise indicated)

	2000	2005	2010	2011	2012	2013	2014	2015
Summary external debt data								
External debt stocks	**320**	**477**	**892**	**1,039**	**1,245**	**1,488**	**1,542**	**1,520**
Long-term external debt	315	463	868	1,017	1,226	1,471	1,527	1,506
Public and publicly guaranteed	315	463	868	1,017	1,226	1,471	1,527	1,506
Official creditors	308	442	816	944	1,108	1,281	1,270	1,247
of which: IMF	1	13	23	20	18	16	14	13
Private creditors	7	22	53	73	118	190	257	259
of which: Bonds	0	0	0	0	0	0	0	0
Private nonguaranteed	..	..	..	..	..	..	..	..
of which: Bonds	..	..	..	..	..	..	..	..
Short-term external debt	4	1	2	2	2	2	2	2
interest arrears on long-term	4	1	2	2	2	2	2	2
Long-term external debt								
Disbursements	**29**	**74**	**208**	**191**	**222**	**244**	**227**	**119**
Public and publicly guaranteed	29	74	208	191	222	244	227	119
Official creditors	29	65	158	165	179	180	132	91
Private creditors	0	9	50	25	43	64	96	29
of which: Bonds	0	0	0	0	0	0	0	0
Private nonguaranteed	..	..	..	..	..	..	..	..
of which: Bonds	..	..	..	..	..	..	..	..
Principal repayments	**11**	**29**	**26**	**26**	**20**	**22**	**24**	**24**
Public and publicly guaranteed	11	29	26	26	20	22	24	24
Official creditors	10	23	22	24	20	22	24	24
Private creditors	2	5	3	2	0	0	0	0
of which: Bonds	0	0	0	0	0	0	0	0
Private nonguaranteed	..	..	..	..	..	..	..	..
of which: Bonds	..	..	..	..	..	..	..	..
Interest payments	**5**	**7**	**8**	**10**	**13**	**16**	**18**	**18**
Public and publicly guaranteed	5	7	8	10	13	16	18	18
Official creditors	4	6	8	9	12	13	14	14
Private creditors	1	1	0	1	2	2	4	4
of which: Bonds	0	0	0	0	0	0	0	0
Private nonguaranteed	..	..	..	..	..	..	..	..
of which: Bonds	..	..	..	..	..	..	..	..
Net financial flows								
Net inflows	**36**	**112**	**275**	**253**	**363**	**342**	**330**	**174**
Net debt inflows	2	49	180	162	199	220	202	95
Official creditors	19	45	134	138	156	156	106	66
of which: World Bank	10	26	22	-2	13	22	45	17
of which: IMF	0	4	-2	-3	-2	-2	-1	0
Private creditors	-18	4	46	23	43	64	96	29
Long-term	-2	4	46	23	43	64	96	29
Bonds	..	..	..	..	..	..	..	..
Banks and other private	-2	4	46	23	43	64	96	29
Short-term	-16	..	..	..	..	..	..	..
Net equity inflows	34	63	95	91	164	121	128	79
Foreign direct investment	34	63	95	91	164	121	128	79
Portfolio equity	..	..	..	..	..	..	..	..
Major economic aggregates								
Gross national income (GNI)	525	938	1,591	1,792	1,677	1,773	1,778	1,556
Exports of goods, services & prim. income	141	373	644	796	788	855	907	686
Imports of goods, services & prim. income	334	695	1,207	1,459	1,293	1,238	1,340	1,013
Primary income on FDI	5	11	56	42	32	17	35	16
Personal transfers & comp. of employees	87	137	131	177	178	176	197	201
International reserves	28	174	382	339	376	475	511	494
Ratios								
External debt stocks to exports (%)	226.2	128.0	138.6	130.5	157.9	174.0	170.0	221.5
External debt stocks to GNI (%)	60.9	50.9	56.1	58.0	74.2	83.9	86.7	97.7
Debt service to exports (%)	11.4	9.6	5.6	4.9	4.6	4.6	4.8	6.2
Short-term to external debt stocks (%)	1.2	0.2	0.2	0.1	0.1	0.1	0.1	0.1
Multilateral to external debt stocks (%)	72.4	78.8	67.0	58.8	51.3	45.8	45.5	47.3
Reserves to external debt stocks (%)	8.8	36.4	42.8	32.6	30.2	31.9	33.1	32.5

CAMBODIA

(US$ million, unless otherwise indicated)

	2000	2005	2010	2011	2012	2013	2014	2015
Summary external debt data								
External debt stocks	**1,946**	**2,769**	**3,685**	**4,227**	**6,283**	**7,132**	**7,916**	**9,319**
Long-term external debt	1,853	2,666	3,177	3,602	5,311	6,040	6,707	7,861
Public and publicly guaranteed	1,853	2,666	2,874	3,279	4,099	4,626	5,051	5,420
Official creditors	1,853	2,666	2,874	3,279	4,099	4,626	5,051	5,420
of which: IMF	93	103	129	129	129	129	122	116
Private creditors	0	0	0	0	0	0	0	0
of which: Bonds	0	0	0	0	0	0	0	0
Private nonguaranteed	..	..	302	323	1,212	1,414	1,657	2,441
of which: Bonds	..	..	..	..	..	..	..	..
Short-term external debt	0	0	379	497	843	963	1,087	1,342
interest arrears on long-term	0	0	0	0	0	0	0	0
Long-term external debt								
Disbursements	**79**	**155**	**454**	**694**	**2,201**	**1,285**	**1,395**	**1,974**
Public and publicly guaranteed	79	155	346	437	869	602	645	600
Official creditors	79	155	346	437	869	602	645	600
Private creditors	0	0	0	0	0	0	0	0
of which: Bonds	0	0	0	0	0	0	0	0
Private nonguaranteed	..	..	108	257	1,333	683	750	1,374
of which: Bonds	..	..	..	..	..	..	..	..
Principal repayments	**0**	**8**	**33**	**277**	**492**	**550**	**585**	**670**
Public and publicly guaranteed	0	8	33	41	47	69	77	80
Official creditors	0	8	33	41	47	69	77	80
Private creditors	0	0	0	0	0	0	0	0
of which: Bonds	0	0	0	0	0	0	0	0
Private nonguaranteed	..	..	0	236	444	481	508	590
of which: Bonds	..	..	..	..	..	..	..	..
Interest payments	**4**	**12**	**27**	**33**	**44**	**56**	**62**	**71**
Public and publicly guaranteed	4	12	26	31	42	52	57	57
Official creditors	4	12	26	31	42	52	57	57
Private creditors	0	0	0	0	0	0	0	0
of which: Bonds	0	0	0	0	0	0	0	0
Private nonguaranteed	..	..	1	2	2	4	5	14
of which: Bonds	..	..	..	..	..	..	..	..
Net financial flows								
Net inflows	**201**	**518**	**1,305**	**1,330**	**3,497**	**2,200**	**2,666**	**3,256**
Net debt inflows	83	138	570	535	2,056	855	935	1,558
Official creditors	83	138	313	396	821	533	568	520
of which: World Bank	37	34	9	12	14	2	22	-11
of which: IMF	4	-9	..	..	..	..	..	..
Private creditors	0	0	257	139	1,234	322	367	1,039
Long-term	..	..	108	21	888	202	243	784
Bonds	..	..	..	..	..	..	..	..
Banks and other private	..	..	108	21	888	202	243	784
Short-term	0	0	149	118	346	120	124	255
Net equity inflows	118	379	735	795	1,441	1,345	1,730	1,698
Foreign direct investment	118	379	735	795	1,441	1,345	1,730	1,698
Portfolio equity	..	..	..	..	..	..	..	..
Major economic aggregates								
Gross national income (GNI)	3,534	6,006	10,728	12,229	13,325	14,575	15,826	17,062
Exports of goods, services & prim. income	1,893	4,094	6,026	7,826	8,893	10,087	11,388	12,515
Imports of goods, services & prim. income	2,453	4,935	7,075	8,882	10,343	12,075	13,638	15,051
Primary income on FDI	123	227	414	460	617	700	945	..
Personal transfers & comp. of employees	103	164	153	160	172	176	377	397
International reserves	502	953	3,255	3,450	4,267	4,516	5,626	6,883
Ratios								
External debt stocks to exports (%)	102.8	67.6	61.2	54.0	70.7	70.7	69.5	74.5
External debt stocks to GNI (%)	55.1	46.1	34.3	34.6	47.2	48.9	50.0	54.6
Debt service to exports (%)	0.7	0.7	1.1	4.1	6.2	6.1	5.8	6.2
Short-term to external debt stocks (%)	0.0	0.0	10.3	11.7	13.4	13.5	13.7	14.4
Multilateral to external debt stocks (%)	19.6	38.3	41.5	37.6	26.0	24.3	21.3	18.0
Reserves to external debt stocks (%)	25.8	34.4	88.3	81.6	67.9	63.3	71.1	73.9

Notes: Long-term private nonguaranteed debt data are estimates based on Central Bank data. Short-term debt is based on Central Bank data. Data include MDRI debt relief.

CAMEROON

(US$ million, unless otherwise indicated)

	2000	2005	2010	2011	2012	2013	2014	2015
Summary external debt data								
External debt stocks	**10,561**	**7,700**	**3,191**	**3,095**	**3,739**	**4,915**	**5,162**	**6,558**
Long-term external debt	9,070	7,059	2,737	2,585	3,142	4,036	4,579	5,931
Public and publicly guaranteed	8,753	6,467	2,160	2,124	2,774	3,811	4,336	5,356
Official creditors	8,436	6,384	2,140	2,100	2,729	3,572	3,946	4,213
of which: IMF	267	307	445	442	440	437	406	358
Private creditors	317	83	20	23	45	239	390	1,143
of which: Bonds	0	0	0	0	0	0	0	750
Private nonguaranteed	317	592	577	461	368	225	243	575
of which: Bonds	..	..	..	..	..	..	..	..
Short-term external debt	1,224	334	9	68	157	442	177	269
interest arrears on long-term	205	280	9	0	24	60	1	0
Long-term external debt								
Disbursements	**286**	**227**	**278**	**178**	**608**	**1,005**	**1,076**	**1,562**
Public and publicly guaranteed	247	130	278	178	608	1,005	1,030	1,505
Official creditors	247	130	272	174	586	814	805	662
Private creditors	0	0	6	5	22	191	225	843
of which: Bonds	0	0	0	0	0	0	17	750
Private nonguaranteed	39	98	0	0	0	0	46	57
of which: Bonds	..	..	..	..	..	..	..	..
Principal repayments	**253**	**537**	**159**	**244**	**173**	**146**	**284**	**231**
Public and publicly guaranteed	166	396	121	133	80	53	256	185
Official creditors	162	396	121	133	79	49	221	135
Private creditors	4	0	0	1	1	4	35	50
of which: Bonds	0	0	0	0	0	0	17	0
Private nonguaranteed	86	141	38	111	93	93	28	47
of which: Bonds	..	..	..	..	..	..	..	..
Interest payments	**215**	**228**	**42**	**86**	**60**	**55**	**146**	**156**
Public and publicly guaranteed	198	178	27	57	35	29	134	114
Official creditors	198	177	27	56	34	28	126	80
Private creditors	1	1	0	1	1	2	8	34
of which: Bonds	0	0	0	0	0	0	0	15
Private nonguaranteed	17	51	15	28	25	25	12	42
of which: Bonds	..	..	..	..	..	..	..	..
Net financial flows								
Net inflows	**5**	**-567**	**644**	**138**	**774**	**1,248**	**1,135**	**2,012**
Net debt inflows	-21	-683	119	1	497	1,104	581	1,392
Official creditors	136	-301	151	40	505	762	579	496
of which: World Bank	-5	-13	75	60	80	152	120	90
of which: IMF	51	-35	0	-1	-2	-4	-5	-31
Private creditors	-157	-382	-32	-39	-8	343	2	896
Long-term	-52	-44	-32	-107	-73	94	208	803
Bonds	..	..	..	..	..	..	..	750
Banks and other private	-52	-44	-32	-107	-73	94	208	53
Short-term	-105	-339	0	68	65	249	-206	93
Net equity inflows	26	116	525	138	277	143	554	620
Foreign direct investment	26	120	525	138	277	143	554	620
Portfolio equity	0	-4	0	0	0	0	..	..
Major economic aggregates								
Gross national income (GNI)	8,694	16,099	23,358	26,284	26,027	28,948	31,761	28,762
Exports of goods, services & prim. income	2,693	4,280	5,701	7,674	7,591	8,226	..	..
Imports of goods, services & prim. income	3,020	5,012	6,703	8,680	8,810	9,658	..	..
Primary income on FDI	41	289	166	282	503	648	..	..
Personal transfers & comp. of employees	22	77	115	219	210	244	244	244
International reserves	212	949	3,643	3,199	3,381	3,472	3,168	3,536
Ratios								
External debt stocks to exports (%)	392.2	179.9	56.0	40.3	49.3	59.8	..	..
External debt stocks to GNI (%)	121.5	47.8	13.7	11.8	14.4	17.0	16.3	22.8
Debt service to exports (%)	20.8	19.1	3.6	4.3	3.1	2.5	..	..
Short-term to external debt stocks (%)	11.6	4.3	0.3	2.2	4.2	9.0	3.4	4.1
Multilateral to external debt stocks (%)	13.4	20.6	24.6	27.6	30.0	27.8	28.4	22.4
Reserves to external debt stocks (%)	2.0	12.3	114.2	103.4	90.4	70.6	61.4	53.9

Notes: Short-term debt is based on data from the BIS. Data include the effects of HIPC and MDRI debt relief.

CENTRAL AFRICAN REPUBLIC

(US$ million, unless otherwise indicated)

	2000	2005	2010	2011	2012	2013	2014	2015
Summary external debt data								
External debt stocks	**869.0**	**1,026.0**	**615.2**	**549.3**	**537.1**	**556.3**	**641.8**	**661.9**
Long-term external debt	797.3	877.2	361.9	271.2	274.3	292.6	380.9	401.3
Public and publicly guaranteed	797.3	877.2	361.9	271.2	274.3	292.6	380.9	401.3
Official creditors	764.8	843.1	325.3	244.1	247.2	266.4	357.2	357.8
of which: IMF	33.6	49.2	172.6	172.0	182.9	181.0	177.3	174.9
Private creditors	32.6	34.1	36.6	27.1	27.1	26.2	23.7	43.5
of which: Bonds	0.0	0.0	0.0	0.0	0.0	0.0	0.0	0.0
Private nonguaranteed	..	..	..	..	..	..	..	..
of which: Bonds	..	..	..	..	..	..	..	..
Short-term external debt	38.1	99.6	80.7	106.1	79.9	82.7	83.6	85.6
interest arrears on long-term	26.1	97.6	77.7	71.1	72.9	76.3	79.6	82.5
Long-term external debt								
Disbursements	**16.1**	**0.0**	**19.2**	**17.1**	**18.4**	**20.2**	**93.9**	**39.1**
Public and publicly guaranteed	16.1	0.0	19.2	17.1	18.4	20.2	93.9	39.1
Official creditors	16.1	0.0	19.2	17.1	18.4	20.2	93.9	19.1
Private creditors	0.0	0.0	0.0	0.0	0.0	0.0	0.0	20.0
of which: Bonds	0.0	0.0	0.0	0.0	0.0	0.0	0.0	0.0
Private nonguaranteed	..	..	..	..	..	..	..	..
of which: Bonds	..	..	..	..	..	..	..	..
Principal repayments	**7.5**	**0.7**	**1.0**	**0.8**	**2.1**	**3.5**	**7.2**	**0.9**
Public and publicly guaranteed	7.5	0.7	1.0	0.8	2.1	3.5	7.2	0.9
Official creditors	7.4	0.7	1.0	0.7	2.1	2.3	5.1	0.9
Private creditors	0.0	0.0	0.0	0.1	0.1	1.2	2.2	0.0
of which: Bonds	0.0	0.0	0.0	0.0	0.0	0.0	0.0	0.0
Private nonguaranteed	..	..	..	..	..	..	..	..
of which: Bonds	..	..	..	..	..	..	..	..
Interest payments	**4.3**	**0.2**	**1.2**	**0.2**	**1.9**	**0.5**	**2.6**	**2.6**
Public and publicly guaranteed	4.3	0.2	1.2	0.2	1.9	0.5	2.6	2.6
Official creditors	4.3	0.2	1.2	0.2	1.9	0.5	2.6	2.6
Private creditors	0.0	0.0	0.0	0.0	0.0	0.0	0.0	0.0
of which: Bonds	0.0	0.0	0.0	0.0	0.0	0.0	0.0	0.0
Private nonguaranteed	..	..	..	..	..	..	..	..
of which: Bonds	..	..	..	..	..	..	..	..
Net financial flows								
Net inflows	**-16.0**	**-3.5**	**92.9**	**85.2**	**68.9**	**15.7**	**95.0**	**45.8**
Net debt inflows	-16.9	-13.6	31.4	48.3	-1.1	13.9	91.5	42.8
Official creditors	7.8	-5.6	31.4	16.4	26.9	15.7	96.2	23.7
of which: World Bank	7.2	..	5.0	5.2	4.2	-0.1	33.1	7.9
of which: IMF	-0.8	-4.9	13.2	..	10.6	-2.3	7.3	5.4
Private creditors	-24.7	-8.0	0.0	31.9	-28.1	-1.8	-4.7	19.1
Long-term	0.0	0.0	0.0	-0.1	-0.1	-1.2	-2.2	20.0
Bonds	..	..	..	..	..	..	..	..
Banks and other private	0.0	0.0	0.0	-0.1	-0.1	-1.2	-2.2	20.0
Short-term	-24.7	-8.0	0.0	32.0	-28.0	-0.6	-2.5	-0.9
Net equity inflows	0.9	10.1	61.5	36.9	70.0	1.9	3.5	3.0
Foreign direct investment	0.9	10.1	61.5	36.9	70.0	1.9	3.5	3.0
Portfolio equity	..	..	..	..	..	..	..	..
Major economic aggregates								
Gross national income (GNI)	901.4	1,340.1	1,995.6	2,222.4	2,195.4	1,499.7	1,698.3	1,510.2
Exports of goods, services & prim. income	..	..	..	..	..	..	..	..
Imports of goods, services & prim. income	..	..	..	..	..	..	..	..
Primary income on FDI	..	..	..	..	..	..	..	..
Personal transfers & comp. of employees	..	..	..	..	..	..	..	..
International reserves	133.3	139.2	181.2	154.5	157.9	193.7	259.6	213.8
Ratios								
External debt stocks to exports (%)	..	..	..	..	..	..	..	..
External debt stocks to GNI (%)	96.4	76.6	30.8	24.7	24.5	37.1	37.8	43.8
Debt service to exports (%)	..	..	..	..	..	..	..	..
Short-term to external debt stocks (%)	4.4	9.7	13.1	19.3	14.9	14.9	13.0	12.9
Multilateral to external debt stocks (%)	67.1	61.2	6.7	6.4	7.9	7.6	10.8	12.9
Reserves to external debt stocks (%)	15.3	13.6	29.5	28.1	29.4	34.8	40.4	32.3

Notes: Short-term debt is based on data from the BIS. Data include the effects of HIPC and MDRI debt relief.

CHAD

(US$ million, unless otherwise indicated)

	2000	2005	2010	2011	2012	2013	2014	2015
Summary external debt data								
External debt stocks	**1,099**	**1,630**	**2,158**	**2,346**	**2,361**	**2,925**	**2,396**	**1,617**
Long-term external debt	986	1,526	2,049	2,235	2,266	2,832	2,291	1,472
Public and publicly guaranteed	986	1,526	2,049	2,235	2,266	2,832	2,291	1,472
Official creditors	971	1,494	2,019	2,211	2,243	2,212	2,096	1,278
of which: IMF	90	93	99	91	87	85	98	137
Private creditors	15	32	30	24	22	620	195	194
of which: Bonds	0	0	0	0	0	0	0	0
Private nonguaranteed	..	..	..	..	..	..	..	..
of which: Bonds	..	..	..	..	..	..	..	..
Short-term external debt	23	11	9	20	8	8	8	8
interest arrears on long-term	10	6	7	8	8	8	8	8
Long-term external debt								
Disbursements	**46**	**143**	**366**	**254**	**95**	**661**	**116**	**43**
Public and publicly guaranteed	46	143	366	254	95	661	116	43
Official creditors	46	143	366	254	95	61	116	43
Private creditors	0	0	0	0	0	600	0	0
of which: Bonds	0	0	0	0	0	0	0	0
Private nonguaranteed	..	..	..	..	..	..	..	..
of which: Bonds	..	..	..	..	..	..	..	..
Principal repayments	**13**	**24**	**45**	**57**	**58**	**95**	**539**	**27**
Public and publicly guaranteed	13	24	45	57	58	95	539	27
Official creditors	13	23	43	51	56	92	114	27
Private creditors	1	1	2	6	2	3	425	0
of which: Bonds	0	0	0	0	0	0	0	0
Private nonguaranteed	..	..	..	..	..	..	..	..
of which: Bonds	..	..	..	..	..	..	..	..
Interest payments	**9**	**16**	**17**	**18**	**21**	**23**	**49**	**9**
Public and publicly guaranteed	9	16	17	18	21	23	49	9
Official creditors	9	16	17	18	21	23	24	9
Private creditors	0	0	0	0	0	0	25	0
of which: Bonds	0	0	0	0	0	0	0	0
Private nonguaranteed	..	..	..	..	..	..	..	..
of which: Bonds	..	..	..	..	..	..	..	..
Net financial flows								
Net inflows	**157**	**12**	**617**	**481**	**601**	**1,084**	**-1,079**	**661**
Net debt inflows	42	111	304	199	21	564	-404	61
Official creditors	46	114	312	194	35	-34	21	61
of which: World Bank	13	58	-16	-17	-17	-21	-17	-6
of which: IMF	13	-7	-11	-8	-4	-3	19	44
Private creditors	-4	-2	-8	4	-14	597	-425	0
Long-term	-1	-1	-2	-6	-2	597	-425	0
Bonds	..	..	..	..	..	..	..	..
Banks and other private	-1	-1	-2	-6	-2	597	-425	0
Short-term	-3	-1	-6	10	-12	0	0	0
Net equity inflows	115	-99	313	282	580	520	-676	600
Foreign direct investment	115	-99	313	282	580	520	-676	600
Portfolio equity	..	..	..	..	..	..	..	..
Major economic aggregates								
Gross national income (GNI)	1,368	5,622	10,302	11,841	12,068	12,359	13,233	10,561
Exports of goods, services & prim. income	..	..	..	..	..	..	..	..
Imports of goods, services & prim. income	..	..	..	..	..	..	..	..
Primary income on FDI	..	..	..	..	..	..	..	..
Personal transfers & comp. of employees	..	..	..	..	..	..	..	..
International reserves	111	226	632	951	1,156	1,183	1,076	369
Ratios								
External debt stocks to exports (%)	..	..	..	..	..	..	..	..
External debt stocks to GNI (%)	80.4	29.0	20.9	19.8	19.6	23.7	18.1	15.3
Debt service to exports (%)	..	..	..	..	..	..	..	..
Short-term to external debt stocks (%)	2.1	0.7	0.4	0.8	0.4	0.3	0.3	0.5
Multilateral to external debt stocks (%)	75.9	84.2	70.9	65.7	65.3	51.4	57.7	35.5
Reserves to external debt stocks (%)	10.1	13.8	29.3	40.5	48.9	40.4	44.9	22.8

Notes: Short-term debt is based on data from the BIS. Data include the effects of HIPC debt relief.

CHINA

(US$ million, unless otherwise indicated)

	2000	2005	2010	2011	2012	2013	2014	2015
Summary external debt data								
External debt stocks	**145,666**	**283,310**	**222,655**	**1,044,355**	**1,138,247**	**1,471,618**	**1,770,543**	**1,418,291**
Long-term external debt	132,278	134,704	211,378	262,263	335,397	383,823	520,964	487,983
Public and publicly guaranteed	94,489	84,212	94,003	104,778	128,593	143,691	171,217	158,402
Official creditors	50,393	52,438	67,204	67,651	66,179	58,529	57,265	45,884
of which: IMF	309	338	10,764	10,731	10,743	10,764	10,127	9,686
Private creditors	44,096	31,774	26,799	37,127	62,414	85,162	113,952	112,518
of which: Bonds	11,371	16,039	12,398	13,404	30,104	36,509	55,403	66,019
Private nonguaranteed	37,789	50,492	117,375	157,485	206,804	240,132	349,748	329,581
of which: Bonds	1,068	3,574	5,561	23,667	44,125	52,353	89,524	123,982
Short-term external debt	13,080	148,267	512	771,361	792,108	1,077,031	1,239,452	920,622
interest arrears on long-term	0	0	0	0	0	0	0	0
Long-term external debt								
Disbursements	**19,006**	**29,228**	**38,569**	**78,621**	**80,331**	**79,893**	**136,867**	**134,139**
Public and publicly guaranteed	11,924	9,776	11,823	37,400	31,880	26,477	41,190	25,556
Official creditors	5,791	2,170	4,348	5,527	3,419	2,713	4,902	2,678
Private creditors	6,133	7,606	7,475	31,874	28,461	23,764	36,287	22,878
of which: Bonds	848	4,208	0	14,016	16,556	6,405	23,695	11,866
Private nonguaranteed	7,082	19,452	26,746	41,220	48,451	53,416	95,678	108,583
of which: Bonds	390	1,622	..	14,189	20,703	23,897	37,740	47,610
Principal repayments	**19,364**	**20,938**	**18,765**	**24,949**	**29,829**	**36,681**	**38,158**	**80,227**
Public and publicly guaranteed	10,237	6,661	11,961	12,199	8,132	9,966	12,597	39,041
Official creditors	4,271	1,415	7,204	5,301	4,491	6,877	5,130	13,556
Private creditors	5,965	5,246	4,757	6,898	3,641	3,089	7,467	25,484
of which: Bonds	443	550	0	2,092	318	0	4,801	1,250
Private nonguaranteed	9,127	14,277	6,803	12,751	21,697	26,715	25,561	41,187
of which: Bonds	534	370	1,459	1,083	1,310	1,821	2,754	13,208
Interest payments	**6,065**	**3,219**	**5,391**	**6,890**	**7,675**	**7,580**	**9,410**	**10,473**
Public and publicly guaranteed	4,141	2,202	1,726	1,792	2,139	1,974	1,707	2,270
Official creditors	2,387	1,376	944	1,070	1,832	1,552	1,083	1,507
Private creditors	1,754	826	783	722	307	422	625	762
of which: Bonds	521	430	393	310	59	151	349	176
Private nonguaranteed	1,924	1,017	3,665	5,097	5,536	5,606	7,703	8,203
of which: Bonds	93	248	672	1,942	2,558	3,593	5,299	6,352
Net financial flows								
Net inflows	**42,243**	**153,012**	**36,758**	**1,080,597**	**315,675**	**626,138**	**523,943**	**-30,327**
Net debt inflows	-2,458	40,787	-220,192	824,520	71,249	328,135	261,130	-264,918
Official creditors	1,519	755	-2,856	226	-1,072	-4,164	-228	-10,878
of which: World Bank	1,263	127	-153	-1,486	-814	-832	-690	-592
of which: IMF	..	..	..	..	..	..	..	..
Private creditors	-3,977	40,032	-217,336	824,294	72,321	332,299	261,358	-254,040
Long-term	-1,877	7,535	22,661	53,446	51,574	47,376	98,937	64,790
Bonds	261	4,910	-1,459	25,029	35,631	28,481	53,880	45,018
Banks and other private	-2,138	2,625	24,120	28,416	15,943	18,895	45,057	19,773
Short-term	-2,100	32,497	-239,997	770,849	20,747	284,923	162,421	-318,830
Net equity inflows	44,700	112,225	256,950	256,076	244,425	298,003	262,813	234,591
Foreign direct investment	37,788	91,656	225,593	250,768	214,523	265,408	210,897	219,627
Portfolio equity	6,912	20,569	31,357	5,308	29,903	32,595	51,916	14,964
Major economic aggregates								
Gross national income (GNI)	1,190,595	2,252,490	6,013,586	7,422,055	8,441,806	9,412,780	10,320,724	10,807,242
Exports of goods, services & prim. income	202,589	812,612	1,746,369	2,153,120	2,342,129	2,539,568	2,763,611	2,657,098
Imports of goods, services & prim. income	188,382	704,099	1,549,244	2,041,534	2,130,171	2,382,630	2,487,623	2,317,819
Primary income on FDI	20,198	47,566	159,637	204,476	171,845	206,381	..	..
Personal transfers & comp. of employees	758	3,337	13,636	16,568	17,066	17,790	29,911	44,445
International reserves	168,278	821,514	2,866,079	3,202,789	3,331,120	3,839,548	3,859,168	3,345,194
Ratios								
External debt stocks to exports (%)	71.9	34.9	12.7	48.5	48.6	57.9	64.1	53.4
External debt stocks to GNI (%)	12.2	12.6	3.7	14.1	13.5	15.6	17.2	13.1
Debt service to exports (%)	13.1	3.4	3.0	2.9	3.1	3.0	2.9	4.7
Short-term to external debt stocks (%)	9.0	52.3	0.2	73.9	69.6	73.2	70.0	64.9
Multilateral to external debt stocks (%)	17.7	9.3	15.8	3.3	3.0	2.3	1.9	2.3
Reserves to external debt stocks (%)	115.5	290.0	1,287.2	306.7	292.7	260.9	218.0	235.9

Notes: Long-term private nonguaranteed and short-term debt data are World Bank staff estimates based on reports provided by the country and market data. 2015 data reflects BPM6 methodology and coverage.

COLOMBIA

(US$ million, unless otherwise indicated)

	2000	2005	2010	2011	2012	2013	2014	2015
Summary external debt data								
External debt stocks	**34,272**	**37,465**	**64,097**	**73,813**	**76,782**	**89,720**	**101,376**	**111,050**
Long-term external debt	31,252	31,665	55,048	62,083	65,313	77,693	88,085	98,092
Public and publicly guaranteed	20,993	22,676	36,970	39,484	43,945	50,947	58,649	66,650
Official creditors	7,909	10,665	16,430	16,921	19,933	21,209	21,906	22,952
of which: IMF	149	163	1,137	1,134	1,135	1,137	1,070	1,023
Private creditors	13,084	12,011	20,539	22,563	24,013	29,739	36,743	43,698
of which: Bonds	8,201	10,927	17,686	20,099	21,729	25,555	31,450	36,482
Private nonguaranteed	10,259	8,989	18,078	22,599	21,368	26,746	29,436	31,442
of which: Bonds	762	370	3,329	2,720	5,320	8,420	8,570	9,170
Short-term external debt	2,871	5,637	7,912	10,596	10,334	10,891	12,221	11,934
interest arrears on long-term	0	0	0	0	0	0	0	0
Long-term external debt								
Disbursements	**3,840**	**6,527**	**12,971**	**16,625**	**17,598**	**20,978**	**19,120**	**19,351**
Public and publicly guaranteed	2,975	4,406	3,631	4,786	7,150	9,295	10,880	10,511
Official creditors	666	1,469	2,265	1,655	4,040	2,463	2,325	2,852
Private creditors	2,310	2,937	1,365	3,131	3,110	6,832	8,555	7,660
of which: Bonds	1,835	2,309	1,335	2,829	2,489	4,778	7,237	5,518
Private nonguaranteed	865	2,121	9,340	11,839	10,448	11,683	8,240	8,840
of which: Bonds	..	..	620	2,720	2,600	3,100	1,750	900
Principal repayments	**2,916**	**7,423**	**6,559**	**6,541**	**11,362**	**6,130**	**10,294**	**9,104**
Public and publicly guaranteed	2,083	4,732	2,311	2,348	2,789	2,012	2,493	1,751
Official creditors	568	2,231	1,123	1,159	1,067	1,114	1,420	1,497
Private creditors	1,515	2,500	1,189	1,189	1,722	898	1,073	253
of which: Bonds	473	1,735	968	481	847	809	1,015	184
Private nonguaranteed	832	2,692	4,248	4,193	8,573	4,118	7,801	7,353
of which: Bonds	110	..	..	..	..	..	1,600	820
Interest payments	**2,039**	**2,597**	**2,837**	**3,202**	**3,393**	**3,288**	**3,982**	**4,307**
Public and publicly guaranteed	1,421	1,959	2,130	2,103	2,157	2,167	2,606	2,871
Official creditors	545	576	559	531	543	571	541	528
Private creditors	875	1,383	1,571	1,571	1,614	1,597	2,065	2,343
of which: Bonds	518	1,294	1,280	1,315	1,395	1,392	1,764	2,023
Private nonguaranteed	618	637	707	1,100	1,236	1,121	1,376	1,436
of which: Bonds	84	36	221	308	202	333	486	470
Net financial flows								
Net inflows	**2,242**	**9,973**	**18,695**	**27,833**	**22,954**	**31,174**	**27,871**	**21,656**
Net debt inflows	-170	-380	10,312	12,769	5,974	15,405	10,156	9,960
Official creditors	98	-763	1,143	496	2,972	1,349	905	1,354
of which: World Bank	24	486	936	84	91	210	542	444
of which: IMF	0	0	0	0	0	0	0	0
Private creditors	-267	383	9,169	12,272	3,001	14,056	9,252	8,606
Long-term	827	-134	5,269	9,588	3,263	13,499	7,921	8,893
Bonds	1,252	574	987	5,069	4,242	7,069	6,372	5,414
Banks and other private	-425	-708	4,282	4,519	-979	6,430	1,549	3,479
Short-term	-1,094	517	3,900	2,684	-262	557	1,331	-287
Net equity inflows	2,412	10,352	8,383	15,064	16,980	15,769	17,715	11,696
Foreign direct investment	2,395	10,267	7,065	12,776	13,801	13,842	13,832	9,936
Portfolio equity	17	86	1,318	2,288	3,180	1,926	3,883	1,760
Major economic aggregates								
Gross national income (GNI)	97,730	141,300	275,802	319,936	354,809	366,035	365,778	286,091
Exports of goods, services & prim. income	16,835	25,787	47,549	66,675	71,884	70,775	67,796	49,740
Imports of goods, services & prim. income	17,675	31,762	60,660	81,232	87,718	87,626	91,730	73,795
Primary income on FDI	655	3,566	9,875	14,866	14,954	13,695	12,045	5,649
Personal transfers & comp. of employees	1,610	3,346	4,031	4,101	4,019	4,450	4,166	4,680
International reserves	8,916	14,787	27,766	31,386	36,444	42,758	46,408	46,104
Ratios								
External debt stocks to exports (%)	203.6	145.3	134.8	110.7	106.8	126.8	149.5	223.3
External debt stocks to GNI (%)	35.1	26.5	23.2	23.1	21.6	24.5	27.7	38.8
Debt service to exports (%)	30.5	39.8	20.5	15.4	21.2	14.0	21.9	28.1
Short-term to external debt stocks (%)	8.4	15.0	12.3	14.4	13.5	12.1	12.1	10.7
Multilateral to external debt stocks (%)	18.9	25.9	24.7	21.6	21.1	18.7	17.0	16.3
Reserves to external debt stocks (%)	26.0	39.5	43.3	42.5	47.5	47.7	45.8	41.5

COMOROS

(US$ million, unless otherwise indicated)

	2000	2005	2010	2011	2012	2013	2014	2015
Summary external debt data								
External debt stocks	**234.5**	**290.1**	**280.6**	**277.9**	**255.7**	**151.1**	**145.0**	**133.4**
Long-term external debt	204.0	255.3	250.7	245.5	223.5	116.6	112.5	103.0
Public and publicly guaranteed	204.0	255.3	250.7	245.5	223.5	116.6	112.5	103.0
Official creditors	204.0	255.3	250.7	245.5	223.5	116.6	112.5	103.0
of which: IMF	2.4	1.0	25.4	27.7	28.0	32.9	30.9	29.2
Private creditors	0.0	0.0	0.0	0.0	0.0	0.0	0.0	0.0
of which: Bonds	0.0	0.0	0.0	0.0	0.0	0.0	0.0	0.0
Private nonguaranteed	..	..	..	..	..	..	..	..
of which: Bonds	..	..	..	..	..	..	..	..
Short-term external debt	28.1	33.7	4.4	4.7	4.1	1.6	1.6	1.3
interest arrears on long-term	19.1	30.7	4.4	4.7	4.1	1.6	1.6	1.3
Long-term external debt								
Disbursements	**2.1**	**3.3**	0.0	0.0	0.0	0.0	0.0	0.0
Public and publicly guaranteed	2.1	3.3	0.0	0.0	0.0	0.0	0.0	0.0
Official creditors	2.1	3.3	0.0	0.0	0.0	0.0	0.0	0.0
Private creditors	0.0	0.0	0.0	0.0	0.0	0.0	0.0	0.0
of which: Bonds	0.0	0.0	0.0	0.0	0.0	0.0	0.0	0.0
Private nonguaranteed	..	..	..	..	..	..	..	..
of which: Bonds	..	..	..	..	..	..	..	..
Principal repayments	**1.2**	**2.6**	**3.1**	**2.2**	**5.1**	**0.3**	**0.5**	**6.6**
Public and publicly guaranteed	1.2	2.6	3.1	2.2	5.1	0.3	0.5	6.6
Official creditors	1.2	2.6	3.1	2.2	5.1	0.3	0.5	6.6
Private creditors	0.0	0.0	0.0	0.0	0.0	0.0	0.0	0.0
of which: Bonds	0.0	0.0	0.0	0.0	0.0	0.0	0.0	0.0
Private nonguaranteed	..	..	..	..	..	..	..	..
of which: Bonds	..	..	..	..	..	..	..	..
Interest payments	**0.8**	**1.3**	**1.1**	**1.7**	**2.3**	**0.1**	**0.1**	**0.1**
Public and publicly guaranteed	0.8	1.3	1.1	1.7	2.3	0.1	0.1	0.1
Official creditors	0.8	1.3	1.1	1.7	2.3	0.1	0.1	0.1
Private creditors	0.0	0.0	0.0	0.0	0.0	0.0	0.0	0.0
of which: Bonds	0.0	0.0	0.0	0.0	0.0	0.0	0.0	0.0
Private nonguaranteed	..	..	..	..	..	..	..	..
of which: Bonds	..	..	..	..	..	..	..	..
Net financial flows								
Net inflows	**2.4**	**1.2**	**7.6**	**23.3**	**0.0**	**8.7**	**4.2**	**-1.8**
Net debt inflows	2.3	0.7	-0.7	0.2	-4.9	4.4	-0.5	-7.0
Official creditors	0.3	0.7	-0.7	0.2	-4.9	4.4	-0.5	-7.0
of which: World Bank	1.4	0.6	-1.7	-0.7	-0.7	0.0	0.0	0.0
of which: IMF	-0.6	..	2.4	2.5	0.2	4.8	..	-0.4
Private creditors	2.0	..	..	..	..	..	..	..
Long-term	..	..	..	..	..	..	..	..
Bonds	..	..	..	..	..	..	..	..
Banks and other private	..	..	..	..	..	..	..	..
Short-term	2.0	0.0	0.0	0.0	0.0	0.0	0.0	0.0
Net equity inflows	0.1	0.6	8.3	23.1	4.9	4.2	4.7	5.1
Foreign direct investment	0.1	0.6	8.3	23.1	4.9	4.2	4.7	5.1
Portfolio equity	..	..	..	..	..	..	..	..
Major economic aggregates								
Gross national income (GNI)	204.2	378.7	515.8	564.8	549.3	597.7	622.5	..
Exports of goods, services & prim. income	..	59.5	90.7	103.4	93.3	109.2	103.8	..
Imports of goods, services & prim. income	..	144.3	275.4	311.6	327.1	354.0	334.6	..
Primary income on FDI	..	1.7	1.8	2.4	2.2	..	..	..
Personal transfers & comp. of employees	..	54.0	87.2	108.0	110.2	115.9	126.0	128.8
International reserves	43.2	85.8	145.3	155.2	194.1	173.4	170.5	199.9
Ratios								
External debt stocks to exports (%)	..	487.1	309.5	268.7	274.0	138.4	139.7	..
External debt stocks to GNI (%)	114.8	76.6	54.4	49.2	46.5	25.3	23.3	..
Debt service to exports (%)	..	6.8	4.7	3.8	12.8	0.4	0.6	..
Short-term to external debt stocks (%)	12.0	11.6	1.6	1.7	1.6	1.1	1.1	0.9
Multilateral to external debt stocks (%)	70.7	71.5	72.7	71.4	67.4	42.9	43.0	44.3
Reserves to external debt stocks (%)	18.4	29.6	51.8	55.8	75.9	114.8	117.5	149.8

Notes: Data include the effects of Paris Club debt restructuring agreements signed in 2010 and 2013, and the HIPC debt relief.

CONGO, DEMOCRATIC REPUBLIC OF

(US$ million, unless otherwise indicated)

	2000	2005	2010	2011	2012	2013	2014	2015
Summary external debt data								
External debt stocks	**11,815**	**10,695**	**6,145**	**5,508**	**5,624**	**6,177**	**5,523**	**5,435**
Long-term external debt	7,880	9,403	4,597	4,022	4,103	4,470	4,149	4,155
Public and publicly guaranteed	7,880	9,403	4,597	4,022	4,103	4,470	4,149	4,155
Official creditors	7,384	9,033	4,472	4,008	4,075	4,452	4,140	4,144
of which: IMF	503	914	1,110	1,258	1,260	1,262	1,188	1,098
Private creditors	496	370	126	14	27	18	9	11
of which: Bonds	3	1	0	0	0	0	0	0
Private nonguaranteed	..	..	..	..	..	..	..	..
of which: Bonds	..	..	..	..	..	..	..	..
Short-term external debt	3,432	377	438	227	262	445	186	183
interest arrears on long-term	3,042	359	267	73	71	71	71	71
Long-term external debt								
Disbursements	**0**	**249**	**78**	**152**	**242**	**495**	**116**	**330**
Public and publicly guaranteed	0	249	78	152	242	495	116	330
Official creditors	0	249	58	152	226	494	116	317
Private creditors	0	0	20	0	17	1	0	13
of which: Bonds	0	0	0	0	0	0	0	0
Private nonguaranteed	..	..	..	..	..	..	..	..
of which: Bonds	..	..	..	..	..	..	..	..
Principal repayments	**0**	**112**	**89**	**133**	**108**	**242**	**260**	**215**
Public and publicly guaranteed	0	112	89	133	108	242	260	215
Official creditors	0	110	85	128	105	232	253	204
Private creditors	0	2	4	5	4	10	8	11
of which: Bonds	0	1	0	0	0	0	0	0
Private nonguaranteed	..	..	..	..	..	..	..	..
of which: Bonds	..	..	..	..	..	..	..	..
Interest payments	**0**	**97**	**125**	**120**	**168**	**153**	**146**	**134**
Public and publicly guaranteed	0	97	125	120	168	153	146	134
Official creditors	0	95	124	120	168	153	146	134
Private creditors	0	1	0	0	0	0	0	0
of which: Bonds	0	0	0	0	0	0	0	0
Private nonguaranteed	..	..	..	..	..	..	..	..
of which: Bonds	..	..	..	..	..	..	..	..
Net financial flows								
Net inflows	**103**	**278**	**177**	**-295**	**-49**	**2,530**	**1,426**	**1,653**
Net debt inflows	31	98	45	158	171	435	-403	73
Official creditors	0	178	-8	180	121	262	-137	74
of which: World Bank	..	226	17	43	73	2	-19	-8
of which: IMF	0	39	19	156	..	..	..	-38
Private creditors	31	-80	54	-22	50	173	-267	-1
Long-term	..	-2	16	-5	13	-10	-8	2
Bonds	..	-1	..	..	..	..	..	..
Banks and other private	..	-2	16	-5	13	-10	-8	2
Short-term	31	-78	38	-17	37	183	-259	-3
Net equity inflows	72	180	131	-453	-220	2,095	1,830	1,579
Foreign direct investment	72	180	131	1,687	3,312	2,098	1,843	1,674
Portfolio equity	..	..	..	-2,140	-3,532	-3	-14	-94
Major economic aggregates								
Gross national income (GNI)	18,700	11,457	19,613	22,553	25,867	27,204	29,742	32,447
Exports of goods, services & prim. income	..	2,756	8,915	10,379	9,049	12,054	12,745	10,463
Imports of goods, services & prim. income	..	3,892	11,931	13,071	12,075	16,428	16,501	13,412
Primary income on FDI	..	..	131	..	..	..	..	..
Personal transfers & comp. of employees	..	9	16	115	12	33	22	5
International reserves	..	131	1,300	1,268	1,633	1,678	1,557	1,216
Ratios								
External debt stocks to exports (%)	..	388.1	68.9	53.1	62.1	51.2	43.3	51.9
External debt stocks to GNI (%)	63.2	93.3	31.3	24.4	21.7	22.7	18.6	16.8
Debt service to exports (%)	..	7.9	3.1	2.5	3.1	3.3	3.2	3.7
Short-term to external debt stocks (%)	29.0	3.5	7.1	4.1	4.7	7.2	3.4	3.4
Multilateral to external debt stocks (%)	18.3	28.5	42.2	43.5	41.7	36.7	35.8	35.4
Reserves to external debt stocks (%)	..	1.2	21.1	23.0	29.0	27.2	28.2	22.4

Notes: Short-term debt is based on data from the BIS. Data include the effects of Paris Club debt restructuring agreement and HIPC and MDRI debt relief.

CONGO, REPUBLIC OF

(US$ million, unless otherwise indicated)

	2000	2005	2010	2011	2012	2013	2014	2015
Summary external debt data								
External debt stocks	**4,676**	**6,293**	**2,410**	**2,632**	**2,837**	**3,449**	**3,903**	**4,204**
Long-term external debt	3,748	5,465	2,063	2,329	2,492	3,072	3,559	3,650
Public and publicly guaranteed	3,748	5,465	2,063	2,329	2,492	3,072	3,559	3,650
Official creditors	2,933	3,287	1,224	1,402	1,479	1,977	2,435	2,563
of which: IMF	54	40	150	155	152	148	134	123
Private creditors	815	2,179	840	927	1,013	1,095	1,124	1,087
of which: Bonds	0	0	454	454	449	436	418	399
Private nonguaranteed	..	..	..	..	..	..	..	..
of which: Bonds	..	..	..	..	..	..	..	..
Short-term external debt	874	788	197	149	193	229	210	431
interest arrears on long-term	664	736	76	61	60	69	68	66
Long-term external debt								
Disbursements	**1**	**183**	**504**	**356**	**472**	**836**	**839**	**324**
Public and publicly guaranteed	1	183	504	356	472	836	839	324
Official creditors	1	183	502	244	251	632	618	324
Private creditors	0	0	2	112	221	204	221	0
of which: Bonds	0	0	0	0	0	0	0	0
Private nonguaranteed	..	..	..	..	..	..	..	..
of which: Bonds	..	..	..	..	..	..	..	..
Principal repayments	**6**	**65**	**116**	**114**	**141**	**265**	**262**	**185**
Public and publicly guaranteed	6	65	116	114	141	265	262	185
Official creditors	6	65	104	92	106	138	135	156
Private creditors	0	0	12	22	35	126	128	29
of which: Bonds	0	0	0	0	5	14	18	18
Private nonguaranteed	..	..	..	..	..	..	..	..
of which: Bonds	..	..	..	..	..	..	..	..
Interest payments	**7**	**34**	**23**	**20**	**23**	**31**	**34**	**30**
Public and publicly guaranteed	7	34	23	20	23	31	34	30
Official creditors	7	34	9	6	7	13	12	13
Private creditors	0	0	14	14	16	18	22	18
of which: Bonds	0	0	14	14	14	16	15	17
Private nonguaranteed	..	..	..	..	..	..	..	..
of which: Bonds	..	..	..	..	..	..	..	..
Net financial flows								
Net inflows	**-107**	**831**	**1,278**	**2,394**	**2,525**	**3,508**	**6,056**	**1,843**
Net debt inflows	-263	30	349	214	373	594	554	357
Official creditors	9	117	400	158	142	489	478	163
of which: World Bank	-3	30	2	2	5	10	10	11
of which: IMF	14	0	2	6	-3	-5	-5	-5
Private creditors	-272	-87	-51	56	231	105	76	194
Long-term	..	..	-11	89	186	78	94	-29
Bonds	..	..	0	0	-5	-14	-18	-18
Banks and other private	..	..	-11	89	190	92	112	-11
Short-term	-272	-87	-40	-33	45	27	-18	223
Net equity inflows	156	801	928	2,180	2,152	2,914	5,502	1,486
Foreign direct investment	156	801	928	2,180	2,152	2,914	5,502	1,486
Portfolio equity	0	..	..	..	..	..	..	..
Major economic aggregates								
Gross national income (GNI)	2,275	4,032	9,024	10,713	10,542	11,050	11,739	8,466
Exports of goods, services & prim. income	2,642	4,983	..	..	..	..	..	..
Imports of goods, services & prim. income	2,013	4,318	..	..	..	..	..	..
Primary income on FDI	466	1,296	..	..	..	..	..	..
Personal transfers & comp. of employees	10	11	..	..	..	..	..	..
International reserves	222	732	4,447	5,641	5,550	5,245	4,926	2,221
Ratios								
External debt stocks to exports (%)	177.0	126.3	..	..	..	..	..	..
External debt stocks to GNI (%)	205.5	156.1	26.7	24.6	26.9	31.2	33.2	49.7
Debt service to exports (%)	1.7	2.3	..	..	..	..	..	..
Short-term to external debt stocks (%)	18.7	12.5	8.2	5.7	6.8	6.7	5.4	10.3
Multilateral to external debt stocks (%)	10.7	8.0	7.9	6.4	5.8	5.4	4.6	4.5
Reserves to external debt stocks (%)	4.7	11.6	184.5	214.3	195.6	152.1	126.2	52.8

Notes: Short-term debt is based on data from the BIS. Data include the effects of Paris Club debt restructuring agreement and HIPC and MDRI debt relief.

COSTA RICA

(US$ million, unless otherwise indicated)

	2000	2005	2010	2011	2012	2013	2014	2015
Summary external debt data								
External debt stocks	**4,692**	**6,485**	**8,154**	**10,271**	**14,310**	**17,135**	**19,640**	**23,667**
Long-term external debt	3,699	4,355	5,482	7,221	11,166	14,483	17,066	20,694
Public and publicly guaranteed	3,513	3,159	3,822	3,968	4,977	7,467	8,737	10,073
Official creditors	1,922	1,368	2,196	2,196	2,192	1,933	2,310	2,708
of which: IMF	31	34	241	240	241	241	227	217
Private creditors	1,591	1,791	1,626	1,773	2,786	5,534	6,427	7,365
of which: Bonds	1,542	1,669	1,435	1,435	2,435	4,185	4,875	5,875
Private nonguaranteed	187	1,195	1,660	3,253	6,189	7,016	8,329	10,621
of which: Bonds	..	..	..	..	..	1,000	1,350	1,350
Short-term external debt	962	2,097	2,431	2,810	2,904	2,411	2,347	2,756
interest arrears on long-term	27	2	0	0	0	0	0	0
Long-term external debt								
Disbursements	**749**	**982**	**1,455**	**1,797**	**3,811**	**5,840**	**4,991**	**4,786**
Public and publicly guaranteed	749	75	928	773	1,784	3,648	2,025	1,625
Official creditors	249	75	845	269	351	418	669	597
Private creditors	500	0	82	504	1,433	3,230	1,356	1,028
of which: Bonds	500	0	0	250	1,250	2,000	1,000	1,000
Private nonguaranteed	0	906	528	1,023	2,026	2,191	2,966	3,161
of which: Bonds	..	..	..	..	..	1,000	350	0
Principal repayments	**392**	**566**	**617**	**1,149**	**1,647**	**2,490**	**2,409**	**1,654**
Public and publicly guaranteed	375	365	342	641	742	1,126	756	285
Official creditors	338	307	256	283	323	646	294	195
Private creditors	37	59	86	357	420	480	462	90
of which: Bonds	30	41	0	250	250	250	310	0
Private nonguaranteed	17	200	275	508	904	1,364	1,653	1,369
of which: Bonds	..	..	..	..	..	0	0	0
Interest payments	**202**	**177**	**313**	**397**	**561**	**728**	**997**	**1,020**
Public and publicly guaranteed	191	105	213	200	202	253	387	815
Official creditors	105	62	86	85	77	70	57	93
Private creditors	86	43	127	115	125	183	330	722
of which: Bonds	80	39	116	105	111	169	260	577
Private nonguaranteed	12	72	100	197	359	475	610	205
of which: Bonds	..	..	..	..	..	0	65	75
Net financial flows								
Net inflows	**1,155**	**1,926**	**2,543**	**2,832**	**3,826**	**5,363**	**4,571**	**5,486**
Net debt inflows	536	841	1,026	1,027	2,257	2,857	2,518	3,541
Official creditors	-89	-231	590	-14	29	-228	375	402
of which: World Bank	-27	-12	512	17	-1	14	5	2
of which: IMF	0	0	0	0	0	0	0	0
Private creditors	625	1,072	437	1,041	2,228	3,085	2,142	3,139
Long-term	446	647	249	662	2,135	3,578	2,207	2,729
Bonds	470	-41	..	..	1,000	2,750	1,040	1,000
Banks and other private	-24	688	249	662	1,135	828	1,167	1,729
Short-term	179	425	188	379	93	-493	-64	409
Net equity inflows	619	1,085	1,516	1,805	1,569	2,505	2,054	1,946
Foreign direct investment	614	1,078	1,508	1,797	1,560	2,491	2,040	1,931
Portfolio equity	5	7	8	9	9	14	14	15
Major economic aggregates								
Gross national income (GNI)	14,694	19,756	35,553	40,648	44,471	48,141	47,914	49,444
Exports of goods, services & prim. income	6,804	9,040	12,736	14,359	15,435	16,061	16,737	17,042
Imports of goods, services & prim. income	7,563	10,200	14,388	16,992	18,254	18,884	19,581	19,831
Primary income on FDI	745	822	1,164	1,409	1,368	1,557	1,661	1,899
Personal transfers & comp. of employees	136	420	531	520	562	596	594	552
International reserves	1,318	2,313	4,627	4,756	6,857	7,331	7,211	7,834
Ratios								
External debt stocks to exports (%)	69.0	71.7	64.0	71.5	92.7	106.7	117.3	138.9
External debt stocks to GNI (%)	31.9	32.8	22.9	25.3	32.2	35.6	41.0	47.9
Debt service to exports (%)	9.6	9.3	7.8	11.3	14.8	20.5	20.7	16.0
Short-term to external debt stocks (%)	20.5	32.3	29.8	27.4	20.3	14.1	11.9	11.6
Multilateral to external debt stocks (%)	29.0	18.1	21.7	17.5	12.9	9.6	10.4	10.2
Reserves to external debt stocks (%)	28.1	35.7	56.7	46.3	47.9	42.8	36.7	33.1

Notes: Long-term private nonguaranteed debt data are World Bank staff estimates based on reports provided by the country. Short-term debt before 2005 is based on data from the BIS.

CÔTE D'IVOIRE

(US$ million, unless otherwise indicated)

Summary external debt data

	2000	2005	2010	2011	2012	2013	2014	2015
External debt stocks	**12,060**	**12,002**	**11,693**	**12,780**	**9,502**	**9,726**	**9,608**	**10,028**
Long-term external debt	10,546	10,867	10,420	11,218	7,500	8,308	8,115	8,520
Public and publicly guaranteed	9,063	9,967	9,403	9,886	5,010	6,241	6,422	7,150
Official creditors	6,669	7,675	9,290	9,755	3,788	3,799	3,278	3,015
of which: IMF	599	252	861	1,090	1,265	1,418	1,492	1,508
Private creditors	2,394	2,292	112	131	1,222	2,442	3,144	4,136
of which: Bonds	2,343	2,159	0	0	0	0	753	1,752
Private nonguaranteed	1,482	900	1,018	1,332	2,490	2,067	1,693	1,370
of which: Bonds	..	..	..	..	..	..	..	..
Short-term external debt	916	883	411	472	737	0	0	0
interest arrears on long-term	79	883	7	5	1	0	0	0

Long-term external debt

	2000	2005	2010	2011	2012	2013	2014	2015
Disbursements	**148**	**55**	**599**	**1,120**	**2,094**	**1,982**	**1,197**	**1,462**
Public and publicly guaranteed	148	21	244	717	1,274	1,982	1,197	1,462
Official creditors	148	21	218	683	95	726	443	462
Private creditors	0	0	26	34	1,178	1,256	754	1,000
of which: Bonds	0	0	0	0	0	0	753	1,000
Private nonguaranteed	0	34	355	402	820	0	0	0
of which: Bonds	..	..	..	..	..	..	..	..
Principal repayments	**442**	**164**	**623**	**568**	**533**	**763**	**641**	**453**
Public and publicly guaranteed	329	21	438	348	267	340	267	129
Official creditors	283	21	438	338	258	305	216	120
Private creditors	46	0	0	9	10	35	51	8
of which: Bonds	46	0	0	0	0	0	0	0
Private nonguaranteed	113	143	185	220	266	423	374	324
of which: Bonds	..	..	..	..	..	..	..	..
Interest payments	**462**	**46**	**114**	**137**	**169**	**279**	**346**	**284**
Public and publicly guaranteed	342	3	58	67	50	188	322	263
Official creditors	189	3	58	67	50	54	36	31
Private creditors	153	0	0	0	0	134	286	231
of which: Bonds	153	0	0	0	0	0	151	97
Private nonguaranteed	120	43	56	70	119	91	24	21
of which: Bonds	..	..	..	..	..	..	..	..

Net financial flows

	2000	2005	2010	2011	2012	2013	2014	2015
Net inflows	**-508**	**117**	**413**	**1,175**	**2,187**	**766**	**1,161**	**1,521**
Net debt inflows	-744	-200	40	853	2,002	632	722	1,091
Official creditors	-174	-90	-176	583	10	570	393	423
of which: World Bank	18	0	-26	-46	-29	51	82	166
of which: IMF	-39	-91	44	238	173	149	166	82
Private creditors	-570	-109	216	270	1,992	62	330	668
Long-term	-159	-109	196	207	1,722	798	330	668
Bonds	-46	..	..	..	..	..	753	1,000
Banks and other private	-113	-109	196	207	1,722	798	-423	-332
Short-term	-411	0	20	63	269	-736	0	0
Net equity inflows	236	316	373	322	185	135	439	430
Foreign direct investment	235	302	371	322	155	134	439	430
Portfolio equity	1	14	2	..	30	1	..	..

Major economic aggregates

	2000	2005	2010	2011	2012	2013	2014	2015
Gross national income (GNI)	9,715	16,433	23,972	24,393	26,178	29,882	32,930	29,424
Exports of goods, services & prim. income	4,512	8,717	12,811	13,859	13,316	13,192	14,106	10,786
Imports of goods, services & prim. income	4,423	8,215	11,907	10,664	13,116	13,175	13,302	11,109
Primary income on FDI	284	370	562	612	578	651	..	..
Personal transfers & comp. of employees	119	163	373	397	367	385	385	385
International reserves	674	1,367	3,624	4,316	3,928	4,243	4,478	4,716

Ratios

	2000	2005	2010	2011	2012	2013	2014	2015
External debt stocks to exports (%)	267.3	137.7	91.3	92.2	71.4	73.7	68.1	93.0
External debt stocks to GNI (%)	124.1	73.0	48.8	52.4	36.3	32.5	29.2	34.1
Debt service to exports (%)	22.7	3.5	5.9	5.3	5.5	7.9	7.1	7.4
Short-term to external debt stocks (%)	7.6	7.4	3.5	3.7	7.8	0.0	0.0	0.0
Multilateral to external debt stocks (%)	24.5	25.7	20.3	18.5	5.6	6.9	7.6	9.3
Reserves to external debt stocks (%)	5.6	11.4	31.0	33.8	41.3	43.6	46.6	47.0

Notes: Long-term private nonguaranteed debt data are World Bank staff estimates. Short-term debt is based on data from the BIS. Data include the effects of Paris Club agreement signed in 2011, 2012 and HIPC and MDRI debt relief.

DJIBOUTI

(US$ million, unless otherwise indicated)

	2000	2005	2010	2011	2012	2013	2014	2015
Summary external debt data								
External debt stocks	**297.7**	**486.5**	**778.5**	**779.1**	**811.7**	**828.3**	**949.5**	**1,222.2**
Long-term external debt	238.3	378.9	621.5	650.8	641.9	672.7	819.6	1,169.1
Public and publicly guaranteed	238.3	378.9	621.5	650.8	641.9	672.7	819.6	1,169.1
Official creditors	238.3	373.3	601.1	633.6	628.1	662.3	811.7	1,164.2
of which: IMF	14.9	20.4	35.5	39.7	57.5	57.6	52.9	49.1
Private creditors	0.0	5.6	20.4	17.2	13.8	10.4	7.9	4.9
of which: Bonds	0.0	0.0	0.0	0.0	0.0	0.0	0.0	0.0
Private nonguaranteed	..	..	..	..	..	..	..	..
of which: Bonds	..	..	..	..	..	..	..	..
Short-term external debt	44.5	87.2	121.5	88.6	112.3	97.9	77.0	4.0
interest arrears on long-term	6.5	9.2	0.5	0.6	1.3	1.4	3.1	4.0
Long-term external debt								
Disbursements	**7.7**	**26.5**	**35.2**	**55.7**	**25.2**	**63.9**	**211.6**	**405.4**
Public and publicly guaranteed	7.7	26.5	35.2	55.7	25.2	63.9	211.6	405.4
Official creditors	7.7	26.5	35.2	55.7	25.2	63.9	211.6	405.4
Private creditors	0.0	0.0	0.0	0.0	0.0	0.0	0.0	0.0
of which: Bonds	0.0	0.0	0.0	0.0	0.0	0.0	0.0	0.0
Private nonguaranteed	..	..	..	..	..	..	..	..
of which: Bonds	..	..	..	..	..	..	..	..
Principal repayments	**8.4**	**11.0**	**22.4**	**26.5**	**31.0**	**31.7**	**27.5**	**28.4**
Public and publicly guaranteed	8.4	11.0	22.4	26.5	31.0	31.7	27.5	28.4
Official creditors	8.4	11.0	20.0	23.6	27.5	28.1	25.5	25.8
Private creditors	0.0	0.0	2.4	2.9	3.5	3.7	2.0	2.7
of which: Bonds	0.0	0.0	0.0	0.0	0.0	0.0	0.0	0.0
Private nonguaranteed	..	..	..	..	..	..	..	..
of which: Bonds	..	..	..	..	..	..	..	..
Interest payments	**2.2**	**3.7**	**8.2**	**9.2**	**9.3**	**9.5**	**9.2**	**15.3**
Public and publicly guaranteed	2.2	3.7	8.2	9.2	9.3	9.5	9.2	15.3
Official creditors	2.2	3.7	7.6	8.6	8.8	9.1	9.0	15.1
Private creditors	0.0	0.0	0.6	0.7	0.5	0.4	0.2	0.1
of which: Bonds	0.0	0.0	0.0	0.0	0.0	0.0	0.0	0.0
Private nonguaranteed	..	..	..	..	..	..	..	..
of which: Bonds	..	..	..	..	..	..	..	..
Net financial flows								
Net inflows	**41.9**	**76.9**	**49.0**	**79.6**	**144.9**	**303.7**	**313.2**	**425.6**
Net debt inflows	38.7	54.7	12.5	0.6	34.9	17.7	160.2	301.6
Official creditors	0.7	14.7	11.9	36.5	15.5	35.9	184.7	378.2
of which: World Bank	3.4	3.4	-0.8	-1.7	-2.0	-3.4	-2.4	-0.7
of which: IMF	1.3	-0.8	-3.3	4.4	17.7	0.0	-1.4	-1.5
Private creditors	38.0	40.0	0.6	-35.9	19.5	-18.2	-24.5	-76.6
Long-term	..	..	-2.4	-2.9	-3.5	-3.7	-2.0	-2.7
Bonds	..	..	..	..	..	..	..	..
Banks and other private	..	..	-2.4	-2.9	-3.5	-3.7	-2.0	-2.7
Short-term	38.0	40.0	3.0	-33.0	23.0	-14.5	-22.6	-74.0
Net equity inflows	3.3	22.2	36.5	79.0	110.0	286.0	153.0	124.0
Foreign direct investment	3.3	22.2	36.5	79.0	110.0	286.0	153.0	124.0
Portfolio equity	..	..	..	..	..	..	..	..
Major economic aggregates								
Gross national income (GNI)	567.0	775.8	..	..	..	..	..	..
Exports of goods, services & prim. income	218.4	319.8	453.6	456.4	503.1	532.8	552.5	631.9
Imports of goods, services & prim. income	287.1	372.3	498.3	702.3	742.4	934.2	1,042.2	1,360.5
Primary income on FDI	4.2	5.9	6.8	18.0	7.2	10.8	5.9	7.4
Personal transfers & comp. of employees	12.3	25.8	32.6	32.4	33.3	35.6	35.5	63.3
International reserves	67.8	89.3	249.0	244.1	248.6	425.0	393.1	364.9
Ratios								
External debt stocks to exports (%)	136.3	152.1	171.6	170.7	161.3	155.5	171.9	193.4
External debt stocks to GNI (%)	52.5	62.7	..	..	..	..	..	..
Debt service to exports (%)	6.9	5.5	7.9	8.6	8.6	8.0	7.1	7.2
Short-term to external debt stocks (%)	14.9	17.9	15.6	11.4	13.8	11.8	8.1	0.3
Multilateral to external debt stocks (%)	46.5	55.2	52.1	55.0	51.8	52.8	45.2	36.4
Reserves to external debt stocks (%)	22.8	18.3	32.0	31.3	30.6	51.3	41.4	29.9

Notes: Short-term debt is based on data from the BIS. Data include the effects of Paris Club debt restructuring agreement signed in 2008.

DOMINICA

(US$ million, unless otherwise indicated)

	2000	2005	2010	2011	2012	2013	2014	2015
Summary external debt data								
External debt stocks	**183.3**	**294.2**	**271.4**	**280.4**	**304.8**	**309.9**	**308.2**	**314.2**
Long-term external debt	163.6	241.3	235.6	247.6	272.7	280.4	281.8	282.1
Public and publicly guaranteed	163.6	241.3	235.6	247.6	272.7	280.4	281.8	282.1
Official creditors	114.3	173.0	173.0	182.3	216.6	227.1	233.0	235.3
of which: IMF	0.8	12.4	30.2	27.3	26.6	23.8	20.9	26.5
Private creditors	49.2	68.2	62.6	65.2	56.0	53.3	48.8	46.8
of which: Bonds	49.2	65.7	57.1	58.9	28.4	28.4	25.7	25.7
Private nonguaranteed	..	..	..	..	..	..	..	..
of which: Bonds	..	..	..	..	..	..	..	..
Short-term external debt	19.0	40.6	5.5	5.6	5.6	5.6	5.5	5.6
interest arrears on long-term	0.0	8.6	1.5	1.5	1.5	1.5	1.5	1.5
Long-term external debt								
Disbursements	**56.2**	**4.5**	**29.7**	**21.1**	**36.3**	**21.5**	**20.2**	**20.9**
Public and publicly guaranteed	56.2	4.5	29.7	21.1	36.3	21.5	20.2	20.9
Official creditors	25.7	4.5	29.7	18.3	36.3	21.5	20.2	20.9
Private creditors	30.5	0.0	0.0	2.8	0.0	0.0	0.0	0.0
of which: Bonds	30.5	0.0	0.0	1.8	0.0	0.0	0.0	0.0
Private nonguaranteed	..	..	..	..	..	..	..	..
of which: Bonds	..	..	..	..	..	..	..	..
Principal repayments	**6.8**	**9.6**	**9.8**	**9.4**	**7.8**	**9.9**	**11.5**	**14.3**
Public and publicly guaranteed	6.8	9.6	9.8	9.4	7.8	9.9	11.5	14.3
Official creditors	6.8	9.6	9.8	9.2	7.6	8.0	9.1	12.3
Private creditors	0.0	0.0	0.1	0.2	0.2	1.9	2.3	2.0
of which: Bonds	0.0	0.0	0.0	0.0	0.0	0.0	0.4	0.1
Private nonguaranteed	..	..	..	..	..	..	..	..
of which: Bonds	..	..	..	..	..	..	..	..
Interest payments	**3.1**	**5.8**	**5.4**	**5.3**	**9.0**	**7.0**	**7.2**	**6.8**
Public and publicly guaranteed	3.1	5.8	5.4	5.3	9.0	7.0	7.2	6.8
Official creditors	2.9	4.3	3.8	3.9	4.2	4.7	5.1	4.8
Private creditors	0.2	1.5	1.6	1.4	4.8	2.3	2.1	2.0
of which: Bonds	0.2	1.5	1.5	1.4	3.8	1.4	1.4	1.4
Private nonguaranteed	..	..	..	..	..	..	..	..
of which: Bonds	..	..	..	..	..	..	..	..
Net financial flows								
Net inflows	**69.2**	**-15.3**	**28.8**	**15.5**	**43.4**	**18.9**	**38.7**	**45.4**
Net debt inflows	49.5	-37.0	18.7	8.7	27.7	8.8	7.1	13.3
Official creditors	18.8	-2.0	18.8	6.1	27.9	10.8	9.5	15.1
of which: World Bank	0.6	0.0	-0.5	-0.1	-0.3	0.7	0.0	0.3
of which: IMF	..	3.2	-1.1	-2.9	-0.8	-2.7	-1.6	6.5
Private creditors	30.7	-35.0	-0.1	2.6	-0.2	-1.9	-2.4	-1.9
Long-term	30.5	0.0	0.0	2.6	-0.2	-1.9	-2.3	-2.0
Bonds	30.5	0.0	0.0	1.8	0.0	0.0	-0.4	-0.1
Banks and other private	..	0.0	-0.1	0.8	-0.2	-1.9	-1.9	-1.9
Short-term	0.2	-35.0	0.0	0.0	0.0	0.0	-0.1	0.1
Net equity inflows	19.6	21.7	10.0	6.8	15.7	10.0	31.6	32.2
Foreign direct investment	19.6	21.7	10.0	6.8	15.7	10.0	31.6	32.2
Portfolio equity	..	..	..	..	..	..	..	..
Major economic aggregates								
Gross national income (GNI)	296.5	341.5	484.4	490.9	475.5	487.1	507.5	497.0
Exports of goods, services & prim. income	149.2	135.3	180.2	195.9	165.0	174.3	221.9	216.6
Imports of goods, services & prim. income	227.1	231.0	280.1	280.3	274.0	267.7	300.0	287.5
Primary income on FDI	33.0	22.7	7.8	5.0	5.1	5.4	..	..
Personal transfers & comp. of employees	13.5	21.8	22.9	22.9	23.2	23.6	26.6	33.2
International reserves	29.4	49.2	76.1	81.1	94.6	87.1	101.4	126.2
Ratios								
External debt stocks to exports (%)	122.9	217.5	150.6	143.2	184.7	177.8	138.9	145.1
External debt stocks to GNI (%)	61.8	86.2	56.0	57.1	64.1	63.6	60.7	63.2
Debt service to exports (%)	7.4	12.9	9.2	9.1	12.6	11.4	9.2	10.8
Short-term to external debt stocks (%)	10.4	13.8	2.0	2.0	1.8	1.8	1.8	1.8
Multilateral to external debt stocks (%)	45.5	42.8	43.1	43.5	42.0	42.4	41.7	42.2
Reserves to external debt stocks (%)	16.0	16.7	28.0	28.9	31.0	28.1	32.9	40.2

DOMINICAN REPUBLIC

(US$ million, unless otherwise indicated)

	2000	2005	2010	2011	2012	2013	2014	2015
Summary external debt data								
External debt stocks	**4,618**	**7,752**	**13,499**	**15,097**	**22,102**	**23,958**	**26,262**	**26,632**
Long-term external debt	3,381	6,419	10,283	11,675	18,835	20,888	22,973	23,119
Public and publicly guaranteed	3,381	6,418	9,441	10,762	11,983	14,175	15,693	15,788
Official creditors	2,625	3,257	6,376	7,119	8,159	9,088	9,024	5,654
of which: IMF	93	446	1,461	1,623	1,513	1,317	803	403
Private creditors	756	3,160	3,065	3,643	3,824	5,086	6,669	10,135
of which: Bonds	506	561	1,134	1,826	1,826	3,312	4,812	8,312
Private nonguaranteed	0	2	843	913	6,852	6,713	7,280	7,330
of which: Bonds	0	0	843	843	1,137	887	1,375	1,575
Short-term external debt	1,144	887	1,754	1,800	1,753	1,753	2,486	3,110
interest arrears on long-term	28	20	0	0	0	0	0	0
Long-term external debt								
Disbursements	**314**	**665**	**2,111**	**2,165**	**2,840**	**3,558**	**3,831**	**6,089**
Public and publicly guaranteed	314	664	2,111	2,120	1,843	3,112	2,828	5,013
Official creditors	150	372	1,176	1,117	1,458	1,554	800	1,071
Private creditors	164	292	935	1,003	385	1,558	2,028	3,942
of which: Bonds	0	0	750	750	0	1,500	1,500	3,500
Private nonguaranteed	..	2	0	45	998	446	1,003	1,076
of which: Bonds	..	..	..	..	550	0	488	200
Principal repayments	**264**	**462**	**799**	**796**	**1,521**	**1,647**	**1,904**	**3,784**
Public and publicly guaranteed	264	462	798	788	625	932	1,223	2,758
Official creditors	223	184	311	376	407	608	847	2,330
Private creditors	40	278	487	412	218	324	376	428
of which: Bonds	4	20	105	58	0	14	0	0
Private nonguaranteed	..	..	0	8	897	714	681	1,026
of which: Bonds	..	..	..	..	431	250	0	0
Interest payments	**211**	**212**	**444**	**584**	**919**	**958**	**821**	**1,021**
Public and publicly guaranteed	211	212	336	473	448	484	573	774
Official creditors	159	109	156	176	198	204	197	192
Private creditors	53	103	181	297	250	280	376	583
of which: Bonds	38	16	76	191	140	172	281	459
Private nonguaranteed	..	0	108	111	471	475	248	247
of which: Bonds	..	..	108	108	90	95	83	124
Net financial flows								
Net inflows	**1,151**	**1,572**	**3,515**	**3,783**	**4,578**	**3,314**	**4,577**	**4,765**
Net debt inflows	281	400	1,695	1,585	1,162	1,714	2,202	2,561
Official creditors	-73	407	1,247	912	941	748	-504	-1,627
of which: World Bank	17	26	116	-14	58	-15	-9	55
of which: IMF	0	220	383	171	-110	-197	-457	-368
Private creditors	355	-7	447	674	221	966	2,707	4,188
Long-term	124	16	448	628	268	966	1,974	3,564
Bonds	-4	-20	645	692	119	1,236	1,988	3,700
Banks and other private	127	35	-197	-64	149	-270	-15	-136
Short-term	231	-23	-1	46	-47	0	733	624
Net equity inflows	869	1,172	1,820	2,198	3,416	1,600	2,375	2,204
Foreign direct investment	869	1,172	1,820	2,198	3,416	1,600	2,375	2,204
Portfolio equity	..	..	..	..	..	..	..	..
Major economic aggregates								
Gross national income (GNI)	22,955	32,100	52,559	56,174	58,246	58,204	60,704	64,059
Exports of goods, services & prim. income	6,202	8,013	13,525	14,889	15,754	16,539	17,476	17,615
Imports of goods, services & prim. income	9,130	11,183	20,983	23,081	23,634	23,222	23,925	23,601
Primary income on FDI	1,068	1,765	1,698	1,949	1,972	2,629	2,745	2,419
Personal transfers & comp. of employees	1,839	2,719	3,887	4,241	4,262	4,486	4,810	5,196
International reserves	627	1,920	3,849	4,086	3,528	4,679	4,840	5,247
Ratios								
External debt stocks to exports (%)	74.5	96.7	99.8	101.4	140.3	144.9	150.3	151.2
External debt stocks to GNI (%)	20.1	24.1	25.7	26.9	37.9	41.2	43.3	41.6
Debt service to exports (%)	8.5	9.1	10.5	10.8	16.5	17.2	18.4	29.7
Short-term to external debt stocks (%)	24.8	11.4	13.0	11.9	7.9	7.3	9.5	11.7
Multilateral to external debt stocks (%)	25.2	23.4	22.8	22.2	16.0	16.3	13.7	15.6
Reserves to external debt stocks (%)	13.6	24.8	28.5	27.1	16.0	19.5	18.4	19.7

Notes: Long-term private nonguaranteed debt data are based on country reports. Short-term debt before 2009 and 2014 onward is based on data from the BIS. Data include the effects of Paris Club debt restructuring agreement signed in 2005.

ECUADOR

(US$ million, unless otherwise indicated)

	2000	2005	2010	2011	2012	2013	2014	2015
Summary external debt data								
External debt stocks	**19,637**	**22,761**	**16,248**	**16,860**	**17,122**	**19,100**	**24,399**	**27,273**
Long-term external debt	18,650	21,116	15,005	16,368	16,630	18,369	23,692	26,598
Public and publicly guaranteed	17,215	16,447	9,924	10,988	10,880	12,575	17,198	19,438
Official creditors	5,973	6,051	7,699	9,036	9,200	11,063	11,626	13,224
of which: IMF	191	125	444	443	443	444	418	400
Private creditors	11,241	10,396	2,225	1,952	1,681	1,512	5,572	6,214
of which: Bonds	10,198	10,094	2,070	1,829	1,589	1,349	3,108	2,218
Private nonguaranteed	1,435	4,668	5,082	5,380	5,750	5,794	6,494	7,160
of which: Bonds	..	..	..	..	..	..	..	..
Short-term external debt	797	1,520	798	50	48	287	289	274
interest arrears on long-term	3	1	37	46	44	43	37	37
Long-term external debt								
Disbursements	**990**	**3,154**	**2,977**	**3,386**	**2,338**	**4,248**	**8,676**	**7,245**
Public and publicly guaranteed	609	991	2,307	2,358	1,352	3,145	6,204	4,636
Official creditors	538	318	2,305	2,358	1,352	3,044	1,866	2,770
Private creditors	71	674	2	1	0	101	4,337	1,867
of which: Bonds	0	650	0	0	0	0	2,000	0
Private nonguaranteed	381	2,162	670	1,028	986	1,102	2,472	2,609
of which: Bonds	..	..	..	..	..	..	..	..
Principal repayments	**1,076**	**3,168**	**1,499**	**2,089**	**2,158**	**2,523**	**3,293**	**4,004**
Public and publicly guaranteed	559	1,043	877	1,300	1,438	1,432	1,521	2,313
Official creditors	399	802	592	1,027	1,167	1,162	1,252	1,101
Private creditors	160	241	285	274	271	270	269	1,212
of which: Bonds	10	120	246	240	240	240	240	890
Private nonguaranteed	517	2,125	623	789	720	1,091	1,772	1,691
of which: Bonds	..	..	..	..	..	..	..	..
Interest payments	**1,186**	**1,067**	**486**	**552**	**689**	**850**	**947**	**1,251**
Public and publicly guaranteed	1,014	882	347	378	497	658	741	1,030
Official creditors	298	277	258	295	417	577	536	530
Private creditors	716	605	89	83	80	81	206	500
of which: Bonds	616	590	80	75	74	70	145	222
Private nonguaranteed	172	185	139	174	193	192	206	221
of which: Bonds	..	..	..	..	..	..	..	..
Net financial flows								
Net inflows	**-117**	**108**	**1,358**	**1,122**	**712**	**2,700**	**6,554**	**4,499**
Net debt inflows	-191	-413	880	540	180	1,964	5,391	3,226
Official creditors	289	-679	1,713	1,331	185	1,882	615	1,668
of which: World Bank	-22	-36	-87	-80	-72	-68	-51	78
of which: IMF	150	-195	0	0	0	0	0	0
Private creditors	-480	266	-833	-791	-6	82	4,777	1,558
Long-term	-226	470	-235	-33	-6	-157	4,768	1,572
Bonds	-10	530	-246	-240	-240	-240	1,760	-890
Banks and other private	-216	-60	11	207	235	83	3,009	2,463
Short-term	-254	-203	-597	-757	0	240	9	-15
Net equity inflows	74	521	478	582	532	736	1,163	1,273
Foreign direct investment	74	519	478	580	528	734	1,162	1,272
Portfolio equity	0	2	0	2	5	2	1	2
Major economic aggregates								
Gross national income (GNI)	16,916	39,692	68,515	78,016	86,620	93,396	99,359	99,127
Exports of goods, services & prim. income	6,163	11,693	19,687	24,754	26,481	27,738	29,056	21,536
Imports of goods, services & prim. income	6,403	13,880	23,754	27,880	29,115	31,069	31,894	25,814
Primary income on FDI	329	1,004	546	701	677	684	666	600
Personal transfers & comp. of employees	1,322	2,460	2,599	2,681	2,476	2,459	2,472	2,388
International reserves	947	1,714	1,435	1,664	1,080	3,328	3,484	2,085
Ratios								
External debt stocks to exports (%)	318.6	194.7	82.5	68.1	64.7	68.9	84.0	126.6
External debt stocks to GNI (%)	116.1	57.3	23.7	21.6	19.8	20.5	24.6	27.5
Debt service to exports (%)	38.5	38.9	10.4	10.7	10.8	12.2	14.6	24.4
Short-term to external debt stocks (%)	4.1	6.7	4.9	0.3	0.3	1.5	1.2	1.0
Multilateral to external debt stocks (%)	18.9	16.1	32.0	30.9	30.2	27.8	23.3	26.2
Reserves to external debt stocks (%)	4.8	7.5	8.8	9.9	6.3	17.4	14.3	7.6

EGYPT, ARAB REPUBLIC OF

(US$ million, unless otherwise indicated)

	2000	2005	2010	2011	2012	2013	2014	2015
Summary external debt data								
External debt stocks	**29,194**	**30,533**	**36,742**	**35,145**	**40,003**	**46,473**	**41,677**	**46,585**
Long-term external debt	24,913	28,683	32,210	30,740	31,965	42,273	37,054	40,915
Public and publicly guaranteed	24,340	28,590	32,156	30,724	31,945	42,261	37,033	40,893
Official creditors	23,790	25,774	28,230	27,446	28,687	36,046	33,407	37,865
of which: IMF	177	194	1,384	1,379	1,381	1,384	1,302	1,245
Private creditors	550	2,816	3,926	3,278	3,258	6,215	3,626	3,028
of which: Bonds	0	1,829	3,333	2,750	2,750	5,850	3,350	2,100
Private nonguaranteed	573	93	54	16	20	12	21	23
of which: Bonds	100	..	..	..	..	..	..	..
Short-term external debt	4,104	1,656	3,149	3,026	6,657	2,816	3,321	4,424
interest arrears on long-term	0	2	0	0	0	0	0	0
Long-term external debt								
Disbursements	**569**	**3,090**	**3,617**	**1,510**	**3,688**	**13,145**	**1,646**	**9,040**
Public and publicly guaranteed	362	3,090	3,612	1,480	3,663	13,127	1,621	9,010
Official creditors	218	1,114	1,903	1,459	3,608	10,002	1,601	8,267
Private creditors	144	1,976	1,709	21	55	3,125	20	744
of which: Bonds	0	1,250	1,500	0	0	3,100	0	0
Private nonguaranteed	207	..	5	30	25	17	25	29
of which: Bonds	..	..	..	..	..	..	..	..
Principal repayments	**1,100**	**1,576**	**2,162**	**2,853**	**2,245**	**2,625**	**5,117**	**4,138**
Public and publicly guaranteed	984	1,576	2,137	2,786	2,224	2,600	5,101	4,110
Official creditors	862	1,346	2,062	2,124	2,149	2,421	2,529	2,798
Private creditors	122	230	75	662	75	179	2,572	1,312
of which: Bonds	0	0	0	583	0	0	2,500	1,250
Private nonguaranteed	116	..	25	68	22	25	16	28
of which: Bonds	..	..	..	..	..	..	..	..
Interest payments	**619**	**621**	**736**	**726**	**680**	**665**	**687**	**704**
Public and publicly guaranteed	603	616	735	726	679	665	686	704
Official creditors	572	547	581	563	557	531	489	511
Private creditors	31	69	154	163	122	134	197	193
of which: Bonds	0	51	141	150	108	121	188	176
Private nonguaranteed	16	4	1	0	0	0	0	0
of which: Bonds	12	..	..	..	..	..	..	..
Net financial flows								
Net inflows	**785**	**7,556**	**10,152**	**-2,660**	**10,122**	**10,503**	**2,131**	**12,904**
Net debt inflows	-720	1,451	2,042	-1,466	5,074	6,678	-2,966	6,005
Official creditors	-644	-232	-160	-665	1,459	7,581	-928	5,469
of which: World Bank	-54	48	649	198	264	275	348	751
of which: IMF	..	..	..	..	..	..	..	..
Private creditors	-75	1,682	2,202	-801	3,615	-902	-2,039	537
Long-term	114	1,746	1,614	-678	-16	2,939	-2,543	-567
Bonds	0	1,250	1,500	-583	0	3,100	-2,500	-1,250
Banks and other private	114	496	114	-95	-16	-161	-43	683
Short-term	-189	-64	588	-123	3,632	-3,841	505	1,103
Net equity inflows	1,504	6,105	8,110	-1,194	5,048	3,825	5,097	6,899
Foreign direct investment	1,235	5,376	6,386	-483	6,031	4,256	4,612	6,885
Portfolio equity	269	729	1,724	-711	-983	-431	485	14
Major economic aggregates								
Gross national income (GNI)	100,770	89,432	214,526	229,952	269,873	278,605	294,203	324,703
Exports of goods, services & prim. income	18,735	32,141	49,365	47,371	48,834	44,992	47,300	37,873
Imports of goods, services & prim. income	23,878	35,787	66,308	68,076	75,597	72,686	80,929	72,861
Primary income on FDI	92	647	5,268	5,079	5,704	6,376	6,089	4,375
Personal transfers & comp. of employees	2,852	5,017	12,453	14,324	19,236	17,833	19,570	18,325
International reserves	13,118	20,609	33,612	14,916	11,628	13,608	11,995	13,282
Ratios								
External debt stocks to exports (%)	155.8	95.0	74.4	74.2	81.9	103.3	88.1	123.0
External debt stocks to GNI (%)	29.0	34.1	17.1	15.3	14.8	16.7	14.2	14.3
Debt service to exports (%)	9.8	7.1	6.1	7.8	6.5	7.6	12.6	13.3
Short-term to external debt stocks (%)	14.1	5.4	8.6	8.6	16.6	6.1	8.0	9.5
Multilateral to external debt stocks (%)	13.4	17.0	25.2	27.2	26.1	23.4	25.9	24.6
Reserves to external debt stocks (%)	44.9	67.5	91.5	42.4	29.1	29.3	28.8	28.5

EL SALVADOR

(US$ million, unless otherwise indicated)

	2000	2005	2010	2011	2012	2013	2014	2015
Summary external debt data								
External debt stocks	**4,535**	**9,317**	**11,060**	**11,996**	**13,035**	**13,539**	**14,533**	**14,982**
Long-term external debt	2,858	7,425	9,972	10,521	11,257	11,434	12,277	12,737
Public and publicly guaranteed	2,746	4,802	6,403	6,538	7,372	7,275	8,055	7,923
Official creditors	2,541	3,083	4,183	4,301	4,339	4,242	4,041	3,909
of which: IMF	33	36	252	251	252	252	237	227
Private creditors	205	1,719	2,220	2,237	3,033	3,033	4,014	4,014
of which: Bonds	82	1,636	2,199	2,217	2,362	2,336	3,269	3,268
Private nonguaranteed	111	2,622	3,569	3,983	3,885	4,159	4,223	4,815
of which: Bonds	..	..	..	..	38	38	38	38
Short-term external debt	1,645	1,856	836	1,223	1,526	1,853	2,018	2,018
interest arrears on long-term	0	0	0	0	0	0	0	0
Long-term external debt								
Disbursements	**372**	**1,222**	**1,055**	**874**	**1,448**	**1,006**	**1,765**	**1,166**
Public and publicly guaranteed	321	682	707	476	1,173	364	1,132	243
Official creditors	201	337	707	476	522	337	281	229
Private creditors	120	345	0	0	652	27	851	13
of which: Bonds	32	343	0	0	0	0	800	0
Private nonguaranteed	51	540	348	398	274	642	633	923
of which: Bonds	..	..	..	..	38	0	0	0
Principal repayments	**163**	**406**	**604**	**757**	**628**	**559**	**679**	**524**
Public and publicly guaranteed	130	245	455	587	453	392	410	331
Official creditors	126	230	388	367	452	391	409	320
Private creditors	4	16	68	220	1	1	1	11
of which: Bonds	0	0	0	219	0	0	0	0
Private nonguaranteed	33	160	149	170	175	167	269	194
of which: Bonds	..	..	..	..	0	0	0	0
Interest payments	**140**	**344**	**465**	**515**	**503**	**532**	**543**	**601**
Public and publicly guaranteed	133	257	350	386	373	403	414	476
Official creditors	124	119	117	119	121	121	116	112
Private creditors	9	139	233	267	252	282	299	363
of which: Bonds	8	133	232	266	251	251	251	315
Private nonguaranteed	7	87	115	129	130	129	129	125
of which: Bonds	..	..	..	..	0	2	0	0
Net financial flows								
Net inflows	**975**	**1,405**	**705**	**673**	**1,656**	**922**	**1,625**	**963**
Net debt inflows	802	892	423	504	1,123	774	1,250	641
Official creditors	75	107	320	109	70	-54	-128	-91
of which: World Bank	16	88	345	98	-31	-20	0	-5
of which: IMF	0	0	0	0	0	0	0	0
Private creditors	726	785	104	395	1,053	827	1,378	731
Long-term	134	709	131	8	749	501	1,213	732
Bonds	32	343	0	-219	38	0	800	0
Banks and other private	102	366	131	228	712	501	414	732
Short-term	592	77	-27	387	304	327	165	0
Net equity inflows	173	512	282	169	533	148	375	322
Foreign direct investment	173	512	282	169	533	148	375	322
Portfolio equity	..	..	..	..	..	..	..	..
Major economic aggregates								
Gross national income (GNI)	12,881	16,604	20,880	22,521	22,922	23,359	23,980	24,713
Exports of goods, services & prim. income	2,650	3,517	5,028	5,940	6,170	6,492	6,550	6,791
Imports of goods, services & prim. income	4,878	7,173	9,190	10,882	11,456	12,161	12,097	12,082
Primary income on FDI	60	181	190	203	577	642	709	726
Personal transfers & comp. of employees	1,764	3,029	3,472	3,644	3,896	3,955	4,151	4,285
International reserves	1,773	1,721	2,568	2,151	2,805	2,476	2,430	2,740
Ratios								
External debt stocks to exports (%)	171.1	264.9	220.0	201.9	211.3	208.6	221.9	220.6
External debt stocks to GNI (%)	35.2	56.1	53.0	53.3	56.9	58.0	60.6	60.6
Debt service to exports (%)	14.2	24.2	21.5	21.6	18.6	17.1	19.0	17.0
Short-term to external debt stocks (%)	36.3	19.9	7.6	10.2	11.7	13.7	13.9	13.5
Multilateral to external debt stocks (%)	42.7	26.3	32.0	30.7	29.0	27.6	24.8	23.3
Reserves to external debt stocks (%)	39.1	18.5	23.2	17.9	21.5	18.3	16.7	18.3

Notes: Long-term private nonguaranteed debt data from 2005 are World Bank staff estimates based on reports provided by the country.

ERITREA

(US$ million, unless otherwise indicated)

	2000	2005	2010	2011	2012	2013	2014	2015
Summary external debt data								
External debt stocks	**329.7**	**757.2**	**1,041.5**	**1,055.2**	**994.1**	**945.4**	**907.7**	**873.1**
Long-term external debt	298.0	723.0	1,002.0	1,013.6	952.1	895.7	829.1	781.5
Public and publicly guaranteed	298.0	723.0	1,002.0	1,013.6	952.1	895.7	829.1	781.5
Official creditors	298.0	690.1	964.1	976.9	914.7	856.6	794.6	750.6
of which: IMF	19.8	21.7	23.3	23.3	23.3	23.3	22.0	21.0
Private creditors	0.0	32.9	38.0	36.8	37.5	39.2	34.5	30.9
of which: Bonds	0.0	0.0	0.0	0.0	0.0	0.0	0.0	0.0
Private nonguaranteed	..	..	..	..	..	..	..	..
of which: Bonds	..	..	..	..	..	..	..	..
Short-term external debt	12.0	12.6	16.2	18.4	18.6	26.3	56.6	70.6
interest arrears on long-term	2.0	1.6	6.2	7.4	12.6	16.3	18.6	20.9
Long-term external debt								
Disbursements	**50.7**	**70.6**	**8.6**	**24.2**	**26.8**	**26.8**	**20.2**	**14.7**
Public and publicly guaranteed	50.7	70.6	8.6	24.2	26.8	26.8	20.2	14.7
Official creditors	50.7	70.6	8.6	24.2	26.8	26.8	20.2	14.7
Private creditors	0.0	0.0	0.0	0.0	0.0	0.0	0.0	0.0
of which: Bonds	0.0	0.0	0.0	0.0	0.0	0.0	0.0	0.0
Private nonguaranteed	..	..	..	..	..	..	..	..
of which: Bonds	..	..	..	..	..	..	..	..
Principal repayments	**0.5**	**11.8**	**13.3**	**14.0**	**86.0**	**81.4**	**41.2**	**29.9**
Public and publicly guaranteed	0.5	11.8	13.3	14.0	86.0	81.4	41.2	29.9
Official creditors	0.5	11.8	13.3	14.0	86.0	81.4	41.2	29.9
Private creditors	0.0	0.0	0.0	0.0	0.0	0.0	0.0	0.0
of which: Bonds	0.0	0.0	0.0	0.0	0.0	0.0	0.0	0.0
Private nonguaranteed	..	..	..	..	..	..	..	..
of which: Bonds	..	..	..	..	..	..	..	..
Interest payments	**2.5**	**8.4**	**9.3**	**7.9**	**8.5**	**6.4**	**4.8**	**4.1**
Public and publicly guaranteed	2.5	8.4	9.3	7.9	8.5	6.4	4.8	4.1
Official creditors	2.5	8.4	9.3	7.9	8.3	6.2	4.7	3.9
Private creditors	0.0	0.0	0.0	0.0	0.2	0.2	0.2	0.2
of which: Bonds	0.0	0.0	0.0	0.0	0.0	0.0	0.0	0.0
Private nonguaranteed	..	..	..	..	..	..	..	..
of which: Bonds	..	..	..	..	..	..	..	..
Net financial flows								
Net inflows	**88.1**	**40.3**	**88.3**	**50.2**	**-22.9**	**-6.7**	**53.5**	**45.7**
Net debt inflows	60.2	38.9	-2.7	11.2	-64.3	-50.5	7.0	-3.6
Official creditors	50.2	58.9	-4.7	10.2	-59.3	-54.5	-21.0	-15.3
of which: World Bank	31.6	56.7	-0.5	12.4	0.0	0.0	0.0	0.0
of which: IMF	0.0	0.0	0.0	0.0	0.0	0.0	0.0	0.0
Private creditors	10.0	-20.0	2.0	1.0	-5.0	4.0	28.0	11.7
Long-term	..	..	..	..	..	..	..	..
Bonds	..	..	..	..	..	..	..	..
Banks and other private	..	..	..	..	..	..	..	..
Short-term	10.0	-20.0	2.0	1.0	-5.0	4.0	28.0	11.7
Net equity inflows	27.9	1.4	91.0	39.0	41.4	43.9	46.5	49.3
Foreign direct investment	27.9	1.4	91.0	39.0	41.4	43.9	46.5	49.3
Portfolio equity	..	..	..	..	..	..	..	..
Major economic aggregates								
Gross national income (GNI)	706.8	1,089.0	2,097.4	2,584.2	..	..	..	..
Exports of goods, services & prim. income	106.9	..	..	..	..	..	..	..
Imports of goods, services & prim. income	510.3	..	..	..	..	..	..	..
Primary income on FDI	4.4	..	..	..	..	..	..	..
Personal transfers & comp. of employees	3.3	..	..	..	..	..	..	..
International reserves	25.5	27.9	114.1	114.8	..	..	..	..
Ratios								
External debt stocks to exports (%)	308.5	..	..	..	..	..	..	..
External debt stocks to GNI (%)	46.6	69.5	49.7	40.8	..	..	..	..
Debt service to exports (%)	4.3	..	..	..	..	..	..	..
Short-term to external debt stocks (%)	3.6	1.7	1.6	1.7	1.9	2.8	6.2	8.1
Multilateral to external debt stocks (%)	46.1	67.4	62.5	63.1	65.8	67.9	65.8	65.6
Reserves to external debt stocks (%)	7.7	3.7	11.0	10.9	..	..	..	..

Notes: Long-term public and publicly guaranteed debt from 2010 are World Bank staff estimates. Short-term debt is based on data from the BIS.

ETHIOPIA

(US$ million, unless otherwise indicated)

	2000	2005	2010	2011	2012	2013	2014	2015
Summary external debt data								
External debt stocks	**5,516**	**6,229**	**7,335**	**8,610**	**10,461**	**12,575**	**16,589**	**20,414**
Long-term external debt	5,339	5,925	6,547	7,945	9,941	11,886	15,846	19,467
Public and publicly guaranteed	5,339	5,925	6,547	7,945	9,941	11,886	15,846	19,467
Official creditors	5,226	5,561	4,638	5,685	7,218	8,980	11,374	13,070
of which: IMF	92	176	485	484	484	485	452	397
Private creditors	113	364	1,909	2,259	2,723	2,905	4,472	6,396
of which: Bonds	0	0	0	0	0	0	1,000	1,000
Private nonguaranteed	..	..	..	..	..	..	..	..
of which: Bonds	..	..	..	..	..	..	..	..
Short-term external debt	86	128	302	181	36	204	292	550
interest arrears on long-term	65	36	30	30	26	28	28	28
Long-term external debt								
Disbursements	**185**	**527**	**1,760**	**1,693**	**2,309**	**2,399**	**4,915**	**4,615**
Public and publicly guaranteed	185	527	1,760	1,693	2,309	2,399	4,915	4,615
Official creditors	184	400	1,021	1,157	1,645	1,889	2,949	2,199
Private creditors	2	127	739	537	664	510	1,966	2,416
of which: Bonds	0	0	0	0	0	0	1,000	0
Private nonguaranteed	..	..	..	..	..	..	..	..
of which: Bonds	..	..	..	..	..	..	..	..
Principal repayments	**72**	**36**	**130**	**259**	**328**	**503**	**567**	**681**
Public and publicly guaranteed	72	36	130	259	328	503	567	681
Official creditors	62	25	39	80	122	162	204	224
Private creditors	10	11	91	179	206	341	364	456
of which: Bonds	0	0	0	0	0	0	0	0
Private nonguaranteed	..	..	..	..	..	..	..	..
of which: Bonds	..	..	..	..	..	..	..	..
Interest payments	**52**	**49**	**50**	**91**	**103**	**159**	**189**	**303**
Public and publicly guaranteed	52	49	50	91	103	159	189	303
Official creditors	48	40	35	52	58	96	130	155
Private creditors	4	10	15	38	46	63	59	147
of which: Bonds	0	0	0	0	0	0	0	66
Private nonguaranteed	..	..	..	..	..	..	..	..
of which: Bonds	..	..	..	..	..	..	..	..
Net financial flows								
Net inflows	**231**	**808**	**2,116**	**1,940**	**2,119**	**3,344**	**6,562**	**6,325**
Net debt inflows	96	542	1,828	1,313	1,840	2,062	4,430	4,158
Official creditors	109	371	1,105	1,077	1,524	1,727	2,741	1,940
of which: World Bank	116	162	385	422	589	842	855	686
of which: IMF	-13	-4	122	0	0	0	-5	-36
Private creditors	-12	171	722	237	317	335	1,690	2,218
Long-term	-8	116	647	358	458	169	1,602	1,960
Bonds	..	..	..	..	..	..	1,000	..
Banks and other private	-8	116	647	358	458	169	602	1,960
Short-term	-4	55	75	-121	-141	166	88	258
Net equity inflows	135	265	288	627	279	1,281	2,132	2,168
Foreign direct investment	135	265	288	627	279	1,281	2,132	2,168
Portfolio equity	..	..	..	..	..	..	..	..
Major economic aggregates								
Gross national income (GNI)	8,182	12,365	29,826	31,883	43,215	47,541	55,459	61,275
Exports of goods, services & prim. income	1,008	1,973	4,652	5,824	6,003	..	..	..
Imports of goods, services & prim. income	1,673	4,943	9,982	11,736	14,235	..	..	..
Primary income on FDI	9	21	35	23	6	..	..	..
Personal transfers & comp. of employees	53	174	345	513	624	624	624	624
International reserves	306	1,043	..	..	..	..	..	..
Ratios								
External debt stocks to exports (%)	547.0	315.7	157.7	147.8	174.3	..	..	..
External debt stocks to GNI (%)	67.4	50.4	24.6	27.0	24.2	26.4	29.9	33.3
Debt service to exports (%)	13.7	4.8	3.9	6.1	7.2	..	..	..
Short-term to external debt stocks (%)	1.6	2.1	4.1	2.1	0.3	1.6	1.8	2.7
Multilateral to external debt stocks (%)	49.9	75.5	38.3	39.6	39.3	42.1	36.0	32.3
Reserves to external debt stocks (%)	5.6	16.7	..	..	..	..	..	..

Notes: Short-term debt is based on data from the BIS. Data include the effects of HIPC and MDRI debt relief.

FIJI

(US$ million, unless otherwise indicated)

Summary external debt data

	2000	2005	2010	2011	2012	2013	2014	2015
External debt stocks	**194.5**	**302.7**	**570.2**	**847.4**	**744.6**	**794.1**	**866.4**	**871.3**
Long-term external debt	174.3	185.4	388.8	544.3	609.4	653.9	701.3	697.4
Public and publicly guaranteed	174.3	185.4	388.3	543.8	608.9	653.5	700.9	697.0
Official creditors	174.2	185.4	238.3	293.8	358.9	403.5	450.9	447.0
of which: IMF	9.1	9.9	103.3	103.0	103.1	103.3	97.2	93.0
Private creditors	0.0	0.0	150.0	250.0	250.0	250.0	250.0	250.0
of which: Bonds	0.0	0.0	150.0	250.0	250.0	250.0	250.0	250.0
Private nonguaranteed	..	..	0.5	0.5	0.5	0.5	0.4	0.4
of which: Bonds	..	..	..	..	..	..	..	..
Short-term external debt	11.2	107.4	78.1	200.1	32.1	36.8	67.9	80.9
interest arrears on long-term	0.2	0.4	0.1	0.1	0.1	0.6	0.0	0.0

Long-term external debt

	2000	2005	2010	2011	2012	2013	2014	2015
Disbursements	**7.1**	**14.1**	**32.6**	**315.4**	**78.3**	**59.8**	**70.5**	**26.0**
Public and publicly guaranteed	7.1	14.1	32.6	315.4	78.2	59.8	70.5	26.0
Official creditors	7.1	14.1	32.6	65.4	78.2	59.8	70.5	26.0
Private creditors	0.0	0.0	0.0	250.0	0.0	0.0	0.0	0.0
of which: Bonds	0.0	0.0	0.0	250.0	0.0	0.0	0.0	0.0
Private nonguaranteed	..	..	0.0	0.0	0.1	0.0	0.0	0.0
of which: Bonds	..	..	..	..	..	..	..	..
Principal repayments	**17.5**	**8.5**	**9.1**	**163.6**	**11.2**	**15.1**	**21.1**	**16.4**
Public and publicly guaranteed	17.5	8.5	9.1	163.6	11.2	15.0	21.0	16.4
Official creditors	17.5	8.5	9.1	13.6	11.2	15.0	21.0	16.4
Private creditors	0.0	0.0	0.0	150.0	0.0	0.0	0.0	0.0
of which: Bonds	0.0	0.0	0.0	150.0	0.0	0.0	0.0	0.0
Private nonguaranteed	..	..	0.0	0.1	0.1	0.1	0.1	0.0
of which: Bonds	..	..	..	..	..	..	..	..
Interest payments	**7.9**	**5.5**	**13.3**	**24.9**	**26.7**	**27.9**	**29.5**	**30.0**
Public and publicly guaranteed	7.9	5.5	13.3	24.9	26.7	27.9	29.5	30.0
Official creditors	7.9	5.5	3.0	3.3	4.2	5.4	7.0	7.5
Private creditors	0.0	0.0	10.3	21.6	22.5	22.5	22.5	22.5
of which: Bonds	0.0	0.0	10.3	21.6	22.5	22.5	22.5	22.5
Private nonguaranteed	..	..	0.0	0.0	0.0	0.0	0.0	0.0
of which: Bonds	..	..	..	..	..	..	..	..

Net financial flows

	2000	2005	2010	2011	2012	2013	2014	2015
Net inflows	**-2.5**	**209.7**	**395.9**	**678.4**	**160.0**	**176.7**	**423.8**	**355.1**
Net debt inflows	0.6	52.5	45.5	273.8	-100.9	49.0	81.0	22.7
Official creditors	-10.4	5.5	23.5	51.8	67.1	44.8	49.5	9.6
of which: World Bank	-6.8	-2.3	0.0	0.0	0.0	0.0	0.0	0.0
of which: IMF	0.0	0.0	0.0	0.0	0.0	0.0	0.0	0.0
Private creditors	11.0	47.0	22.0	222.0	-168.0	4.3	31.5	13.0
Long-term	0.0	..	0.0	100.0	0.0	0.0	-0.1	0.0
Bonds	..	..	..	100.0	..	..	..	..
Banks and other private	0.0	..	0.0	0.0	0.0	0.0	-0.1	0.0
Short-term	11.0	47.0	22.0	122.0	-168.0	4.3	31.6	13.0
Net equity inflows	-3.1	157.2	350.4	404.6	261.0	127.7	342.8	332.4
Foreign direct investment	-3.1	155.5	350.3	404.6	261.0	127.7	342.8	332.4
Portfolio equity	..	1.7	0.1	-0.1	..	..	..	..

Major economic aggregates

	2000	2005	2010	2011	2012	2013	2014	2015
Gross national income (GNI)	1,717.4	3,050.1	3,043.1	3,660.4	3,835.1	4,115.6	4,332.9	4,167.6
Exports of goods, services & prim. income	1,021.5	1,692.3	1,887.6	2,341.4	2,503.2	2,465.9	2,544.8	2,207.9
Imports of goods, services & prim. income	1,134.8	2,038.6	2,186.3	2,679.3	2,771.2	3,077.4	3,125.6	2,540.4
Primary income on FDI	7.5	132.8	143.4	171.2	168.2	122.3	230.2	209.1
Personal transfers & comp. of employees	43.3	203.3	175.6	160.4	190.6	203.6	220.9	251.3
International reserves	411.8	320.9	719.4	832.2	920.0	940.9	915.2	917.9

Ratios

	2000	2005	2010	2011	2012	2013	2014	2015
External debt stocks to exports (%)	19.0	17.9	30.2	36.2	29.7	32.2	34.0	39.5
External debt stocks to GNI (%)	11.3	9.9	18.7	23.1	19.4	19.3	20.0	20.9
Debt service to exports (%)	2.6	0.9	1.2	8.2	1.6	1.8	2.0	2.2
Short-term to external debt stocks (%)	5.8	35.5	13.7	23.6	4.3	4.6	7.8	9.3
Multilateral to external debt stocks (%)	45.6	30.3	19.9	14.7	18.0	17.5	15.9	14.9
Reserves to external debt stocks (%)	211.7	106.0	126.2	98.2	123.6	118.5	105.6	105.4

Notes: Long-term private nonguaranteed debt data for 2012 are World Bank staff estimates. Short-term debt is based on data from the BIS.

GABON

(US$ million, unless otherwise indicated)

	2000	2005	2010	2011	2012	2013	2014	2015
Summary external debt data								
External debt stocks	**3,920**	**3,897**	**2,524**	**2,798**	**2,870**	**4,323**	**4,303**	**5,097**
Long-term external debt	3,457	3,564	2,128	2,388	2,533	3,824	4,018	4,436
Public and publicly guaranteed	3,457	3,564	2,128	2,388	2,533	3,824	4,018	4,436
Official creditors	3,338	3,444	884	929	981	1,257	1,416	1,468
of which: IMF	107	88	226	225	225	226	213	203
Private creditors	119	119	1,244	1,459	1,552	2,567	2,602	2,968
of which: Bonds	0	0	879	879	875	1,718	1,718	2,218
Private nonguaranteed	..	..	..	..	..	..	..	..
of which: Bonds	..	..	..	..	..	..	..	..
Short-term external debt	355	245	170	185	111	273	73	458
interest arrears on long-term	63	186	0	0	0	0	0	2
Long-term external debt								
Disbursements	**34**	**18**	**466**	**549**	**385**	**2,112**	**598**	**780**
Public and publicly guaranteed	34	18	466	549	385	2,112	598	780
Official creditors	13	18	189	216	165	317	301	181
Private creditors	21	0	276	333	221	1,795	297	598
of which: Bonds	0	0	0	0	0	1,500	0	500
Private nonguaranteed	..	..	..	..	..	..	..	..
of which: Bonds	..	..	..	..	..	..	..	..
Principal repayments	**188**	**112**	**291**	**256**	**259**	**879**	**239**	**201**
Public and publicly guaranteed	188	112	291	256	259	879	239	201
Official creditors	160	63	171	165	118	66	78	59
Private creditors	27	48	120	91	142	813	161	142
of which: Bonds	0	0	23	0	4	657	0	0
Private nonguaranteed	..	..	..	..	..	..	..	..
of which: Bonds	..	..	..	..	..	..	..	..
Interest payments	**124**	**52**	**131**	**127**	**130**	**246**	**159**	**190**
Public and publicly guaranteed	124	52	131	127	130	246	159	190
Official creditors	118	46	32	30	28	31	30	33
Private creditors	7	7	99	97	102	215	130	157
of which: Bonds	0	0	74	72	73	191	114	131
Private nonguaranteed	..	..	..	..	..	..	..	..
of which: Bonds	..	..	..	..	..	..	..	..
Net financial flows								
Net inflows	**-208**	**262**	**741**	**1,003**	**884**	**2,166**	**1,170**	**1,585**
Net debt inflows	-363	-59	242	307	52	1,394	159	961
Official creditors	-140	-70	19	51	47	251	223	122
of which: World Bank	-4	-7	6	14	-2	1	1	24
of which: IMF	8	-25	0	0	0	0	0	0
Private creditors	-223	11	223	257	5	1,144	-64	839
Long-term	-7	-48	156	242	79	982	136	456
Bonds	..	..	-23	..	-4	843	..	500
Banks and other private	-7	-48	178	242	83	138	136	-44
Short-term	-216	59	67	15	-74	162	-200	383
Net equity inflows	154	321	499	696	832	771	1,011	624
Foreign direct investment	154	321	499	696	832	771	1,011	624
Portfolio equity	..	..	..	..	..	..	..	..
Major economic aggregates								
Gross national income (GNI)	4,289	8,501	12,472	15,691	15,458	15,886	17,233	13,482
Exports of goods, services & prim. income	3,541	5,639	..	..	..	..	..	..
Imports of goods, services & prim. income	2,477	3,387	..	..	..	..	..	..
Primary income on FDI	473	765	..	..	..	..	..	..
Personal transfers & comp. of employees	6	11	..	..	..	..	..	..
International reserves	190	669	1,736	2,157	2,352	3,004	2,478	1,863
Ratios								
External debt stocks to exports (%)	110.7	69.1	..	..	..	..	..	..
External debt stocks to GNI (%)	91.4	45.8	20.2	17.8	18.6	27.2	25.0	37.8
Debt service to exports (%)	10.0	3.4	..	..	..	..	..	..
Short-term to external debt stocks (%)	9.1	6.3	6.7	6.6	3.9	6.3	1.7	9.0
Multilateral to external debt stocks (%)	11.9	10.1	15.5	16.4	17.2	12.0	12.0	9.1
Reserves to external debt stocks (%)	4.8	17.2	68.8	77.1	81.9	69.5	57.6	36.6

Notes: Long-term public and publicly guaranteed debt data before 2008 are World Bank staff estimates based on reports provided by the country. Short-term debt is based on data from the BIS. Data include the effects of Paris Club debt buyback agreement signed in 2007.

GAMBIA, THE

(US$ million, unless otherwise indicated)

	2000	2005	2010	2011	2012	2013	2014	2015
Summary external debt data								
External debt stocks	**490.1**	**667.1**	**550.5**	**512.7**	**548.1**	**553.4**	**524.2**	**526.8**
Long-term external debt	438.0	616.5	428.9	430.9	431.1	446.1	423.9	426.8
Public and publicly guaranteed	438.0	616.5	428.9	430.9	431.1	446.1	423.9	426.8
Official creditors	437.0	616.5	422.5	426.8	421.5	435.2	415.0	420.7
of which: IMF	24.8	28.1	77.0	80.3	94.4	95.5	86.8	88.4
Private creditors	1.0	0.0	6.4	4.1	9.6	11.0	8.9	6.2
of which: Bonds	0.0	0.0	0.0	0.0	0.0	0.0	0.0	0.0
Private nonguaranteed	..	..	..	..	..	..	..	..
of which: Bonds	..	..	..	..	..	..	..	..
Short-term external debt	27.3	22.4	44.7	1.4	22.6	11.8	13.5	11.5
interest arrears on long-term	0.0	1.4	2.7	1.4	1.6	1.8	3.5	2.8
Long-term external debt								
Disbursements	**20.7**	**54.3**	**43.3**	**24.3**	**25.2**	**37.0**	**39.6**	**42.7**
Public and publicly guaranteed	20.7	54.3	43.3	24.3	25.2	37.0	39.6	42.7
Official creditors	20.7	54.3	36.9	24.3	17.9	33.9	38.3	42.7
Private creditors	0.0	0.0	6.4	0.0	7.3	3.1	1.3	0.0
of which: Bonds	0.0	0.0	0.0	0.0	0.0	0.0	0.0	0.0
Private nonguaranteed	..	..	..	..	..	..	..	..
of which: Bonds	..	..	..	..	..	..	..	..
Principal repayments	**12.7**	**16.1**	**16.8**	**19.8**	**19.1**	**21.7**	**38.9**	**27.8**
Public and publicly guaranteed	12.7	16.1	16.8	19.8	19.1	21.7	38.9	27.8
Official creditors	12.3	15.8	13.5	17.5	17.0	19.6	36.9	26.0
Private creditors	0.4	0.3	3.2	2.2	2.1	2.2	2.1	1.8
of which: Bonds	0.0	0.0	0.0	0.0	0.0	0.0	0.0	0.0
Private nonguaranteed	..	..	..	..	..	..	..	..
of which: Bonds	..	..	..	..	..	..	..	..
Interest payments	**6.0**	**9.4**	**6.6**	**6.7**	**6.5**	**5.5**	**5.2**	**5.1**
Public and publicly guaranteed	6.0	9.4	6.6	6.7	6.5	5.5	5.2	5.1
Official creditors	5.9	9.4	6.6	6.6	6.3	5.3	5.1	5.0
Private creditors	0.1	0.0	0.0	0.1	0.2	0.1	0.1	0.1
of which: Bonds	0.0	0.0	0.0	0.0	0.0	0.0	0.0	0.0
Private nonguaranteed	..	..	..	..	..	..	..	..
of which: Bonds	..	..	..	..	..	..	..	..
Net financial flows								
Net inflows	**20.6**	**86.9**	**67.9**	**2.4**	**74.6**	**42.8**	**25.8**	**29.7**
Net debt inflows	20.6	33.2	30.5	-33.8	41.1	5.1	-2.6	19.1
Official creditors	15.8	36.5	26.4	10.4	14.9	15.2	-1.8	22.2
of which: World Bank	5.4	15.6	1.9	-0.8	-1.2	-1.2	-0.5	-0.2
of which: IMF	7.5	-2.0	3.0	3.7	13.9	0.8	-3.2	5.5
Private creditors	4.8	-3.3	4.2	-44.2	26.3	-10.1	-0.8	-3.1
Long-term	-0.4	-0.3	3.2	-2.2	5.3	0.9	-0.8	-1.8
Bonds	..	..	..	..	..	..	..	..
Banks and other private	-0.4	-0.3	3.2	-2.2	5.3	0.9	-0.8	-1.8
Short-term	5.2	-3.0	1.0	-42.0	21.0	-11.0	0.0	-1.3
Net equity inflows	..	53.7	37.4	36.2	33.5	37.6	28.4	10.6
Foreign direct investment	..	53.7	37.4	36.2	33.5	37.6	28.4	10.6
Portfolio equity	..	..	..	..	..	..	..	..
Major economic aggregates								
Gross national income (GNI)	752.7	591.8	944.4	888.5	893.9	881.4	822.1	..
Exports of goods, services & prim. income	..	189.8	284.9	318.9	343.8	..	..	..
Imports of goods, services & prim. income	..	305.0	341.3	392.8	467.6	..	..	..
Primary income on FDI	..	26.9	11.5	11.3	10.2	..	..	..
Personal transfers & comp. of employees	..	59.3	115.7	107.9	141.0	137.1	152.5	155.9
International reserves	109.4	98.3	201.6	223.2	236.2	210.6	159.3	..
Ratios								
External debt stocks to exports (%)	..	351.5	193.2	160.7	159.5	..	..	..
External debt stocks to GNI (%)	65.1	112.7	58.3	57.7	61.3	62.8	63.8	..
Debt service to exports (%)	..	15.1	8.5	8.4	7.6	..	..	..
Short-term to external debt stocks (%)	5.6	3.4	8.1	0.3	4.1	2.1	2.6	2.2
Multilateral to external debt stocks (%)	70.1	75.3	54.9	60.8	57.2	57.8	59.6	58.6
Reserves to external debt stocks (%)	22.3	14.7	36.6	43.5	43.1	38.0	30.4	0.0

Notes: Short-term debt is based on data from the BIS. Data include the effects of HIPC and MDRI debt relief.

GEORGIA

(US$ million, unless otherwise indicated)

	2000	2005	2010	2011	2012	2013	2014	2015
Summary external debt data								
External debt stocks	**1,826**	**2,151**	**9,656**	**11,360**	**12,398**	**13,467**	**14,035**	**14,854**
Long-term external debt	1,316	1,663	7,284	8,605	9,274	10,806	11,464	12,444
Public and publicly guaranteed	1,274	1,531	4,141	4,343	4,876	5,227	5,454	5,664
Official creditors	1,272	1,529	2,450	2,706	3,097	3,384	3,526	3,712
of which: IMF	466	438	1,272	1,210	965	580	420	330
Private creditors	2	2	1,691	1,637	1,778	1,843	1,928	1,952
of which: Bonds	0	0	750	815	1,065	1,000	1,000	750
Private nonguaranteed	42	132	3,143	4,262	4,399	5,579	6,010	6,781
of which: Bonds	..	..	..	..	750	750	750	900
Short-term external debt	44	50	1,101	1,546	2,159	2,081	2,151	2,080
interest arrears on long-term	1	11	7	84	366	363	375	20
Long-term external debt								
Disbursements	**65**	**146**	**1,190**	**1,785**	**1,625**	**1,236**	**1,299**	**2,276**
Public and publicly guaranteed	37	76	815	843	690	332	458	464
Official creditors	37	76	401	343	431	326	458	455
Private creditors	0	0	414	500	258	6	0	9
of which: Bonds	0	0	250	500	250	0	0	0
Private nonguaranteed	28	69	375	942	935	904	841	1,812
of which: Bonds	..	..	..	..	750	0	0	150
Principal repayments	**42**	**103**	**510**	**1,199**	**933**	**811**	**1,113**	**1,319**
Public and publicly guaranteed	41	80	169	620	165	238	97	368
Official creditors	41	80	71	67	48	56	97	118
Private creditors	0	0	97	553	118	182	0	250
of which: Bonds	0	0	0	435	0	65	0	250
Private nonguaranteed	2	23	342	579	768	573	1,016	952
of which: Bonds	..	..	..	..	0	0	0	0
Interest payments	**43**	**28**	**247**	**307**	**404**	**415**	**382**	**631**
Public and publicly guaranteed	42	24	87	139	112	130	121	130
Official creditors	42	24	39	35	38	43	45	44
Private creditors	0	0	47	104	73	87	76	86
of which: Bonds	0	0	38	94	64	79	76	76
Private nonguaranteed	1	4	160	167	292	286	260	501
of which: Bonds	..	..	..	..	29	58	58	70
Net financial flows								
Net inflows	**133**	**356**	**1,807**	**1,728**	**1,760**	**935**	**1,825**	**2,475**
Net debt inflows	33	-30	1,131	895	778	-34	112	1,168
Official creditors	-29	-17	605	216	139	-113	229	264
of which: World Bank	18	52	126	140	147	99	109	133
of which: IMF	-26	-13	275	-60	-244	-383	-132	-73
Private creditors	62	-14	526	679	639	79	-117	904
Long-term	26	46	350	310	308	154	-175	619
Bonds	..	..	250	65	1,000	-65	0	-100
Banks and other private	26	46	100	245	-692	219	-175	719
Short-term	36	-60	176	369	331	-76	58	285
Net equity inflows	100	386	676	833	981	969	1,713	1,306
Foreign direct investment	100	383	698	840	908	968	1,503	1,302
Portfolio equity	..	3	-22	-7	74	1	210	5
Major economic aggregates								
Gross national income (GNI)	3,175	6,473	11,279	14,012	15,700	15,835	16,358	13,582
Exports of goods, services & prim. income	994	2,415	4,591	6,000	7,099	8,097	8,066	7,020
Imports of goods, services & prim. income	1,420	3,469	6,887	9,171	10,359	10,497	11,250	10,251
Primary income on FDI	36	116	470	800	747	770	750	580
Personal transfers & comp. of employees	206	446	1,184	1,547	1,770	1,945	1,986	1,459
International reserves	116	479	2,264	2,818	2,873	2,823	2,699	2,521
Ratios								
External debt stocks to exports (%)	183.7	89.1	210.3	189.3	174.7	166.3	174.0	211.6
External debt stocks to GNI (%)	57.5	33.2	85.6	81.1	79.0	85.0	85.8	109.4
Debt service to exports (%)	12.7	8.1	17.5	26.8	22.9	21.0	22.2	29.7
Short-term to external debt stocks (%)	2.4	2.3	11.4	13.6	17.4	15.5	15.3	14.0
Multilateral to external debt stocks (%)	26.2	38.1	18.7	17.8	18.6	18.9	19.6	19.9
Reserves to external debt stocks (%)	6.4	22.2	23.4	24.8	23.2	21.0	19.2	17.0

GHANA

(US$ million, unless otherwise indicated)

	2000	2005	2010	2011	2012	2013	2014	2015
Summary external debt data								
External debt stocks	**6,743**	**7,334**	**9,114**	**11,226**	**12,837**	**16,626**	**18,363**	**20,677**
Long-term external debt	5,839	6,055	6,085	7,366	8,882	11,753	14,161	16,090
Public and publicly guaranteed	5,582	6,055	6,085	7,366	8,882	11,753	13,908	15,837
Official creditors	5,023	5,492	4,214	5,130	6,319	7,449	8,154	8,782
of which: IMF	375	507	937	1,101	1,253	1,223	1,120	1,242
Private creditors	559	563	1,872	2,235	2,562	4,304	5,754	7,055
of which: Bonds	0	0	750	750	750	1,531	2,531	3,531
Private nonguaranteed	257	..	..	..	..	..	253	253
of which: Bonds	250	..	..	..	..	..	253	253
Short-term external debt	530	772	2,092	2,759	2,703	3,651	3,082	3,345
interest arrears on long-term	27	38	28	105	144	231	171	206
Long-term external debt								
Disbursements	**457**	**558**	**1,310**	**1,537**	**1,755**	**3,367**	**3,296**	**2,853**
Public and publicly guaranteed	457	558	1,310	1,537	1,755	3,367	3,043	2,853
Official creditors	351	483	998	1,025	1,279	1,260	1,237	1,125
Private creditors	106	74	312	512	475	2,107	1,805	1,728
of which: Bonds	0	0	0	0	0	1,000	1,000	1,000
Private nonguaranteed	..	..	..	..	..	..	253	0
of which: Bonds	..	..	..	..	..	..	253	0
Principal repayments	**274**	**190**	**166**	**207**	**278**	**577**	**442**	**552**
Public and publicly guaranteed	271	190	166	207	278	577	442	552
Official creditors	171	127	74	88	117	166	229	240
Private creditors	100	63	92	120	161	411	213	312
of which: Bonds	0	0	0	0	0	219	0	0
Private nonguaranteed	3	..	..	..	..	..	0	0
of which: Bonds	..	..	..	..	..	..	0	0
Interest payments	**117**	**88**	**160**	**98**	**174**	**317**	**300**	**381**
Public and publicly guaranteed	103	88	160	98	174	317	300	375
Official creditors	75	57	72	61	83	153	88	89
Private creditors	28	30	88	37	91	164	212	286
of which: Bonds	0	0	64	0	32	54	124	192
Private nonguaranteed	14	..	..	..	..	..	0	6
of which: Bonds	14	..	..	..	..	..	0	6
Net financial flows								
Net inflows	**152**	**757**	**4,385**	**5,340**	**4,826**	**6,845**	**5,676**	**5,893**
Net debt inflows	-14	612	1,840	2,091	1,532	3,618	2,313	2,700
Official creditors	179	364	1,049	1,109	1,312	1,062	976	1,058
of which: World Bank	171	289	305	412	253	300	296	475
of which: IMF	-2	7	124	171	150	-32	-32	172
Private creditors	-193	247	791	982	220	2,556	1,336	1,643
Long-term	2	11	220	392	314	1,696	1,845	1,416
Bonds	..	..	..	..	..	781	1,253	1,000
Banks and other private	2	11	220	392	314	915	592	416
Short-term	-195	236	571	590	-95	860	-509	227
Net equity inflows	166	145	2,545	3,248	3,295	3,227	3,363	3,192
Foreign direct investment	166	145	2,527	3,248	3,295	3,227	3,363	3,192
Portfolio equity	..	..	18	1	..	..	..	..
Major economic aggregates								
Gross national income (GNI)	4,836	10,601	31,641	38,336	39,810	46,454	36,899	36,732
Exports of goods, services & prim. income	2,456	3,952	9,490	14,651	16,867	16,490	15,372	16,893
Imports of goods, services & prim. income	3,473	6,851	14,560	20,790	24,184	24,134	21,075	22,300
Primary income on FDI	17	94	396	1,062	1,961	1,219	1,341	813
Personal transfers & comp. of employees	32	99	136	2,135	2,155	1,864	2,008	4,982
International reserves	232	1,753	4,763	5,483	5,368	5,249	..	..
Ratios								
External debt stocks to exports (%)	274.5	185.6	96.0	76.6	76.1	100.8	119.5	122.4
External debt stocks to GNI (%)	139.4	69.2	28.8	29.3	32.2	35.8	49.8	56.3
Debt service to exports (%)	19.0	8.6	4.0	2.4	3.2	6.1	5.4	6.2
Short-term to external debt stocks (%)	7.9	10.5	22.9	24.6	21.1	22.0	16.8	16.2
Multilateral to external debt stocks (%)	54.3	68.8	30.1	29.2	28.7	24.4	22.6	22.2
Reserves to external debt stocks (%)	3.4	23.9	52.3	48.8	41.8	31.6	..	..

Notes: Long-term private nonguaranteed debt data only cover bonds. Short-term debt is based on data from the BIS. Data include the effects of MDRI debt relief.

GRENADA

(US$ million, unless otherwise indicated)

	2000	2005	2010	2011	2012	2013	2014	2015
Summary external debt data								
External debt stocks	**199.4**	**408.4**	**606.2**	**578.0**	**636.3**	**612.5**	**663.7**	**685.8**
Long-term external debt	180.7	391.4	522.4	516.3	519.0	518.9	539.0	571.4
Public and publicly guaranteed	180.7	391.4	522.4	516.3	519.0	518.9	539.0	571.4
Official creditors	116.8	172.5	277.7	273.2	275.8	275.8	295.9	329.4
of which: IMF	1.2	9.7	46.3	45.9	45.5	45.1	45.7	44.8
Private creditors	63.9	218.9	244.7	243.1	243.1	243.1	243.1	242.0
of which: Bonds	27.4	214.3	239.4	239.4	239.4	239.4	239.4	239.4
Private nonguaranteed	..	..	..	..	..	..	..	..
of which: Bonds	..	..	..	..	..	..	..	..
Short-term external debt	17.5	7.4	37.6	15.8	71.9	48.5	79.0	69.6
interest arrears on long-term	4.5	4.4	14.6	15.8	39.9	48.5	58.1	57.8
Long-term external debt								
Disbursements	**77.6**	**38.5**	**21.1**	**6.3**	**8.7**	**28.3**	**33.7**	**50.9**
Public and publicly guaranteed	77.6	38.5	21.1	6.3	8.7	28.3	33.7	50.9
Official creditors	19.8	38.5	21.1	6.3	8.7	28.3	33.7	50.9
Private creditors	57.8	0.0	0.0	0.0	0.0	0.0	0.0	0.0
of which: Bonds	26.6	0.0	0.0	0.0	0.0	0.0	0.0	0.0
Private nonguaranteed	..	..	..	..	..	..	..	..
of which: Bonds	..	..	..	..	..	..	..	..
Principal repayments	**10.1**	**5.7**	**15.4**	**13.5**	**6.3**	**28.6**	**11.2**	**14.5**
Public and publicly guaranteed	10.1	5.7	15.4	13.5	6.3	28.6	11.2	14.5
Official creditors	6.4	5.3	11.0	10.6	6.3	28.6	11.2	13.5
Private creditors	3.7	0.4	4.4	2.9	0.0	0.0	0.0	1.1
of which: Bonds	0.0	0.0	0.0	0.0	0.0	0.0	0.0	0.0
Private nonguaranteed	..	..	..	..	..	..	..	..
of which: Bonds	..	..	..	..	..	..	..	..
Interest payments	**3.4**	**3.3**	**11.7**	**12.2**	**8.9**	**6.9**	**11.2**	**8.4**
Public and publicly guaranteed	3.4	3.3	11.7	12.2	8.9	6.9	11.2	8.4
Official creditors	2.3	3.3	5.7	6.4	3.6	5.8	5.7	5.6
Private creditors	1.1	0.0	5.9	5.9	5.3	1.0	5.5	2.8
of which: Bonds	0.0	0.0	5.9	5.8	5.3	1.0	5.5	2.8
Private nonguaranteed	..	..	..	..	..	..	..	..
of which: Bonds	..	..	..	..	..	..	..	..
Net financial flows								
Net inflows	**73.9**	**26.4**	**52.4**	**-1.0**	**50.4**	**25.1**	**85.1**	**89.0**
Net debt inflows	59.4	-23.2	10.1	-30.4	33.9	-32.8	46.8	28.4
Official creditors	13.4	33.2	16.5	-4.5	1.9	-0.8	25.9	38.5
of which: World Bank	2.6	5.6	8.6	-0.2	1.9	4.2	15.0	18.1
of which: IMF	..	..	6.4	-0.2	-0.5	-0.5	3.4	1.1
Private creditors	45.9	-56.4	-6.4	-25.9	32.0	-32.0	20.9	-10.2
Long-term	54.1	-0.4	-4.4	-2.9	0.0	0.0	0.0	-1.1
Bonds	26.6	0.0	0.0	0.0	0.0	0.0	0.0	0.0
Banks and other private	27.5	-0.4	-4.4	-2.9	0.0	0.0	0.0	-1.1
Short-term	-8.1	-56.0	-2.0	-23.0	32.0	-32.0	20.9	-9.1
Net equity inflows	14.5	49.6	42.3	29.4	16.5	58.0	38.2	60.7
Foreign direct investment	14.5	49.6	42.3	29.4	16.5	58.0	38.2	60.7
Portfolio equity	..	..	..	..	..	..	..	..
Major economic aggregates								
Gross national income (GNI)	486.3	667.1	731.1	747.0	765.6	813.0	878.7	944.2
Exports of goods, services & prim. income	240.8	160.3	190.9	202.0	213.5	216.7	240.6	244.6
Imports of goods, services & prim. income	349.0	435.9	426.6	433.0	437.0	455.9	443.6	458.5
Primary income on FDI	27.8	22.7	30.8	20.6	18.8	19.6	..	..
Personal transfers & comp. of employees	24.2	26.8	28.5	28.9	29.3	29.6	31.6	32.2
International reserves	57.7	94.3	119.2	120.7	119.5	150.6	169.9	198.0
Ratios								
External debt stocks to exports (%)	82.8	254.8	317.5	286.2	298.1	282.6	275.8	280.4
External debt stocks to GNI (%)	41.0	61.2	82.9	77.4	83.1	75.3	75.5	72.6
Debt service to exports (%)	6.0	6.6	14.4	13.0	7.5	16.8	10.6	11.4
Short-term to external debt stocks (%)	8.8	1.8	6.2	2.7	11.3	7.9	11.9	10.2
Multilateral to external debt stocks (%)	31.8	27.2	31.0	32.2	29.7	31.4	31.7	35.8
Reserves to external debt stocks (%)	28.9	23.1	19.7	20.9	18.8	24.6	25.6	28.9

Notes: Short-term debt is based on data from the BIS.

GUATEMALA

(US$ million, unless otherwise indicated)

	2000	2005	2010	2011	2012	2013	2014	2015
Summary external debt data								
External debt stocks	**3,948**	**9,506**	**15,039**	**16,277**	**15,130**	**17,263**	**19,286**	**20,182**
Long-term external debt	2,740	8,014	13,144	13,703	14,127	16,239	18,235	19,174
Public and publicly guaranteed	2,598	3,720	5,555	5,349	6,301	7,069	6,965	7,472
Official creditors	2,156	2,484	4,600	4,719	4,971	5,322	5,216	5,713
of which: IMF	36	40	309	308	309	309	291	278
Private creditors	442	1,237	955	630	1,330	1,748	1,749	1,759
of which: Bonds	245	1,105	955	630	1,330	1,730	1,730	1,730
Private nonguaranteed	142	4,294	7,589	8,354	7,826	9,170	11,270	11,701
of which: Bonds	..	50	5	155	355	355	1,155	1,150
Short-term external debt	1,172	1,453	1,585	2,265	695	714	760	730
interest arrears on long-term	317	414	0	0	0	0	0	0
Long-term external debt								
Disbursements	**220**	**1,639**	**1,471**	**1,025**	**1,449**	**4,441**	**3,287**	**2,809**
Public and publicly guaranteed	220	144	879	393	1,249	1,400	259	1,292
Official creditors	220	144	879	393	549	682	258	1,281
Private creditors	0	0	0	0	700	718	2	11
of which: Bonds	0	0	0	0	700	700	0	0
Private nonguaranteed	0	1,495	592	633	200	3,041	3,028	1,516
of which: Bonds	..	0	0	150	200	0	800	0
Principal repayments	**192**	**570**	**949**	**1,347**	**981**	**2,328**	**1,254**	**1,433**
Public and publicly guaranteed	172	200	264	604	273	596	325	349
Official creditors	139	199	264	279	273	296	325	347
Private creditors	32	1	0	325	0	300	0	2
of which: Bonds	31	0	0	325	0	300	0	0
Private nonguaranteed	20	371	685	743	708	1,732	928	1,084
of which: Bonds	..	0	0	0	0	0	0	5
Interest payments	**153**	**420**	**636**	**684**	**598**	**585**	**719**	**676**
Public and publicly guaranteed	134	203	284	284	274	274	280	288
Official creditors	112	102	196	196	199	207	212	219
Private creditors	23	101	88	88	75	67	68	69
of which: Bonds	22	101	88	88	75	67	67	67
Private nonguaranteed	19	217	352	401	324	310	439	388
of which: Bonds	..	5	0	7	20	26	54	54
Net financial flows								
Net inflows	**-737**	**1,298**	**1,808**	**1,376**	**-45**	**3,028**	**3,032**	**3,016**
Net debt inflows	62	906	881	359	-1,102	2,133	2,080	1,345
Official creditors	80	-56	615	114	276	386	-67	934
of which: World Bank	38	1	260	20	2	154	-51	694
of which: IMF	..	..	..	..	..	..	..	..
Private creditors	-18	961	266	245	-1,379	1,746	2,147	411
Long-term	-52	1,124	-93	-435	192	1,727	2,101	441
Bonds	-31	0	0	-175	900	400	800	-5
Banks and other private	-22	1,125	-93	-260	-708	1,327	1,301	446
Short-term	34	-163	359	680	-1,570	19	46	-31
Net equity inflows	-799	392	926	1,018	1,058	895	952	1,671
Foreign direct investment	-799	392	907	968	1,026	880	958	1,706
Portfolio equity	..	..	19	49	32	16	-6	-34
Major economic aggregates								
Gross national income (GNI)	19,065	26,727	40,127	46,004	49,091	52,644	57,169	62,176
Exports of goods, services & prim. income	4,076	7,069	11,165	13,171	12,985	13,178	14,376	14,141
Imports of goods, services & prim. income	5,991	11,886	16,674	19,904	19,939	20,642	22,051	21,423
Primary income on FDI	248	370	1,001	1,453	1,112	986	1,324	1,355
Personal transfers & comp. of employees	596	3,067	4,232	4,524	5,031	5,379	5,838	6,587
International reserves	1,746	3,664	5,637	5,835	6,325	7,002	7,064	7,511
Ratios								
External debt stocks to exports (%)	96.9	134.5	134.7	123.6	116.5	131.0	134.2	142.7
External debt stocks to GNI (%)	20.7	35.6	37.5	35.4	30.8	32.8	33.7	32.5
Debt service to exports (%)	9.7	14.8	14.4	15.7	12.7	22.3	14.0	15.2
Short-term to external debt stocks (%)	29.7	15.3	10.5	13.9	4.6	4.1	3.9	3.6
Multilateral to external debt stocks (%)	38.5	21.5	28.2	26.9	30.8	29.0	25.0	26.2
Reserves to external debt stocks (%)	44.2	38.5	37.5	35.8	41.8	40.6	36.6	37.2

Notes: Long-term private nonguaranteed debt data are World Bank staff estimates based on reports provided by the country. Short-term debt before 2012 is based on data from the BIS.

GUINEA

(US$ million, unless otherwise indicated)

	2000	2005	2010	2011	2012	2013	2014	2015
Summary external debt data								
External debt stocks	**3,092**	**3,363**	**3,381**	**3,329**	**1,381**	**1,404**	**1,420**	**1,389**
Long-term external debt	2,650	3,078	3,045	3,069	1,053	1,044	1,017	930
Public and publicly guaranteed	2,650	3,078	3,045	3,069	1,053	1,044	1,017	930
Official creditors	2,621	2,887	2,913	2,954	955	956	950	880
of which: IMF	136	113	205	199	215	243	321	340
Private creditors	29	190	132	115	98	88	67	50
of which: Bonds	0	159	114	97	86	76	55	38
Private nonguaranteed	..	..	..	..	..	..	..	..
of which: Bonds	..	..	..	..	..	..	..	..
Short-term external debt	306	172	131	61	114	117	82	120
interest arrears on long-term	81	84	56	61	40	37	37	35
Long-term external debt								
Disbursements	**71**	**249**	**32**	**33**	**43**	**55**	**99**	**22**
Public and publicly guaranteed	71	249	32	33	43	55	99	22
Official creditors	71	247	32	33	43	55	99	22
Private creditors	0	1	0	0	0	0	0	0
of which: Bonds	0	0	0	0	0	0	0	0
Private nonguaranteed	..	..	..	..	..	..	..	..
of which: Bonds	..	..	..	..	..	..	..	..
Principal repayments	**91**	**97**	**65**	**154**	**108**	**69**	**63**	**58**
Public and publicly guaranteed	91	97	65	154	108	69	63	58
Official creditors	91	84	52	140	95	56	50	47
Private creditors	0	12	13	14	13	13	13	11
of which: Bonds	0	12	13	14	13	13	13	11
Private nonguaranteed	..	..	..	..	..	..	..	..
of which: Bonds	..	..	..	..	..	..	..	..
Interest payments	**41**	**50**	**21**	**36**	**21**	**13**	**12**	**10**
Public and publicly guaranteed	41	50	21	36	21	13	12	10
Official creditors	41	50	21	36	21	13	12	10
Private creditors	0	0	0	0	0	0	0	0
of which: Bonds	0	0	0	0	0	0	0	0
Private nonguaranteed	..	..	..	..	..	..	..	..
of which: Bonds	..	..	..	..	..	..	..	..
Net financial flows								
Net inflows	**-22**	**319**	**133**	**753**	**630**	**155**	**165**	**122**
Net debt inflows	-32	214	31	-202	25	20	97	37
Official creditors	-28	137	-30	-113	-36	27	145	8
of which: World Bank	17	22	0	-81	-30	9	39	-2
of which: IMF	-8	-26	-10	-6	16	28	96	33
Private creditors	-4	77	62	-89	61	-8	-48	29
Long-term	0	-11	-13	-14	-13	-13	-13	-11
Bonds	..	-12	-13	-14	-13	-13	-13	-11
Banks and other private	..	1	..	..	..	..	..	..
Short-term	-4	88	75	-75	74	6	-35	40
Net equity inflows	10	105	101	955	605	135	68	85
Foreign direct investment	10	105	101	955	605	135	68	85
Portfolio equity	..	..	..	..	..	..	..	..
Major economic aggregates								
Gross national income (GNI)	2,922	2,658	4,302	4,625	5,235	5,778	6,134	6,226
Exports of goods, services & prim. income	758	929	1,549	1,528	2,118	1,993	2,152	2,416
Imports of goods, services & prim. income	973	1,079	1,892	2,829	3,289	3,242	3,151	2,874
Primary income on FDI	8	..	0	26	39	47	..	..
Personal transfers & comp. of employees	1	42	46	65	66	93	93	93
International reserves	148	95	..	103	155	174	293	249
Ratios								
External debt stocks to exports (%)	408.1	362.0	218.4	217.9	65.2	70.5	66.0	57.5
External debt stocks to GNI (%)	105.8	126.5	78.6	72.0	26.4	24.3	23.1	22.3
Debt service to exports (%)	20.7	18.8	6.3	12.8	8.0	4.2	3.5	4.1
Short-term to external debt stocks (%)	9.9	5.1	3.9	1.8	8.2	8.3	5.8	8.6
Multilateral to external debt stocks (%)	52.1	53.3	55.1	57.5	44.6	44.7	45.7	43.9
Reserves to external debt stocks (%)	4.8	2.8	0.0	3.1	11.2	12.4	20.6	17.9

Notes: Short-term debt is based on data from the BIS. Data include the effects of Paris Club debt restructuring agreement signed in 2010, 2012 and HIPC debt relief.

GUINEA-BISSAU

(US$ million, unless otherwise indicated)

	2000	2005	2010	2011	2012	2013	2014	2015
Summary external debt data								
External debt stocks	**948.8**	**1,022.7**	**1,129.5**	**283.7**	**279.5**	**277.4**	**271.4**	**314.9**
Long-term external debt	822.1	888.8	978.2	218.5	213.4	212.2	203.2	223.8
Public and publicly guaranteed	822.1	888.8	978.2	218.5	213.4	212.2	203.2	223.8
Official creditors	822.1	888.8	978.2	218.5	213.4	212.2	203.2	223.8
of which: IMF	26.3	13.2	24.7	32.0	32.0	32.1	35.3	37.7
Private creditors	0.0	0.0	0.0	0.0	0.0	0.0	0.0	0.0
of which: Bonds	0.0	0.0	0.0	0.0	0.0	0.0	0.0	0.0
Private nonguaranteed	..	..	..	..	..	..	..	..
of which: Bonds	..	..	..	..	..	..	..	..
Short-term external debt	100.4	120.7	126.6	33.1	34.1	33.1	32.9	53.3
interest arrears on long-term	87.4	118.7	125.6	33.1	33.1	33.1	32.9	32.6
Long-term external debt								
Disbursements	**13.6**	**15.6**	**4.0**	**9.1**	**2.7**	**1.0**	**2.5**	**29.8**
Public and publicly guaranteed	13.6	15.6	4.0	9.1	2.7	1.0	2.5	29.8
Official creditors	13.6	15.6	4.0	9.1	2.7	1.0	2.5	29.8
Private creditors	0.0	0.0	0.0	0.0	0.0	0.0	0.0	0.0
of which: Bonds	0.0	0.0	0.0	0.0	0.0	0.0	0.0	0.0
Private nonguaranteed	..	..	..	..	..	..	..	..
of which: Bonds	..	..	..	..	..	..	..	..
Principal repayments	**2.6**	**1.0**	**5.9**	**4.5**	**6.3**	**1.1**	**1.4**	**1.4**
Public and publicly guaranteed	2.6	1.0	5.9	4.5	6.3	1.1	1.4	1.4
Official creditors	2.4	1.0	5.9	4.5	6.3	1.1	1.4	1.4
Private creditors	0.2	0.0	0.0	0.0	0.0	0.0	0.0	0.0
of which: Bonds	0.0	0.0	0.0	0.0	0.0	0.0	0.0	0.0
Private nonguaranteed	..	..	..	..	..	..	..	..
of which: Bonds	..	..	..	..	..	..	..	..
Interest payments	**1.6**	**2.0**	**3.3**	**0.5**	**0.6**	**0.4**	**0.5**	**0.8**
Public and publicly guaranteed	1.6	2.0	3.3	0.5	0.6	0.4	0.5	0.8
Official creditors	1.6	2.0	3.3	0.5	0.6	0.4	0.5	0.8
Private creditors	0.0	0.0	0.0	0.0	0.0	0.0	0.0	0.0
of which: Bonds	0.0	0.0	0.0	0.0	0.0	0.0	0.0	0.0
Private nonguaranteed	..	..	..	..	..	..	..	..
of which: Bonds	..	..	..	..	..	..	..	..
Net financial flows								
Net inflows	**30.1**	**16.4**	**28.7**	**36.2**	**4.0**	**18.6**	**35.3**	**71.4**
Net debt inflows	29.4	10.4	-0.3	11.2	-2.7	-1.1	6.4	53.0
Official creditors	19.6	11.4	5.8	12.2	-3.7	-0.1	6.4	32.4
of which: World Bank	11.3	10.6	-1.0	0.0	0.0	0.0	2.2	3.3
of which: IMF	8.4	-3.1	7.6	7.6	0.0	0.0	5.4	4.0
Private creditors	9.8	-1.0	-6.0	-1.0	1.0	-1.0	0.0	20.7
Long-term	-0.2	0.0	0.0	0.0	0.0	0.0	0.0	0.0
Bonds	..	..	..	..	..	..	..	..
Banks and other private	-0.2	..	..	..	..	..	..	..
Short-term	10.0	-1.0	-6.0	-1.0	1.0	-1.0	0.0	20.7
Net equity inflows	0.7	5.9	28.9	25.1	6.6	19.6	28.9	18.3
Foreign direct investment	0.7	5.9	26.2	25.0	6.6	19.6	28.9	18.3
Portfolio equity	..	..	2.7	0.0	..	..	..	..
Major economic aggregates								
Gross national income (GNI)	357.8	575.4	846.6	1,104.8	994.7	1,025.8	1,104.9	1,053.0
Exports of goods, services & prim. income	..	95.2	183.8	297.9	156.3	201.2	275.9	310.4
Imports of goods, services & prim. income	..	156.9	314.7	373.7	290.5	288.3	356.3	309.3
Primary income on FDI	..	..	5.7	31.8	31.2	8.2	..	..
Personal transfers & comp. of employees	8.0	19.9	45.9	52.1	45.6	63.8	63.8	63.8
International reserves	66.8	79.8	156.4	220.0	164.6	186.3	287.0	332.1
Ratios								
External debt stocks to exports (%)	..	1073.9	614.6	95.2	178.8	137.9	98.4	101.4
External debt stocks to GNI (%)	265.2	177.7	133.4	25.7	28.1	27.0	24.6	29.9
Debt service to exports (%)	..	6.7	9.5	1.7	4.4	0.8	0.7	0.8
Short-term to external debt stocks (%)	10.6	11.8	11.2	11.7	12.2	11.9	12.1	16.9
Multilateral to external debt stocks (%)	41.8	45.5	44.9	40.4	39.6	39.5	37.5	39.2
Reserves to external debt stocks (%)	7.0	7.8	13.8	77.6	58.9	67.1	105.7	105.5

Notes: Short-term debt is based on data from the BIS. Data include the effects of Paris Club debt restructuring agreement and HIPC and MDRI debt relief.

GUYANA

(US$ million, unless otherwise indicated)

	2000	2005	2010	2011	2012	2013	2014	2015
Summary external debt data								
External debt stocks	**1,374**	**1,239**	**1,408**	**2,007**	**1,974**	**2,302**	**2,343**	**1,639**
Long-term external debt	1,129	1,043	885	1,054	1,215	1,116	1,284	1,201
Public and publicly guaranteed	1,125	1,041	885	1,054	1,215	1,116	1,099	1,031
Official creditors	1,080	1,033	864	1,034	1,194	1,095	1,078	1,010
of which: IMF	136	112	190	182	171	160	140	125
Private creditors	45	9	21	21	21	21	21	21
of which: Bonds	27	0	0	0	0	0	0	0
Private nonguaranteed	4	2	0	0	0	0	185	170
of which: Bonds	..	..	..	..	..	..	..	..
Short-term external debt	109	84	333	770	588	1,026	919	313
interest arrears on long-term	67	82	103	107	111	111	108	108
Long-term external debt								
Disbursements	**64**	**104**	**123**	**188**	**279**	**200**	**355**	**74**
Public and publicly guaranteed	64	104	123	188	279	200	170	74
Official creditors	64	104	123	188	279	200	170	74
Private creditors	0	0	0	0	0	0	0	0
of which: Bonds	0	0	0	0	0	0	0	0
Private nonguaranteed	0	0	0	0	0	0	185	0
of which: Bonds	..	..	..	..	..	..	..	..
Principal repayments	**23**	**16**	**16**	**20**	**119**	**21**	**24**	**44**
Public and publicly guaranteed	22	15	16	20	119	21	24	29
Official creditors	22	15	16	20	119	21	24	29
Private creditors	0	0	0	0	0	0	0	0
of which: Bonds	0	0	0	0	0	0	0	0
Private nonguaranteed	0	0	0	0	0	0	0	15
of which: Bonds	..	..	..	..	..	..	..	..
Interest payments	**26**	**10**	**11**	**13**	**13**	**14**	**16**	**17**
Public and publicly guaranteed	26	10	11	13	13	14	16	17
Official creditors	26	10	11	13	13	14	16	17
Private creditors	0	0	0	0	0	0	0	0
of which: Bonds	0	0	0	0	0	0	0	0
Private nonguaranteed	0	0	0	0	0	0	0	0
of which: Bonds	..	..	..	..	..	..	..	..
Net financial flows								
Net inflows	**26**	**113**	**20**	**639**	**5**	**634**	**249**	**-566**
Net debt inflows	11	95	-19	593	-37	605	216	-585
Official creditors	34	108	106	160	149	168	135	36
of which: World Bank	2	1	0	1	1	2	2	7
of which: IMF	-7	20	-1	-7	-11	-11	-11	-9
Private creditors	-24	-13	-125	433	-186	438	82	-621
Long-term	0	-1	0	0	0	0	185	-15
Bonds	..	..	..	..	..	0	..	..
Banks and other private	0	-1	0	0	..	0	185	-15
Short-term	-23	-12	-125	433	-186	438	-103	-606
Net equity inflows	16	18	39	46	42	28	33	19
Foreign direct investment	16	18	39	46	42	28	33	19
Portfolio equity	..	..	..	..	..	..	..	..
Major economic aggregates								
Gross national income (GNI)	661	777	2,272	2,567	2,875	3,019	3,046	3,174
Exports of goods, services & prim. income	684	697	1,197	1,479	1,764	1,594	1,403	1,370
Imports of goods, services & prim. income	813	960	1,814	2,265	2,550	2,403	2,246	1,931
Primary income on FDI	6	7	13	18	10	5	5	6
Personal transfers & comp. of employees	27	201	368	412	469	328	330	294
International reserves	305	252	782	802	864	784	668	532
Ratios								
External debt stocks to exports (%)	201.0	177.8	117.6	135.7	111.9	144.5	167.0	119.6
External debt stocks to GNI (%)	208.1	159.5	62.0	78.2	68.7	76.3	76.9	51.6
Debt service to exports (%)	10.2	5.0	2.6	3.1	8.6	4.9	4.7	6.4
Short-term to external debt stocks (%)	8.0	6.8	23.7	38.4	29.8	44.6	39.2	19.1
Multilateral to external debt stocks (%)	43.7	68.7	35.6	27.5	30.7	28.7	29.0	42.0
Reserves to external debt stocks (%)	22.2	20.3	55.5	40.0	43.8	34.0	28.5	32.5

Notes: Long-term private nonguaranteed debt data for 2014 and 2015 are World Bank staff estimates based on market data. Short-term debt is based on data from the BIS. Principal payment shown from 2012 include rice for oil deal. Data include the effects of HIPC and MDRI debt relief.

HAITI

(US$ million, unless otherwise indicated)

	2000	2005	2010	2011	2012	2013	2014	2015
Summary external debt data								
External debt stocks	**1,203**	**1,347**	**957**	**771**	**1,156**	**1,559**	**1,940**	**2,084**
Long-term external debt	1,056	1,278	822	623	986	1,381	1,762	1,903
Public and publicly guaranteed	1,056	1,278	822	623	986	1,378	1,759	1,900
Official creditors	1,056	1,278	822	623	986	1,378	1,759	1,900
of which: IMF	57	41	135	148	169	178	177	178
Private creditors	0	0	0	0	0	0	0	0
of which: Bonds	0	0	0	0	0	0	0	0
Private nonguaranteed	..	..	..	..	..	3	3	3
of which: Bonds	..	..	..	..	..	..	..	..
Short-term external debt	90	28	0	0	0	0	1	4
interest arrears on long-term	1	15	0	0	0	0	1	4
Long-term external debt								
Disbursements	**51**	**77**	**288**	**357**	**360**	**401**	**408**	**173**
Public and publicly guaranteed	51	77	288	357	360	398	408	173
Official creditors	51	77	288	357	360	398	408	173
Private creditors	0	0	0	0	0	0	0	0
of which: Bonds	0	0	0	0	0	0	0	0
Private nonguaranteed	..	..	..	..	..	3	0	0
of which: Bonds	..	..	..	..	..	..	..	..
Principal repayments	**19**	**34**	**122**	**2**	**0**	**6**	**18**	**27**
Public and publicly guaranteed	19	34	122	2	0	6	18	27
Official creditors	19	34	122	2	0	6	18	27
Private creditors	0	0	0	0	0	0	0	0
of which: Bonds	0	0	0	0	0	0	0	0
Private nonguaranteed	..	..	..	..	..	0	0	0
of which: Bonds	..	..	..	..	..	..	..	..
Interest payments	**15**	**17**	**8**	**3**	**3**	**4**	**5**	**8**
Public and publicly guaranteed	15	17	8	3	3	4	5	7
Official creditors	15	17	8	3	3	4	5	7
Private creditors	0	0	0	0	0	0	0	0
of which: Bonds	0	0	0	0	0	0	0	0
Private nonguaranteed	..	..	..	..	..	0	0	0
of which: Bonds	..	..	..	..	..	..	..	..
Net financial flows								
Net inflows	**33**	**47**	**468**	**487**	**538**	**565**	**494**	**265**
Net debt inflows	20	21	290	368	382	405	395	156
Official creditors	26	55	290	368	382	402	395	156
of which: World Bank	1	-5	-36	..	..	..	..	..
of which: IMF	-6	11	125	13	22	10	5	10
Private creditors	-6	-34	..	..	..	3	0	0
Long-term	..	..	..	..	..	3	0	0
Bonds	..	..	..	..	..	..	..	..
Banks and other private	..	..	..	..	..	3	0	0
Short-term	-6	-34	0	0	0	0	0	0
Net equity inflows	13	26	178	119	156	160	99	109
Foreign direct investment	13	26	178	119	156	160	99	109
Portfolio equity	..	..	..	..	..	..	..	..
Major economic aggregates								
Gross national income (GNI)	..	4,387	6,645	7,555	7,945	8,485	8,789	8,887
Exports of goods, services & prim. income	504	605	1,049	1,356	1,400	1,612	1,684	1,777
Imports of goods, services & prim. income	1,378	1,888	4,298	4,437	4,199	4,433	4,777	4,449
Primary income on FDI	..	..	..	..	..	..	..	..
Personal transfers & comp. of employees	578	986	1,474	1,551	1,612	1,781	1,977	2,196
International reserves	182	218	1,891	1,880	2,164	2,448	1,965	1,916
Ratios								
External debt stocks to exports (%)	238.9	222.6	91.2	56.8	82.5	96.7	115.2	117.3
External debt stocks to GNI (%)	..	30.7	14.4	10.2	14.5	18.4	22.1	23.5
Debt service to exports (%)	9.2	9.5	12.5	0.4	0.3	0.7	1.4	2.0
Short-term to external debt stocks (%)	7.5	2.1	0.0	0.0	0.0	0.0	0.0	0.2
Multilateral to external debt stocks (%)	76.4	79.9	58.2	10.0	6.8	5.0	4.1	3.9
Reserves to external debt stocks (%)	15.1	16.2	197.7	243.9	187.2	157.0	101.3	91.9

Notes: Long-term private nonguaranteed debt data only cover IDB loans. Short-term debt before 2007 is based on data from the BIS. Data include the effects of Paris Club restructuring agreements signed in 2006 and 2009 and HIPC and MDRI debt relief.

HONDURAS

(US$ million, unless otherwise indicated)

	2000	2005	2010	2011	2012	2013	2014	2015
Summary external debt data								
External debt stocks	**5,614**	**5,170**	**3,977**	**4,388**	**5,055**	**6,831**	**7,329**	**7,584**
Long-term external debt	5,000	4,654	3,382	3,905	4,444	6,116	6,640	6,920
Public and publicly guaranteed	4,440	4,145	2,803	3,186	3,646	5,170	5,528	5,879
Official creditors	4,315	4,072	2,714	3,102	3,541	3,980	4,231	4,598
of which: IMF	241	195	220	215	209	203	185	173
Private creditors	125	73	89	85	106	1,190	1,297	1,280
of which: Bonds	0	0	50	50	50	1,051	1,051	1,051
Private nonguaranteed	560	509	579	719	798	946	1,112	1,042
of which: Bonds	..	..	..	..	..	..	..	..
Short-term external debt	374	321	374	267	402	512	504	491
interest arrears on long-term	35	12	11	6	6	4	3	3
Long-term external debt								
Disbursements	**347**	**481**	**904**	**1,554**	**1,348**	**2,444**	**898**	**1,453**
Public and publicly guaranteed	163	302	452	558	513	1,602	580	561
Official creditors	159	297	452	558	493	521	455	561
Private creditors	4	4	0	0	20	1,082	125	0
of which: Bonds	0	0	0	0	0	1,001	0	0
Private nonguaranteed	184	179	452	996	835	841	318	893
of which: Bonds	..	..	..	..	..	..	..	..
Principal repayments	**259**	**267**	**452**	**922**	**824**	**783**	**491**	**1,061**
Public and publicly guaranteed	93	141	62	65	58	82	110	139
Official creditors	92	139	60	62	58	81	107	135
Private creditors	1	2	2	3	1	1	3	4
of which: Bonds	0	0	0	0	0	0	0	0
Private nonguaranteed	166	126	390	856	766	701	381	922
of which: Bonds	..	..	..	..	..	..	..	..
Interest payments	**108**	**83**	**56**	**77**	**89**	**130**	**198**	**215**
Public and publicly guaranteed	77	64	46	59	70	111	178	193
Official creditors	77	62	45	58	70	81	92	101
Private creditors	0	1	1	1	0	30	86	91
of which: Bonds	0	0	0	0	0	29	82	82
Private nonguaranteed	31	20	10	19	19	19	20	22
of which: Bonds	..	..	..	..	..	..	..	..
Net financial flows								
Net inflows	**261**	**690**	**1,022**	**1,526**	**1,671**	**3,594**	**1,202**	**1,349**
Net debt inflows	41	153	575	526	652	1,768	392	375
Official creditors	84	158	391	491	429	434	342	422
of which: World Bank	9	73	109	133	77	87	91	68
of which: IMF	16	0	-2	-5	-6	-6	-6	-4
Private creditors	-42	-4	184	35	223	1,334	51	-46
Long-term	20	56	60	137	88	1,221	59	-34
Bonds	..	..	..	..	..	1,001	..	..
Banks and other private	20	56	60	137	88	220	59	-34
Short-term	-63	-61	124	-102	134	113	-8	-13
Net equity inflows	219	537	447	1,000	1,019	1,827	810	974
Foreign direct investment	219	537	469	958	1,006	820	789	974
Portfolio equity	..	..	-22	42	13	1,007	20	-1
Major economic aggregates								
Gross national income (GNI)	6,885	9,219	15,110	16,769	17,247	17,193	18,058	18,771
Exports of goods, services & prim. income	2,694	3,817	4,993	6,290	6,729	6,307	6,644	6,690
Imports of goods, services & prim. income	3,740	6,016	8,556	10,836	11,598	11,475	11,661	11,816
Primary income on FDI	160	479	681	910	1,192	1,208	1,129	1,183
Personal transfers & comp. of employees	474	1,805	2,618	2,811	2,920	3,098	3,370	3,666
International reserves	1,313	2,327	2,671	2,750	2,495	2,982	3,432	3,731
Ratios								
External debt stocks to exports (%)	208.4	135.5	79.6	69.8	75.1	108.3	110.3	113.4
External debt stocks to GNI (%)	81.5	56.1	26.3	26.2	29.3	39.7	40.6	40.4
Debt service to exports (%)	14.8	10.1	10.3	16.0	13.7	14.7	10.6	19.2
Short-term to external debt stocks (%)	6.7	6.2	9.4	6.1	7.9	7.5	6.9	6.5
Multilateral to external debt stocks (%)	49.6	61.7	47.7	53.2	54.5	47.3	48.2	49.8
Reserves to external debt stocks (%)	23.4	45.0	67.2	62.7	49.4	43.7	46.8	49.2

Notes: Data include the effects of HIPC and MDRI debt relief.

INDIA

(US$ million, unless otherwise indicated)

	2000	2005	2010	2011	2012	2013	2014	2015
Summary external debt data								
External debt stocks	**101,131**	**121,195**	**290,428**	**334,399**	**392,625**	**427,296**	**457,553**	**479,559**
Long-term external debt	96,782	111,406	227,853	250,240	293,162	328,464	366,215	392,483
Public and publicly guaranteed	81,196	54,726	100,563	107,926	133,206	133,380	161,829	175,718
Official creditors	51,730	50,058	72,499	75,601	75,304	73,698	71,700	71,683
of which: IMF	888	974	6,127	6,108	6,114	6,127	5,764	5,513
Private creditors	29,466	4,668	28,065	32,324	57,901	59,682	90,129	104,035
of which: Bonds	10,240	1,360	14,700	16,517	24,007	21,910	50,811	59,512
Private nonguaranteed	15,586	56,680	127,290	142,314	159,956	195,084	204,386	216,765
of which: Bonds	1,515	5,761	13,217	10,861	7,848	8,286	6,214	7,909
Short-term external debt	3,462	8,816	56,448	78,052	93,349	92,706	85,574	81,563
interest arrears on long-term	0	0	0	0	0	0	0	0
Long-term external debt								
Disbursements	**10,556**	**19,380**	**43,406**	**42,850**	**49,929**	**70,314**	**130,044**	**66,347**
Public and publicly guaranteed	10,256	6,630	24,337	13,642	17,269	14,108	47,038	27,219
Official creditors	3,270	3,824	8,379	6,599	5,170	5,253	6,226	6,026
Private creditors	6,986	2,805	15,958	7,043	12,099	8,855	40,812	21,193
of which: Bonds	5,520	1,714	11,050	2,032	7,478	2,045	29,116	8,702
Private nonguaranteed	300	12,751	19,069	29,207	32,661	56,206	83,006	39,129
of which: Bonds	..	2,920	1,288	737	665	1,224	819	2,770
Principal repayments	**6,425**	**19,384**	**19,018**	**22,227**	**21,202**	**28,931**	**80,774**	**37,406**
Public and publicly guaranteed	6,176	12,469	5,164	6,823	6,183	10,756	14,235	11,774
Official creditors	3,217	2,701	3,159	3,879	3,665	3,970	4,134	4,596
Private creditors	2,959	9,769	2,005	2,943	2,519	6,786	10,101	7,178
of which: Bonds	0	8,457	148	200	0	4,153	150	0
Private nonguaranteed	249	6,914	13,854	15,405	15,019	18,176	66,538	25,632
of which: Bonds	35	117	1,851	2,847	3,678	833	2,347	767
Interest payments	**3,993**	**4,196**	**4,675**	**6,206**	**7,774**	**8,629**	**10,970**	**9,815**
Public and publicly guaranteed	3,363	3,022	1,063	1,210	1,396	1,446	1,839	1,899
Official creditors	1,422	1,062	797	873	900	802	757	749
Private creditors	1,941	1,960	266	337	496	644	1,082	1,150
of which: Bonds	143	1,799	39	51	121	158	256	296
Private nonguaranteed	630	1,174	3,612	4,996	6,378	7,183	9,131	7,916
of which: Bonds	224	141	421	848	516	518	375	349
Net financial flows								
Net inflows	**9,700**	**21,369**	**92,032**	**72,821**	**90,006**	**87,344**	**86,109**	**66,525**
Net debt inflows	3,635	1,949	34,233	42,226	44,025	40,739	42,138	24,929
Official creditors	28	1,124	5,221	2,720	1,505	1,283	2,091	1,430
of which: World Bank	677	1,336	3,027	1,149	9	-30	543	262
of which: IMF	-25	0	0	0	0	0	0	0
Private creditors	3,607	825	29,013	39,506	42,520	39,456	40,047	23,500
Long-term	4,078	-1,127	19,168	17,902	27,223	40,099	47,179	27,511
Bonds	5,485	-3,940	10,339	-278	4,465	-1,717	27,437	10,705
Banks and other private	-1,407	2,813	8,829	18,180	22,758	41,816	19,741	16,806
Short-term	-471	1,952	9,845	21,604	15,297	-643	-7,132	-4,012
Net equity inflows	6,066	19,421	57,799	30,594	45,981	46,604	43,971	41,595
Foreign direct investment	3,584	7,269	27,357	34,643	23,172	26,713	31,602	39,663
Portfolio equity	2,481	12,151	30,442	-4,048	22,809	19,892	12,369	1,933
Major economic aggregates								
Gross national income (GNI)	471,633	828,316	1,690,504	1,799,897	1,803,547	1,840,087	2,018,326	2,049,502
Exports of goods, services & prim. income	62,453	160,228	357,996	456,523	453,744	479,503	498,220	443,164
Imports of goods, services & prim. income	80,489	194,154	464,622	579,253	610,650	593,441	591,134	529,774
Primary income on FDI	..	5,244	21,763	23,760	16,389	12,555	14,027	13,684
Personal transfers & comp. of employees	12,883	22,125	53,480	62,499	68,821	69,970	70,389	68,910
International reserves	37,902	131,924	275,277	271,285	270,587	276,493	303,455	334,311
Ratios								
External debt stocks to exports (%)	161.9	75.6	81.1	73.2	86.5	89.1	91.8	108.2
External debt stocks to GNI (%)	21.4	14.6	17.2	18.6	21.8	23.2	22.7	23.4
Debt service to exports (%)	17.1	14.9	6.8	6.4	6.7	8.1	18.5	10.9
Short-term to external debt stocks (%)	3.4	7.3	19.4	23.3	23.8	21.7	18.7	17.0
Multilateral to external debt stocks (%)	30.1	25.9	16.0	14.6	12.8	11.9	11.1	10.5
Reserves to external debt stocks (%)	37.5	108.9	94.8	81.1	68.9	64.7	66.3	69.7

Notes: External debt data prior to 2003 are revised from fiscal year to calendar year. Long-term public and publicly guaranteed bonds include Foreign Institutional Investor debt (FII) as reported by the Reserve Bank of India.

INDONESIA

(US$ million, unless otherwise indicated)

	2000	2005	2010	2011	2012	2013	2014	2015
Summary external debt data								
External debt stocks	**144,032**	**142,120**	**198,268**	**219,619**	**252,555**	**265,453**	**292,969**	**308,540**
Long-term external debt	111,195	122,949	162,171	178,405	205,258	216,293	244,140	266,903
Public and publicly guaranteed	70,025	77,705	103,387	108,786	128,044	128,832	142,818	160,038
Official creditors	55,259	59,945	66,486	66,502	61,518	55,865	50,858	50,977
of which: IMF	11,149	8,148	3,050	3,041	3,044	3,050	2,869	2,744
Private creditors	14,766	17,760	36,901	42,283	66,526	72,967	91,960	109,060
of which: Bonds	971	7,492	29,348	35,501	60,551	67,179	82,967	97,134
Private nonguaranteed	41,169	45,244	58,783	69,620	77,214	87,461	101,322	106,866
of which: Bonds	6,337	7,858	7,787	14,112	9,337	11,117	12,617	15,671
Short-term external debt	21,688	11,023	33,047	38,173	44,253	46,110	45,960	38,892
interest arrears on long-term	4,632	0	0	0	0	0	0	0
Long-term external debt								
Disbursements	**6,057**	**13,881**	**34,335**	**39,430**	**55,702**	**50,567**	**69,894**	**60,090**
Public and publicly guaranteed	3,707	5,015	14,345	9,820	18,942	13,330	28,092	20,418
Official creditors	3,444	2,581	6,587	3,782	3,202	3,883	3,188	5,219
Private creditors	263	2,434	7,758	6,038	15,740	9,447	24,904	15,199
of which: Bonds	0	2,095	5,640	5,775	15,536	8,647	20,550	9,718
Private nonguaranteed	2,350	8,866	19,990	29,609	36,761	37,237	41,802	39,673
of which: Bonds	350	194	195	295	1,470	2,590	1,215	1,179
Principal repayments	**9,297**	**15,746**	**23,975**	**25,164**	**29,527**	**32,041**	**37,558**	**45,163**
Public and publicly guaranteed	3,897	6,232	5,846	6,132	6,430	5,964	8,617	9,029
Official creditors	1,615	3,539	5,214	5,156	5,152	4,925	4,999	4,600
Private creditors	2,282	2,692	632	976	1,278	1,039	3,618	4,429
of which: Bonds	0	310	0	0	230	0	2,745	2,095
Private nonguaranteed	5,400	9,515	18,129	19,032	23,097	26,077	28,941	36,134
of which: Bonds	2,400	267	411	1,771	1,560	510	715	130
Interest payments	**5,702**	**2,957**	**4,944**	**5,532**	**5,951**	**7,967**	**8,253**	**9,769**
Public and publicly guaranteed	3,767	1,945	3,034	3,485	3,475	3,966	4,487	5,248
Official creditors	2,604	1,189	1,586	1,508	1,376	1,169	1,301	909
Private creditors	1,163	755	1,448	1,977	2,098	2,796	3,186	4,339
of which: Bonds	72	159	1,225	1,655	1,811	2,549	2,948	4,107
Private nonguaranteed	1,935	1,012	1,910	2,048	2,477	4,001	3,766	4,521
of which: Bonds	735	113	81	1,145	1,104	1,083	1,185	1,211
Net financial flows								
Net inflows	**-1,720**	**1,036**	**33,936**	**35,343**	**52,568**	**38,530**	**57,738**	**21,821**
Net debt inflows	-1,590	-6,611	19,358	19,391	32,256	20,382	32,186	7,860
Official creditors	2,951	-2,103	1,373	-1,374	-1,950	-1,042	-1,811	618
of which: World Bank	323	-765	1,287	633	672	764	733	2,059
of which: IMF	1,123	-1,145	0	0	0	0	0	0
Private creditors	-4,542	-4,508	17,985	20,765	34,205	21,424	33,996	7,241
Long-term	-5,069	-906	8,987	15,639	28,125	19,567	34,147	14,309
Bonds	-2,050	1,711	5,424	4,299	15,216	10,727	18,306	8,672
Banks and other private	-3,019	-2,617	3,563	11,340	12,909	8,840	15,841	5,637
Short-term	527	-3,602	8,998	5,126	6,080	1,857	-150	-7,068
Net equity inflows	-129	7,647	14,578	15,952	20,312	18,148	25,553	13,961
Foreign direct investment	892	7,812	12,447	16,278	18,615	20,004	22,293	15,508
Portfolio equity	-1,021	-165	2,132	-326	1,698	-1,856	3,259	-1,547
Major economic aggregates								
Gross national income (GNI)	150,317	271,958	734,396	866,422	891,242	885,469	860,795	833,906
Exports of goods, services & prim. income	73,079	97,017	168,570	215,578	213,656	207,635	200,953	173,420
Imports of goods, services & prim. income	66,903	101,533	168,056	218,103	242,168	240,922	233,683	196,625
Primary income on FDI	3,574	9,525	12,844	17,975	18,166	17,395	19,460	18,231
Personal transfers & comp. of employees	1,190	5,420	6,916	6,924	7,212	7,614	8,551	9,659
International reserves	28,502	33,140	92,908	106,539	108,837	96,364	108,836	103,268
Ratios								
External debt stocks to exports (%)	197.1	146.5	117.6	101.9	118.2	127.8	145.8	177.9
External debt stocks to GNI (%)	95.8	52.3	27.0	25.3	28.3	30.0	34.0	37.0
Debt service to exports (%)	22.8	20.9	17.4	14.4	16.8	19.5	23.1	32.1
Short-term to external debt stocks (%)	15.1	7.8	16.7	17.4	17.5	17.4	15.7	12.6
Multilateral to external debt stocks (%)	13.8	13.0	11.4	10.4	9.1	8.6	7.8	8.2
Reserves to external debt stocks (%)	19.8	23.3	46.9	48.5	43.1	36.3	37.1	33.5

IRAN, ISLAMIC REPUBLIC OF

(US$ million, unless otherwise indicated)

	2000	2005	2010	2011	2012	2013	2014	2015
Summary external debt data								
External debt stocks	**8,024**	**21,543**	**20,030**	**17,344**	**7,406**	**7,006**	**5,441**	**6,322**
Long-term external debt	4,709	10,506	6,156	4,814	4,271	4,025	3,042	2,326
Public and publicly guaranteed	4,709	10,506	6,156	4,814	4,271	4,025	3,042	2,326
Official creditors	1,664	2,121	2,066	1,672	1,484	1,193	921	636
of which: IMF	308	352	2,261	2,209	2,192	2,204	1,967	1,976
Private creditors	3,045	8,384	4,090	3,142	2,787	2,832	2,121	1,691
of which: Bonds	0	0	0	0	0	0	0	0
Private nonguaranteed	..	..	..	..	..	..	..	..
of which: Bonds	..	..	..	..	..	..	..	..
Short-term external debt	3,008	10,686	11,613	10,320	943	777	432	2,019
interest arrears on long-term	0	0	0	0	0	0	0	0
Long-term external debt								
Disbursements	**1,469**	**2,740**	**252**	**216**	**18**	**22**	**0**	**2**
Public and publicly guaranteed	1,469	2,740	252	216	18	22	0	2
Official creditors	477	703	105	31	15	18	0	2
Private creditors	993	2,037	147	185	3	4	0	0
of which: Bonds	0	0	0	0	0	0	0	0
Private nonguaranteed	..	..	..	..	..	..	..	..
of which: Bonds	..	..	..	..	..	..	..	..
Principal repayments	**2,345**	**1,734**	**1,575**	**1,389**	**446**	**396**	**463**	**742**
Public and publicly guaranteed	2,345	1,734	1,575	1,389	446	396	463	742
Official creditors	1,785	329	331	429	188	272	238	287
Private creditors	561	1,405	1,245	960	258	124	224	455
of which: Bonds	0	0	0	0	0	0	0	0
Private nonguaranteed	..	..	..	..	..	..	..	..
of which: Bonds	..	..	..	..	..	..	..	..
Interest payments	**391**	**418**	**139**	**110**	**35**	**33**	**33**	**39**
Public and publicly guaranteed	391	418	139	110	35	33	33	39
Official creditors	190	104	54	47	17	25	26	14
Private creditors	202	314	85	63	18	8	7	25
of which: Bonds	0	0	0	0	0	0	0	0
Private nonguaranteed	..	..	..	..	..	..	..	..
of which: Bonds	..	..	..	..	..	..	..	..
Net financial flows								
Net inflows	**-1,446**	**4,329**	**5,151**	**1,810**	**-5,143**	**2,510**	**1,298**	**2,897**
Net debt inflows	-1,485	1,440	1,502	-2,466	-9,805	-540	-808	847
Official creditors	-1,308	374	-225	-399	-173	-255	-238	-285
of which: World Bank	44	102	64	-62	-37	-124	-96	-55
of which: IMF	0	0	0	0	0	0	0	0
Private creditors	-177	1,066	1,728	-2,068	-9,632	-286	-569	1,132
Long-term	432	633	-1,098	-775	-255	-120	-224	-455
Bonds	..	..	..	..	..	..	..	..
Banks and other private	432	633	-1,098	-775	-255	-120	-224	-455
Short-term	-609	433	2,826	-1,293	-9,377	-166	-345	1,587
Net equity inflows	39	2,889	3,649	4,277	4,662	3,050	2,105	2,050
Foreign direct investment	39	2,889	3,649	4,277	4,662	3,050	2,105	2,050
Portfolio equity	..	..	..	..	..	..	..	..
Major economic aggregates								
Gross national income (GNI)	109,482	219,436	467,870	592,134	588,882	512,851	426,269	..
Exports of goods, services & prim. income	30,131	50,757	98,191	123,593	156,380	108,880	104,416	98,356
Imports of goods, services & prim. income	18,107	50,115	88,815	96,224	98,279	85,966	78,518	83,006
Primary income on FDI	..	..	..	..	..	..	..	..
Personal transfers & comp. of employees	536	1,032	1,181	727	846	882	865	872
International reserves	..	..	..	..	..	..	..	..
Ratios								
External debt stocks to exports (%)	26.6	42.4	20.4	14.0	4.7	6.4	5.2	6.4
External debt stocks to GNI (%)	7.3	9.8	4.3	2.9	1.3	1.4	1.3	..
Debt service to exports (%)	9.7	5.5	1.9	1.3	0.4	0.4	0.5	0.8
Short-term to external debt stocks (%)	37.5	49.6	58.0	59.5	12.7	11.1	7.9	31.9
Multilateral to external debt stocks (%)	6.3	1.8	4.2	4.4	9.6	8.6	9.1	7.0
Reserves to external debt stocks (%)	..	..	..	..	..	..	..	..

Notes: Fiscal year-end for external debt data is March. Short-term debt is based on Central Bank data.

JAMAICA

(US$ million, unless otherwise indicated)

	2000	2005	2010	2011	2012	2013	2014	2015
Summary external debt data								
External debt stocks	**4,828**	**6,627**	**14,193**	**14,332**	**14,309**	**12,951**	**14,078**	**14,122**
Long-term external debt	3,922	5,953	11,916	12,111	11,309	10,272	11,563	11,608
Public and publicly guaranteed	3,819	5,563	7,609	7,768	7,399	7,452	7,992	9,649
Official creditors	2,492	2,150	3,271	3,225	3,197	3,349	3,437	3,594
of which: IMF	113	58	1,188	1,234	1,235	1,239	1,046	1,025
Private creditors	1,327	3,413	4,338	4,543	4,202	4,103	4,555	6,055
of which: Bonds	1,004	3,043	3,786	4,027	3,724	3,686	4,181	5,750
Private nonguaranteed	103	390	4,307	4,343	3,910	2,820	3,571	1,959
of which: Bonds	..	300	4,290	4,290	3,840	2,750	2,750	1,175
Short-term external debt	793	616	1,089	988	1,765	1,440	1,469	1,489
interest arrears on long-term	150	224	214	197	126	40	47	24
Long-term external debt								
Disbursements	**905**	**1,350**	**2,360**	**1,208**	**2,047**	**1,411**	**1,920**	**3,325**
Public and publicly guaranteed	905	1,043	1,285	1,170	279	410	1,167	2,397
Official creditors	312	91	1,075	418	239	384	316	369
Private creditors	593	953	210	753	40	26	851	2,028
of which: Bonds	553	875	0	694	0	0	800	2,000
Private nonguaranteed	0	307	1,075	37	1,768	1,001	752	928
of which: Bonds	..	300	1,075	0	1,750	1,000	0	925
Principal repayments	**426**	**552**	**346**	**728**	**1,083**	**359**	**509**	**3,238**
Public and publicly guaranteed	362	543	337	726	633	358	507	698
Official creditors	275	233	212	199	249	235	195	188
Private creditors	87	311	125	527	384	123	312	511
of which: Bonds	13	256	68	438	302	48	238	431
Private nonguaranteed	64	9	9	2	451	1	1	2,539
of which: Bonds	55	0	0	0	450	0	0	2,500
Interest payments	**209**	**387**	**829**	**900**	**690**	**562**	**612**	**666**
Public and publicly guaranteed	196	361	489	492	462	416	406	427
Official creditors	121	84	100	109	68	69	68	67
Private creditors	75	277	388	383	394	347	338	359
of which: Bonds	50	265	375	368	379	333	325	344
Private nonguaranteed	13	26	341	408	228	146	206	239
of which: Bonds	2	21	340	406	226	141	201	232
Net financial flows								
Net inflows	**829**	**978**	**3,326**	**645**	**2,303**	**1,393**	**2,002**	**1,044**
Net debt inflows	439	319	3,143	446	1,812	814	1,307	154
Official creditors	18	-143	1,641	269	-10	151	-6	206
of which: World Bank	37	-22	181	90	-10	120	-23	74
of which: IMF	-19	-1	778	50	0	2	-126	25
Private creditors	421	461	1,501	177	1,821	663	1,313	-52
Long-term	443	940	1,151	261	973	903	1,290	-94
Bonds	485	919	1,007	256	998	952	562	-6
Banks and other private	-43	22	145	5	-24	-49	729	-88
Short-term	-21	-479	350	-84	848	-240	23	42
Net equity inflows	390	660	183	199	492	579	695	890
Foreign direct investment	390	660	183	199	413	593	554	794
Portfolio equity	..	..	..	..	78	-14	141	95
Major economic aggregates								
Gross national income (GNI)	8,586	10,530	12,704	13,938	14,633	14,007	13,641	13,693
Exports of goods, services & prim. income	3,782	4,322	4,248	4,508	4,835	4,608	4,692	4,631
Imports of goods, services & prim. income	4,970	6,972	7,192	8,567	8,362	8,123	8,042	7,332
Primary income on FDI	290	454	127	112	121	138	161	253
Personal transfers & comp. of employees	878	1,762	2,026	2,106	2,168	2,172	2,269	2,361
International reserves	1,054	2,170	2,501	2,282	1,996	1,818	2,473	2,914
Ratios								
External debt stocks to exports (%)	127.7	153.3	334.2	317.9	296.0	281.0	300.0	305.0
External debt stocks to GNI (%)	56.2	62.9	111.7	102.8	97.8	92.5	103.2	103.1
Debt service to exports (%)	18.8	22.5	28.0	36.7	37.4	26.4	33.2	87.8
Short-term to external debt stocks (%)	16.4	9.3	7.7	6.9	12.3	11.1	10.4	10.5
Multilateral to external debt stocks (%)	25.6	20.3	16.6	17.6	17.3	20.0	19.1	20.3
Reserves to external debt stocks (%)	21.8	32.7	17.6	15.9	14.0	14.0	17.6	20.6

Notes: Short-term debt is based on data from the BIS.

JORDAN

(US$ million, unless otherwise indicated)

	2000	2005	2010	2011	2012	2013	2014	2015
Summary external debt data								
External debt stocks	**11,063**	**12,904**	**17,073**	**17,669**	**18,484**	**23,173**	**24,281**	**25,746**
Long-term external debt	6,183	6,901	7,767	7,818	8,105	11,000	11,800	13,070
Public and publicly guaranteed	6,183	6,878	6,502	6,317	6,302	8,855	9,688	10,976
Official creditors	5,243	6,483	5,452	5,291	5,308	5,494	5,352	5,424
of which: IMF	484	260	257	257	642	1,300	1,593	2,070
Private creditors	940	395	1,050	1,026	994	3,361	4,335	5,552
of which: Bonds	583	145	881	866	852	3,237	4,223	5,458
Private nonguaranteed	..	24	1,265	1,501	1,803	2,145	2,113	2,094
of which: Bonds	..	..	..	..	..	..	..	..
Short-term external debt	4,396	5,742	9,049	9,594	9,737	10,873	10,888	10,605
interest arrears on long-term	102	0	1	1	1	1	1	1
Long-term external debt								
Disbursements	**176**	**434**	**1,538**	**475**	**1,010**	**3,644**	**2,275**	**3,210**
Public and publicly guaranteed	176	434	1,388	325	711	3,308	1,978	2,951
Official creditors	176	269	626	325	711	908	978	951
Private creditors	0	165	762	0	0	2,400	1,000	2,000
of which: Bonds	0	145	750	0	0	2,400	1,000	2,000
Private nonguaranteed	..	..	150	150	299	336	297	258
of which: Bonds	..	..	..	..	..	..	..	..
Principal repayments	**308**	**366**	**513**	**599**	**615**	**606**	**910**	**1,594**
Public and publicly guaranteed	308	341	487	574	585	566	873	1,537
Official creditors	238	323	463	548	557	538	852	754
Private creditors	70	19	25	26	28	28	22	783
of which: Bonds	10	10	15	15	15	15	15	765
Private nonguaranteed	..	25	26	25	30	40	37	57
of which: Bonds	..	..	..	..	..	..	..	..
Interest payments	**239**	**161**	**163**	**194**	**189**	**189**	**280**	**312**
Public and publicly guaranteed	239	160	147	171	165	162	254	282
Official creditors	162	157	124	130	126	113	124	114
Private creditors	77	4	22	41	39	49	130	168
of which: Bonds	43	0	19	39	37	48	129	167
Private nonguaranteed	..	1	16	23	24	27	26	30
of which: Bonds	..	..	..	..	..	..	..	..
Net financial flows								
Net inflows	**4,268**	**2,479**	**3,219**	**2,016**	**2,487**	**6,788**	**3,746**	**3,175**
Net debt inflows	3,371	325	1,551	421	921	4,824	1,768	1,886
Official creditors	-73	-131	159	-223	537	1,020	515	749
of which: World Bank	-17	-28	-71	-85	165	28	252	156
of which: IMF	-11	-77	-4	0	383	650	389	552
Private creditors	3,445	456	1,392	644	384	3,804	1,253	1,137
Long-term	-70	121	862	99	241	2,667	1,239	1,419
Bonds	-10	135	736	-15	-15	2,386	986	1,236
Banks and other private	-60	-14	126	113	255	282	253	183
Short-term	3,515	335	530	545	143	1,136	14	-282
Net equity inflows	896	2,154	1,668	1,595	1,566	1,964	1,978	1,289
Foreign direct investment	913	1,984	1,688	1,486	1,513	1,806	2,009	1,275
Portfolio equity	-17	169	-21	109	53	158	-31	15
Major economic aggregates								
Gross national income (GNI)	8,558	12,925	26,218	28,576	30,549	33,255	35,410	37,040
Exports of goods, services & prim. income	4,207	7,426	13,639	14,454	14,998	15,021	16,405	14,872
Imports of goods, services & prim. income	6,363	12,314	19,343	22,276	24,054	25,304	26,282	23,761
Primary income on FDI	32	72	813	713	821	845	903	794
Personal transfers & comp. of employees	1,845	2,421	3,623	3,684	3,848	5,343	6,370	5,348
International reserves	3,331	5,250	13,057	11,467	8,090	13,224	15,299	15,162
Ratios								
External debt stocks to exports (%)	263.0	173.8	125.2	122.2	123.2	154.3	148.0	173.1
External debt stocks to GNI (%)	129.3	99.8	65.1	61.8	60.5	69.7	68.6	69.5
Debt service to exports (%)	20.1	11.9	5.9	6.6	6.3	6.2	8.2	14.3
Short-term to external debt stocks (%)	39.7	44.5	53.0	54.3	52.7	46.9	44.8	41.2
Multilateral to external debt stocks (%)	15.4	14.8	14.8	13.6	13.8	12.7	12.4	11.6
Reserves to external debt stocks (%)	30.1	40.7	76.5	64.9	43.8	57.1	63.0	58.9

Notes: Long-term private nonguaranteed debt data from 2001 are based on reports provided by the country. Short-term debt before 1999 is based on data from the BIS.

KAZAKHSTAN

(US$ million, unless otherwise indicated)

	2000	2005	2010	2011	2012	2013	2014	2015
Summary external debt data								
External debt stocks	**12,890**	**43,857**	**119,145**	**124,317**	**135,498**	**149,653**	**157,651**	**154,288**
Long-term external debt	11,481	35,263	109,751	115,033	125,883	139,627	147,372	147,363
Public and publicly guaranteed	3,623	2,177	3,845	4,675	7,375	12,266	15,080	20,070
Official creditors	2,239	1,780	3,845	4,675	5,065	5,331	5,645	6,635
of which: IMF	448	491	529	528	528	529	498	476
Private creditors	1,384	396	0	0	2,310	6,935	9,435	13,435
of which: Bonds	1,000	350	0	0	2,300	6,925	9,425	13,425
Private nonguaranteed	7,859	33,087	105,905	110,358	118,508	127,361	132,292	127,293
of which: Bonds	100	7,550	21,044	17,995	15,098	11,790	13,682	6,683
Short-term external debt	961	8,102	8,864	8,756	9,086	9,497	9,781	6,448
interest arrears on long-term	0	0	0	0	0	0	67	0
Long-term external debt								
Disbursements	**3,063**	**17,207**	**45,054**	**32,740**	**31,396**	**45,774**	**39,152**	**34,731**
Public and publicly guaranteed	623	197	1,522	920	3,050	5,445	3,376	5,511
Official creditors	168	197	1,522	920	740	820	876	1,511
Private creditors	455	0	0	0	2,310	4,625	2,500	4,000
of which: Bonds	350	0	0	0	2,300	4,625	2,500	4,000
Private nonguaranteed	2,440	17,010	43,532	31,821	28,346	40,329	35,776	29,220
of which: Bonds	0	3,050	450	800	560	6,684	6,692	1,712
Principal repayments	**2,155**	**11,417**	**34,639**	**26,226**	**20,862**	**28,341**	**27,854**	**31,266**
Public and publicly guaranteed	216	1,090	278	134	254	409	459	326
Official creditors	133	1,018	278	134	254	409	459	326
Private creditors	83	72	1	0	0	0	0	0
of which: Bonds	0	0	0	0	0	0	0	0
Private nonguaranteed	1,939	10,327	34,360	26,092	20,607	27,932	27,395	30,940
of which: Bonds	0	0	1,503	3,789	3,457	4,210	3,092	8,709
Interest payments	**713**	**1,521**	**4,517**	**5,921**	**2,033**	**2,257**	**2,980**	**3,467**
Public and publicly guaranteed	235	146	54	61	75	147	405	525
Official creditors	124	102	54	61	75	68	57	61
Private creditors	112	44	0	0	0	79	348	464
of which: Bonds	90	39	0	0	0	78	347	463
Private nonguaranteed	478	1,376	4,463	5,860	1,957	2,110	2,575	2,942
of which: Bonds	11	543	1,525	1,343	1,115	655	1,115	1,578
Net financial flows								
Net inflows	**1,827**	**10,336**	**16,591**	**12,320**	**17,563**	**22,727**	**16,040**	**2,172**
Net debt inflows	1,061	9,950	12,295	6,406	10,865	17,844	11,516	199
Official creditors	-407	-820	1,244	786	486	411	417	1,184
of which: World Bank	30	-621	1,283	478	333	456	332	-32
of which: IMF	-442	0	0	0	0	0	0	0
Private creditors	1,469	10,770	11,050	5,620	10,379	17,432	11,099	-986
Long-term	873	6,610	9,171	5,729	10,048	17,022	10,881	2,280
Bonds	350	3,050	-1,053	-2,989	-597	7,100	6,101	-2,998
Banks and other private	523	3,560	10,224	8,717	10,645	9,922	4,780	5,278
Short-term	595	4,160	1,879	-109	331	410	218	-3,266
Net equity inflows	766	386	4,296	5,914	6,698	4,883	4,524	1,973
Foreign direct investment	746	237	4,162	5,907	7,117	4,818	4,659	1,967
Portfolio equity	19	150	134	8	-418	65	-135	6
Major economic aggregates								
Gross national income (GNI)	17,038	51,757	128,676	172,656	187,763	218,608	204,769	172,845
Exports of goods, services & prim. income	10,480	31,380	68,212	91,764	93,849	93,214	88,961	54,915
Imports of goods, services & prim. income	10,363	32,008	66,337	81,300	91,751	90,730	81,672	58,799
Primary income on FDI	1,046	4,805	17,997	25,213	24,753	22,511	19,764	8,772
Personal transfers & comp. of employees	67	62	226	180	178	207	229	194
International reserves	1,594	6,084	25,223	25,179	22,132	19,127	21,814	20,299
Ratios								
External debt stocks to exports (%)	123.0	139.8	174.7	135.5	144.4	160.5	177.2	281.0
External debt stocks to GNI (%)	75.7	84.7	92.6	72.0	72.2	68.5	77.0	89.3
Debt service to exports (%)	32.4	41.9	57.9	35.4	24.7	33.2	35.0	63.6
Short-term to external debt stocks (%)	7.5	18.5	7.4	7.0	6.7	6.3	6.2	4.2
Multilateral to external debt stocks (%)	11.5	2.0	2.3	2.9	3.1	3.1	3.2	3.9
Reserves to external debt stocks (%)	12.4	13.9	21.2	20.3	16.3	12.8	13.8	13.2

KENYA

(US$ million, unless otherwise indicated)

	2000	2005	2010	2011	2012	2013	2014	2015
Summary external debt data								
External debt stocks	**6,148**	**6,487**	**8,848**	**10,163**	**11,894**	**13,721**	**16,683**	**19,148**
Long-term external debt	5,217	5,785	6,989	7,771	9,024	9,830	13,355	15,324
Public and publicly guaranteed	5,042	5,785	6,989	7,771	9,024	9,830	13,355	15,324
Official creditors	4,560	5,422	6,679	7,451	8,086	8,885	10,301	11,559
of which: IMF	175	212	817	1,100	1,293	1,471	1,328	1,205
Private creditors	482	363	311	320	938	946	3,053	3,766
of which: Bonds	0	0	0	0	0	0	2,750	2,750
Private nonguaranteed	175	..	..	..	..	..	..	..
of which: Bonds	..	..	..	..	..	..	..	..
Short-term external debt	757	490	1,041	1,293	1,577	2,420	2,001	2,619
interest arrears on long-term	47	21	80	100	93	111	84	89
Long-term external debt								
Disbursements	**333**	**169**	**530**	**1,073**	**1,682**	**1,235**	**5,142**	**2,748**
Public and publicly guaranteed	333	169	530	1,073	1,682	1,235	5,142	2,748
Official creditors	248	140	519	1,050	1,005	1,221	2,386	1,994
Private creditors	85	28	12	23	677	14	2,756	754
of which: Bonds	0	0	0	0	0	0	2,750	0
Private nonguaranteed	..	..	..	..	..	..	..	..
of which: Bonds	..	..	..	..	..	..	..	..
Principal repayments	**407**	**439**	**260**	**290**	**357**	**338**	**949**	**349**
Public and publicly guaranteed	362	429	260	290	357	338	949	349
Official creditors	241	356	256	283	347	321	330	329
Private creditors	121	74	4	7	10	17	619	20
of which: Bonds	0	0	0	0	0	0	0	0
Private nonguaranteed	45	10	..	..	..	..	..	..
of which: Bonds	..	..	..	..	..	..	..	..
Interest payments	**100**	**73**	**90**	**93**	**171**	**225**	**197**	**276**
Public and publicly guaranteed	81	73	90	93	171	225	197	276
Official creditors	55	67	90	92	144	189	168	210
Private creditors	27	6	1	1	26	36	29	66
of which: Bonds	0	0	0	0	0	0	0	44
Private nonguaranteed	19	0	..	..	..	..	..	..
of which: Bonds	..	..	..	..	..	..	..	..
Net financial flows								
Net inflows	**5**	**-386**	**430**	**1,368**	**1,881**	**2,226**	**5,164**	**4,393**
Net debt inflows	-72	-394	318	1,309	1,807	1,895	3,743	2,946
Official creditors	9	-149	237	1,060	848	1,074	1,997	1,600
of which: World Bank	101	-21	132	165	193	383	475	366
of which: IMF	2	67	-26	293	191	174	-59	-66
Private creditors	-81	-246	81	249	958	821	1,746	1,347
Long-term	-81	-56	8	17	668	-4	2,137	734
Bonds	..	..	..	..	..	..	2,750	..
Banks and other private	-81	-56	8	17	668	-4	-613	734
Short-term	0	-190	73	232	291	825	-391	612
Net equity inflows	77	9	111	60	75	331	1,421	1,446
Foreign direct investment	83	6	89	40	49	71	467	1,437
Portfolio equity	-6	3	22	20	26	260	954	9
Major economic aggregates								
Gross national income (GNI)	12,576	18,732	39,852	41,960	50,263	54,792	60,990	62,953
Exports of goods, services & prim. income	2,821	5,416	9,127	10,130	11,205	10,951	11,290	10,790
Imports of goods, services & prim. income	3,941	6,921	13,823	16,631	18,270	18,959	21,407	18,547
Primary income on FDI	29	35	60	105	111	124	214	..
Personal transfers & comp. of employees	538	425	686	934	1,211	1,304	1,441	1,560
International reserves	898	1,799	4,320	4,264	5,711	6,598	7,911	7,548
Ratios								
External debt stocks to exports (%)	218.0	119.8	96.9	100.3	106.1	125.3	147.8	177.5
External debt stocks to GNI (%)	48.9	34.6	22.2	24.2	23.7	25.0	27.4	30.4
Debt service to exports (%)	21.0	10.0	4.4	4.3	5.3	5.9	10.9	6.8
Short-term to external debt stocks (%)	12.3	7.6	11.8	12.7	13.3	17.6	12.0	13.7
Multilateral to external debt stocks (%)	46.1	53.0	46.6	45.4	43.0	42.4	37.3	35.2
Reserves to external debt stocks (%)	14.6	27.7	48.8	42.0	48.0	48.1	47.4	39.4

Notes: Short-term debt is based on data from the BIS.

KOSOVO

(US$ million, unless otherwise indicated)

	2000	2005	2010	2011	2012	2013	2014	2015
Summary external debt data								
External debt stocks	..	..	**1,456**	**1,700**	**2,002**	**2,221**	**2,242**	**2,158**
Long-term external debt	..	..	886	1,130	1,116	1,315	1,258	1,263
Public and publicly guaranteed	..	..	319	299	295	300	273	265
Official creditors	..	..	319	299	295	300	271	246
of which: IMF	..	..	114	114	234	231	204	216
Private creditors	..	..	0	0	0	0	2	19
of which: Bonds	..	..	0	0	0	0	0	0
Private nonguaranteed	..	..	567	830	822	1,015	985	998
of which: Bonds	..	..	0	0	0	0	0	0
Short-term external debt	..	..	455	456	652	675	780	679
interest arrears on long-term	..	..	0	0	0	0	0	0
Long-term external debt								
Disbursements	..	..	**169**	**158**	**109**	**145**	**76**	**111**
Public and publicly guaranteed	..	..	0	7	5	8	22	33
Official creditors	..	..	0	7	5	8	19	16
Private creditors	..	..	0	0	0	0	3	18
of which: Bonds	..	..	0	0	0	0	0	0
Private nonguaranteed	..	..	169	152	105	136	54	78
of which: Bonds	..	..	..	..	..	..	..	..
Principal repayments	..	..	**76**	**85**	**94**	**101**	**93**	**79**
Public and publicly guaranteed	..	..	14	17	15	15	15	14
Official creditors	..	..	14	17	15	15	15	14
Private creditors	..	..	0	0	0	0	0	0
of which: Bonds	..	..	0	0	0	0	0	0
Private nonguaranteed	..	..	61	68	79	86	78	65
of which: Bonds	..	..	..	..	..	..	..	..
Interest payments	..	..	**34**	**38**	**33**	**42**	**44**	**62**
Public and publicly guaranteed	..	..	11	12	11	12	12	10
Official creditors	..	..	11	12	11	12	12	10
Private creditors	..	..	0	0	0	0	0	0
of which: Bonds	..	..	0	0	0	0	0	0
Private nonguaranteed	..	..	23	26	22	29	32	52
of which: Bonds	..	..	..	..	..	..	..	..
Net financial flows								
Net inflows	..	..	**196**	**552**	**592**	**285**	**636**	**219**
Net debt inflows	..	..	-244	75	331	63	73	-48
Official creditors	..	..	14	-10	109	-10	-10	23
of which: World Bank	..	..	-14	-10	-10	-9	-6	-5
of which: IMF	..	..	29	..	119	-4	-14	21
Private creditors	..	..	-258	85	221	74	83	-71
Long-term	..	..	108	84	25	51	-22	30
Bonds	..	..	..	..	..	..	..	..
Banks and other private	..	..	108	84	25	51	-22	30
Short-term	..	..	-366	1	196	23	105	-101
Net equity inflows	..	..	439	478	261	222	563	266
Foreign direct investment	..	..	439	478	260	223	154	270
Portfolio equity	..	..	..	..	1	-1	409	-4
Major economic aggregates								
Gross national income (GNI)	..	..	5,919	6,851	6,698	7,234	7,536	6,472
Exports of goods, services & prim. income	..	..	1,333	1,670	1,477	1,520	1,731	1,487
Imports of goods, services & prim. income	..	..	3,377	4,018	3,495	3,596	3,861	3,343
Primary income on FDI	..	..	130	148	65	97	98	132
Personal transfers & comp. of employees	..	..	997	1,122	1,059	1,122	1,192	1,068
International reserves	..	..	846	742	1,108	1,103	906	938
Ratios								
External debt stocks to exports (%)	..	..	109.2	101.8	135.6	146.1	129.5	145.2
External debt stocks to GNI (%)	..	..	24.6	24.8	29.9	30.7	29.8	33.3
Debt service to exports (%)	..	..	8.3	7.4	8.6	9.7	8.8	10.8
Short-term to external debt stocks (%)	..	..	31.3	26.8	32.6	30.4	34.8	31.5
Multilateral to external debt stocks (%)	..	..	21.9	17.6	14.7	13.4	11.6	10.6
Reserves to external debt stocks (%)	..	..	58.2	43.6	55.3	49.7	40.4	43.5

KYRGYZ REPUBLIC

(US$ million, unless otherwise indicated)

	2000	2005	2010	2011	2012	2013	2014	2015
Summary external debt data								
External debt stocks	**1,938**	**2,257**	**4,114**	**5,486**	**6,026**	**6,804**	**7,257**	**7,504**
Long-term external debt	1,510	1,825	3,612	4,986	5,492	6,163	6,636	6,854
Public and publicly guaranteed	1,220	1,665	2,442	2,618	2,840	2,945	3,222	3,393
Official creditors	1,184	1,665	2,442	2,618	2,840	2,945	3,222	3,393
of which: IMF	298	299	307	312	321	333	308	306
Private creditors	37	0	0	0	0	0	0	0
of which: Bonds	0	0	0	0	0	0	0	0
Private nonguaranteed	290	161	1,171	2,368	2,652	3,218	3,414	3,461
of which: Bonds	..	..	..	..	..	..	..	..
Short-term external debt	129	132	195	188	214	308	313	345
interest arrears on long-term	10	3	12	3	4	1	1	0
Long-term external debt								
Disbursements	**161**	**132**	**668**	**746**	**853**	**916**	**927**	**596**
Public and publicly guaranteed	153	76	147	211	344	386	479	302
Official creditors	149	76	147	211	344	386	479	302
Private creditors	4	0	0	0	0	0	0	0
of which: Bonds	0	0	0	0	0	0	0	0
Private nonguaranteed	8	56	521	535	510	530	449	294
of which: Bonds	..	..	..	..	..	..	..	..
Principal repayments	**86**	**73**	**462**	**314**	**266**	**305**	**309**	**319**
Public and publicly guaranteed	17	16	38	44	41	44	57	73
Official creditors	13	16	38	44	41	44	57	73
Private creditors	4	0	0	0	0	0	0	0
of which: Bonds	0	0	0	0	0	0	0	0
Private nonguaranteed	69	57	424	270	226	261	252	247
of which: Bonds	..	..	..	..	..	..	..	..
Interest payments	**69**	**21**	**69**	**70**	**58**	**63**	**69**	**70**
Public and publicly guaranteed	23	12	23	40	32	34	41	43
Official creditors	20	12	23	40	32	34	41	43
Private creditors	2	0	0	0	0	0	0	0
of which: Bonds	0	0	0	0	0	0	0	0
Private nonguaranteed	47	9	46	29	25	29	28	27
of which: Bonds	..	..	..	..	..	..	..	..
Net financial flows								
Net inflows	**178**	**-103**	**193**	**992**	**733**	**880**	**972**	**1,211**
Net debt inflows	152	-150	-20	439	620	719	617	322
Official creditors	143	47	121	173	311	354	416	241
of which: World Bank	52	29	5	13	14	21	17	9
of which: IMF	7	-13	12	6	8	12	-6	11
Private creditors	9	-196	-141	266	309	365	201	81
Long-term	-60	-1	97	265	284	269	196	47
Bonds	..	..	..	..	..	..	..	..
Banks and other private	-60	-1	97	265	284	269	196	47
Short-term	69	-195	-238	1	25	97	5	34
Net equity inflows	26	47	213	553	112	161	355	890
Foreign direct investment	26	47	231	547	112	162	355	890
Portfolio equity	..	0	-18	5	0	-2	0	0
Major economic aggregates								
Gross national income (GNI)	1,288	2,372	4,489	5,539	6,436	7,045	7,240	6,330
Exports of goods, services & prim. income	590	963	2,273	3,236	3,533	3,856	3,315	2,625
Imports of goods, services & prim. income	753	1,501	4,112	5,551	6,619	7,103	6,791	4,979
Primary income on FDI	37	36	289	611	112	348	227	191
Personal transfers & comp. of employees	2	313	1,266	1,709	2,031	2,278	2,243	1,688
International reserves	239	570	1,604	1,703	1,903	2,099	1,805	1,634
Ratios								
External debt stocks to exports (%)	328.5	234.4	181.0	169.6	170.6	176.5	218.9	285.9
External debt stocks to GNI (%)	150.5	95.1	91.7	99.0	93.6	96.6	100.2	118.6
Debt service to exports (%)	30.2	14.8	24.5	12.7	9.8	10.1	12.1	15.7
Short-term to external debt stocks (%)	6.7	5.9	4.7	3.4	3.5	4.5	4.3	4.6
Multilateral to external debt stocks (%)	37.3	48.7	31.5	24.5	23.0	21.0	18.8	17.9
Reserves to external debt stocks (%)	12.3	25.2	39.0	31.0	31.6	30.8	24.9	21.8

Notes: Long-term private nonguaranteed debt data are World Bank staff estimates based on reports provided by the country.

LAO PEOPLE'S DEMOCRATIC REPUBLIC

(US$ million, unless otherwise indicated)

	2000	2005	2010	2011	2012	2013	2014	2015
Summary external debt data								
External debt stocks	**2,531**	**3,279**	**6,525**	**7,542**	**8,181**	**9,425**	**10,188**	**11,645**
Long-term external debt	2,474	3,179	6,381	7,402	8,042	8,545	9,291	10,854
Public and publicly guaranteed	2,474	2,354	3,771	4,277	4,542	5,146	5,625	6,657
Official creditors	2,474	2,354	3,768	4,272	4,536	4,995	5,305	5,726
of which: IMF	55	43	88	83	79	78	73	70
Private creditors	0	0	3	5	7	151	320	930
of which: Bonds	0	0	0	0	0	143	300	838
Private nonguaranteed	..	825	2,610	3,125	3,500	3,398	3,666	4,198
of which: Bonds	..	..	..	..	..	..	246	246
Short-term external debt	2	57	56	57	59	802	823	721
interest arrears on long-term	0	0	0	0	0	0	0	0
Long-term external debt								
Disbursements	**82**	**544**	**427**	**1,086**	**867**	**1,613**	**1,611**	**1,946**
Public and publicly guaranteed	82	222	282	471	417	803	765	1,322
Official creditors	82	222	280	468	416	658	595	708
Private creditors	0	0	3	3	1	145	170	614
of which: Bonds	0	0	0	0	0	143	157	538
Private nonguaranteed	..	321	144	615	450	810	846	624
of which: Bonds	..	..	..	..	..	..	246	..
Principal repayments	**23**	**80**	**217**	**208**	**174**	**197**	**223**	**232**
Public and publicly guaranteed	23	40	59	108	99	106	128	140
Official creditors	23	40	59	108	99	106	128	140
Private creditors	0	0	0	0	0	0	0	0
of which: Bonds	0	0	0	0	0	0	0	0
Private nonguaranteed	..	40	159	100	75	92	95	92
of which: Bonds	..	..	..	..	..	..	..	..
Interest payments	**9**	**48**	**78**	**101**	**87**	**133**	**140**	**159**
Public and publicly guaranteed	9	15	28	51	57	75	94	104
Official creditors	9	15	28	51	57	74	89	94
Private creditors	0	0	0	0	0	1	5	10
of which: Bonds	0	0	0	0	0	1	5	10
Private nonguaranteed	..	32	50	50	30	58	47	55
of which: Bonds	..	..	..	..	..	..	..	4
Net financial flows								
Net inflows	**87**	**540**	**388**	**1,186**	**992**	**2,590**	**2,327**	**2,690**
Net debt inflows	54	512	56	874	692	2,157	1,409	1,611
Official creditors	52	177	216	355	314	551	467	568
of which: World Bank	17	26	-13	-15	-19	-10	-21	-21
of which: IMF	-8	-6	-6	-5	-3	-1	..	..
Private creditors	2	335	-160	519	378	1,606	942	1,043
Long-term	..	281	-12	518	376	863	921	1,145
Bonds	..	..	..	..	..	143	403	538
Banks and other private	..	281	-12	518	376	719	518	607
Short-term	2	54	-148	1	2	743	21	-103
Net equity inflows	34	28	333	312	300	433	918	1,079
Foreign direct investment	34	28	279	301	294	427	913	1,079
Portfolio equity	..	..	54	11	6	7	4	0
Major economic aggregates								
Gross national income (GNI)	1,660	2,670	6,713	7,690	8,751	10,550	11,132	11,690
Exports of goods, services & prim. income	513	762	2,308	2,452	2,917	3,118	3,474	3,671
Imports of goods, services & prim. income	638	1,003	2,457	2,881	3,582	3,731	4,940	6,120
Primary income on FDI	..	25	44	16	52	52	22	86
Personal transfers & comp. of employees	1	1	42	110	59	60	40	93
International reserves	139	234	703	741	799	722	875	1,043
Ratios								
External debt stocks to exports (%)	493.1	430.1	282.7	307.6	280.4	302.3	293.3	317.3
External debt stocks to GNI (%)	152.4	122.8	97.2	98.1	93.5	89.3	91.5	99.6
Debt service to exports (%)	8.0	17.8	13.1	12.8	9.1	10.8	10.7	10.9
Short-term to external debt stocks (%)	0.1	1.7	0.9	0.8	0.7	8.5	8.1	6.2
Multilateral to external debt stocks (%)	41.7	48.9	33.2	28.4	24.7	20.1	16.8	13.7
Reserves to external debt stocks (%)	5.5	7.1	10.8	9.8	9.8	7.7	8.6	9.0

Notes: Long-term private nonguaranteed debt data are World Bank staff estimates. Short-term debt is based on data from the BIS.

LEBANON

(US$ million, unless otherwise indicated)

	2000	2005	2010	2011	2012	2013	2014	2015
Summary external debt data								
External debt stocks	**10,073**	**22,722**	**24,676**	**24,826**	**29,135**	**30,918**	**29,943**	**30,896**
Long-term external debt	7,704	19,877	20,713	21,101	24,691	26,124	25,344	26,905
Public and publicly guaranteed	6,968	18,866	20,213	20,601	23,991	25,424	24,644	26,205
Official creditors	1,290	2,172	2,226	2,088	1,997	1,734	1,458	1,287
of which: IMF	6	6	395	355	317	298	280	268
Private creditors	5,677	16,694	17,987	18,513	21,994	23,690	23,186	24,918
of which: Bonds	5,260	16,142	17,422	17,966	21,489	23,298	22,855	24,645
Private nonguaranteed	736	1,011	500	500	700	700	700	700
of which: Bonds	736	1,011	500	500	700	700	700	700
Short-term external debt	2,364	2,838	3,567	3,370	4,127	4,496	4,318	3,723
interest arrears on long-term	0	0	0	0	0	0	0	0
Long-term external debt								
Disbursements	**2,445**	**3,179**	**2,143**	**4,174**	**6,221**	**3,185**	**1,674**	**3,911**
Public and publicly guaranteed	2,330	2,649	2,143	4,174	5,721	3,185	1,674	3,911
Official creditors	238	106	199	206	226	136	90	108
Private creditors	2,092	2,543	1,943	3,968	5,495	3,049	1,584	3,803
of which: Bonds	2,031	2,500	1,925	3,954	5,478	2,992	1,575	3,800
Private nonguaranteed	115	530	0	0	500	0	0	0
of which: Bonds	115	530	0	0	500	0	0	0
Principal repayments	**884**	**2,172**	**2,632**	**3,743**	**2,642**	**1,801**	**2,254**	**2,205**
Public and publicly guaranteed	834	1,907	2,462	3,743	2,342	1,801	2,254	2,205
Official creditors	74	143	298	328	318	415	257	202
Private creditors	760	1,764	2,164	3,415	2,024	1,386	1,997	2,003
of which: Bonds	400	1,695	2,151	3,385	1,965	1,209	1,944	1,954
Private nonguaranteed	50	265	170	0	300	0	0	0
of which: Bonds	50	265	170	0	300	0	0	0
Interest payments	**475**	**1,287**	**1,454**	**1,491**	**1,484**	**1,618**	**1,664**	**1,652**
Public and publicly guaranteed	418	1,197	1,403	1,453	1,446	1,577	1,622	1,610
Official creditors	57	92	100	82	75	72	62	49
Private creditors	361	1,106	1,303	1,372	1,371	1,505	1,560	1,562
of which: Bonds	300	1,087	1,289	1,359	1,359	1,495	1,550	1,554
Private nonguaranteed	57	90	51	38	38	42	42	42
of which: Bonds	57	90	51	38	38	42	42	42
Net financial flows								
Net inflows	**1,723**	**4,317**	**4,494**	**3,539**	**7,261**	**4,473**	**2,246**	**2,897**
Net debt inflows	1,723	258	60	194	4,298	1,734	-758	1,110
Official creditors	164	-37	-117	-161	-130	-299	-167	-95
of which: World Bank	26	-6	3	-21	-48	-43	-25	14
of which: IMF	0	0	-19	-40	-39	-19	0	0
Private creditors	1,559	296	177	356	4,428	2,032	-591	1,205
Long-term	1,397	1,045	-391	553	3,671	1,663	-413	1,800
Bonds	1,696	1,070	-396	569	3,714	1,782	-369	1,846
Banks and other private	-299	-26	5	-16	-43	-119	-43	-46
Short-term	162	-749	568	-197	757	369	-178	-595
Net equity inflows	..	4,059	4,434	3,345	2,963	2,739	3,004	1,787
Foreign direct investment	..	2,624	4,280	3,490	3,155	2,702	2,904	2,340
Portfolio equity	..	1,436	154	-145	-191	38	100	-553
Major economic aggregates								
Gross national income (GNI)	17,581	21,101	37,501	40,194	43,242	44,021	46,072	47,716
Exports of goods, services & prim. income	..	14,958	22,177	26,687	21,812	21,943	21,349	21,766
Imports of goods, services & prim. income	..	18,768	32,179	34,071	33,155	34,771	35,297	33,293
Primary income on FDI	..	95	209	184	195	505	335	423
Personal transfers & comp. of employees	..	4,924	6,914	6,913	6,671	7,567	7,191	7,481
International reserves	5,944	11,887	31,514	33,741	37,186	36,748	39,547	38,756
Ratios								
External debt stocks to exports (%)	..	151.9	111.3	93.0	133.6	140.9	140.3	141.9
External debt stocks to GNI (%)	57.3	107.7	65.8	61.8	67.4	70.2	65.0	64.7
Debt service to exports (%)	..	24.3	18.7	20.0	19.3	16.0	18.6	18.0
Short-term to external debt stocks (%)	23.5	12.5	14.5	13.6	14.2	14.5	14.4	12.1
Multilateral to external debt stocks (%)	8.8	5.2	5.3	5.0	3.9	3.3	2.9	2.5
Reserves to external debt stocks (%)	59.0	52.3	127.7	135.9	127.6	118.9	132.1	125.4

Notes: Long-term private nonguaranteed debt only cover Bonds. Short-term debt is based on data from the BIS.

LESOTHO

(US$ million, unless otherwise indicated)

	2000	2005	2010	2011	2012	2013	2014	2015
Summary external debt data								
External debt stocks	**769.7**	**666.3**	**779.0**	**802.9**	**861.9**	**887.7**	**879.1**	**879.8**
Long-term external debt	656.7	618.9	700.2	718.5	746.7	757.5	758.0	765.2
Public and publicly guaranteed	656.7	618.9	700.2	718.5	746.7	757.5	758.0	765.2
Official creditors	580.9	590.6	686.6	706.9	735.5	747.5	749.4	761.7
of which: IMF	16.0	40.4	78.8	80.3	115.2	130.2	121.0	114.6
Private creditors	75.8	28.4	13.6	11.7	11.2	10.0	8.6	3.5
of which: Bonds	0.0	0.0	0.0	0.0	0.0	0.0	0.0	0.0
Private nonguaranteed	..	..	..	..	..	..	..	..
of which: Bonds	..	..	..	..	..	..	..	..
Short-term external debt	97.0	7.0	0.0	4.0	0.0	0.0	0.1	0.1
interest arrears on long-term	0.0	0.0	0.0	0.0	0.0	0.0	0.1	0.1
Long-term external debt								
Disbursements	**69.4**	**21.1**	**42.4**	**44.4**	**55.1**	**40.0**	**74.0**	**71.1**
Public and publicly guaranteed	69.4	21.1	42.4	44.4	55.1	40.0	74.0	71.1
Official creditors	67.4	21.1	42.4	44.4	55.1	40.0	74.0	71.1
Private creditors	2.0	0.0	0.0	0.0	0.0	0.0	0.0	0.0
of which: Bonds	0.0	0.0	0.0	0.0	0.0	0.0	0.0	0.0
Private nonguaranteed	..	..	..	..	..	..	..	..
of which: Bonds	..	..	..	..	..	..	..	..
Principal repayments	**33.2**	**65.3**	**19.4**	**23.3**	**24.3**	**27.2**	**27.2**	**30.3**
Public and publicly guaranteed	33.2	65.3	19.4	23.3	24.3	27.2	27.2	30.3
Official creditors	26.4	32.0	19.1	23.0	24.0	26.9	26.9	25.9
Private creditors	6.8	33.3	0.3	0.3	0.3	0.3	0.3	4.4
of which: Bonds	0.0	0.0	0.0	0.0	0.0	0.0	0.0	0.0
Private nonguaranteed	..	..	..	..	..	..	..	..
of which: Bonds	..	..	..	..	..	..	..	..
Interest payments	**22.9**	**13.7**	**7.5**	**8.8**	**9.2**	**9.9**	**11.6**	**19.7**
Public and publicly guaranteed	22.9	13.7	7.5	8.8	9.2	9.9	11.6	19.7
Official creditors	16.0	7.7	6.4	7.8	8.3	9.1	10.9	19.2
Private creditors	7.0	6.0	1.0	1.0	0.9	0.7	0.7	0.6
of which: Bonds	0.0	0.0	0.0	0.0	0.0	0.0	0.0	0.0
Private nonguaranteed	..	..	..	..	..	..	..	..
of which: Bonds	..	..	..	..	..	..	..	..
Net financial flows								
Net inflows	**156.4**	**-16.2**	**71.1**	**-32.9**	**6.0**	**-21.8**	**47.6**	**71.8**
Net debt inflows	124.0	-45.2	24.4	26.9	61.4	27.4	45.2	39.8
Official creditors	35.9	-10.9	27.7	23.2	65.6	27.7	45.5	44.1
of which: World Bank	11.2	4.6	21.5	-6.6	-6.9	-8.4	2.2	2.4
of which: IMF	-5.2	..	4.4	1.8	34.5	14.7	-1.6	-1.1
Private creditors	88.1	-34.3	-3.3	3.7	-4.3	-0.3	-0.3	-4.4
Long-term	-4.9	-33.3	-0.3	-0.3	-0.3	-0.3	-0.3	-4.4
Bonds	..	..	..	..	..	..	..	..
Banks and other private	-4.9	-33.3	-0.3	-0.3	-0.3	-0.3	-0.3	-4.4
Short-term	93.0	-1.0	-3.0	4.0	-4.0	0.0	0.0	0.0
Net equity inflows	32.4	29.0	46.6	-59.8	-55.4	-49.3	2.5	32.0
Foreign direct investment	32.4	29.0	46.6	-60.2	-55.7	-49.6	2.2	31.8
Portfolio equity	..	0.0	..	0.4	0.4	0.3	0.3	0.3
Major economic aggregates								
Gross national income (GNI)	1,014.4	1,869.4	2,594.0	3,124.2	2,861.5	2,862.9	2,605.0	..
Exports of goods, services & prim. income	823.4	1,391.2	1,667.7	1,947.8	1,632.0	1,420.1	1,316.1	1,339.4
Imports of goods, services & prim. income	1,136.5	1,702.2	2,499.5	2,839.4	2,888.2	2,423.9	2,306.8	2,187.9
Primary income on FDI	71.3	6.6	76.6	187.2	173.4	154.3	142.4	125.7
Personal transfers & comp. of employees	477.6	599.4	610.1	649.3	554.6	462.9	380.2	365.6
International reserves	417.9	519.1	1,071.0	919.1	1,027.9	1,055.2	1,070.8	904.2
Ratios								
External debt stocks to exports (%)	93.5	47.9	46.7	41.2	52.8	62.5	66.8	65.7
External debt stocks to GNI (%)	75.9	35.6	30.0	25.7	30.1	31.0	33.7	..
Debt service to exports (%)	7.5	5.7	2.1	2.0	2.3	2.8	3.1	3.8
Short-term to external debt stocks (%)	12.6	1.1	0.0	0.5	0.0	0.0	0.0	0.0
Multilateral to external debt stocks (%)	61.8	77.8	80.1	79.6	75.8	74.1	72.9	73.6
Reserves to external debt stocks (%)	54.3	77.9	137.5	114.5	119.3	118.9	121.8	102.8

Notes: Large interest payment was made during 2007 to a creditor country to settle a long standing claim. Short-term debt is based on data from the BIS.

LIBERIA

(US$ million, unless otherwise indicated)

	2000	2005	2010	2011	2012	2013	2014	2015
Summary external debt data								
External debt stocks	**2,836.3**	**3,950.6**	**418.9**	**448.4**	**487.2**	**530.5**	**680.5**	**836.3**
Long-term external debt	1,104.0	1,179.1	183.1	188.0	208.5	229.2	353.2	504.2
Public and publicly guaranteed	1,104.0	1,179.1	183.1	188.0	208.5	229.2	295.2	433.2
Official creditors	907.3	981.3	183.1	188.0	208.5	229.2	295.2	433.2
of which: IMF	319.7	349.7	235.3	248.2	266.7	289.9	327.2	332.1
Private creditors	196.8	197.7	0.0	0.0	0.0	0.0	0.0	0.0
of which: Bonds	0.0	0.0	0.0	0.0	0.0	0.0	0.0	0.0
Private nonguaranteed	..	..	..	..	..	..	58.0	71.0
of which: Bonds	..	..	..	..	..	..	..	..
Short-term external debt	1,412.6	2,421.8	0.4	12.2	12.0	11.4	0.0	0.0
interest arrears on long-term	1,412.6	2,421.8	0.4	12.2	12.0	11.4	0.0	0.0
Long-term external debt								
Disbursements	**0.0**	**0.0**	**0.0**	**20.3**	**23.1**	**35.1**	**138.5**	**165.6**
Public and publicly guaranteed	0.0	0.0	0.0	20.3	23.1	35.1	80.5	149.6
Official creditors	0.0	0.0	0.0	20.3	23.1	35.1	80.5	149.6
Private creditors	0.0	0.0	0.0	0.0	0.0	0.0	0.0	0.0
of which: Bonds	0.0	0.0	0.0	0.0	0.0	0.0	0.0	0.0
Private nonguaranteed	..	..	..	..	..	..	58.0	16.0
of which: Bonds	..	..	..	..	..	..	..	..
Principal repayments	**0.0**	**0.0**	**3.7**	**2.6**	**3.5**	**4.6**	**5.6**	**5.2**
Public and publicly guaranteed	0.0	0.0	3.7	2.6	3.5	4.6	5.6	2.2
Official creditors	0.0	0.0	3.7	2.6	3.5	4.6	5.6	2.2
Private creditors	0.0	0.0	0.0	0.0	0.0	0.0	0.0	0.0
of which: Bonds	0.0	0.0	0.0	0.0	0.0	0.0	0.0	0.0
Private nonguaranteed	..	..	..	..	..	..	0.0	3.0
of which: Bonds	..	..	..	..	..	..	..	..
Interest payments	**0.0**	**0.0**	**0.6**	**0.4**	**1.1**	**1.5**	**8.6**	**2.7**
Public and publicly guaranteed	0.0	0.0	0.6	0.4	1.1	1.5	8.6	2.7
Official creditors	0.0	0.0	0.6	0.4	1.1	1.5	8.6	2.7
Private creditors	0.0	0.0	0.0	0.0	0.0	0.0	0.0	0.0
of which: Bonds	0.0	0.0	0.0	0.0	0.0	0.0	0.0	0.0
Private nonguaranteed	..	..	..	..	..	..	0.0	0.0
of which: Bonds	..	..	..	..	..	..	..	..
Net financial flows								
Net inflows	**20.2**	**3.5**	**9.8**	**62.3**	**684.3**	**753.2**	**667.3**	**551.8**
Net debt inflows	-0.6	-0.1	9.8	31.8	37.7	53.0	190.0	179.8
Official creditors	-0.6	-0.1	9.8	31.8	37.7	53.0	132.0	166.8
of which: World Bank	..	..	-1.7	14.3	23.1	21.6	48.9	67.2
of which: IMF	-0.6	-0.1	13.6	14.0	18.1	22.5	57.1	19.4
Private creditors	..	..	..	..	..	..	58.0	13.0
Long-term	..	..	..	..	..	..	58.0	13.0
Bonds	..	..	..	..	..	..	..	..
Banks and other private	..	..	..	..	..	..	58.0	13.0
Short-term	..	..	..	..	..	..	..	..
Net equity inflows	20.8	3.5	0.0	30.5	646.6	700.3	477.3	372.0
Foreign direct investment	20.8	3.5	0.0	30.5	646.6	700.3	477.3	372.0
Portfolio equity	..	..	..	..	..	..	..	..
Major economic aggregates								
Gross national income (GNI)	427.7	394.4	1,113.3	1,420.6	1,473.5	1,645.0	1,680.0	1,773.0
Exports of goods, services & prim. income	..	354.7	430.4	1,351.8	709.6	850.0	719.5	540.3
Imports of goods, services & prim. income	..	1,317.7	1,804.7	3,325.3	2,317.1	2,362.0	3,615.1	2,983.4
Primary income on FDI	..	7.1	0.1	11.7	232.2	252.9	477.3	372.0
Personal transfers & comp. of employees	..	31.9	31.4	360.0	515.8	383.4	505.7	640.8
International reserves	0.3	25.4	465.9	512.8	497.2	493.1	499.0	522.6
Ratios								
External debt stocks to exports (%)	..	1113.7	97.3	33.2	68.7	62.4	94.6	154.8
External debt stocks to GNI (%)	663.2	1001.7	37.6	31.6	33.1	32.2	40.5	47.2
Debt service to exports (%)	..	0.5	1.4	0.2	0.6	0.8	2.4	8.2
Short-term to external debt stocks (%)	49.8	61.3	0.1	2.7	2.5	2.1	0.0	0.0
Multilateral to external debt stocks (%)	13.9	11.1	15.1	13.3	16.7	21.5	26.7	38.2
Reserves to external debt stocks (%)	0.0	0.6	111.2	114.4	102.1	93.0	73.3	62.5

Notes: Historical long-term public and publicly guaranteed debt data before 2011 are revised based on reports provided by the country. Data include the effects of Paris Club rescheduling agreement signed in 2008 and 2010, and HIPC and MDRI debt relief.

MACEDONIA, FYR

(US$ million, unless otherwise indicated)

	2000	2005	2010	2011	2012	2013	2014	2015
Summary external debt data								
External debt stocks	**1,480**	**2,981**	**5,159**	**6,131**	**6,469**	**6,737**	**7,233**	**6,942**
Long-term external debt	1,333	2,108	3,840	4,132	4,376	4,941	5,741	5,634
Public and publicly guaranteed	1,206	1,637	1,880	2,110	2,270	2,572	3,140	3,097
Official creditors	921	1,202	1,369	1,392	1,453	1,596	1,691	1,668
of which: IMF	92	74	101	403	404	404	273	91
Private creditors	284	435	512	717	817	976	1,449	1,429
of which: Bonds	0	177	434	421	429	207	789	838
Private nonguaranteed	127	471	1,959	2,022	2,106	2,368	2,602	2,537
of which: Bonds	..	..	..	..	..	..	..	..
Short-term external debt	55	800	1,218	1,597	1,690	1,392	1,218	1,217
interest arrears on long-term	4	9	64	80	109	129	125	131
Long-term external debt								
Disbursements	**151**	**318**	**596**	**968**	**637**	**1,063**	**1,492**	**1,082**
Public and publicly guaranteed	98	293	197	414	303	694	1,078	571
Official creditors	96	104	190	155	176	305	430	260
Private creditors	1	189	7	259	127	389	647	311
of which: Bonds	0	187	0	0	0	0	644	299
Private nonguaranteed	54	25	399	555	334	369	415	512
of which: Bonds	..	..	..	..	..	..	..	..
Principal repayments	**74**	**171**	**443**	**739**	**479**	**734**	**657**	**699**
Public and publicly guaranteed	25	81	98	126	168	462	183	327
Official creditors	23	67	90	103	124	192	159	147
Private creditors	2	14	9	23	44	270	24	180
of which: Bonds	0	0	0	0	0	235	0	166
Private nonguaranteed	49	90	344	614	310	272	475	373
of which: Bonds	..	..	..	..	..	..	..	..
Interest payments	**37**	**54**	**128**	**129**	**125**	**117**	**150**	**128**
Public and publicly guaranteed	30	41	56	60	64	64	60	78
Official creditors	20	32	22	24	23	19	22	23
Private creditors	10	9	35	36	41	45	38	55
of which: Bonds	0	0	32	33	31	21	9	30
Private nonguaranteed	7	13	71	70	60	54	89	51
of which: Bonds	..	..	..	..	..	..	..	..
Net financial flows								
Net inflows	**265**	**326**	**123**	**1,465**	**358**	**207**	**408**	**121**
Net debt inflows	59	117	-75	902	222	12	553	204
Official creditors	58	42	101	362	51	113	159	-60
of which: World Bank	48	49	53	23	1	34	38	-6
of which: IMF	-16	5	0	311	0	0	-112	-172
Private creditors	2	75	-176	539	171	-101	394	264
Long-term	5	109	53	177	108	216	563	271
Bonds	0	187	0	0	0	-235	644	133
Banks and other private	5	-78	53	177	108	451	-80	137
Short-term	-3	-34	-229	362	64	-317	-170	-7
Net equity inflows	206	209	198	563	136	195	-145	-83
Foreign direct investment	206	155	202	572	142	196	-141	-74
Portfolio equity	..	54	-4	-8	-6	-1	-4	-9
Major economic aggregates								
Gross national income (GNI)	3,703	6,149	9,276	10,307	9,534	10,561	11,106	9,840
Exports of goods, services & prim. income	1,178	2,190	3,801	5,019	4,521	4,916	5,627	5,058
Imports of goods, services & prim. income	1,890	3,393	5,789	7,347	6,922	7,149	7,803	7,018
Primary income on FDI	31	142	230	272	265	363	311	371
Personal transfers & comp. of employees	81	227	388	434	394	376	367	307
International reserves	429	1,229	1,970	2,331	2,528	2,485	2,701	2,239
Ratios								
External debt stocks to exports (%)	125.7	136.2	135.7	122.2	143.1	137.0	128.5	137.3
External debt stocks to GNI (%)	40.0	48.5	55.6	59.5	67.9	63.8	65.1	70.6
Debt service to exports (%)	11.8	12.5	16.4	18.8	15.0	18.6	17.3	20.8
Short-term to external debt stocks (%)	3.7	26.8	23.6	26.0	26.1	20.7	16.8	17.5
Multilateral to external debt stocks (%)	38.5	30.7	21.8	18.9	18.9	20.0	18.4	18.3
Reserves to external debt stocks (%)	29.0	41.2	38.2	38.0	39.1	36.9	37.3	32.2

MADAGASCAR

(US$ million, unless otherwise indicated)

	2000	2005	2010	2011	2012	2013	2014	2015
Summary external debt data								
External debt stocks	**4,726**	**3,519**	**2,699**	**2,810**	**2,930**	**2,872**	**2,852**	**2,985**
Long-term external debt	4,295	3,180	1,997	2,106	2,200	2,271	2,299	2,500
Public and publicly guaranteed	4,295	3,180	1,982	2,093	2,191	2,263	2,294	2,486
Official creditors	4,256	3,171	1,975	2,086	2,181	2,229	2,260	2,392
of which: IMF	129	240	278	273	267	256	267	281
Private creditors	39	9	7	7	10	34	33	94
of which: Bonds	0	0	0	0	0	0	0	0
Private nonguaranteed	..	..	15	12	10	8	5	13
of which: Bonds	..	..	..	..	..	..	..	..
Short-term external debt	301	99	425	430	463	345	286	205
interest arrears on long-term	204	72	188	188	192	52	43	42
Long-term external debt								
Disbursements	**150**	**249**	**198**	**137**	**138**	**149**	**189**	**322**
Public and publicly guaranteed	150	249	198	137	138	149	189	322
Official creditors	150	249	197	137	135	146	187	249
Private creditors	0	0	0	0	3	3	2	73
of which: Bonds	0	0	0	0	0	0	0	0
Private nonguaranteed	..	..	..	..	..	..	..	..
of which: Bonds	..	..	..	..	..	..	..	..
Principal repayments	**74**	**38**	**37**	**25**	**44**	**48**	**54**	**49**
Public and publicly guaranteed	74	38	36	24	42	48	53	48
Official creditors	73	37	36	24	42	48	53	38
Private creditors	0	1	0	0	0	0	0	10
of which: Bonds	0	0	0	0	0	0	0	0
Private nonguaranteed	..	..	1	1	2	1	1	1
of which: Bonds	..	..	..	..	..	..	..	..
Interest payments	**28**	**28**	**16**	**16**	**17**	**17**	**19**	**19**
Public and publicly guaranteed	28	28	16	16	17	17	18	19
Official creditors	28	28	16	16	17	17	18	19
Private creditors	0	0	0	0	0	0	0	0
of which: Bonds	0	0	0	0	0	0	0	0
Private nonguaranteed	..	..	0	0	0	0	0	0
of which: Bonds	..	..	..	..	..	..	..	..
Net financial flows								
Net inflows	**128**	**297**	**0**	**155**	**157**	**144**	**462**	**736**
Net debt inflows	45	244	-65	115	116	112	112	219
Official creditors	122	218	160	109	87	87	161	237
of which: World Bank	77	209	75	42	47	80	118	107
of which: IMF	45	6	-2	-4	-7	-11	27	26
Private creditors	-77	26	-225	5	29	24	-49	-19
Long-term	0	-1	-1	-1	1	2	1	62
Bonds	..	..	..	..	..	..	..	..
Banks and other private	0	-1	-1	-1	1	2	1	62
Short-term	-76	27	-224	6	29	22	-50	-80
Net equity inflows	83	53	65	41	41	32	351	517
Foreign direct investment	83	53	65	41	41	32	351	517
Portfolio equity	..	..	0	..	..	..	..	..
Major economic aggregates								
Gross national income (GNI)	3,807	4,960	8,637	9,737	9,605	10,278	10,712	9,604
Exports of goods, services & prim. income	845	1,353	2,241	2,733	2,867	3,205	3,513	..
Imports of goods, services & prim. income	1,219	2,251	3,616	4,016	4,223	4,461	4,272	..
Primary income on FDI	4	65	120	162	276	249	..	..
Personal transfers & comp. of employees	11	115	547	398	397	427	427	427
International reserves	285	481	1,023	1,135	1,053	776	774	832
Ratios								
External debt stocks to exports (%)	559.0	260.2	120.5	102.8	102.2	89.6	81.2	..
External debt stocks to GNI (%)	124.1	70.9	31.3	28.9	30.5	27.9	26.6	31.1
Debt service to exports (%)	13.9	5.9	2.7	1.8	2.5	2.5	2.7	..
Short-term to external debt stocks (%)	6.4	2.8	15.7	15.3	15.8	12.0	10.0	6.9
Multilateral to external debt stocks (%)	38.7	80.6	57.0	57.2	57.4	62.6	65.3	64.5
Reserves to external debt stocks (%)	6.0	13.7	37.9	40.4	35.9	27.0	27.1	27.9

Notes: Data include the effects of HIPC and MDRI debt relief.

MALAWI

(US$ million, unless otherwise indicated)

	2000	2005	2010	2011	2012	2013	2014	2015
Summary external debt data								
External debt stocks	**2,716**	**3,196**	**1,021**	**1,213**	**1,329**	**1,560**	**1,658**	**1,735**
Long-term external debt	2,545	3,062	729	929	1,025	1,244	1,364	1,454
Public and publicly guaranteed	2,545	3,062	729	929	1,025	1,244	1,364	1,454
Official creditors	2,527	3,044	724	923	1,019	1,238	1,362	1,454
of which: IMF	97	91	248	247	283	295	273	255
Private creditors	18	18	5	5	5	6	2	1
of which: Bonds	0	0	0	0	0	0	0	0
Private nonguaranteed	..	..	..	..	..	..	..	..
of which: Bonds	..	..	..	..	..	..	..	..
Short-term external debt	75	43	43	38	21	21	22	26
interest arrears on long-term	37	34	0	0	0	0	1	0
Long-term external debt								
Disbursements	**119**	**89**	**81**	**208**	**109**	**230**	**211**	**175**
Public and publicly guaranteed	119	89	81	208	109	230	211	175
Official creditors	119	89	81	208	109	230	211	175
Private creditors	0	0	0	0	0	0	0	0
of which: Bonds	0	0	0	0	0	0	0	0
Private nonguaranteed	..	..	..	..	..	..	..	..
of which: Bonds	..	..	..	..	..	..	..	..
Principal repayments	**33**	**38**	**13**	**14**	**15**	**22**	**24**	**26**
Public and publicly guaranteed	33	38	13	14	15	22	24	26
Official creditors	33	35	13	14	15	22	21	25
Private creditors	0	3	0	0	0	0	3	1
of which: Bonds	0	0	0	0	0	0	0	0
Private nonguaranteed	..	..	..	..	..	..	..	..
of which: Bonds	..	..	..	..	..	..	..	..
Interest payments	**18**	**22**	**7**	**7**	**9**	**14**	**15**	**16**
Public and publicly guaranteed	18	22	7	7	9	14	15	16
Official creditors	18	22	7	7	9	14	15	16
Private creditors	0	0	0	0	0	0	0	0
of which: Bonds	0	0	0	0	0	0	0	0
Private nonguaranteed	..	..	..	..	..	..	..	..
of which: Bonds	..	..	..	..	..	..	..	..
Net financial flows								
Net inflows	**106**	**128**	**199**	**631**	**-106**	**476**	**560**	**428**
Net debt inflows	80	43	65	188	113	220	181	149
Official creditors	85	47	89	193	130	220	184	145
of which: World Bank	74	32	34	34	49	94	117	114
of which: IMF	-1	-6	21	-1	36	12	-6	-6
Private creditors	-6	-4	-24	-5	-17	0	-3	4
Long-term	0	-3	0	0	0	0	-3	-1
Bonds	..	..	..	..	..	..	..	..
Banks and other private	..	-3	0	0	0	0	-3	-1
Short-term	-6	-1	-24	-5	-17	0	0	5
Net equity inflows	26	84	134	443	-219	257	379	279
Foreign direct investment	26	88	133	441	-220	256	378	279
Portfolio equity	..	-4	1	2	0	0	0	0
Major economic aggregates								
Gross national income (GNI)	1,707	3,616	6,851	7,888	5,893	5,357	5,887	6,348
Exports of goods, services & prim. income	471	609	1,224	1,606	1,385	1,398	1,645	1,548
Imports of goods, services & prim. income	680	1,390	2,835	3,262	2,599	3,226	3,317	2,753
Primary income on FDI	15	52	173	362	23	245	276	297
Personal transfers & comp. of employees	1	23	22	25	28	34	38	34
International reserves	243	159	307	197	223	413	602	..
Ratios								
External debt stocks to exports (%)	577.1	524.6	83.4	75.6	96.0	111.6	100.8	112.1
External debt stocks to GNI (%)	159.1	88.4	14.9	15.4	22.6	29.1	28.2	27.3
Debt service to exports (%)	13.5	12.5	1.7	1.4	2.1	3.2	4.0	4.3
Short-term to external debt stocks (%)	2.8	1.4	4.2	3.1	1.6	1.3	1.3	1.5
Multilateral to external debt stocks (%)	75.3	80.1	57.4	52.3	53.2	53.4	55.8	58.4
Reserves to external debt stocks (%)	8.9	5.0	30.1	16.3	16.8	26.5	36.3	..

Notes: Short-term debt is based on data from the BIS. Data include the effects of Paris Club rescheduling agreement signed in 2006 and HIPC and MDRI debt relief.

MALAYSIA

(US$ million, unless otherwise indicated)

	2000	2005	2010	2011	2012	2013	2014	2015
Summary external debt data								
External debt stocks	**41,946**	**64,911**	**133,800**	**144,898**	**193,880**	**188,795**	**196,587**	**190,951**
Long-term external debt	37,192	51,537	80,450	78,128	99,201	107,005	115,255	112,619
Public and publicly guaranteed	19,125	34,387	61,858	60,647	67,392	68,540	67,757	66,385
Official creditors	4,950	6,542	3,750	3,263	2,980	2,463	2,071	1,805
of which: IMF	181	199	2,073	2,067	2,069	2,073	1,950	1,865
Private creditors	14,175	27,845	58,108	57,384	64,412	66,077	65,686	64,580
of which: Bonds	9,836	24,585	51,638	52,735	61,762	64,777	64,422	63,628
Private nonguaranteed	18,067	17,150	18,593	17,481	31,809	38,465	47,498	46,234
of which: Bonds	18,067	17,150	18,593	17,481	30,213	37,321	40,738	46,194
Short-term external debt	4,573	13,176	51,276	64,704	92,610	79,717	79,382	76,467
interest arrears on long-term	0	0	0	0	0	0	0	0
Long-term external debt								
Disbursements	**5,921**	**10,378**	**9,938**	**12,354**	**24,260**	**18,687**	**22,312**	**23,776**
Public and publicly guaranteed	3,460	6,195	6,014	3,311	8,870	6,936	4,636	13,723
Official creditors	1,446	981	18	10	514	56	0	0
Private creditors	2,015	5,215	5,996	3,301	8,356	6,881	4,635	13,723
of which: Bonds	1,061	5,164	2,339	2,892	8,033	6,834	4,398	13,481
Private nonguaranteed	2,461	4,183	3,923	9,043	15,390	11,751	17,677	10,053
of which: Bonds	2,461	4,183	3,923	9,043	13,794	11,416	11,611	10,053
Principal repayments	**4,146**	**7,192**	**3,564**	**4,551**	**4,171**	**8,821**	**9,852**	**10,532**
Public and publicly guaranteed	2,017	4,752	1,863	3,608	3,304	1,681	2,547	6,635
Official creditors	840	1,218	688	625	604	300	269	266
Private creditors	1,176	3,534	1,176	2,983	2,701	1,381	2,277	6,369
of which: Bonds	200	2,036	0	750	380	9	2,009	5,823
Private nonguaranteed	2,129	2,440	1,701	943	867	7,139	7,305	3,897
of which: Bonds	2,129	2,440	1,701	943	867	6,352	6,880	3,217
Interest payments	**2,021**	**1,858**	**1,708**	**1,563**	**2,053**	**2,451**	**2,537**	**2,556**
Public and publicly guaranteed	1,159	1,208	1,024	1,017	1,293	1,251	1,235	1,146
Official creditors	259	314	97	86	79	69	72	62
Private creditors	900	894	927	931	1,214	1,182	1,163	1,084
of which: Bonds	599	746	771	853	1,084	1,117	1,138	1,052
Private nonguaranteed	862	650	684	545	760	1,200	1,302	1,410
of which: Bonds	862	650	684	545	760	1,190	1,300	1,407
Net financial flows								
Net inflows	**4,124**	**7,962**	**23,015**	**33,429**	**57,234**	**9,089**	**23,004**	**21,451**
Net debt inflows	337	4,929	13,955	21,231	47,995	-3,027	12,126	10,329
Official creditors	606	-238	-669	-614	-90	-245	-269	-266
of which: World Bank	-86	-92	-38	0	..	..	..	..
of which: IMF	..	..	..	..	..	..	..	..
Private creditors	-269	5,167	14,625	21,846	48,085	-2,782	12,396	10,596
Long-term	1,170	3,424	7,043	8,418	20,179	10,111	12,730	13,511
Bonds	1,192	4,870	4,561	10,243	20,580	11,889	7,121	14,495
Banks and other private	-23	-1,447	2,482	-1,825	-401	-1,778	5,609	-984
Short-term	-1,439	1,744	7,581	13,428	27,906	-12,894	-334	-2,915
Net equity inflows	3,788	3,033	9,060	12,198	9,239	12,115	10,877	11,121
Foreign direct investment	3,788	4,232	9,060	12,198	9,239	12,115	10,877	11,121
Portfolio equity	..	-1,200	..	..	..	..	..	..
Major economic aggregates								
Gross national income (GNI)	86,182	137,212	246,904	290,893	302,839	312,561	326,700	287,975
Exports of goods, services & prim. income	114,272	166,725	234,007	271,150	263,076	259,477	265,588	223,013
Imports of goods, services & prim. income	103,860	142,268	201,594	231,775	240,783	242,715	245,415	208,412
Primary income on FDI	7,173	8,330	15,298	18,105	18,389	18,030	19,020	13,164
Personal transfers & comp. of employees	342	1,117	1,103	1,211	1,294	1,423	1,580	1,643
International reserves	28,330	69,858	104,884	131,780	137,784	133,444	114,572	93,979
Ratios								
External debt stocks to exports (%)	36.7	38.9	57.2	53.4	73.7	72.8	74.0	85.6
External debt stocks to GNI (%)	48.7	47.3	54.2	49.8	64.0	60.4	60.2	66.3
Debt service to exports (%)	5.6	5.6	2.4	2.4	2.5	4.5	4.9	6.1
Short-term to external debt stocks (%)	10.9	20.3	38.3	44.7	47.8	42.2	40.4	40.0
Multilateral to external debt stocks (%)	3.1	1.4	0.2	0.1	0.1	0.1	0.1	0.0
Reserves to external debt stocks (%)	67.5	107.6	78.4	90.9	71.1	70.7	58.3	49.2

Notes: Long-term public and publicly guaranteed, long-term private nonguaranteed, and short-term debt data are World Bank staff estimates based on reports.

MALDIVES

(US$ million, unless otherwise indicated)

	2000	2005	2010	2011	2012	2013	2014	2015
Summary external debt data								
External debt stocks	**203.0**	**362.3**	**916.6**	**882.0**	**890.0**	**900.5**	**1,054.1**	**943.0**
Long-term external debt	184.7	299.8	743.1	717.1	761.4	789.8	892.7	786.2
Public and publicly guaranteed	184.7	299.8	627.8	675.2	720.9	748.0	703.3	633.2
Official creditors	154.8	250.2	522.3	565.3	633.5	669.0	647.9	595.0
of which: IMF	0.4	6.3	27.6	27.5	27.6	22.1	14.9	13.1
Private creditors	29.9	49.6	105.5	109.9	87.3	79.1	55.4	38.3
of which: Bonds	0.0	0.0	0.0	0.0	0.0	0.0	0.0	0.0
Private nonguaranteed	..	..	115.2	41.9	40.5	41.8	189.3	153.0
of which: Bonds	..	..	..	..	..	..	..	..
Short-term external debt	18.0	56.3	145.9	137.3	101.0	88.6	146.6	143.7
interest arrears on long-term	0.0	0.3	2.9	1.3	3.0	5.6	3.6	2.6
Long-term external debt								
Disbursements	**13.6**	**45.9**	**168.5**	**124.5**	**113.3**	**77.0**	**199.5**	**23.5**
Public and publicly guaranteed	13.6	45.9	142.4	115.9	113.3	77.0	49.5	23.5
Official creditors	6.3	29.5	108.4	82.9	111.7	70.4	49.4	23.5
Private creditors	7.3	16.3	34.0	33.0	1.6	6.6	0.1	0.0
of which: Bonds	0.0	0.0	0.0	0.0	0.0	0.0	0.0	0.0
Private nonguaranteed	..	..	26.1	8.6	0.0	0.0	150.0	0.0
of which: Bonds	..	..	..	..	..	..	..	..
Principal repayments	**13.9**	**22.1**	**59.8**	**70.3**	**67.7**	**57.3**	**66.6**	**96.9**
Public and publicly guaranteed	13.9	22.1	50.9	66.3	66.3	55.1	64.2	60.5
Official creditors	6.7	13.1	27.1	40.9	41.1	37.5	47.5	48.1
Private creditors	7.3	9.0	23.9	25.4	25.2	17.7	16.7	12.5
of which: Bonds	0.0	0.0	0.0	0.0	0.0	0.0	0.0	0.0
Private nonguaranteed	..	..	8.9	3.9	1.4	2.2	2.5	36.3
of which: Bonds	..	..	..	..	..	..	..	..
Interest payments	**4.7**	**7.1**	**10.6**	**11.0**	**10.4**	**9.6**	**11.6**	**9.5**
Public and publicly guaranteed	4.7	7.1	9.2	10.4	10.1	9.2	11.0	8.4
Official creditors	2.6	4.8	5.4	6.2	6.9	7.4	10.3	7.8
Private creditors	2.2	2.2	3.7	4.2	3.2	1.7	0.8	0.6
of which: Bonds	0.0	0.0	0.0	0.0	0.0	0.0	0.0	0.0
Private nonguaranteed	..	..	1.5	0.5	0.3	0.4	0.6	1.1
of which: Bonds	..	..	..	..	..	..	..	..
Net financial flows								
Net inflows	**15.2**	**106.8**	**-138.3**	**473.1**	**233.5**	**360.2**	**518.9**	**247.4**
Net debt inflows	-7.2	53.8	-344.3	47.2	7.6	-0.8	186.6	-76.5
Official creditors	-0.4	22.5	88.3	42.0	70.6	27.4	-4.3	-25.7
of which: World Bank	3.0	3.6	15.7	4.6	1.9	2.2	-2.1	-1.9
of which: IMF	0.0	6.1	7.0	0.0	0.0	-5.5	-6.2	-1.1
Private creditors	-6.8	31.3	-432.6	5.2	-63.1	-28.2	190.9	-50.8
Long-term	0.0	7.3	27.4	12.2	-25.1	-13.2	130.9	-48.8
Bonds	..	..	..	..	..	..	..	..
Banks and other private	0.0	7.3	27.4	12.2	-25.1	-13.2	130.9	-48.8
Short-term	-6.8	24.0	-460.0	-7.0	-38.0	-15.0	60.0	-1.9
Net equity inflows	22.3	53.0	206.0	425.8	226.0	361.0	332.2	323.9
Foreign direct investment	22.3	53.0	216.5	423.5	228.0	360.8	333.4	323.9
Portfolio equity	..	..	-10.4	2.3	-2.0	0.2	-1.2	..
Major economic aggregates								
Gross national income (GNI)	594.3	1,088.9	2,012.1	2,138.6	2,242.3	2,430.7	2,693.2	2,813.9
Exports of goods, services & prim. income	467.5	495.4	2,011.5	2,454.4	2,497.4	2,927.3	3,321.7	3,151.1
Imports of goods, services & prim. income	492.0	910.4	2,008.5	2,596.1	2,422.8	2,767.5	3,114.9	3,081.2
Primary income on FDI	34.4	31.0	271.9	266.5	234.5	333.9	314.1	306.9
Personal transfers & comp. of employees	2.2	2.3	3.2	3.0	3.1	3.3	3.5	3.6
International reserves	122.8	189.0	364.3	348.7	318.3	381.9	627.4	575.8
Ratios								
External debt stocks to exports (%)	43.4	73.1	45.6	35.9	35.6	30.8	31.7	29.9
External debt stocks to GNI (%)	34.2	33.3	45.6	41.2	39.7	37.0	39.1	33.5
Debt service to exports (%)	4.2	6.3	4.0	3.6	3.3	2.5	2.6	3.5
Short-term to external debt stocks (%)	8.9	15.5	15.9	15.6	11.3	9.8	13.9	15.2
Multilateral to external debt stocks (%)	58.5	47.4	32.8	34.0	35.6	34.7	27.3	28.1
Reserves to external debt stocks (%)	60.5	52.2	39.7	39.5	35.8	42.4	59.5	61.1

Notes: Long-term private nonguaranteed data from 2006 are World Bank staff estimates based on reports provided by the country. Short-term debt is based on data from the BIS.

MALI

(US$ million, unless otherwise indicated)

	2000	2005	2010	2011	2012	2013	2014	2015
Summary external debt data								
External debt stocks	**2,981**	**3,196**	**2,456**	**2,922**	**3,056**	**3,424**	**3,430**	**3,668**
Long-term external debt	2,671	3,036	2,263	2,499	2,780	3,080	3,107	3,331
Public and publicly guaranteed	2,671	3,036	2,263	2,499	2,780	3,080	3,107	3,331
Official creditors	2,671	3,032	2,258	2,495	2,776	3,077	3,106	3,330
of which: IMF	196	132	187	230	237	277	264	256
Private creditors	0	5	5	4	3	3	1	1
of which: Bonds	0	0	0	0	0	0	0	0
Private nonguaranteed	..	..	..	..	..	..	..	..
of which: Bonds	..	..	..	..	..	..	..	..
Short-term external debt	114	27	6	193	39	67	58	81
interest arrears on long-term	42	6	0	18	26	29	29	30
Long-term external debt								
Disbursements	**100**	**280**	**304**	**292**	**277**	**348**	**301**	**453**
Public and publicly guaranteed	100	280	304	292	277	348	301	453
Official creditors	100	277	304	292	277	348	301	453
Private creditors	0	3	0	0	0	0	0	0
of which: Bonds	0	0	0	0	0	0	0	0
Private nonguaranteed	..	..	..	..	..	..	..	..
of which: Bonds	..	..	..	..	..	..	..	..
Principal repayments	**50**	**52**	**39**	**41**	**34**	**69**	**64**	**65**
Public and publicly guaranteed	50	52	39	41	34	69	64	65
Official creditors	50	52	38	39	33	67	63	64
Private creditors	0	0	1	1	0	1	1	1
of which: Bonds	0	0	0	0	0	0	0	0
Private nonguaranteed	..	..	..	..	..	..	..	..
of which: Bonds	..	..	..	..	..	..	..	..
Interest payments	**18**	**27**	**21**	**25**	**24**	**27**	**26**	**32**
Public and publicly guaranteed	18	27	21	25	24	27	26	32
Official creditors	18	27	21	25	24	27	26	32
Private creditors	0	0	0	0	0	0	0	0
of which: Bonds	0	0	0	0	0	0	0	0
Private nonguaranteed	..	..	..	..	..	..	..	..
of which: Bonds	..	..	..	..	..	..	..	..
Net financial flows								
Net inflows	**-6**	**360**	**627**	**860**	**273**	**437**	**433**	**566**
Net debt inflows	-31	191	253	466	89	343	231	413
Official creditors	42	210	272	298	251	319	241	392
of which: World Bank	42	102	151	148	69	149	105	172
of which: IMF	-7	-15	6	45	7	38	4	3
Private creditors	-73	-20	-19	168	-162	24	-10	21
Long-term	..	3	-1	-1	0	-1	-1	-1
Bonds	..	..	..	..	..	..	..	..
Banks and other private	..	3	-1	-1	0	-1	-1	-1
Short-term	-73	-23	-18	169	-162	25	-9	22
Net equity inflows	25	169	374	395	185	94	201	153
Foreign direct investment	24	160	373	393	189	95	199	153
Portfolio equity	0	9	1	2	-4	-1	2	..
Major economic aggregates								
Gross national income (GNI)	2,924	6,038	10,260	12,516	11,941	12,813	14,004	12,706
Exports of goods, services & prim. income	664	1,443	2,508	2,859	3,427	3,384	3,330	2,507
Imports of goods, services & prim. income	1,045	2,108	4,236	4,371	4,495	5,794	5,942	4,926
Primary income on FDI	76	190	402	407	445	393	367	..
Personal transfers & comp. of employees	73	177	473	784	827	895	920	895
International reserves	382	854	1,344	1,379	1,341	1,306	861	624
Ratios								
External debt stocks to exports (%)	449.2	221.5	97.9	102.2	89.2	101.2	103.0	146.3
External debt stocks to GNI (%)	102.0	52.9	23.9	23.3	25.6	26.7	24.5	28.9
Debt service to exports (%)	14.1	6.9	2.5	2.4	1.7	3.0	3.0	4.2
Short-term to external debt stocks (%)	3.8	0.9	0.2	6.6	1.3	2.0	1.7	2.2
Multilateral to external debt stocks (%)	50.8	70.1	72.6	68.2	69.8	70.3	69.5	69.2
Reserves to external debt stocks (%)	12.8	26.7	54.7	47.2	43.9	38.1	25.1	17.0

Notes: Short-term debt is based on data from the BIS. The data for Principal Arrears on long-term are revised from 2001. Data include the effects of HIPC and MDRI debt relief.

MAURITANIA

(US$ million, unless otherwise indicated)

	2000	2005	2010	2011	2012	2013	2014	2015
Summary external debt data								
External debt stocks	**2,390**	**2,321**	**2,683**	**2,815**	**3,308**	**3,529**	**3,518**	**3,691**
Long-term external debt	2,029	2,071	2,301	2,485	2,901	3,102	3,131	3,254
Public and publicly guaranteed	2,029	2,071	2,301	2,485	2,901	3,102	3,131	3,254
Official creditors	2,009	2,048	2,300	2,485	2,901	3,102	3,131	3,254
of which: IMF	111	83	145	178	211	226	210	196
Private creditors	19	23	1	0	0	0	0	0
of which: Bonds	0	0	0	0	0	0	0	0
Private nonguaranteed	..	..	..	..	..	..	..	..
of which: Bonds	..	..	..	..	..	..	..	..
Short-term external debt	251	167	237	151	196	201	178	240
interest arrears on long-term	112	109	76	77	76	75	73	70
Long-term external debt								
Disbursements	**115**	**143**	**390**	**256**	**452**	**296**	**298**	**345**
Public and publicly guaranteed	115	143	390	256	452	296	298	345
Official creditors	115	128	390	256	452	296	298	345
Private creditors	0	15	0	0	0	0	0	0
of which: Bonds	0	0	0	0	0	0	0	0
Private nonguaranteed	..	..	..	..	..	..	..	..
of which: Bonds	..	..	..	..	..	..	..	..
Principal repayments	**46**	**33**	**76**	**79**	**85**	**106**	**154**	**123**
Public and publicly guaranteed	46	33	76	79	85	106	154	123
Official creditors	43	31	65	78	85	106	154	123
Private creditors	2	1	11	1	0	0	0	0
of which: Bonds	0	0	0	0	0	0	0	0
Private nonguaranteed	..	..	..	..	..	..	..	..
of which: Bonds	..	..	..	..	..	..	..	..
Interest payments	**20**	**20**	**35**	**41**	**55**	**54**	**62**	**85**
Public and publicly guaranteed	20	20	35	41	55	54	62	85
Official creditors	18	19	34	41	55	54	62	85
Private creditors	2	1	1	0	0	0	0	0
of which: Bonds	0	0	0	0	0	0	0	0
Private nonguaranteed	..	..	..	..	..	..	..	..
of which: Bonds	..	..	..	..	..	..	..	..
Net financial flows								
Net inflows	**102**	**904**	**581**	**714**	**1,831**	**1,336**	**623**	**784**
Net debt inflows	62	92	451	125	445	210	120	282
Official creditors	74	87	359	214	399	204	141	217
of which: World Bank	55	40	39	31	38	8	9	6
of which: IMF	2	-10	34	35	33	14	-3	-4
Private creditors	-11	5	92	-88	46	6	-21	65
Long-term	-2	14	-11	-1	..	..	..	..
Bonds	..	..	..	..	..	..	..	..
Banks and other private	-2	14	-11	-1	..	..	..	..
Short-term	-9	-9	103	-87	46	6	-21	65
Net equity inflows	40	812	131	589	1,386	1,126	503	502
Foreign direct investment	40	812	131	589	1,386	1,126	503	502
Portfolio equity	..	..	..	..	..	..	..	..
Major economic aggregates								
Gross national income (GNI)	1,307	2,249	4,269	5,011	5,041	5,443	5,189	..
Exports of goods, services & prim. income	..	..	2,306	3,124	2,911	2,957	2,235	1,712
Imports of goods, services & prim. income	..	..	2,787	3,522	4,448	4,360	3,822	2,846
Primary income on FDI	..	..	..	..	..	..	..	..
Personal transfers & comp. of employees	..	..	..	..	..	..	..	..
International reserves	46	64	272	485	949	..	..	..
Ratios								
External debt stocks to exports (%)	..	..	116.4	90.1	113.6	119.3	157.4	215.6
External debt stocks to GNI (%)	182.8	103.2	62.9	56.2	65.6	64.8	67.8	..
Debt service to exports (%)	..	..	4.9	3.9	4.9	5.6	9.9	12.6
Short-term to external debt stocks (%)	10.5	7.2	8.8	5.4	5.9	5.7	5.1	6.5
Multilateral to external debt stocks (%)	41.6	60.8	50.3	51.1	48.1	47.5	50.6	51.4
Reserves to external debt stocks (%)	1.9	2.8	10.1	17.2	28.7	..	..	..

Notes: Short-term debt is based on data from the BIS. Data include the effects of MDRI debt relief.

MAURITIUS

(US$ million, unless otherwise indicated)

	2000	2005	2010	2011	2012	2013	2014	2015
Summary external debt data								
External debt stocks	**967**	**805**	**2,734**	**9,533**	**10,111**	**13,317**	**15,202**	**14,643**
Long-term external debt	946	782	1,107	7,677	7,121	10,259	11,469	11,060
Public and publicly guaranteed	828	716	1,007	1,171	1,368	1,735	1,812	1,718
Official creditors	494	504	888	1,096	1,295	1,674	1,767	1,685
of which: IMF	21	23	149	149	149	149	140	134
Private creditors	334	213	119	75	73	61	45	34
of which: Bonds	0	0	0	0	0	0	0	0
Private nonguaranteed	118	66	100	6,505	5,752	8,523	9,657	9,341
of which: Bonds	0	0	0	0	0	0	0	0
Short-term external debt	0	0	1,478	1,707	2,842	2,909	3,593	3,449
interest arrears on long-term	0	0	0	0	1	0	1	1
Long-term external debt								
Disbursements	**128**	**138**	**425**	**4,625**	**3,717**	**6,386**	**4,479**	**2,776**
Public and publicly guaranteed	119	126	356	296	248	405	290	75
Official creditors	43	62	293	268	237	405	290	75
Private creditors	76	64	63	28	11	0	0	0
of which: Bonds	0	0	0	0	0	0	0	0
Private nonguaranteed	9	11	69	4,329	3,469	5,981	4,190	2,701
of which: Bonds	..	..	..	..	..	..	..	..
Principal repayments	**401**	**197**	**118**	**3,336**	**3,025**	**3,271**	**3,164**	**3,108**
Public and publicly guaranteed	385	176	69	72	59	61	108	92
Official creditors	55	87	45	49	45	45	98	85
Private creditors	330	89	24	23	15	15	9	7
of which: Bonds	150	0	0	0	0	0	0	0
Private nonguaranteed	16	21	49	3,264	2,966	3,210	3,056	3,016
of which: Bonds	..	..	..	..	..	..	..	..
Interest payments	**52**	**30**	**18**	**77**	**71**	**75**	**297**	**228**
Public and publicly guaranteed	51	30	17	22	25	25	29	27
Official creditors	23	19	15	20	24	24	28	26
Private creditors	29	10	2	2	2	1	1	0
of which: Bonds	5	0	0	0	0	0	0	0
Private nonguaranteed	1	0	1	55	46	50	269	201
of which: Bonds	..	..	..	..	..	..	..	..
Net financial flows								
Net inflows	**-11**	**18**	**922**	**1,952**	**2,415**	**3,476**	**2,417**	**-268**
Net debt inflows	-273	-59	492	1,519	1,826	3,183	1,999	-477
Official creditors	-12	-24	249	219	193	360	191	-10
of which: World Bank	-15	-7	-4	46	28	49	17	-24
of which: IMF	0	0	0	0	0	0	0	0
Private creditors	-261	-35	243	1,300	1,633	2,823	1,807	-466
Long-term	-261	-35	58	1,070	500	2,756	1,124	-322
Bonds	-150	0	0	0	0	0	0	0
Banks and other private	-111	-35	58	1,070	500	2,756	1,124	-322
Short-term	..	..	185	230	1,134	67	683	-144
Net equity inflows	262	77	430	433	589	293	418	208
Foreign direct investment	266	42	430	433	589	293	418	208
Portfolio equity	-4	36	..	..	..	..	..	..
Major economic aggregates								
Gross national income (GNI)	4,553	6,276	9,835	11,282	11,483	12,065	12,434	11,399
Exports of goods, services & prim. income	2,671	3,899	10,189	6,983	8,048	12,268	13,075	11,773
Imports of goods, services & prim. income	2,772	4,284	11,378	8,664	9,017	12,926	13,579	12,113
Primary income on FDI	8	34	4,639	601	1,074	4,331	4,204	4,020
Personal transfers & comp. of employees	177	1	1	1	1	1	1	1
International reserves	897	1,340	2,442	2,583	2,837	3,340	3,615	3,957
Ratios								
External debt stocks to exports (%)	36.2	20.6	26.8	136.5	125.6	108.5	116.3	124.4
External debt stocks to GNI (%)	21.2	12.8	27.8	84.5	88.1	110.4	122.3	128.5
Debt service to exports (%)	17.0	5.8	1.5	49.3	39.0	27.6	26.8	28.9
Short-term to external debt stocks (%)	0.0	0.0	54.0	17.9	28.1	21.8	23.6	23.6
Multilateral to external debt stocks (%)	22.3	31.1	18.3	6.1	6.2	6.6	6.3	6.1
Reserves to external debt stocks (%)	92.8	166.4	89.3	27.1	28.1	25.1	23.8	27

Notes: 2009-2010 long-term private nonguaranteed debt data are based on reports provided by the country and do not include offshore liabilities and 2011-2015 are World Bank staff estimates based on reports provided by the country. Short-term debt data are based on reports provided by the country and include offshore liabilities.

MEXICO

(US$ million, unless otherwise indicated)

	2000	2005	2010	2011	2012	2013	2014	2015
Summary external debt data								
External debt stocks	**152,558**	**170,823**	**245,906**	**291,784**	**349,269**	**406,227**	**441,564**	**426,334**
Long-term external debt	133,248	148,208	198,455	234,974	268,962	309,325	346,281	352,624
Public and publicly guaranteed	82,767	115,549	145,925	164,302	195,894	220,022	247,366	259,275
Official creditors	20,892	19,092	25,975	28,212	29,949	31,417	32,010	31,545
of which: IMF	378	415	4,391	4,377	4,382	4,391	4,131	3,951
Private creditors	61,875	96,457	119,950	136,090	165,945	188,604	215,357	227,730
of which: Bonds	53,693	75,294	97,656	115,543	147,704	158,176	184,210	195,362
Private nonguaranteed	50,481	32,658	52,529	70,672	73,067	89,303	98,914	93,349
of which: Bonds	20,644	16,943	32,898	47,393	54,967	80,400	84,752	77,863
Short-term external debt	18,932	22,201	43,061	52,434	75,925	92,511	91,152	69,759
interest arrears on long-term	0	0	0	0	0	0	0	0
Long-term external debt								
Disbursements	**32,830**	**29,393**	**54,656**	**57,106**	**92,931**	**87,459**	**67,023**	**49,800**
Public and publicly guaranteed	11,483	18,588	41,812	31,458	42,349	39,658	41,413	27,850
Official creditors	2,855	2,309	6,166	4,568	3,142	2,876	2,600	1,674
Private creditors	8,628	16,278	35,646	26,890	39,207	36,783	38,813	26,176
of which: Bonds	7,368	13,541	26,489	24,189	36,167	17,413	34,479	20,392
Private nonguaranteed	21,346	10,806	12,844	25,649	50,582	47,801	25,610	21,950
of which: Bonds	3,346	6,669	11,298	18,065	31,005	43,355	17,759	14,519
Principal repayments	**39,455**	**25,101**	**21,683**	**28,708**	**35,413**	**20,201**	**29,393**	**31,909**
Public and publicly guaranteed	16,825	15,686	13,941	12,383	8,501	12,210	9,000	11,857
Official creditors	3,386	2,530	1,679	1,947	1,490	1,427	1,477	1,574
Private creditors	13,439	13,155	12,263	10,436	7,011	10,783	7,523	10,282
of which: Bonds	9,256	9,989	7,118	5,851	1,703	3,630	4,591	5,959
Private nonguaranteed	22,630	9,416	7,742	16,325	26,912	7,991	20,393	20,052
of which: Bonds	3,552	2,645	2,826	2,216	3,723	2,190	9,166	12,148
Interest payments	**12,226**	**9,410**	**8,345**	**10,887**	**32,204**	**16,660**	**15,280**	**18,790**
Public and publicly guaranteed	7,974	7,545	5,859	7,318	28,709	10,289	10,262	14,477
Official creditors	1,554	860	627	730	756	765	746	711
Private creditors	6,420	6,685	5,232	6,587	27,954	9,524	9,517	13,765
of which: Bonds	4,897	6,247	4,927	6,258	27,633	9,197	8,714	12,980
Private nonguaranteed	4,251	1,866	2,486	3,570	3,495	6,372	5,017	4,313
of which: Bonds	1,620	957	1,379	1,761	1,849	4,606	3,446	3,596
Net financial flows								
Net inflows	**-2,865**	**28,110**	**71,371**	**50,759**	**105,258**	**121,990**	**61,927**	**23,202**
Net debt inflows	-16,055	6,181	50,480	37,771	81,010	83,844	36,271	-3,502
Official creditors	-4,830	-221	4,487	2,620	1,651	1,449	1,122	100
of which: World Bank	418	-382	2,256	1,264	1,040	360	-68	-135
of which: IMF	-4,299	0	0	0	0	0	0	0
Private creditors	-11,225	6,402	45,992	35,150	79,359	82,395	35,149	-3,602
Long-term	-6,095	4,513	28,486	25,778	55,867	65,809	36,508	17,791
Bonds	-2,094	7,576	27,843	34,187	61,745	54,948	38,481	16,804
Banks and other private	-4,001	-3,063	643	-8,410	-5,879	10,861	-1,973	987
Short-term	-5,130	1,889	17,506	9,373	23,492	16,586	-1,359	-21,393
Net equity inflows	13,189	21,929	20,891	12,989	24,248	38,146	25,656	26,704
Foreign direct investment	12,743	18,576	20,518	19,555	14,371	39,089	20,822	23,103
Portfolio equity	447	3,353	373	-6,566	9,877	-943	4,833	3,601
Major economic aggregates								
Gross national income (GNI)	668,631	850,654	1,061,247	1,173,921	1,184,279	1,242,781	1,285,931	1,135,773
Exports of goods, services & prim. income	185,853	235,187	324,906	376,155	400,742	412,243	430,054	412,103
Imports of goods, services & prim. income	211,599	266,378	351,663	413,113	440,257	464,874	479,218	469,111
Primary income on FDI	6,086	8,608	9,907	13,710	18,499	28,633	19,540	15,618
Personal transfers & comp. of employees	7,525	22,742	22,080	23,588	23,366	23,433	24,462	26,164
International reserves	35,509	74,054	120,265	143,991	160,413	175,432	190,923	173,458
Ratios								
External debt stocks to exports (%)	82.1	72.6	75.7	77.6	87.2	98.5	102.7	103.5
External debt stocks to GNI (%)	22.8	20.1	23.2	24.9	29.5	32.7	34.3	37.5
Debt service to exports (%)	31.9	15.5	10.1	11.2	17.7	10.1	11.5	13.2
Short-term to external debt stocks (%)	12.4	13.0	17.5	18.0	21.7	22.8	20.6	16.4
Multilateral to external debt stocks (%)	11.3	9.8	8.7	8.0	7.3	6.7	6.3	6.6
Reserves to external debt stocks (%)	23.3	43.4	48.9	49.3	45.9	43.2	43.2	40.7

MOLDOVA

(US$ million, unless otherwise indicated)

	2000	2005	2010	2011	2012	2013	2014	2015
Summary external debt data								
External debt stocks	**1,842**	**2,219**	**4,725**	**5,217**	**5,783**	**6,560**	**6,569**	**6,338**
Long-term external debt	1,053	1,238	2,745	2,907	3,228	3,603	3,677	4,206
Public and publicly guaranteed	856	698	839	865	965	997	1,027	1,069
Official creditors	749	664	823	844	936	968	1,001	1,047
of which: IMF	308	264	509	655	793	773	699	628
Private creditors	107	34	16	21	29	29	26	22
of which: Bonds	75	25	0	0	0	0	0	0
Private nonguaranteed	197	540	1,906	2,042	2,263	2,606	2,650	3,137
of which: Bonds	..	..	..	..	..	..	..	..
Short-term external debt	481	718	1,471	1,655	1,762	2,184	2,193	1,504
interest arrears on long-term	14	56	37	42	52	56	60	81
Long-term external debt								
Disbursements	**164**	**237**	**464**	**539**	**662**	**683**	**438**	**310**
Public and publicly guaranteed	54	26	94	103	157	109	162	137
Official creditors	52	26	89	89	135	94	155	134
Private creditors	2	0	5	14	21	15	7	3
of which: Bonds	0	0	0	0	0	0	0	0
Private nonguaranteed	110	211	370	436	505	574	276	173
of which: Bonds	..	..	..	..	..	..	..	..
Principal repayments	**58**	**163**	**306**	**368**	**467**	**543**	**455**	**312**
Public and publicly guaranteed	30	42	55	71	65	84	61	41
Official creditors	27	35	47	63	51	67	54	36
Private creditors	3	7	8	8	14	16	8	5
of which: Bonds	0	6	0	0	0	0	0	0
Private nonguaranteed	28	120	251	297	402	459	394	271
of which: Bonds	..	..	..	..	..	..	..	..
Interest payments	**47**	**42**	**49**	**58**	**55**	**66**	**63**	**43**
Public and publicly guaranteed	40	22	16	16	17	17	17	15
Official creditors	28	20	16	16	15	16	16	14
Private creditors	11	2	1	0	1	1	1	0
of which: Bonds	7	2	0	0	0	0	0	0
Private nonguaranteed	7	20	33	42	38	49	47	28
of which: Bonds	..	..	..	..	..	..	..	..
Net financial flows								
Net inflows	**644**	**265**	**617**	**738**	**576**	**727**	**166**	**-515**
Net debt inflows	560	157	439	503	428	537	-43	-752
Official creditors	12	-31	217	177	221	5	72	57
of which: World Bank	31	10	42	32	52	7	30	27
of which: IMF	-12	-22	175	152	137	-22	-29	-41
Private creditors	547	188	223	325	207	532	-115	-809
Long-term	82	84	117	145	111	113	-119	-100
Bonds	0	-6	0	0	0	0	0	0
Banks and other private	82	90	117	145	111	113	-119	-100
Short-term	465	104	106	180	96	418	4	-709
Net equity inflows	84	108	177	236	148	190	209	237
Foreign direct investment	81	107	172	231	134	180	199	233
Portfolio equity	3	1	6	5	14	10	10	3
Major economic aggregates								
Gross national income (GNI)	1,310	3,347	6,297	7,593	8,101	8,850	8,815	6,958
Exports of goods, services & prim. income	699	1,871	2,719	3,674	3,756	4,195	4,070	3,292
Imports of goods, services & prim. income	1,008	2,673	4,463	5,922	5,898	6,315	6,165	4,798
Primary income on FDI	3	45	152	257	117	165	134	224
Personal transfers & comp. of employees	178	915	1,753	1,813	1,986	2,192	2,076	1,540
International reserves	222	597	1,718	1,965	2,511	2,818	2,154	1,754
Ratios								
External debt stocks to exports (%)	263.3	118.6	173.8	142.0	154.0	156.4	161.4	192.5
External debt stocks to GNI (%)	140.6	66.3	75.0	68.7	71.4	74.1	74.5	91.1
Debt service to exports (%)	22.5	13.6	14.5	12.7	15.3	16.1	14.6	12.9
Short-term to external debt stocks (%)	26.1	32.3	31.1	31.7	30.5	33.3	33.4	23.7
Multilateral to external debt stocks (%)	22.1	18.4	12.0	11.9	12.8	12.2	12.9	13.8
Reserves to external debt stocks (%)	12.1	26.9	36.4	37.7	43.4	43.0	32.8	27.7

MONGOLIA

(US$ million, unless otherwise indicated)

	2000	2005	2010	2011	2012	2013	2014	2015
Summary external debt data								
External debt stocks	**960**	**1,396**	**5,928**	**9,627**	**15,385**	**18,893**	**20,826**	**21,542**
Long-term external debt	833	1,267	5,290	8,775	14,248	17,189	18,379	19,040
Public and publicly guaranteed	833	1,267	1,782	1,826	3,243	3,540	3,498	3,596
Official creditors	831	1,266	1,775	1,814	1,734	2,035	1,995	2,096
of which: IMF	114	105	273	268	234	140	73	68
Private creditors	3	0	7	12	1,508	1,505	1,503	1,500
of which: Bonds	0	0	0	0	1,500	1,500	1,500	1,500
Private nonguaranteed	..	..	3,508	6,949	11,006	13,650	14,881	15,444
of which: Bonds	..	..	..	..	900	900	919	1,119
Short-term external debt	13	25	365	583	903	1,563	2,374	2,435
interest arrears on long-term	2	0	0	0	0	4	0	0
Long-term external debt								
Disbursements	**75**	**91**	**2,929**	**3,554**	**6,422**	**3,867**	**2,057**	**2,031**
Public and publicly guaranteed	75	91	66	87	1,558	425	179	223
Official creditors	75	91	66	83	58	425	179	223
Private creditors	0	0	0	5	1,500	0	0	0
of which: Bonds	0	0	0	0	1,500	0	0	0
Private nonguaranteed	..	..	2,863	3,466	4,864	3,442	1,877	1,808
of which: Bonds	..	..	..	..	900	0	19	500
Principal repayments	**22**	**17**	**139**	**78**	**898**	**885**	**869**	**1,323**
Public and publicly guaranteed	22	17	122	54	84	71	63	61
Official creditors	19	17	44	54	80	68	60	58
Private creditors	3	0	77	0	4	3	3	3
of which: Bonds	0	0	75	0	0	0	0	0
Private nonguaranteed	..	..	18	24	814	814	807	1,262
of which: Bonds	..	..	..	..	0	0	0	300
Interest payments	**9**	**15**	**89**	**155**	**258**	**396**	**309**	**388**
Public and publicly guaranteed	9	15	20	20	21	59	23	18
Official creditors	9	15	19	20	21	22	22	18
Private creditors	0	0	1	0	0	38	1	1
of which: Bonds	0	0	1	0	0	38	1	1
Private nonguaranteed	..	..	70	134	236	337	286	369
of which: Bonds	..	..	..	..	27	79	80	104
Net financial flows								
Net inflows	**99**	**111**	**4,938**	**5,198**	**7,311**	**3,926**	**1,971**	**957**
Net debt inflows	45	-73	2,925	3,689	5,808	3,546	1,941	767
Official creditors	58	69	40	24	-58	264	58	163
of which: World Bank	14	12	17	47	20	4	6	4
of which: IMF	1	-6	19	-4	-35	-93	-61	-3
Private creditors	-12	-142	2,885	3,665	5,866	3,282	1,883	604
Long-term	-3	0	2,768	3,447	5,547	2,625	1,068	543
Bonds	..	..	-75	..	2,400	0	19	200
Banks and other private	-3	0	2,843	3,447	3,147	2,625	1,049	343
Short-term	-9	-142	117	218	319	657	815	61
Net equity inflows	54	185	2,012	1,509	1,503	380	30	190
Foreign direct investment	54	185	1,332	1,499	1,487	377	31	192
Portfolio equity	..	..	680	9	15	3	-1	-2
Major economic aggregates								
Gross national income (GNI)	1,132	2,472	6,591	9,566	11,343	11,872	11,233	10,680
Exports of goods, services & prim. income	627	1,494	3,423	5,481	5,402	5,030	6,406	5,375
Imports of goods, services & prim. income	791	1,635	4,496	8,478	9,004	8,364	7,954	6,088
Primary income on FDI	9	41	465	630	594	282	469	533
Personal transfers & comp. of employees	12	180	266	279	320	256	255	265
International reserves	179	333	2,197	2,275	3,930	2,096	1,540	1,247
Ratios								
External debt stocks to exports (%)	153.2	93.5	173.2	175.6	284.8	375.6	325.1	400.8
External debt stocks to GNI (%)	84.8	56.5	89.9	100.6	135.6	159.1	185.4	201.7
Debt service to exports (%)	6.6	3.0	7.0	4.6	22.4	27.9	20.0	32.6
Short-term to external debt stocks (%)	1.3	1.8	6.2	6.1	5.9	8.3	11.4	11.3
Multilateral to external debt stocks (%)	48.1	56.4	18.1	11.6	7.4	6.0	5.2	5.3
Reserves to external debt stocks (%)	18.6	23.9	37.1	23.6	25.5	11.1	7.4	5.8

Notes: Long-term private nonguaranteed debt data from 2008 are World Bank staff estimates based on reports provided by the country. Short-term debt before 2008 is based on data from the BIS.

MONTENEGRO

(US$ million, unless otherwise indicated)

	2000	2005	2010	2011	2012	2013	2014	2015
Summary external debt data								
External debt stocks	..	..	**1,603**	**2,357**	**2,834**	**3,086**	**2,537**	**2,665**
Long-term external debt	..	..	1,378	1,863	2,256	2,505	2,448	2,630
Public and publicly guaranteed	..	..	1,359	1,809	2,188	2,428	2,368	2,555
Official creditors	..	..	846	1,016	1,172	1,206	1,087	1,137
of which: IMF	..	..	40	40	40	40	37	36
Private creditors	..	..	512	792	1,016	1,222	1,281	1,418
of which: Bonds	..	..	267	492	501	634	786	1,043
Private nonguaranteed	..	..	19	54	68	77	80	75
of which: Bonds	..	..	0	0	0	0	0	0
Short-term external debt	..	..	186	455	538	541	52	0
interest arrears on long-term	..	..	..	..	..	..	..	..
Long-term external debt								
Disbursements	..	..	**395**	**664**	**526**	**422**	**523**	**829**
Public and publicly guaranteed	..	..	383	623	506	402	494	803
Official creditors	..	..	35	262	187	76	93	234
Private creditors	..	..	348	361	319	326	401	569
of which: Bonds	..	..	265	248	0	107	360	555
Private nonguaranteed	..	..	12	40	21	20	29	25
of which: Bonds	..	..	..	..	..	..	..	..
Principal repayments	..	..	**61**	**127**	**174**	**269**	**184**	**410**
Public and publicly guaranteed	..	..	60	125	166	255	168	388
Official creditors	..	..	33	43	48	85	92	92
Private creditors	..	..	27	81	118	170	76	295
of which: Bonds	..	..	0	0	0	0	11	210
Private nonguaranteed	..	..	2	2	8	14	16	23
of which: Bonds	..	..	..	..	..	..	..	..
Interest payments	..	..	**34**	**79**	**87**	**98**	**92**	**89**
Public and publicly guaranteed	..	..	33	78	86	97	91	87
Official creditors	..	..	20	24	24	31	25	24
Private creditors	..	..	13	55	63	66	66	64
of which: Bonds	..	..	0	22	37	39	39	45
Private nonguaranteed	..	..	1	1	1	1	1	1
of which: Bonds	..	..	..	..	..	..	..	..
Net financial flows								
Net inflows	..	..	**-129**	**1,228**	**970**	**500**	**138**	**842**
Net debt inflows	..	..	-687	806	435	156	-150	366
Official creditors	..	..	2	218	139	-9	1	142
of which: World Bank	..	..	-3	-2	88	-5	-12	-15
of which: IMF	..	..	0	0	0	0	0	0
Private creditors	..	..	-689	587	297	164	-151	225
Long-term	..	..	332	318	214	161	338	277
Bonds	..	..	265	248	0	107	349	344
Banks and other private	..	..	67	70	214	54	-11	-68
Short-term	..	..	-1,021	269	83	3	-489	-52
Net equity inflows	..	..	558	423	535	344	288	476
Foreign direct investment	..	..	566	438	535	330	272	465
Portfolio equity	..	..	-8	-15	0	14	16	10
Major economic aggregates								
Gross national income (GNI)	..	..	4,110	4,575	4,157	4,552	4,649	4,096
Exports of goods, services & prim. income	..	..	1,722	2,198	1,975	2,125	2,142	1,982
Imports of goods, services & prim. income	..	..	2,826	3,152	2,918	2,938	2,992	2,624
Primary income on FDI	..	..	99	45	33	28	71	45
Personal transfers & comp. of employees	..	..	301	343	333	423	431	381
International reserves	..	..	556	393	459	584	661	734
Ratios								
External debt stocks to exports (%)	..	..	93.1	107.2	143.5	145.2	118.5	134.5
External debt stocks to GNI (%)	..	..	39.0	51.5	68.2	67.8	54.6	65.1
Debt service to exports (%)	..	..	5.7	9.7	13.6	17.6	13.1	25.2
Short-term to external debt stocks (%)	..	..	11.6	19.3	19.0	17.5	2.0	0.0
Multilateral to external debt stocks (%)	..	..	34.7	28.7	27.9	27.0	28.7	23.4
Reserves to external debt stocks (%)	..	..	34.7	16.7	16.2	18.9	26.1	27.5

Notes: Short-term debt is based on data from the BIS.

MOROCCO

(US$ million, unless otherwise indicated)

	2000	2005	2010	2011	2012	2013	2014	2015
Summary external debt data								
External debt stocks	**20,790**	**16,254**	**27,259**	**29,924**	**33,836**	**39,263**	**42,809**	**42,989**
Long-term external debt	19,106	15,449	23,647	25,225	28,805	33,048	34,389	35,343
Public and publicly guaranteed	17,244	12,398	21,059	22,392	25,106	28,280	29,817	29,728
Official creditors	12,759	10,075	17,278	18,637	19,823	21,869	20,753	20,028
of which: IMF	112	122	865	862	863	865	813	778
Private creditors	4,485	2,323	3,780	3,755	5,283	6,411	9,064	9,701
of which: Bonds	152	472	1,336	1,294	2,819	3,629	5,314	5,189
Private nonguaranteed	1,862	3,051	2,589	2,833	3,699	4,768	4,572	5,615
of which: Bonds	..	..	..	..	..	..	..	..
Short-term external debt	1,573	682	2,747	3,837	4,167	5,351	7,607	6,867
interest arrears on long-term	122	0	0	0	0	0	0	0
Long-term external debt								
Disbursements	**1,638**	**2,456**	**4,999**	**4,506**	**6,122**	**7,486**	**8,200**	**6,062**
Public and publicly guaranteed	980	1,658	3,882	3,285	4,114	4,407	6,113	3,712
Official creditors	631	1,562	2,258	2,995	2,477	3,176	2,666	2,372
Private creditors	349	97	1,625	290	1,636	1,231	3,447	1,340
of which: Bonds	0	0	1,327	0	1,500	750	1,850	0
Private nonguaranteed	658	798	1,116	1,222	2,008	3,079	2,087	2,350
of which: Bonds	..	..	..	..	..	..	..	..
Principal repayments	**1,632**	**2,139**	**2,423**	**2,424**	**2,770**	**3,998**	**3,714**	**2,462**
Public and publicly guaranteed	1,593	1,881	1,270	1,470	1,572	1,821	1,873	1,658
Official creditors	928	1,303	1,086	1,277	1,392	1,557	1,648	1,465
Private creditors	666	578	184	193	180	264	225	193
of which: Bonds	30	41	0	0	0	0	0	0
Private nonguaranteed	39	258	1,154	955	1,198	2,177	1,841	804
of which: Bonds	..	..	..	..	..	..	..	..
Interest payments	**949**	**569**	**850**	**758**	**787**	**1,015**	**953**	**981**
Public and publicly guaranteed	877	501	819	723	751	908	892	872
Official creditors	548	388	731	571	586	659	510	456
Private creditors	329	113	88	152	165	249	381	416
of which: Bonds	14	25	0	62	57	130	255	266
Private nonguaranteed	71	68	31	35	35	107	62	110
of which: Bonds	..	..	..	..	..	..	..	..
Net financial flows								
Net inflows	**-216**	**1,845**	**4,613**	**5,414**	**5,666**	**7,928**	**9,876**	**5,100**
Net debt inflows	-449	831	3,112	3,172	3,683	4,671	6,742	2,860
Official creditors	-296	259	1,172	1,718	1,085	1,619	1,018	908
of which: World Bank	-170	-48	68	502	39	1,108	304	533
of which: IMF	0	0	0	0	0	0	0	0
Private creditors	-153	573	1,940	1,454	2,598	3,053	5,724	1,953
Long-term	302	59	1,403	364	2,267	1,869	3,468	2,693
Bonds	-30	-41	1,327	..	1,500	750	1,850	..
Banks and other private	332	99	77	364	767	1,119	1,618	2,693
Short-term	-455	514	537	1,090	330	1,183	2,256	-740
Net equity inflows	233	1,013	1,501	2,242	1,984	3,256	3,134	2,240
Foreign direct investment	215	950	1,369	2,076	2,092	3,213	3,134	2,240
Portfolio equity	18	64	132	166	-108	43	..	..
Major economic aggregates								
Gross national income (GNI)	38,094	62,069	91,933	99,661	96,282	105,779	107,524	98,539
Exports of goods, services & prim. income	9,127	17,281	27,913	32,649	32,954	33,086	36,415	33,814
Imports of goods, services & prim. income	12,085	21,616	39,109	48,764	49,913	49,667	52,707	43,624
Primary income on FDI	268	594	1,445	2,086	2,092	1,279	2,219	1,419
Personal transfers & comp. of employees	2,161	4,589	6,423	7,256	6,508	6,882	8,094	6,904
International reserves	4,823	16,187	22,960	19,333	16,211	18,197	19,672	22,254
Ratios								
External debt stocks to exports (%)	227.8	94.1	97.7	91.7	102.7	118.7	117.6	127.1
External debt stocks to GNI (%)	54.6	26.2	29.7	30.0	35.1	37.1	39.8	43.6
Debt service to exports (%)	29.7	15.8	11.8	9.9	10.9	15.3	13.1	10.5
Short-term to external debt stocks (%)	7.6	4.2	10.1	12.8	12.3	13.6	17.8	16.0
Multilateral to external debt stocks (%)	29.3	35.9	37.2	37.8	35.6	36.1	31.1	30.0
Reserves to external debt stocks (%)	23.2	99.6	84.2	64.6	47.9	46.3	46.0	51.8

Notes: Short-term debt before 2009 is based on data from the BIS.

MOZAMBIQUE

(US$ million, unless otherwise indicated)

	2000	2005	2010	2011	2012	2013	2014	2015
Summary external debt data								
External debt stocks	**5,613**	**4,392**	**4,130**	**4,649**	**5,490**	**7,895**	**8,695**	**10,056**
Long-term external debt	4,693	3,366	3,170	4,032	4,793	6,826	7,930	8,903
Public and publicly guaranteed	4,693	3,366	3,170	4,032	4,793	6,826	7,930	8,903
Official creditors	4,682	3,364	3,072	3,802	4,530	5,695	6,435	6,913
of which: IMF	361	312	357	355	353	351	327	399
Private creditors	11	2	98	230	262	1,131	1,495	1,991
of which: Bonds	0	0	0	0	0	850	850	850
Private nonguaranteed	..	..	..	..	..	..	..	..
of which: Bonds	..	..	..	..	..	..	..	..
Short-term external debt	560	714	603	262	344	719	438	754
interest arrears on long-term	404	525	504	133	174	330	133	213
Long-term external debt								
Disbursements	**131**	**326**	**375**	**613**	**768**	**1,982**	**1,556**	**1,370**
Public and publicly guaranteed	131	326	375	613	768	1,982	1,556	1,370
Official creditors	131	326	296	462	737	1,110	1,150	766
Private creditors	0	0	79	151	31	872	405	605
of which: Bonds	0	0	0	0	0	850	0	0
Private nonguaranteed	..	..	..	..	..	..	..	..
of which: Bonds	..	..	..	..	..	..	..	..
Principal repayments	**34**	**18**	**38**	**37**	**49**	**98**	**102**	**176**
Public and publicly guaranteed	34	18	38	37	49	98	102	176
Official creditors	33	18	30	30	45	84	90	90
Private creditors	1	0	8	6	4	14	11	86
of which: Bonds	0	0	0	0	0	0	0	0
Private nonguaranteed	..	..	..	..	..	..	..	..
of which: Bonds	..	..	..	..	..	..	..	..
Interest payments	**20**	**22**	**48**	**31**	**33**	**55**	**105**	**190**
Public and publicly guaranteed	20	22	48	31	33	55	105	190
Official creditors	20	22	48	31	33	53	64	79
Private creditors	0	0	0	0	0	2	41	110
of which: Bonds	0	0	0	0	0	0	27	54
Private nonguaranteed	..	..	..	..	..	..	..	..
of which: Bonds	..	..	..	..	..	..	..	..
Net financial flows								
Net inflows	**223**	**186**	**701**	**2,007**	**974**	**3,059**	**1,920**	**2,646**
Net debt inflows	83	125	290	605	758	2,100	1,367	1,518
Official creditors	157	297	288	430	690	1,023	1,057	763
of which: World Bank	96	222	158	93	227	369	240	280
of which: IMF	60	-11	21	-2	-2	-3	-3	87
Private creditors	-74	-172	3	174	68	1,077	310	755
Long-term	-1	..	71	144	27	858	394	519
Bonds	..	..	..	..	..	850	0	0
Banks and other private	-1	..	71	144	27	8	394	519
Short-term	-73	-172	-68	30	41	219	-84	236
Net equity inflows	139	60	410	1,402	216	959	553	1,128
Foreign direct investment	139	60	410	1,402	216	959	553	1,128
Portfolio equity	..	0	0	0	..	0	..	..
Major economic aggregates								
Gross national income (GNI)	4,824	7,364	9,813	12,941	14,495	15,960	16,744	14,468
Exports of goods, services & prim. income	769	2,186	2,713	3,668	4,781	4,902	4,769	4,248
Imports of goods, services & prim. income	1,763	3,350	5,220	8,001	12,609	12,577	11,939	10,935
Primary income on FDI	0	284	218	272	46	54	49	60
Personal transfers & comp. of employees	37	59	116	130	174	152	155	196
International reserves	723	1,054	2,159	2,469	2,770	3,142	3,010	2,411
Ratios								
External debt stocks to exports (%)	730.3	200.9	152.2	126.7	114.8	161.1	182.3	236.7
External debt stocks to GNI (%)	116.4	59.6	42.1	35.9	37.9	49.5	51.9	69.5
Debt service to exports (%)	9.4	3.2	3.3	2.0	1.8	3.3	4.5	9.5
Short-term to external debt stocks (%)	10.0	16.3	14.6	5.6	6.3	9.1	5.0	7.5
Multilateral to external debt stocks (%)	19.7	52.9	52.5	52.7	50.6	40.9	38.4	35.2
Reserves to external debt stocks (%)	12.9	24.0	52.3	53.1	50.5	39.8	34.6	24.0

Notes: Short-term debt is based on data from the BIS. Data include HIPC and MDRI debt relief.

MYANMAR

(US$ million, unless otherwise indicated)

	2000	2005	2010	2011	2012	2013	2014	2015
Summary external debt data								
External debt stocks	**5,875**	**6,674**	**8,217**	**8,192**	**7,840**	**7,251**	**6,266**	**6,401**
Long-term external debt	5,328	5,815	6,646	6,620	6,486	5,978	5,175	5,306
Public and publicly guaranteed	5,328	5,815	6,646	6,620	6,486	5,978	5,175	5,240
Official creditors	4,283	4,721	6,034	6,014	5,895	5,399	4,650	4,716
of which: IMF	55	63	390	381	378	380	339	341
Private creditors	1,045	1,094	612	605	591	579	525	525
of which: Bonds	0	0	0	0	0	0	0	0
Private nonguaranteed	..	..	..	..	..	..	..	66
of which: Bonds	..	..	..	..	..	..	..	..
Short-term external debt	492	796	1,181	1,191	977	893	752	754
interest arrears on long-term	492	796	1,181	1,191	977	893	752	754
Long-term external debt								
Disbursements	**38**	**1**	**0**	**0**	**931**	**0**	**18**	**178**
Public and publicly guaranteed	38	1	0	0	931	0	18	93
Official creditors	35	1	0	0	931	0	18	93
Private creditors	3	0	0	0	0	0	0	0
of which: Bonds	0	0	0	0	0	0	0	0
Private nonguaranteed	..	..	..	..	..	..	..	85
of which: Bonds	..	..	..	..	..	..	..	..
Principal repayments	**6**	**3**	**2**	**1**	**764**	**54**	**49**	**64**
Public and publicly guaranteed	6	3	2	1	764	54	49	46
Official creditors	2	3	2	1	764	54	49	46
Private creditors	4	0	0	0	0	0	0	0
of which: Bonds	0	0	0	0	0	0	0	0
Private nonguaranteed	..	..	..	..	..	..	..	19
of which: Bonds	..	..	..	..	..	..	..	..
Interest payments	**1**	**0**	**1**	**1**	**179**	**13**	**13**	**12**
Public and publicly guaranteed	1	0	1	1	179	13	13	11
Official creditors	0	0	1	1	179	13	13	11
Private creditors	0	0	0	0	0	0	0	0
of which: Bonds	0	0	0	0	0	0	0	0
Private nonguaranteed	..	..	..	..	..	..	..	0
of which: Bonds	..	..	..	..	..	..	..	..
Net financial flows								
Net inflows	**286**	**233**	**899**	**2,519**	**1,501**	**2,201**	**1,367**	**3,251**
Net debt inflows	31	-2	-2	-1	167	-54	-31	113
Official creditors	33	-2	-2	-1	167	-54	-31	47
of which: World Bank	0	0	0	0	89	-26	-8	53
of which: IMF	0	0	0	0	0	0	0	0
Private creditors	-2	..	..	..	..	..	..	66
Long-term	-2	..	..	..	..	..	..	66
Bonds	..	..	..	..	..	..	..	..
Banks and other private	-2	..	..	..	..	..	..	66
Short-term	..	..	..	..	..	..	..	..
Net equity inflows	255	235	901	2,520	1,334	2,255	1,398	3,137
Foreign direct investment	255	235	901	2,520	1,334	2,255	1,398	3,137
Portfolio equity	..	..	..	..	..	..	..	..
Major economic aggregates								
Gross national income (GNI)	..	..	..	..	73,934	57,366	62,194	..
Exports of goods, services & prim. income	2,145	3,838	7,851	8,658	9,745	12,387	13,452	14,163
Imports of goods, services & prim. income	2,627	3,429	6,516	10,614	11,555	13,925	18,291	20,617
Primary income on FDI	135	1,388	1,816	1,955	2,396	2,011	3,705	4,068
Personal transfers & comp. of employees	102	129	115	127	275	1,644	279	387
International reserves	223	771	5,717	7,004	6,964	..	..	..
Ratios								
External debt stocks to exports (%)	273.9	173.9	104.7	94.6	80.5	58.5	46.6	45.2
External debt stocks to GNI (%)	..	..	..	..	10.6	12.6	10.1	..
Debt service to exports (%)	0.4	0.1	0.0	0.0	9.7	0.5	0.5	0.5
Short-term to external debt stocks (%)	8.4	11.9	14.4	14.5	12.5	12.3	12.0	11.8
Multilateral to external debt stocks (%)	19.5	18.4	17.2	17.1	19.0	20.2	20.6	21.3
Reserves to external debt stocks (%)	3.8	11.5	69.6	85.5	88.8	0.0	0.0	0.0

Notes: Fiscal year-end for external debt data is March. Long-term public and publicly guaranteed, long-term private nonguaranteed debt data are World Bank staff estimates based on the original terms of the loans.

NEPAL

(US$ million, unless otherwise indicated)

	2000	2005	2010	2011	2012	2013	2014	2015
Summary external debt data								
External debt stocks	**2,878**	**3,191**	**3,789**	**3,828**	**3,888**	**4,088**	**4,010**	**4,155**
Long-term external debt	2,826	3,112	3,509	3,530	3,571	3,649	3,512	3,612
Public and publicly guaranteed	2,826	3,112	3,509	3,530	3,571	3,649	3,512	3,612
Official creditors	2,821	3,108	3,506	3,528	3,569	3,648	3,511	3,612
of which: IMF	23	32	219	214	204	189	165	194
Private creditors	5	5	3	2	2	2	1	0
of which: Bonds	0	0	0	0	0	0	0	0
Private nonguaranteed	..	..	..	..	..	..	..	..
of which: Bonds	..	..	..	..	..	..	..	..
Short-term external debt	29	47	61	84	113	250	333	349
interest arrears on long-term	0	0	0	0	0	0	0	0
Long-term external debt								
Disbursements	**154**	**196**	**126**	**174**	**235**	**265**	**243**	**405**
Public and publicly guaranteed	154	196	126	174	235	265	243	405
Official creditors	154	196	126	174	235	265	243	405
Private creditors	0	0	0	0	0	0	0	0
of which: Bonds	0	0	0	0	0	0	0	0
Private nonguaranteed	..	..	..	..	..	..	..	..
of which: Bonds	..	..	..	..	..	..	..	..
Principal repayments	**67**	**86**	**148**	**154**	**175**	**165**	**171**	**165**
Public and publicly guaranteed	67	86	148	154	175	165	171	165
Official creditors	60	85	148	153	175	164	171	165
Private creditors	7	1	0	1	0	1	0	0
of which: Bonds	0	0	0	0	0	0	0	0
Private nonguaranteed	0	0	0	0	0	0	0	0
of which: Bonds	0	0	0	0	0	0	0	0
Interest payments	**28**	**30**	**32**	**35**	**33**	**36**	**40**	**32**
Public and publicly guaranteed	28	30	32	35	33	36	40	32
Official creditors	27	30	32	35	33	36	40	32
Private creditors	1	0	0	0	0	0	0	0
of which: Bonds	0	0	0	0	0	0	0	0
Private nonguaranteed	..	..	..	..	..	..	..	..
of which: Bonds	..	..	..	..	..	..	..	..
Net financial flows								
Net inflows	**69**	**124**	**121**	**133**	**170**	**296**	**173**	**311**
Net debt inflows	69	121	34	39	78	221	142	292
Official creditors	90	111	17	16	50	85	60	276
of which: World Bank	33	3	-33	4	31	91	53	185
of which: IMF	-4	..	39	-4	-10	-15	-13	36
Private creditors	-21	10	17	22	29	136	83	16
Long-term	-7	-1	0	-1	0	-1	0	0
Bonds	..	..	..	..	..	..	..	..
Banks and other private	-7	-1	0	-1	0	-1	0	0
Short-term	-14	11	17	23	29	137	83	17
Net equity inflows	0	2	88	94	92	74	30	19
Foreign direct investment	0	2	88	94	92	74	30	19
Portfolio equity	..	..	..	..	..	..	..	..
Major economic aggregates								
Gross national income (GNI)	5,514	8,153	16,125	19,018	19,003	19,393	19,971	21,217
Exports of goods, services & prim. income	1,354	1,423	1,781	2,150	2,177	2,516	2,803	2,681
Imports of goods, services & prim. income	1,825	2,803	5,995	6,588	6,969	7,618	8,844	7,799
Primary income on FDI	..	57	50	59	34	25	26	49
Personal transfers & comp. of employees	111	1,212	3,464	4,217	4,793	5,589	5,889	6,730
International reserves	945	1,499	2,937	3,631	4,307	5,293	6,027	7,937
Ratios								
External debt stocks to exports (%)	212.5	224.2	212.7	178.0	178.6	162.5	143.1	155.0
External debt stocks to GNI (%)	52.2	39.1	23.5	20.1	20.5	21.1	20.1	19.6
Debt service to exports (%)	7.6	8.5	10.6	9.2	10.3	8.8	8.3	8.3
Short-term to external debt stocks (%)	1.0	1.5	1.6	2.2	2.9	6.1	8.3	8.4
Multilateral to external debt stocks (%)	85.4	85.8	82.7	82.2	80.8	79.0	77.4	77.2
Reserves to external debt stocks (%)	32.9	47.0	77.5	94.8	110.8	129.5	150.3	191.0

Notes: Short-term debt before 2013 is based on data from the BIS.

NICARAGUA

(US$ million, unless otherwise indicated)

	2000	2005	2010	2011	2012	2013	2014	2015
Summary external debt data								
External debt stocks	**6,822**	**5,000**	**7,002**	**7,924**	**8,950**	**9,777**	**10,213**	**10,490**
Long-term external debt	5,716	4,231	5,251	6,108	6,895	7,743	8,408	8,994
Public and publicly guaranteed	5,435	3,939	2,683	2,846	3,055	3,295	3,564	3,943
Official creditors	5,219	3,867	2,680	2,843	3,051	3,291	3,561	3,940
of which: IMF	194	229	359	373	361	345	303	264
Private creditors	216	72	3	3	3	3	3	3
of which: Bonds	0	0	0	0	0	0	0	0
Private nonguaranteed	281	292	2,567	3,262	3,840	4,448	4,844	5,051
of which: Bonds	..	..	..	..	..	..	..	..
Short-term external debt	912	540	1,392	1,443	1,695	1,690	1,501	1,232
interest arrears on long-term	790	364	495	506	518	528	537	547
Long-term external debt								
Disbursements	**511**	**287**	**1,186**	**1,399**	**1,219**	**1,246**	**1,191**	**1,199**
Public and publicly guaranteed	226	226	267	239	258	287	401	385
Official creditors	220	226	267	239	258	287	401	385
Private creditors	6	0	0	0	0	0	0	0
of which: Bonds	0	0	0	0	0	0	0	0
Private nonguaranteed	285	61	919	1,159	961	960	790	814
of which: Bonds	..	..	..	..	..	..	..	..
Principal repayments	**184**	**110**	**456**	**540**	**453**	**456**	**532**	**596**
Public and publicly guaranteed	71	64	56	63	53	54	63	72
Official creditors	62	64	56	63	53	53	63	71
Private creditors	8	0	0	0	0	0	0	0
of which: Bonds	0	0	0	0	0	0	0	0
Private nonguaranteed	114	47	400	477	400	403	469	524
of which: Bonds	..	..	..	..	..	..	..	..
Interest payments	**91**	**46**	**104**	**121**	**144**	**150**	**155**	**186**
Public and publicly guaranteed	79	44	33	39	39	45	56	60
Official creditors	76	44	33	39	39	45	56	60
Private creditors	3	0	0	0	0	0	0	0
of which: Bonds	0	0	0	0	0	0	0	0
Private nonguaranteed	12	2	70	82	105	106	100	126
of which: Bonds	..	..	..	..	..	..	..	..
Net financial flows								
Net inflows	**617**	**451**	**1,628**	**1,850**	**1,759**	**1,574**	**1,324**	**1,131**
Net debt inflows	350	210	1,138	914	992	759	440	296
Official creditors	179	153	230	191	192	217	316	287
of which: World Bank	81	63	36	29	24	34	23	32
of which: IMF	21	-9	20	15	-13	-16	-22	-27
Private creditors	172	57	907	722	800	542	124	9
Long-term	169	14	518	683	561	557	321	289
Bonds	..	..	..	..	..	..	..	..
Banks and other private	169	14	518	683	561	557	321	289
Short-term	3	43	389	40	240	-15	-197	-280
Net equity inflows	267	241	490	936	767	816	884	835
Foreign direct investment	267	241	490	936	768	816	884	835
Portfolio equity	..	..	..	..	0	..	..	..
Major economic aggregates								
Gross national income (GNI)	4,906	6,171	8,500	9,503	10,113	10,547	11,476	12,351
Exports of goods, services & prim. income	984	1,434	3,379	4,192	4,760	4,674	5,031	4,802
Imports of goods, services & prim. income	2,330	3,075	5,330	6,599	7,169	7,223	7,394	7,396
Primary income on FDI	69	82	135	146	177	169	160	161
Personal transfers & comp. of employees	320	616	825	914	1,016	1,081	1,140	1,198
International reserves	488	728	1,799	1,892	1,887	1,993	2,276	2,492
Ratios								
External debt stocks to exports (%)	693.1	348.7	207.3	189.1	188.0	209.2	203.0	218.4
External debt stocks to GNI (%)	139.1	81.0	82.4	83.4	88.5	92.7	89.0	84.9
Debt service to exports (%)	29.4	12.1	17.3	16.7	13.6	14.1	14.8	17.5
Short-term to external debt stocks (%)	13.4	10.8	19.9	18.2	18.9	17.3	14.7	11.7
Multilateral to external debt stocks (%)	32.0	56.8	23.6	23.4	23.2	23.7	25.0	27.0
Reserves to external debt stocks (%)	7.2	14.6	25.7	23.9	21.1	20.4	22.3	23.8

Notes: Short-term debt before 2006 is based on data from the BIS. Data include the effects of HIPC and MDRI debt relief.

NIGER

(US$ million, unless otherwise indicated)

	2000	2005	2010	2011	2012	2013	2014	2015
Summary external debt data								
External debt stocks	**1,721**	**1,966**	**1,550**	**2,236**	**2,352**	**2,660**	**2,668**	**2,892**
Long-term external debt	1,563	1,785	1,220	1,928	2,090	2,322	2,352	2,550
Public and publicly guaranteed	1,495	1,753	1,220	1,928	2,090	2,322	2,352	2,550
Official creditors	1,495	1,753	1,220	1,928	2,090	2,322	2,352	2,550
of which: IMF	86	141	158	153	164	173	202	237
Private creditors	0	0	0	0	0	0	0	0
of which: Bonds	0	0	0	0	0	0	0	0
Private nonguaranteed	68	33	..	..	..	..	..	..
of which: Bonds	..	..	..	..	..	..	..	..
Short-term external debt	72	40	172	155	98	165	114	105
interest arrears on long-term	60	37	23	20	23	118	76	98
Long-term external debt								
Disbursements	**76**	**122**	**283**	**746**	**170**	**252**	**160**	**380**
Public and publicly guaranteed	76	122	283	746	170	252	160	380
Official creditors	76	122	283	746	170	252	160	380
Private creditors	0	0	0	0	0	0	0	0
of which: Bonds	0	0	0	0	0	0	0	0
Private nonguaranteed	0	0	0	..	..	..	..	..
of which: Bonds	..	..	..	..	..	..	..	..
Principal repayments	**14**	**22**	**14**	**18**	**19**	**27**	**32**	**59**
Public and publicly guaranteed	12	15	7	18	19	27	32	59
Official creditors	12	15	7	18	19	27	32	59
Private creditors	0	0	0	0	0	0	0	0
of which: Bonds	0	0	0	0	0	0	0	0
Private nonguaranteed	2	7	7	..	..	..	..	..
of which: Bonds	..	..	..	..	..	..	..	..
Interest payments	**8**	**13**	**8**	**10**	**10**	**13**	**19**	**20**
Public and publicly guaranteed	8	11	8	10	10	13	19	20
Official creditors	8	11	8	10	10	13	19	20
Private creditors	0	0	0	0	0	0	0	0
of which: Bonds	0	0	0	0	0	0	0	0
Private nonguaranteed	0	2	0	..	..	..	..	..
of which: Bonds	..	..	..	..	..	..	..	..
Net financial flows								
Net inflows	**53**	**133**	**316**	**1,767**	**647**	**652**	**583**	**859**
Net debt inflows	52	109	309	709	101	206	159	334
Official creditors	73	119	281	723	161	234	168	365
of which: World Bank	60	65	14	82	92	100	61	76
of which: IMF	9	12	5	-5	11	9	41	44
Private creditors	-22	-10	28	-14	-60	-28	-9	-31
Long-term	-2	-7	-7	..	..	..	..	..
Bonds	..	..	..	..	..	..	..	..
Banks and other private	-2	-7	-7	..	..	..	..	..
Short-term	-20	-3	35	-14	-60	-28	-9	-31
Net equity inflows	1	23	7	1,058	546	446	424	525
Foreign direct investment	1	23	0	1,062	526	446	410	525
Portfolio equity	0	1	6	-4	20	..	14	..
Major economic aggregates								
Gross national income (GNI)	1,782	3,396	5,674	6,362	6,807	7,483	8,094	7,079
Exports of goods, services & prim. income	334	602	1,332	1,433	1,665	1,820	1,847	1,192
Imports of goods, services & prim. income	485	1,095	2,916	3,208	3,015	3,265	3,384	2,812
Primary income on FDI	2	21	17	60	179	181	..	..
Personal transfers & comp. of employees	14	66	134	166	152	146	146	146
International reserves	81	251	760	673	1,015	1,167	1,281	1,039
Ratios								
External debt stocks to exports (%)	515.7	326.5	116.4	156.0	141.3	146.2	144.4	242.6
External debt stocks to GNI (%)	96.6	57.9	27.3	35.1	34.5	35.6	33.0	40.8
Debt service to exports (%)	8.0	6.8	1.8	2.4	2.2	2.7	3.4	7.5
Short-term to external debt stocks (%)	4.2	2.0	11.1	7.0	4.2	6.2	4.3	3.6
Multilateral to external debt stocks (%)	59.8	79.0	42.9	36.8	40.4	41.4	42.6	49.0
Reserves to external debt stocks (%)	4.7	12.8	49.1	30.1	43.1	43.9	48.0	35.9

Notes: Short-term debt is based on data from the BIS. Data include the effects of HIPC and MDRI debt relief.

NIGERIA

(US$ million, unless otherwise indicated)

	2000	2005	2010	2011	2012	2013	2014	2015
Summary external debt data								
External debt stocks	**32,374**	**25,755**	**15,484**	**17,663**	**18,127**	**21,144**	**24,756**	**29,029**
Long-term external debt	31,049	25,527	12,904	15,091	15,552	18,563	22,328	26,707
Public and publicly guaranteed	30,042	20,248	4,691	5,937	6,680	8,286	9,133	10,633
Official creditors	26,596	18,039	4,691	5,437	6,180	7,286	8,133	9,633
of which: IMF	205	225	2,580	2,572	2,575	2,580	2,427	2,322
Private creditors	3,446	2,209	0	500	500	1,000	1,000	1,000
of which: Bonds	2,051	1,442	0	500	500	1,000	1,000	1,000
Private nonguaranteed	1,007	5,279	8,213	9,155	8,872	10,277	13,195	16,075
of which: Bonds	..	..	..	500	850	2,125	4,475	5,275
Short-term external debt	1,120	3	0	0	0	1	0	0
interest arrears on long-term	43	3	0	0	0	1	0	0
Long-term external debt								
Disbursements	**946**	**2,449**	**1,117**	**2,681**	**1,586**	**3,274**	**8,436**	**5,548**
Public and publicly guaranteed	153	379	1,057	1,587	833	1,870	1,378	1,658
Official creditors	153	345	1,057	1,087	833	1,370	1,378	1,658
Private creditors	0	34	0	500	0	500	0	0
of which: Bonds	0	0	0	500	0	500	0	0
Private nonguaranteed	792	2,070	61	1,093	752	1,404	7,058	3,890
of which: Bonds	..	..	..	500	350	1,275	2,350	800
Principal repayments	**1,092**	**3,863**	**1,189**	**426**	**1,192**	**226**	**4,278**	**1,104**
Public and publicly guaranteed	1,057	3,863	248	274	158	226	138	94
Official creditors	915	3,685	244	274	158	226	138	94
Private creditors	142	179	4	0	0	0	0	0
of which: Bonds	0	0	0	0	0	0	0	0
Private nonguaranteed	35	0	942	152	1,035	0	4,140	1,010
of which: Bonds	..	..	..	0	0	0	0	0
Interest payments	**690**	**4,937**	**59**	**96**	**144**	**267**	**267**	**364**
Public and publicly guaranteed	673	4,937	59	77	94	168	126	171
Official creditors	516	4,717	59	61	60	71	80	123
Private creditors	157	220	0	17	34	97	46	49
of which: Bonds	128	170	0	17	34	97	46	49
Private nonguaranteed	18	0	0	19	50	99	141	193
of which: Bonds	..	..	..	19	50	99	141	193
Net financial flows								
Net inflows	**1,235**	**4,319**	**8,048**	**13,414**	**17,355**	**14,115**	**9,837**	**7,017**
Net debt inflows	95	-1,414	-72	2,255	393	3,049	4,157	4,444
Official creditors	-762	-3,340	813	813	675	1,144	1,239	1,564
of which: World Bank	-191	22	905	567	472	630	860	733
of which: IMF	..	..	..	..	..	..	..	..
Private creditors	857	1,925	-885	1,441	-282	1,904	2,918	2,880
Long-term	616	1,925	-885	1,441	-282	1,904	2,918	2,880
Bonds	0	0	0	1,000	350	1,775	2,350	800
Banks and other private	616	1,925	-885	441	-632	129	568	2,080
Short-term	241	0	0	0	0	0	0	0
Net equity inflows	1,140	5,733	8,120	11,160	16,962	11,066	5,679	2,573
Foreign direct investment	1,140	4,983	5,966	8,589	7,003	5,534	4,643	3,060
Portfolio equity	..	751	2,153	2,571	9,959	5,532	1,037	-487
Major economic aggregates								
Gross national income (GNI)	40,238	98,881	349,460	388,904	438,689	489,237	549,333	465,480
Exports of goods, services & prim. income	21,183	57,149	83,697	103,336	99,481	100,300	85,523	51,029
Imports of goods, services & prim. income	15,383	35,773	91,290	114,474	103,917	103,056	106,375	87,385
Primary income on FDI	2,279	2,603	19,958	23,070	22,277	25,257	19,509	12,725
Personal transfers & comp. of employees	1,392	14,640	19,745	20,617	20,543	20,797	20,829	21,060
International reserves	9,911	28,280	34,919	35,212	46,405	45,427	36,669	30,606
Ratios								
External debt stocks to exports (%)	152.8	45.1	18.5	17.1	18.2	21.1	28.9	56.9
External debt stocks to GNI (%)	80.5	26.0	4.4	4.5	4.1	4.3	4.5	6.2
Debt service to exports (%)	8.8	15.4	1.5	0.5	1.3	0.5	5.3	2.9
Short-term to external debt stocks (%)	3.5	0.0	0.0	0.0	0.0	0.0	0.0	0.0
Multilateral to external debt stocks (%)	10.3	9.9	27.8	27.2	29.6	29.5	27.2	26.8
Reserves to external debt stocks (%)	30.6	109.8	225.5	199.4	256.0	214.9	148.1	105.4

Notes: Long-term public and publicly guaranteed debt data for 2015 are World Bank staff estimates based on the original terms of the loans. Long-term private nonguaranteed debt data from 2005 are estimates based on Central Bank data. Short-term debt is revised from 2001 based on reports provided by the country.

PAKISTAN

(US$ million, unless otherwise indicated)

	2000	2005	2010	2011	2012	2013	2014	2015
Summary external debt data								
External debt stocks	**33,022**	**34,018**	**64,003**	**65,520**	**62,144**	**60,057**	**62,262**	**65,482**
Long-term external debt	29,752	31,053	49,412	51,494	50,658	49,440	51,723	54,990
Public and publicly guaranteed	27,192	30,089	43,403	45,129	44,738	43,305	45,944	48,212
Official creditors	25,134	28,907	41,604	43,362	43,009	41,614	40,523	40,799
of which: IMF	1,751	1,735	10,258	9,962	7,684	5,113	5,001	6,359
Private creditors	2,058	1,182	1,799	1,768	1,729	1,690	5,422	7,413
of which: Bonds	623	1,100	1,550	1,550	1,550	1,550	4,550	5,050
Private nonguaranteed	2,560	964	6,009	6,365	5,920	6,135	5,779	6,778
of which: Bonds	45	600	250	250	250	12	12	12
Short-term external debt	1,519	1,230	4,333	4,065	3,802	5,505	5,538	4,133
interest arrears on long-term	0	0	0	0	0	0	0	0
Long-term external debt								
Disbursements	**1,647**	**2,831**	**5,474**	**3,210**	**2,312**	**4,163**	**7,746**	**6,621**
Public and publicly guaranteed	1,530	2,231	1,854	2,572	2,312	2,418	7,144	5,407
Official creditors	1,526	1,619	1,852	2,572	2,312	2,418	3,376	3,169
Private creditors	4	612	1	0	0	0	3,768	2,238
of which: Bonds	0	600	0	0	0	0	3,000	500
Private nonguaranteed	117	600	3,620	638	0	1,746	602	1,214
of which: Bonds	0	600	0	0	0	12	0	0
Principal repayments	**1,588**	**1,466**	**3,009**	**1,665**	**1,527**	**3,361**	**2,671**	**2,101**
Public and publicly guaranteed	1,143	1,139	2,133	1,383	1,395	1,830	1,713	1,886
Official creditors	1,106	996	1,425	1,351	1,356	1,791	1,674	1,663
Private creditors	37	143	707	32	39	39	39	223
of which: Bonds	0	108	600	0	0	0	0	0
Private nonguaranteed	445	327	876	282	132	1,531	958	215
of which: Bonds	0	0	600	0	0	250	0	0
Interest payments	**858**	**681**	**840**	**784**	**752**	**914**	**946**	**1,125**
Public and publicly guaranteed	642	605	781	711	686	666	678	920
Official creditors	528	554	649	594	583	582	489	569
Private creditors	114	50	131	117	103	84	188	351
of which: Bonds	61	47	120	111	99	81	155	309
Private nonguaranteed	217	76	59	73	65	248	269	205
of which: Bonds	2	3	30	22	22	11	0	0
Net financial flows								
Net inflows	**2**	**3,760**	**9,225**	**2,410**	**-434**	**1,590**	**7,972**	**6,114**
Net debt inflows	-341	1,108	6,692	1,005	-1,752	-57	5,308	4,706
Official creditors	331	381	1,787	950	-1,319	-1,936	1,902	3,096
of which: World Bank	10	419	78	601	268	113	1,167	1,310
of which: IMF	-89	-242	1,360	-272	-2,275	-2,562	200	1,591
Private creditors	-672	727	4,906	56	-433	1,879	3,406	1,609
Long-term	-361	742	2,038	324	-171	176	3,374	3,014
Bonds	0	1,092	-1,200	0	0	-238	3,000	500
Banks and other private	-361	-350	3,238	324	-171	414	374	2,514
Short-term	-311	-15	2,867	-269	-263	1,703	33	-1,404
Net equity inflows	343	2,652	2,533	1,405	1,318	1,647	2,664	1,408
Foreign direct investment	308	2,201	2,022	1,380	1,140	1,536	1,899	884
Portfolio equity	35	451	511	25	178	111	765	524
Major economic aggregates								
Gross national income (GNI)	73,025	111,767	184,164	223,348	236,253	243,148	257,256	286,512
Exports of goods, services & prim. income	10,115	19,763	28,737	32,279	31,963	30,544	31,107	29,171
Imports of goods, services & prim. income	14,362	32,448	43,884	51,089	52,876	53,631	55,931	52,877
Primary income on FDI	429	1,872	2,140	2,102	2,373	2,908	3,181	3,334
Personal transfers & comp. of employees	1,075	4,280	9,690	12,263	14,007	14,629	17,244	19,306
International reserves	1,513	10,033	14,346	14,528	10,242	5,156	11,807	17,830
Ratios								
External debt stocks to exports (%)	326.5	172.1	222.7	203.0	194.4	196.6	200.2	224.5
External debt stocks to GNI (%)	45.2	30.4	34.8	29.3	26.3	24.7	24.2	22.9
Debt service to exports (%)	28.4	12.5	14.9	9.1	14.8	26.3	18.2	12.9
Short-term to external debt stocks (%)	4.6	3.6	6.8	6.2	6.1	9.2	8.9	6.3
Multilateral to external debt stocks (%)	40.9	46.9	38.5	38.8	40.4	39.9	38.2	37.3
Reserves to external debt stocks (%)	4.6	29.5	22.4	22.2	16.5	8.6	19.0	27.2

Notes: Long-term private nonguaranteed debt data from 2006 are World Bank staff estimates based on the reports provided by the country. Short-term debt before 2010 is based on data from the BIS and thereafter short-term debt is World Bank staff estimates based on Central Bank data.

PANAMA

(US$ million, unless otherwise indicated)

	2000	2005	2010	2011	2012	2013	2014	2015
Summary external debt data								
External debt stocks	**6,608**	**8,694**	**48,882**	**57,056**	**61,429**	**68,348**	**78,023**	**87,724**
Long-term external debt	6,483	8,632	23,692	28,176	30,242	32,682	39,161	44,099
Public and publicly guaranteed	5,703	6,890	10,420	10,890	10,790	12,212	14,087	15,410
Official creditors	1,289	1,306	2,126	2,399	2,733	3,214	3,809	4,372
of which: IMF	124	61	303	302	303	303	285	273
Private creditors	4,414	5,584	8,293	8,491	8,057	8,998	10,278	11,037
of which: Bonds	4,141	5,505	8,071	8,272	7,725	8,306	9,506	10,377
Private nonguaranteed	780	1,742	13,272	17,286	19,452	20,470	25,074	28,689
of which: Bonds	266	635	911	1,261	2,061	3,671	5,506	6,608
Short-term external debt	1	0	24,887	28,577	30,885	35,363	38,577	43,353
interest arrears on long-term	1	0	0	0	0	0	0	0
Long-term external debt								
Disbursements	**724**	**1,595**	**2,220**	**5,228**	**3,095**	**2,929**	**6,495**	**5,841**
Public and publicly guaranteed	486	1,325	440	973	652	2,314	2,479	2,062
Official creditors	97	94	440	438	537	704	1,122	812
Private creditors	388	1,231	0	535	114	1,610	1,357	1,250
of which: Bonds	370	1,230	0	535	0	1,250	1,250	1,250
Private nonguaranteed	238	270	1,780	4,255	2,443	615	4,016	3,779
of which: Bonds	0	150	0	350	800	270	969	450
Principal repayments	**411**	**1,403**	**556**	**754**	**1,194**	**1,029**	**714**	**969**
Public and publicly guaranteed	386	1,152	170	511	917	764	215	731
Official creditors	109	139	165	175	174	179	188	240
Private creditors	277	1,013	5	336	742	584	27	491
of which: Bonds	120	995	0	333	741	584	0	379
Private nonguaranteed	25	251	386	243	278	266	499	239
of which: Bonds	0	0	150	0	0	0	220	0
Interest payments	**418**	**618**	**797**	**817**	**783**	**922**	**965**	**986**
Public and publicly guaranteed	365	531	670	701	697	669	691	752
Official creditors	79	59	75	76	77	85	93	116
Private creditors	287	471	595	624	620	585	597	636
of which: Bonds	264	467	592	621	606	567	558	616
Private nonguaranteed	53	87	126	116	86	252	274	234
of which: Bonds	24	44	83	73	42	205	226	195
Net financial flows								
Net inflows	**707**	**652**	**5,235**	**10,093**	**6,612**	**9,771**	**12,976**	**13,810**
Net debt inflows	261	182	3,267	8,164	4,208	6,378	8,996	9,647
Official creditors	-63	-55	275	263	363	524	934	573
of which: World Bank	-2	-31	-15	-21	90	89	504	270
of which: IMF	-52	-10	0	0	0	0	0	0
Private creditors	324	237	2,993	7,901	3,845	5,854	8,062	9,075
Long-term	324	237	1,389	4,210	1,538	1,375	4,848	4,299
Bonds	249	385	-150	552	59	936	1,999	1,321
Banks and other private	75	-148	1,539	3,658	1,479	439	2,849	2,978
Short-term	0	0	1,604	3,691	2,307	4,478	3,214	4,776
Net equity inflows	447	470	1,967	1,929	2,404	3,394	3,980	4,163
Foreign direct investment	447	470	1,967	1,929	2,404	3,394	3,980	4,163
Portfolio equity	..	..	..	..	..	..	..	..
Major economic aggregates								
Gross national income (GNI)	11,732	15,444	26,105	31,903	37,408	41,932	45,875	48,643
Exports of goods, services & prim. income	9,384	11,578	21,993	28,978	32,355	31,933	30,221	29,402
Imports of goods, services & prim. income	10,233	12,883	25,244	33,671	36,620	36,397	35,136	32,673
Primary income on FDI	562	1,048	2,176	2,025	2,426	3,033	2,989	3,802
Personal transfers & comp. of employees	16	130	410	368	411	452	760	560
International reserves	723	1,211	2,714	2,304	2,466	2,848	4,032	3,378
Ratios								
External debt stocks to exports (%)	70.4	75.1	222.3	196.9	189.9	214.0	258.2	298.4
External debt stocks to GNI (%)	56.3	56.3	187.3	178.8	164.2	163.0	170.1	180.3
Debt service to exports (%)	9.5	17.6	6.2	5.4	6.1	6.1	7.3	8.9
Short-term to external debt stocks (%)	0.0	0.0	50.9	50.1	50.3	51.7	49.4	49.4
Multilateral to external debt stocks (%)	15.5	12.8	3.7	3.6	3.9	4.3	4.6	4.7
Reserves to external debt stocks (%)	10.9	13.9	5.6	4.0	4.0	4.2	5.2	3.9

Notes: Long-term private nonguaranteed debt data before 2008 only cover Inter-American Development Bank and Bonds, from 2008 to 2013 data are world Bank Staff estimates based on National Institute of Statistics and Census data while from 2014, data are based on reports provided by the country.

PAPUA NEW GUINEA

(US$ million, unless otherwise indicated)

	2000	2005	2010	2011	2012	2013	2014	2015
Summary external debt data								
External debt stocks	**2,325**	**1,871**	**5,987**	**12,584**	**14,922**	**21,610**	**20,429**	**20,031**
Long-term external debt	2,204	1,651	5,380	12,268	14,468	21,102	19,439	19,439
Public and publicly guaranteed	1,454	1,264	1,042	1,069	1,130	1,256	1,369	1,501
Official creditors	1,394	1,213	1,009	1,043	1,114	1,248	1,368	1,500
of which: IMF	51	13	193	193	193	193	182	174
Private creditors	60	51	33	26	16	8	1	1
of which: Bonds	0	0	0	0	0	0	0	0
Private nonguaranteed	750	387	4,337	11,199	13,338	19,847	18,070	17,937
of which: Bonds	..	..	..	..	..	..	..	..
Short-term external debt	70	207	414	123	261	314	808	418
interest arrears on long-term	0	0	0	0	0	0	0	0
Long-term external debt								
Disbursements	**254**	**335**	**3,153**	**8,158**	**2,717**	**7,692**	**1,028**	**562**
Public and publicly guaranteed	219	45	37	94	161	231	244	242
Official creditors	206	44	37	94	161	231	244	242
Private creditors	13	1	0	0	0	0	0	0
of which: Bonds	0	0	0	0	0	0	0	0
Private nonguaranteed	35	290	3,116	8,064	2,556	7,461	784	320
of which: Bonds	..	..	..	..	..	..	..	..
Principal repayments	**196**	**183**	**758**	**1,076**	**349**	**1,028**	**822**	**519**
Public and publicly guaranteed	115	114	67	79	78	75	74	67
Official creditors	96	93	60	71	70	69	68	66
Private creditors	19	21	7	8	8	7	6	0
of which: Bonds	0	0	0	0	0	0	0	0
Private nonguaranteed	80	69	691	997	271	953	748	452
of which: Bonds	..	..	..	..	..	..	..	..
Interest payments	**85**	**54**	**50**	**104**	**131**	**231**	**336**	**575**
Public and publicly guaranteed	54	38	16	19	18	18	20	21
Official creditors	50	36	16	19	18	17	20	21
Private creditors	5	2	1	1	0	0	0	0
of which: Bonds	0	0	0	0	0	0	0	0
Private nonguaranteed	31	16	33	85	113	213	317	555
of which: Bonds	..	..	..	..	..	..	..	..
Net financial flows								
Net inflows	**146**	**249**	**2,726**	**6,482**	**2,443**	**6,735**	**664**	**-320**
Net debt inflows	50	218	2,697	6,790	2,506	6,717	700	-347
Official creditors	128	-110	-23	23	91	162	176	176
of which: World Bank	12	-7	-6	2	10	9	14	5
of which: IMF	19	-61	..	..	..	..	..	..
Private creditors	-78	327	2,720	6,768	2,415	6,555	524	-522
Long-term	-51	200	2,418	7,059	2,277	6,502	30	-133
Bonds	..	..	..	..	..	..	..	..
Banks and other private	-51	200	2,418	7,059	2,277	6,502	30	-133
Short-term	-27	127	302	-291	138	53	494	-390
Net equity inflows	96	31	28	-309	-64	18	-36	27
Foreign direct investment	96	31	28	-309	-64	18	-30	28
Portfolio equity	..	..	..	..	..	..	-6	-1
Major economic aggregates								
Gross national income (GNI)	3,303	4,528	9,124	12,322	14,662	14,768	16,527	..
Exports of goods, services & prim. income	2,369	3,649	6,097	7,380	6,856	6,407	8,984	9,742
Imports of goods, services & prim. income	2,013	3,368	6,920	7,796	9,274	9,990	6,712	4,159
Primary income on FDI	198	511	466	350	566	391	209	257
Personal transfers & comp. of employees	7	7	3	17	14	14	10	10
International reserves	287	718	3,033	4,256	3,930	2,775	2,254	1,692
Ratios								
External debt stocks to exports (%)	98.2	51.3	98.2	170.5	217.7	337.3	227.4	205.6
External debt stocks to GNI (%)	70.4	41.3	65.6	102.1	101.8	146.3	123.6	..
Debt service to exports (%)	12.9	8.4	13.3	16.0	7.0	19.9	13.0	11.3
Short-term to external debt stocks (%)	3.0	11.1	6.9	1.0	1.7	1.5	4.0	2.1
Multilateral to external debt stocks (%)	35.5	44.7	11.9	5.6	5.2	4.4	5.0	5.4
Reserves to external debt stocks (%)	12.3	38.4	50.7	33.8	26.3	12.8	11.0	8.4

Notes: Short-term debt is based on data from the BIS.

PARAGUAY

(US$ million, unless otherwise indicated)

	2000	2005	2010	2011	2012	2013	2014	2015
Summary external debt data								
External debt stocks	**3,106**	**8,279**	**15,895**	**15,573**	**16,040**	**15,706**	**16,493**	**16,162**
Long-term external debt	2,539	4,880	11,375	11,045	11,233	10,839	11,513	11,228
Public and publicly guaranteed	2,089	2,267	2,383	2,321	2,262	2,700	3,720	4,033
Official creditors	1,641	1,846	2,116	2,088	2,068	2,045	2,104	2,150
of which: IMF	18	20	147	146	146	147	138	132
Private creditors	449	421	267	233	194	655	1,616	1,883
of which: Bonds	0	0	0	0	0	500	1,500	1,780
Private nonguaranteed	450	2,614	8,992	8,724	8,971	8,139	7,794	7,194
of which: Bonds	..	..	..	..	500	500	800	800
Short-term external debt	549	3,379	4,373	4,382	4,661	4,721	4,841	4,802
interest arrears on long-term	11	0	0	0	0	0	0	0
Long-term external debt								
Disbursements	**192**	**1,292**	**1,912**	**512**	**1,670**	**1,023**	**3,499**	**1,471**
Public and publicly guaranteed	192	144	308	163	227	712	1,261	496
Official creditors	192	141	308	163	227	212	261	216
Private creditors	0	3	0	0	0	500	1,000	280
of which: Bonds	0	0	0	0	0	500	1,000	280
Private nonguaranteed	0	1,147	1,605	349	1,443	310	2,238	975
of which: Bonds	..	..	..	..	500	0	300	0
Principal repayments	**207**	**332**	**313**	**711**	**1,738**	**1,351**	**2,778**	**1,580**
Public and publicly guaranteed	114	206	239	244	240	208	195	171
Official creditors	107	176	224	211	201	169	156	158
Private creditors	7	29	15	34	39	39	39	13
of which: Bonds	0	0	0	0	0	0	0	0
Private nonguaranteed	93	126	75	467	1,497	1,143	2,583	1,409
of which: Bonds	..	..	..	..	0	0	0	0
Interest payments	**116**	**115**	**131**	**140**	**179**	**236**	**227**	**535**
Public and publicly guaranteed	100	94	65	66	59	65	77	135
Official creditors	70	77	63	61	55	51	51	50
Private creditors	30	17	2	4	4	15	26	85
of which: Bonds	0	0	0	0	0	12	23	84
Private nonguaranteed	16	21	66	75	120	170	149	400
of which: Bonds	..	..	..	..	38	38	50	0
Net financial flows								
Net inflows	**-113**	**1,073**	**1,998**	**86**	**887**	**125**	**1,325**	**179**
Net debt inflows	-218	1,041	1,911	-190	211	-269	842	-148
Official creditors	85	-35	84	-47	26	43	105	58
of which: World Bank	26	-10	-26	-14	86	1	38	51
of which: IMF	..	..	..	..	..	..	..	..
Private creditors	-303	1,077	1,827	-143	185	-312	737	-206
Long-term	-100	995	1,515	-151	-94	-371	616	-167
Bonds	..	..	..	..	500	500	1,300	280
Banks and other private	-100	995	1,515	-151	-594	-871	-684	-447
Short-term	-203	81	312	9	279	60	121	-39
Net equity inflows	105	32	87	277	677	394	484	328
Foreign direct investment	105	32	87	277	677	394	484	328
Portfolio equity	..	..	..	..	..	..	..	..
Major economic aggregates								
Gross national income (GNI)	7,085	7,360	18,618	23,793	22,950	27,287	29,344	26,082
Exports of goods, services & prim. income	3,972	5,182	11,135	13,336	12,384	14,413	13,898	11,660
Imports of goods, services & prim. income	4,396	5,473	11,749	13,940	13,644	14,655	14,631	12,795
Primary income on FDI	84	158	759	641	1,069	1,084	965	899
Personal transfers & comp. of employees	152	161	410	541	634	623	507	554
International reserves	763	1,297	4,137	4,950	4,557	5,556	6,669	5,659
Ratios								
External debt stocks to exports (%)	78.2	159.8	142.8	116.8	129.5	109.0	118.7	138.6
External debt stocks to GNI (%)	43.8	112.5	85.4	65.5	69.9	57.6	56.2	62.0
Debt service to exports (%)	9.0	9.2	4.1	6.5	15.7	11.6	21.9	18.6
Short-term to external debt stocks (%)	17.7	40.8	27.5	28.1	29.1	30.1	29.4	29.7
Multilateral to external debt stocks (%)	37.7	15.2	9.5	9.7	10.0	10.6	10.8	11.6
Reserves to external debt stocks (%)	24.6	15.7	26.0	31.8	28.4	35.4	40.4	35.0

Notes: Long-term private nonguaranteed debt data from 2002 are estimates based on Central Bank data. Short-term debt is based on data from the BIS until 2002 and on Central Bank data from 2003.

PERU

(US$ million, unless otherwise indicated)

	2000	2005	2010	2011	2012	2013	2014	2015
Summary external debt data								
External debt stocks	**28,834**	**29,514**	**42,154**	**45,012**	**54,150**	**56,803**	**61,270**	**65,938**
Long-term external debt	24,229	26,114	34,822	37,751	44,680	49,414	53,408	58,018
Public and publicly guaranteed	19,291	22,542	20,009	20,142	19,966	17,219	15,903	19,407
Official creditors	14,461	13,836	10,555	10,721	9,982	7,646	7,236	7,883
of which: IMF	677	188	939	936	937	939	884	845
Private creditors	4,830	8,706	9,454	9,422	9,984	9,573	8,667	11,524
of which: Bonds	3,727	8,390	9,311	9,299	9,894	9,511	8,625	11,496
Private nonguaranteed	4,938	3,572	14,813	17,608	24,714	32,195	37,505	38,611
of which: Bonds	150	1,230	727	1,705	4,665	9,885	13,571	15,250
Short-term external debt	3,928	3,212	6,393	6,325	8,532	6,450	6,978	7,075
interest arrears on long-term	14	4	1	0	0	0	0	0
Long-term external debt								
Disbursements	**2,066**	**3,721**	**5,425**	**3,386**	**6,865**	**5,793**	**8,015**	**8,918**
Public and publicly guaranteed	1,489	2,635	3,862	1,003	1,347	376	449	4,865
Official creditors	1,454	985	1,601	1,003	447	376	449	1,350
Private creditors	35	1,650	2,261	0	900	0	0	3,515
of which: Bonds	0	1,650	2,261	0	900	0	0	3,515
Private nonguaranteed	577	1,086	1,563	2,382	5,518	5,417	7,565	4,052
of which: Bonds	0	1,080	0	1,705	2,960	5,220	3,686	1,679
Principal repayments	**1,003**	**4,193**	**4,060**	**2,128**	**2,758**	**5,130**	**3,283**	**2,734**
Public and publicly guaranteed	986	3,037	3,490	892	1,348	2,846	1,008	909
Official creditors	840	2,922	2,971	867	1,013	2,431	620	624
Private creditors	146	114	518	25	335	415	388	285
of which: Bonds	0	90	497	0	312	400	374	271
Private nonguaranteed	17	1,156	570	1,236	1,410	2,284	2,275	1,825
of which: Bonds	0	0	0	727	0	0	0	0
Interest payments	**1,175**	**1,718**	**2,550**	**1,789**	**3,007**	**1,581**	**1,688**	**1,875**
Public and publicly guaranteed	1,106	1,404	1,096	1,001	969	951	864	810
Official creditors	918	807	346	288	275	243	142	136
Private creditors	188	596	750	712	694	708	722	675
of which: Bonds	179	568	742	705	688	704	719	672
Private nonguaranteed	69	314	1,454	788	2,038	630	824	1,065
of which: Bonds	11	56	284	463	176	392	589	814
Net financial flows								
Net inflows	**1,216**	**3,298**	**10,822**	**6,887**	**18,598**	**5,389**	**10,645**	**12,228**
Net debt inflows	283	-50	2,974	1,191	6,314	-1,419	5,260	6,280
Official creditors	473	-1,976	-1,370	136	-566	-2,055	-171	726
of which: World Bank	173	-17	119	-232	-298	-611	17	877
of which: IMF	-141	-40	0	0	0	0	0	0
Private creditors	-190	1,927	4,344	1,055	6,880	636	5,431	5,554
Long-term	448	1,465	2,735	1,121	4,673	2,718	4,903	5,457
Bonds	0	2,640	1,764	978	3,548	4,820	3,312	4,922
Banks and other private	448	-1,175	971	143	1,125	-2,102	1,591	535
Short-term	-638	461	1,608	-67	2,207	-2,082	528	97
Net equity inflows	933	3,348	7,849	5,696	12,284	6,808	5,385	5,947
Foreign direct investment	810	2,579	7,762	5,548	12,426	6,223	5,464	6,007
Portfolio equity	123	769	87	147	-142	585	-79	-60
Major economic aggregates								
Gross national income (GNI)	49,571	69,883	137,317	157,217	180,304	191,398	193,527	185,261
Exports of goods, services & prim. income	8,942	20,006	39,986	51,052	52,743	49,248	46,292	41,030
Imports of goods, services & prim. income	11,489	20,631	46,794	57,430	61,287	61,067	58,697	52,791
Primary income on FDI	344	4,030	10,714	12,511	11,403	9,301	7,964	5,225
Personal transfers & comp. of employees	718	1,440	2,534	2,697	2,788	2,707	2,639	2,725
International reserves	8,374	13,599	42,648	47,206	62,300	64,423	61,185	60,413
Ratios								
External debt stocks to exports (%)	322.5	147.5	105.4	88.2	102.7	115.3	132.4	160.7
External debt stocks to GNI (%)	58.2	42.2	30.7	28.6	30.0	29.7	31.7	35.6
Debt service to exports (%)	28.9	30.4	16.7	7.9	11.1	13.8	10.9	11.5
Short-term to external debt stocks (%)	13.6	10.9	15.2	14.1	15.8	11.4	11.4	10.7
Multilateral to external debt stocks (%)	19.3	26.8	18.7	17.7	14.0	10.0	9.2	9.7
Reserves to external debt stocks (%)	29.0	46.1	101.2	104.9	115.1	113.4	99.9	91.6

Notes: Long-term private nonguaranteed debt data are World Bank staff estimates based on reports provided by the country.

PHILIPPINES

(US$ million, unless otherwise indicated)

	2000	2005	2010	2011	2012	2013	2014	2015
Summary external debt data								
External debt stocks	**58,456**	**58,693**	**65,303**	**66,063**	**69,372**	**66,202**	**77,104**	**77,725**
Long-term external debt	50,777	51,742	53,500	52,726	51,632	48,003	59,641	61,465
Public and publicly guaranteed	33,744	35,364	45,039	44,582	43,050	38,593	37,459	36,145
Official creditors	19,890	18,580	23,208	23,585	21,932	18,532	17,470	18,239
of which: IMF	2,183	555	1,290	1,287	1,288	1,290	1,214	1,161
Private creditors	13,855	16,784	21,831	20,997	21,118	20,061	19,989	17,906
of which: Bonds	10,466	14,290	20,534	19,722	19,966	19,151	19,277	17,324
Private nonguaranteed	17,033	16,378	8,462	8,144	8,582	9,410	22,183	25,320
of which: Bonds	2,856	2,975	1,651	1,579	2,600	6,250	7,325	9,537
Short-term external debt	5,495	6,395	10,512	12,050	16,452	16,909	16,248	15,099
interest arrears on long-term	0	0	0	0	0	0	0	0
Long-term external debt								
Disbursements	**5,747**	**5,544**	**10,928**	**7,959**	**5,761**	**4,617**	**16,507**	**12,262**
Public and publicly guaranteed	5,228	3,874	8,251	5,004	3,829	824	3,283	6,548
Official creditors	1,528	1,144	1,370	1,709	1,436	772	1,738	2,298
Private creditors	3,701	2,730	6,881	3,295	2,393	51	1,546	4,250
of which: Bonds	2,630	2,384	6,680	3,121	2,241	0	1,500	4,250
Private nonguaranteed	519	1,670	2,677	2,954	1,933	3,793	13,224	5,714
of which: Bonds	5	250	0	1,075	1,525	3,650	1,075	2,287
Principal repayments	**4,047**	**5,748**	**8,341**	**6,311**	**2,728**	**2,918**	**3,046**	**4,842**
Public and publicly guaranteed	2,515	3,353	6,813	4,887	2,632	2,767	2,595	3,333
Official creditors	1,572	1,788	1,818	2,007	1,757	2,184	1,546	1,398
Private creditors	943	1,566	4,996	2,880	875	583	1,049	1,934
of which: Bonds	395	1,209	4,807	2,669	655	366	892	1,834
Private nonguaranteed	1,533	2,395	1,527	1,424	96	151	451	1,509
of which: Bonds	445	333	174	158	0	0	0	75
Interest payments	**2,469**	**3,152**	**3,112**	**3,195**	**2,975**	**2,923**	**3,054**	**3,258**
Public and publicly guaranteed	1,882	2,409	2,977	2,850	2,846	2,662	2,547	2,431
Official creditors	841	584	498	489	431	341	295	252
Private creditors	1,041	1,825	2,479	2,361	2,415	2,320	2,253	2,179
of which: Bonds	880	1,725	2,441	2,323	2,379	2,289	2,227	2,160
Private nonguaranteed	586	743	135	345	129	261	506	826
of which: Bonds	479	283	25	147	107	243	385	452
Net financial flows								
Net inflows	**3,348**	**2,569**	**9,716**	**5,756**	**12,012**	**3,205**	**16,473**	**8,116**
Net debt inflows	2,551	828	9,097	3,186	7,435	2,155	12,801	6,272
Official creditors	261	-961	-447	-299	-321	-1,412	192	900
of which: World Bank	-190	-253	52	690	67	297	283	731
of which: IMF	305	-317	0	0	0	0	0	0
Private creditors	2,290	1,788	9,544	3,484	7,755	3,567	12,609	5,372
Long-term	1,744	439	3,035	1,946	3,354	3,111	13,270	6,521
Bonds	1,796	1,092	1,700	1,369	3,111	3,284	1,683	4,629
Banks and other private	-52	-653	1,335	576	243	-174	11,587	1,892
Short-term	546	1,349	6,509	1,539	4,402	457	-661	-1,149
Net equity inflows	797	1,741	619	2,570	4,577	1,050	3,672	1,844
Foreign direct investment	999	1,321	-214	1,531	2,824	1,084	2,476	2,588
Portfolio equity	-202	420	833	1,040	1,753	-34	1,196	-744
Major economic aggregates								
Gross national income (GNI)	94,969	129,804	265,931	268,494	301,388	330,990	345,248	352,993
Exports of goods, services & prim. income	30,797	38,514	61,241	64,792	75,080	76,206	84,101	82,024
Imports of goods, services & prim. income	38,668	48,158	71,658	77,716	87,631	85,896	96,127	97,837
Primary income on FDI	230	1,382	2,417	2,910	3,955	3,518	4,277	4,125
Personal transfers & comp. of employees	6,924	13,733	21,557	23,054	24,610	26,717	28,691	29,799
International reserves	13,090	15,926	55,363	67,290	73,478	75,689	72,057	73,964
Ratios								
External debt stocks to exports (%)	189.8	152.4	106.6	102.0	92.4	86.9	91.7	94.8
External debt stocks to GNI (%)	61.6	45.2	24.6	24.6	23.0	20.0	22.3	22.0
Debt service to exports (%)	22.9	24.7	18.7	14.7	7.6	7.7	7.3	9.9
Short-term to external debt stocks (%)	9.4	10.9	16.1	18.2	23.7	25.5	21.1	19.4
Multilateral to external debt stocks (%)	12.3	11.3	12.8	13.7	13.5	12.9	11.7	13.1
Reserves to external debt stocks (%)	22.4	27.1	84.8	101.9	105.9	114.3	93.5	95.2

Notes: Long-term private nonguaranteed debt data no longer include unregistered debt and are revised from 2005 based on the reports provided by the country.

ROMANIA

(US$ million, unless otherwise indicated)

	2000	2005	2010	2011	2012	2013	2014	2015
Summary external debt data								
External debt stocks	**11,259**	**38,884**	**115,393**	**119,601**	**120,826**	**123,954**	**111,824**	**95,955**
Long-term external debt	9,945	31,102	81,627	82,365	88,755	98,870	96,190	81,419
Public and publicly guaranteed	6,583	13,330	20,801	24,869	29,495	35,574	36,792	32,574
Official creditors	4,149	6,152	14,280	16,887	17,395	19,178	16,863	13,794
of which: IMF	552	369	16,609	17,738	15,748	9,540	3,352	1,498
Private creditors	2,434	7,177	6,520	7,982	12,100	16,395	19,929	18,780
of which: Bonds	736	2,123	3,006	4,852	10,166	14,783	18,802	17,998
Private nonguaranteed	3,362	17,773	60,826	57,496	59,260	63,296	59,398	48,845
of which: Bonds	..	..	..	117	288	4,707	328	235
Short-term external debt	762	7,413	17,157	19,498	16,323	15,544	12,282	13,039
interest arrears on long-term	12	13	1	1	1	1	0	0
Long-term external debt								
Disbursements	**3,144**	**12,909**	**17,435**	**17,847**	**20,958**	**21,721**	**19,249**	**15,465**
Public and publicly guaranteed	1,937	2,637	5,623	6,177	6,507	6,379	6,263	3,569
Official creditors	1,083	1,016	4,128	3,900	1,263	2,154	716	1,349
Private creditors	854	1,621	1,495	2,277	5,244	4,225	5,547	2,220
of which: Bonds	139	623	1,327	2,070	5,117	4,186	5,540	2,218
Private nonguaranteed	1,207	10,272	11,812	11,670	14,451	15,342	12,986	11,896
of which: Bonds	..	..	..	83	38	135	382	222
Principal repayments	**1,706**	**5,170**	**15,784**	**15,729**	**15,998**	**19,679**	**16,143**	**19,789**
Public and publicly guaranteed	984	1,697	2,150	1,274	2,190	1,341	1,183	4,726
Official creditors	493	590	668	767	853	935	842	2,826
Private creditors	491	1,107	1,482	507	1,337	406	340	1,900
of which: Bonds	0	374	929	0	0	0	0	1,664
Private nonguaranteed	721	3,473	13,633	14,454	13,808	18,338	14,961	15,064
of which: Bonds	75	..	..	0	4	0	364	261
Interest payments	**632**	**1,247**	**2,180**	**2,454**	**2,313**	**2,230**	**2,243**	**1,978**
Public and publicly guaranteed	439	672	617	751	971	1,155	1,324	1,318
Official creditors	269	229	297	421	471	464	462	399
Private creditors	171	443	320	330	500	691	861	919
of which: Bonds	45	184	156	171	362	648	832	901
Private nonguaranteed	193	575	1,563	1,703	1,342	1,076	919	660
of which: Bonds	7	..	..	3	6	6	7	4
Net financial flows								
Net inflows	**2,834**	**15,646**	**10,890**	**7,654**	**1,271**	**-627**	**-1,763**	**-1,281**
Net debt inflows	1,843	10,619	8,489	5,672	-212	-4,917	-6,052	-5,293
Official creditors	608	275	9,124	4,346	-1,587	-4,962	-6,023	-3,201
of which: World Bank	293	77	-75	789	-21	769	199	572
of which: IMF	18	-152	5,664	1,213	-1,997	-6,181	-5,897	-1,725
Private creditors	1,235	10,344	-635	1,327	1,375	45	-29	-2,091
Long-term	849	7,312	-1,808	-1,015	4,550	824	3,233	-2,847
Bonds	64	249	398	2,153	5,151	4,320	5,557	516
Banks and other private	785	7,063	-2,207	-3,167	-601	-3,497	-2,325	-3,363
Short-term	386	3,032	1,174	2,341	-3,175	-779	-3,262	756
Net equity inflows	991	5,028	2,400	1,981	1,483	4,290	4,289	4,011
Foreign direct investment	933	4,795	2,397	2,020	1,074	3,236	3,754	3,650
Portfolio equity	58	232	3	-38	408	1,054	535	362
Major economic aggregates								
Gross national income (GNI)	37,177	96,805	165,463	182,295	168,704	187,417	196,798	173,811
Exports of goods, services & prim. income	12,230	25,560	55,642	70,591	66,746	79,466	85,307	75,611
Imports of goods, services & prim. income	14,445	38,547	68,302	83,764	78,427	85,132	88,917	80,801
Primary income on FDI	72	2,935	665	719	1,713	3,837	2,478	4,185
Personal transfers & comp. of employees	96	952	641	694	733	3,519	3,381	3,085
International reserves	2,470	19,872	43,361	42,939	41,162	44,811	39,165	35,167
Ratios								
External debt stocks to exports (%)	92.1	152.1	207.4	169.4	181.0	156.0	131.1	126.9
External debt stocks to GNI (%)	30.3	40.2	69.7	65.6	71.6	66.1	56.8	55.2
Debt service to exports (%)	20.5	27.0	33.2	26.8	31.4	36.3	28.8	31.4
Short-term to external debt stocks (%)	6.8	19.1	14.9	16.3	13.5	12.5	11.0	13.6
Multilateral to external debt stocks (%)	29.9	14.4	11.6	13.4	13.7	14.9	14.6	13.8
Reserves to external debt stocks (%)	21.9	51.1	37.6	35.9	34.1	36.2	35.0	36.6

RUSSIAN FEDERATION

(US$ million, unless otherwise indicated)

	2000	2005	2010	2011	2012	2013	2014	2015
Summary external debt data								
External debt stocks	**146,665**	**249,832**	**417,892**	**544,358**	**591,835**	**668,508**	**549,631**	**467,720**
Long-term external debt	112,033	214,595	348,894	465,714	501,167	575,724	479,663	417,710
Public and publicly guaranteed	90,270	76,006	165,621	195,424	209,984	273,793	228,351	194,156
Official creditors	70,954	34,729	7,592	5,286	4,351	3,529	2,846	2,442
of which: IMF	19,002	8,107	8,735	8,708	8,717	8,735	8,217	7,860
Private creditors	19,316	41,277	158,028	190,137	205,634	270,264	225,504	191,714
of which: Bonds	15,543	29,005	25,510	31,560	52,769	59,360	38,997	30,567
Private nonguaranteed	21,762	138,589	183,273	270,291	291,182	301,931	251,313	223,555
of which: Bonds	1,412	12,956	2,100	12,792	11,092	14,407	11,492	11,639
Short-term external debt	15,630	27,131	60,263	69,936	81,952	84,050	61,750	42,150
interest arrears on long-term	4,530	3,151	56	52	52	50	50	50
Long-term external debt								
Disbursements	**1,416**	**48,438**	**70,301**	**93,720**	**120,192**	**83,980**	**9,718**	**12,163**
Public and publicly guaranteed	1,036	12,100	49,805	30,008	27,956	64,547	591	5,579
Official creditors	776	441	1,320	169	107	72	67	81
Private creditors	261	11,659	48,486	29,838	27,849	64,475	524	5,499
of which: Bonds	0	1,495	9,665	10,299	21,200	15,060	0	1,125
Private nonguaranteed	380	36,338	20,496	63,712	92,237	19,433	9,126	6,584
of which: Bonds	75	7,226	..	10,692	3,299	3,120	1,640	1,620
Principal repayments	**3,333**	**29,121**	**42,977**	**33,072**	**30,864**	**34,182**	**68,673**	**81,737**
Public and publicly guaranteed	2,031	23,151	30,004	20,968	13,404	18,889	45,822	40,618
Official creditors	1,206	18,695	1,096	2,480	1,044	896	740	476
Private creditors	825	4,456	28,908	18,488	12,360	17,993	45,082	40,142
of which: Bonds	268	3,765	5,805	5,016	0	8,512	20,188	10,427
Private nonguaranteed	1,302	5,971	12,973	12,105	17,459	15,293	22,851	41,120
of which: Bonds	825	822	186	..	4,999	2,620	4,555	1,473
Interest payments	**3,759**	**7,002**	**12,291**	**10,956**	**18,390**	**15,716**	**19,092**	**18,462**
Public and publicly guaranteed	2,682	4,521	1,707	2,964	3,011	3,177	3,630	2,974
Official creditors	1,227	2,339	62	96	85	68	54	45
Private creditors	1,454	2,182	1,645	2,867	2,926	3,109	3,576	2,929
of which: Bonds	1,320	2,095	791	1,961	1,856	2,340	2,301	1,791
Private nonguaranteed	1,077	2,481	10,584	7,992	15,379	12,540	15,462	15,488
of which: Bonds	165	907	..	137	331	527	597	616
Net financial flows								
Net inflows	**-980**	**29,430**	**58,660**	**93,686**	**126,017**	**76,630**	**-71,123**	**-84,368**
Net debt inflows	-2,805	16,562	34,862	70,324	101,345	51,898	-81,255	-89,174
Official creditors	-3,318	-21,642	224	-2,311	-937	-825	-673	-395
of which: World Bank	274	-528	-596	-556	-456	-405	-328	-146
of which: IMF	-2,888	-3,389	..	..	..	..	..	..
Private creditors	513	38,204	34,638	72,635	102,282	52,722	-80,583	-88,779
Long-term	-1,487	37,570	27,100	62,958	90,266	50,622	-58,283	-69,179
Bonds	-1,018	4,134	3,674	15,976	19,500	7,048	-23,103	-9,155
Banks and other private	-469	33,437	23,426	46,982	70,766	43,575	-35,180	-60,024
Short-term	2,000	634	7,538	9,677	12,016	2,100	-22,300	-19,600
Net equity inflows	1,825	12,868	23,798	23,362	24,672	24,732	10,133	4,807
Foreign direct investment	1,674	13,032	28,684	33,157	23,510	32,358	23,099	10,345
Portfolio equity	150	-163	-4,885	-9,796	1,162	-7,625	-12,966	-5,538
Major economic aggregates								
Gross national income (GNI)	252,972	745,491	1,477,813	1,971,439	2,101,980	2,151,067	1,963,844	1,289,956
Exports of goods, services & prim. income	115,273	286,351	479,897	616,135	637,532	634,135	609,723	430,549
Imports of goods, services & prim. income	69,960	200,317	406,127	513,137	560,117	591,432	544,032	355,925
Primary income on FDI	884	19,506	48,561	61,600	67,174	69,362	68,604	41,124
Personal transfers & comp. of employees	500	3,437	5,250	6,103	5,788	6,751	7,777	6,870
International reserves	24,264	175,891	443,586	453,948	486,577	469,603	339,370	319,835
Ratios								
External debt stocks to exports (%)	127.2	87.2	87.1	88.4	92.8	105.4	90.1	108.6
External debt stocks to GNI (%)	58.0	33.5	28.3	27.6	28.2	31.1	28.0	36.3
Debt service to exports (%)	10.1	14.2	11.6	7.2	7.8	8.0	14.5	23.3
Short-term to external debt stocks (%)	10.7	10.9	14.4	12.8	13.8	12.6	11.2	9.0
Multilateral to external debt stocks (%)	4.8	2.3	0.7	0.4	0.3	0.2	0.2	0.2
Reserves to external debt stocks (%)	16.5	70.4	106.1	83.4	82.2	70.2	61.7	68.4

Notes: Long-term public and publicly guaranteed and long-term private nonguaranteed debt are World Bank staff estimates based on reports provided by the country.

RWANDA

(US$ million, unless otherwise indicated)

	2000	2005	2010	2011	2012	2013	2014	2015
Summary external debt data								
External debt stocks	**1,290**	**1,526**	**906**	**1,216**	**1,263**	**1,694**	**2,022**	**2,244**
Long-term external debt	1,148	1,415	759	971	1,045	1,553	1,877	2,121
Public and publicly guaranteed	1,148	1,415	759	971	1,045	1,553	1,877	2,121
Official creditors	1,147	1,415	759	971	1,045	1,153	1,355	1,660
of which: IMF	104	97	133	132	131	130	119	112
Private creditors	1	0	0	0	0	400	522	460
of which: Bonds	0	0	0	0	0	400	400	400
Private nonguaranteed	..	..	..	..	..	..	..	..
of which: Bonds	..	..	..	..	..	..	..	..
Short-term external debt	38	15	14	112	86	11	25	11
interest arrears on long-term	16	13	0	0	0	0	0	0
Long-term external debt								
Disbursements	**40**	**85**	**63**	**230**	**94**	**527**	**409**	**379**
Public and publicly guaranteed	40	85	63	230	94	527	409	379
Official creditors	40	85	63	230	94	127	287	379
Private creditors	0	0	0	0	0	400	122	0
of which: Bonds	0	0	0	0	0	400	0	0
Private nonguaranteed	..	..	..	..	..	..	..	..
of which: Bonds	..	..	..	..	..	..	..	..
Principal repayments	**13**	**13**	**8**	**12**	**13**	**14**	**15**	**79**
Public and publicly guaranteed	13	13	8	12	13	14	15	79
Official creditors	13	13	8	12	13	14	15	17
Private creditors	0	0	0	0	0	0	0	62
of which: Bonds	0	0	0	0	0	0	0	0
Private nonguaranteed	..	..	..	..	..	..	..	..
of which: Bonds	..	..	..	..	..	..	..	..
Interest payments	**8**	**10**	**6**	**7**	**8**	**24**	**38**	**26**
Public and publicly guaranteed	8	10	6	7	8	24	38	26
Official creditors	8	10	6	7	8	10	11	13
Private creditors	0	0	0	0	0	14	27	13
of which: Bonds	0	0	0	0	0	14	27	13
Private nonguaranteed	..	..	..	..	..	..	..	..
of which: Bonds	..	..	..	..	..	..	..	..
Net financial flows								
Net inflows	**33**	**82**	**122**	**453**	**220**	**551**	**530**	**436**
Net debt inflows	25	72	58	315	54	436	405	283
Official creditors	41	70	54	217	80	111	269	359
of which: World Bank	31	47	9	136	38	41	167	285
of which: IMF	14	-2	0	-1	-1	-2	-3	-3
Private creditors	-16	2	4	98	-26	325	136	-75
Long-term	..	..	..	..	..	400	122	-62
Bonds	..	..	..	..	..	400	..	..
Banks and other private	..	..	..	..	..	..	122	-62
Short-term	-16	2	4	98	-26	-75	14	-14
Net equity inflows	8	11	64	138	167	115	125	152
Foreign direct investment	8	11	42	106	160	113	124	151
Portfolio equity	..	..	21	31	7	2	1	1
Major economic aggregates								
Gross national income (GNI)	1,719	2,554	5,656	6,348	7,125	7,386	7,755	7,913
Exports of goods, services & prim. income	142	260	639	933	1,027	1,299	1,256	1,415
Imports of goods, services & prim. income	452	693	1,708	2,273	2,570	2,915	2,825	3,036
Primary income on FDI	3	5	4	12	1	..	22	46
Personal transfers & comp. of employees	7	9	106	174	182	123	128	161
International reserves	191	406	813	1,050	848	1,070	1,066	1,030
Ratios								
External debt stocks to exports (%)	911.5	586.8	141.9	130.3	123.0	130.4	160.9	158.5
External debt stocks to GNI (%)	75.0	59.8	16.0	19.1	17.7	22.9	26.1	28.4
Debt service to exports (%)	25.7	10.9	2.3	2.1	2.2	3.2	4.5	7.7
Short-term to external debt stocks (%)	3.0	1.0	1.6	9.2	6.8	0.7	1.2	0.5
Multilateral to external debt stocks (%)	77.3	89.0	70.5	67.4	69.4	55.2	54.5	60.9
Reserves to external debt stocks (%)	14.8	26.6	89.7	86.4	67.2	63.2	52.7	45.9

Notes: Short-term debt is based on data from the BIS. Data include the effects of HIPC and MDRI debt relief.

SAMOA

(US$ million, unless otherwise indicated)

	2000	2005	2010	2011	2012	2013	2014	2015
Summary external debt data								
External debt stocks	**139.2**	**169.1**	**325.1**	**368.3**	**422.9**	**447.2**	**450.2**	**437.4**
Long-term external debt	137.7	167.5	299.1	342.4	396.9	412.3	417.3	407.6
Public and publicly guaranteed	137.7	167.5	299.1	342.4	396.9	412.3	417.3	407.6
Official creditors	137.7	167.5	299.1	342.4	396.9	412.3	417.3	407.6
of which: IMF	1.5	1.6	26.0	25.9	26.0	34.9	32.9	29.8
Private creditors	0.0	0.0	0.0	0.0	0.0	0.0	0.0	0.0
of which: Bonds	0.0	0.0	0.0	0.0	0.0	0.0	0.0	0.0
Private nonguaranteed	..	..	..	..	..	..	..	..
of which: Bonds	..	..	..	..	..	..	..	..
Short-term external debt	0.0	0.0	0.0	0.0	0.0	0.0	0.0	0.0
interest arrears on long-term	0.0	0.0	0.0	0.0	0.0	0.0	0.0	0.0
Long-term external debt								
Disbursements	**6.7**	**10.4**	**78.9**	**47.6**	**64.3**	**26.0**	**36.5**	**23.3**
Public and publicly guaranteed	6.7	10.4	78.9	47.6	64.3	26.0	36.5	23.3
Official creditors	6.7	10.4	78.9	47.6	64.3	26.0	36.5	23.3
Private creditors	0.0	0.0	0.0	0.0	0.0	0.0	0.0	0.0
of which: Bonds	0.0	0.0	0.0	0.0	0.0	0.0	0.0	0.0
Private nonguaranteed	..	..	..	..	..	..	..	..
of which: Bonds	..	..	..	..	..	..	..	..
Principal repayments	**4.2**	**4.3**	**7.2**	**7.7**	**8.6**	**9.7**	**13.4**	**13.7**
Public and publicly guaranteed	4.2	4.3	7.2	7.7	8.6	9.7	13.4	13.7
Official creditors	4.2	4.3	7.2	7.7	8.6	9.7	13.4	13.7
Private creditors	0.0	0.0	0.0	0.0	0.0	0.0	0.0	0.0
of which: Bonds	0.0	0.0	0.0	0.0	0.0	0.0	0.0	0.0
Private nonguaranteed	..	..	..	..	..	..	..	..
of which: Bonds	..	..	..	..	..	..	..	..
Interest payments	**1.3**	**1.5**	**3.3**	**4.1**	**4.7**	**5.2**	**5.7**	**5.6**
Public and publicly guaranteed	1.3	1.5	3.3	4.1	4.7	5.2	5.7	5.6
Official creditors	1.3	1.5	3.3	4.1	4.7	5.2	5.7	5.6
Private creditors	0.0	0.0	0.0	0.0	0.0	0.0	0.0	0.0
of which: Bonds	0.0	0.0	0.0	0.0	0.0	0.0	0.0	0.0
Private nonguaranteed	..	..	..	..	..	..	..	..
of which: Bonds	..	..	..	..	..	..	..	..
Net financial flows								
Net inflows	**0.9**	**9.9**	**70.3**	**48.8**	**69.6**	**49.4**	**45.7**	**23.5**
Net debt inflows	2.5	6.1	71.6	39.8	55.7	25.2	23.1	7.9
Official creditors	2.5	6.1	71.6	39.8	55.7	25.2	23.1	7.9
of which: World Bank	5.0	6.7	19.9	0.9	2.8	0.6	-1.9	4.5
of which: IMF	0.0	0.0	0.0	0.0	0.0	8.8	0.0	-1.6
Private creditors	..	..	..	..	..	..	..	..
Long-term	..	..	..	..	..	..	..	..
Bonds	..	..	..	..	..	..	..	..
Banks and other private	..	..	..	..	..	..	..	..
Short-term	..	..	..	..	..	..	..	..
Net equity inflows	-1.5	3.8	-1.3	9.0	13.9	24.2	22.6	15.6
Foreign direct investment	-1.5	3.8	-1.3	9.0	13.9	24.2	22.6	15.6
Portfolio equity	..	..	..	..	..	..	..	..
Major economic aggregates								
Gross national income (GNI)	269.0	441.4	638.1	734.4	767.3	763.0	774.3	735.4
Exports of goods, services & prim. income	..	147.3	201.8	211.8	238.0	249.2	242.0	191.5
Imports of goods, services & prim. income	..	300.2	392.7	463.1	423.7	464.1	455.4	328.2
Primary income on FDI	..	30.0	23.7	29.2	23.3	32.2	26.0	..
Personal transfers & comp. of employees	45.0	81.6	138.5	159.6	177.7	164.6	140.5	154.2
International reserves	63.7	81.8	209.4	166.8	168.7	170.7	140.7	139.4
Ratios								
External debt stocks to exports (%)	..	114.8	161.1	173.9	177.7	179.5	186.0	228.4
External debt stocks to GNI (%)	51.7	38.3	50.9	50.2	55.1	58.6	58.1	59.5
Debt service to exports (%)	..	3.9	5.3	5.6	5.6	6.0	7.9	11.0
Short-term to external debt stocks (%)	..	..	..	..	..	..	..	..
Multilateral to external debt stocks (%)	92.9	91.7	67.4	60.8	56.7	53.8	49.2	48.9
Reserves to external debt stocks (%)	45.7	48.4	64.4	45.3	39.9	38.2	31.2	31.9

Notes: Short-term debt data are excluded since BIS data include debt liabilities of offshore centers located in the country. BIS short-term debt data for 2013, 2014, and 2015 are $3.2 billion, $4.5 billion and $4.6 billion respectively.

SÃO TOMÉ AND PRÍNCIPE

(US$ million, unless otherwise indicated)

	2000	2005	2010	2011	2012	2013	2014	2015
Summary external debt data								
External debt stocks	**304.8**	**335.6**	**181.1**	**231.0**	**201.6**	**214.4**	**212.9**	**249.4**
Long-term external debt	278.3	317.1	145.3	189.2	169.3	183.3	186.5	224.6
Public and publicly guaranteed	278.3	317.1	145.3	189.2	169.3	183.3	186.5	224.6
Official creditors	278.3	317.1	145.3	189.2	169.3	183.3	186.5	224.6
of which: IMF	3.3	4.1	15.9	15.8	16.4	17.0	14.9	14.2
Private creditors	0.0	0.0	0.0	0.0	0.0	0.0	0.0	0.0
of which: Bonds	0.0	0.0	0.0	0.0	0.0	0.0	0.0	0.0
Private nonguaranteed	..	..	..	..	..	..	..	..
of which: Bonds	..	..	..	..	..	..	..	..
Short-term external debt	23.3	14.4	19.9	25.9	15.9	14.1	11.6	10.6
interest arrears on long-term	11.3	14.4	5.9	5.9	7.9	8.1	6.6	6.5
Long-term external debt								
Disbursements	**9.4**	**5.4**	**19.8**	**47.6**	**3.1**	**16.0**	**26.1**	**45.3**
Public and publicly guaranteed	9.4	5.4	19.8	47.6	3.1	16.0	26.1	45.3
Official creditors	9.4	5.4	19.8	47.6	3.1	16.0	26.1	45.3
Private creditors	0.0	0.0	0.0	0.0	0.0	0.0	0.0	0.0
of which: Bonds	0.0	0.0	0.0	0.0	0.0	0.0	0.0	0.0
Private nonguaranteed	..	..	..	..	..	..	..	..
of which: Bonds	..	..	..	..	..	..	..	..
Principal repayments	**2.2**	**4.4**	**1.2**	**1.1**	**10.8**	**4.8**	**11.1**	**0.7**
Public and publicly guaranteed	2.2	4.4	1.2	1.1	10.8	4.8	11.1	0.7
Official creditors	2.2	4.4	1.2	1.1	10.8	4.8	11.1	0.7
Private creditors	0.0	0.0	0.0	0.0	0.0	0.0	0.0	0.0
of which: Bonds	0.0	0.0	0.0	0.0	0.0	0.0	0.0	0.0
Private nonguaranteed	..	..	..	..	..	..	..	..
of which: Bonds	..	..	..	..	..	..	..	..
Interest payments	**1.2**	**2.1**	**0.3**	**0.3**	**0.5**	**0.5**	**1.1**	**1.0**
Public and publicly guaranteed	1.2	2.1	0.3	0.3	0.5	0.5	1.1	1.0
Official creditors	1.2	2.1	0.3	0.3	0.5	0.5	1.1	1.0
Private creditors	0.0	0.0	0.0	0.0	0.0	0.0	0.0	0.0
of which: Bonds	0.0	0.0	0.0	0.0	0.0	0.0	0.0	0.0
Private nonguaranteed	..	..	..	..	..	..	..	..
of which: Bonds	..	..	..	..	..	..	..	..
Net financial flows								
Net inflows	**13.5**	**17.2**	**72.7**	**84.6**	**3.3**	**18.6**	**30.0**	**69.6**
Net debt inflows	9.7	1.5	22.1	52.5	-19.1	9.8	12.9	43.6
Official creditors	9.7	1.5	19.1	46.5	-7.1	11.8	13.9	44.6
of which: World Bank	1.3	2.5	0.1	0.0	0.0	0.0	-0.1	-0.2
of which: IMF	2.5	0.5	0.6	0.0	0.6	0.5	-1.1	-0.1
Private creditors	..	..	3.0	6.0	-12.0	-2.0	-1.0	-1.0
Long-term	..	..	..	..	..	..	..	..
Bonds	..	..	..	..	..	..	..	..
Banks and other private	0.0	0.0	0.0	0.0	0.0	0.0	0.0	0.0
Short-term	0.0	0.0	3.0	6.0	-12.0	-2.0	-1.0	-1.0
Net equity inflows	3.8	15.7	50.6	32.2	22.5	8.9	17.1	26.0
Foreign direct investment	3.8	15.7	50.6	32.2	22.5	8.8	17.1	26.1
Portfolio equity	..	..	..	..	..	0.0	..	-0.1
Major economic aggregates								
Gross national income (GNI)	..	123.3	194.8	239.6	263.4	303.1	334.1	..
Exports of goods, services & prim. income	16.8	17.9	26.2	31.2	34.0	54.4	99.7	97.0
Imports of goods, services & prim. income	41.2	57.6	122.8	149.4	147.0	180.2	235.0	190.1
Primary income on FDI	..	..	..	..	..	..	0.2	1.0
Personal transfers & comp. of employees	0.5	1.5	6.4	6.9	6.4	26.6	26.8	20.0
International reserves	11.6	26.7	48.2	52.3	51.6	63.8	63.4	72.6
Ratios								
External debt stocks to exports (%)	1811.4	1873.4	690.9	740.1	593.7	393.8	213.7	257.1
External debt stocks to GNI (%)	..	272.3	93.0	96.4	76.6	70.7	63.7	..
Debt service to exports (%)	25.8	37.2	6.3	5.3	33.5	11.0	13.4	2.8
Short-term to external debt stocks (%)	7.6	4.3	11.0	11.2	7.9	6.6	5.4	4.2
Multilateral to external debt stocks (%)	55.5	58.8	20.6	18.0	18.7	17.6	17.7	15.1
Reserves to external debt stocks (%)	3.8	8.0	26.6	22.6	25.6	29.8	29.8	29.1

Notes: Short-term debt is based on data from the BIS. Data include HIPC and MDRI debt relief.

SENEGAL

(US$ million, unless otherwise indicated)

	2000	2005	2010	2011	2012	2013	2014	2015
Summary external debt data								
External debt stocks	**3,653**	**3,862**	**3,909**	**4,325**	**4,906**	**5,226**	**5,620**	**5,893**
Long-term external debt	3,221	3,643	3,458	3,879	4,464	4,788	5,225	5,549
Public and publicly guaranteed	3,208	3,501	3,150	3,614	4,198	4,517	4,953	5,320
Official creditors	3,203	3,492	2,950	3,114	3,696	4,015	4,011	4,123
of which: IMF	286	183	451	447	442	438	395	344
Private creditors	5	9	200	500	502	502	942	1,198
of which: Bonds	0	0	200	500	500	500	931	886
Private nonguaranteed	13	141	308	265	266	271	272	229
of which: Bonds	..	..	..	..	..	..	..	..
Short-term external debt	146	36	0	0	0	0	0	0
interest arrears on long-term	1	0	0	0	0	0	0	0
Long-term external debt								
Disbursements	**137**	**382**	**434**	**1,009**	**747**	**535**	**992**	**643**
Public and publicly guaranteed	136	333	352	928	672	409	871	595
Official creditors	131	333	352	428	670	409	361	456
Private creditors	5	0	0	500	2	0	510	138
of which: Bonds	0	0	0	500	0	0	500	0
Private nonguaranteed	1	49	83	81	74	126	122	49
of which: Bonds	..	..	..	..	..	..	..	..
Principal repayments	**127**	**112**	**229**	**236**	**211**	**268**	**214**	**193**
Public and publicly guaranteed	125	83	84	139	138	147	116	101
Official creditors	124	81	83	139	138	147	106	101
Private creditors	0	2	2	0	0	0	10	0
of which: Bonds	0	0	0	0	0	0	10	0
Private nonguaranteed	3	29	144	96	73	121	97	92
of which: Bonds	..	..	..	..	..	..	..	..
Interest payments	**58**	**55**	**75**	**122**	**102**	**128**	**126**	**150**
Public and publicly guaranteed	58	45	64	108	85	107	109	138
Official creditors	58	44	46	57	48	61	64	63
Private creditors	0	1	18	51	37	46	45	75
of which: Bonds	0	0	18	51	37	46	45	64
Private nonguaranteed	0	10	11	15	17	21	17	12
of which: Bonds	..	..	..	..	..	..	..	..
Net financial flows								
Net inflows	**-106**	**388**	**544**	**1,081**	**805**	**574**	**1,175**	**761**
Net debt inflows	-153	242	254	770	530	262	761	416
Official creditors	5	224	318	286	527	256	237	321
of which: World Bank	78	171	109	172	137	131	138	162
of which: IMF	-2	-28	49	-3	-5	-5	-18	-34
Private creditors	-158	18	-63	485	3	5	524	95
Long-term	3	18	-63	485	3	5	524	95
Bonds	..	..	..	500	..	..	490	..
Banks and other private	3	18	-63	-15	3	5	35	95
Short-term	-161	0	0	0	0	0	0	0
Net equity inflows	47	146	290	310	275	312	414	345
Foreign direct investment	49	152	267	296	276	311	403	345
Portfolio equity	-2	-6	23	14	-1	1	11	..
Major economic aggregates								
Gross national income (GNI)	4,589	8,551	12,799	14,274	13,865	14,606	15,459	13,553
Exports of goods, services & prim. income	1,391	2,562	3,418	4,055	4,210	4,493	4,593	3,598
Imports of goods, services & prim. income	1,938	3,991	5,557	6,969	7,496	7,907	7,900	6,528
Primary income on FDI	84	173	135	209	244	306	342	..
Personal transfers & comp. of employees	233	789	1,478	1,614	1,576	1,777	1,929	1,614
International reserves	388	1,186	2,047	1,946	2,082	2,253	2,038	2,012
Ratios								
External debt stocks to exports (%)	262.6	150.7	114.4	106.7	116.5	116.3	122.4	163.8
External debt stocks to GNI (%)	79.6	45.2	30.5	30.3	35.4	35.8	36.4	43.5
Debt service to exports (%)	16.2	7.9	8.9	8.9	7.6	8.9	7.8	10.5
Short-term to external debt stocks (%)	4.0	0.9	0.0	0.0	0.0	0.0	0.0	0.0
Multilateral to external debt stocks (%)	52.4	72.9	50.5	51.8	51.5	53.5	48.8	47.0
Reserves to external debt stocks (%)	10.6	30.7	52.4	45.0	42.4	43.1	36.3	34.1

Notes: Short-term debt before 2009 is based on data from the BIS.

SERBIA

(US$ million, unless otherwise indicated)

	2000	2005	2010	2011	2012	2013	2014	2015
Summary external debt data								
External debt stocks	**11,573**	**16,159**	**32,935**	**31,724**	**34,444**	**36,397**	**33,079**	**30,807**
Long-term external debt	6,789	12,970	27,417	27,779	30,910	34,180	31,710	29,291
Public and publicly guaranteed	6,178	7,756	9,504	11,339	13,701	16,722	16,569	16,343
Official creditors	4,243	6,679	8,172	8,738	9,324	10,085	9,114	8,961
of which: IMF	226	947	2,720	2,783	2,517	1,647	830	633
Private creditors	1,935	1,077	1,332	2,601	4,378	6,637	7,454	7,382
of which: Bonds	0	0	0	1,000	2,750	5,250	6,250	6,250
Private nonguaranteed	611	5,214	17,912	16,440	17,208	17,457	15,142	12,948
of which: Bonds	0	0	165	165	0	641	878	1,041
Short-term external debt	4,558	2,242	2,798	1,162	1,018	571	539	884
interest arrears on long-term	3,668	728	352	324	367	279	419	557
Long-term external debt								
Disbursements	**222**	**2,904**	**4,617**	**6,280**	**6,382**	**8,973**	**4,976**	**3,115**
Public and publicly guaranteed	222	311	1,388	2,541	2,854	3,789	1,893	1,381
Official creditors	187	311	1,149	1,137	965	999	765	1,240
Private creditors	35	0	239	1,404	1,889	2,789	1,128	141
of which: Bonds	0	0	0	1,000	1,750	2,500	1,000	0
Private nonguaranteed	0	2,593	3,230	3,739	3,528	5,184	3,083	1,734
of which: Bonds	0	0	0	0	0	641	237	162
Principal repayments	**0**	**570**	**3,431**	**4,257**	**4,756**	**6,296**	**6,321**	**2,987**
Public and publicly guaranteed	0	48	351	451	623	1,149	904	834
Official creditors	0	48	275	350	494	580	706	701
Private creditors	0	0	76	101	129	568	198	133
of which: Bonds	0	0	0	0	0	0	0	0
Private nonguaranteed	0	522	3,081	3,806	4,133	5,147	5,417	2,153
of which: Bonds	0	0	0	0	165	0	0	0
Interest payments	**0**	**367**	**759**	**905**	**978**	**1,269**	**1,234**	**1,116**
Public and publicly guaranteed	0	237	321	348	430	617	615	593
Official creditors	0	194	241	257	268	313	228	199
Private creditors	0	44	80	91	162	303	387	394
of which: Bonds	0	0	0	0	73	221	318	337
Private nonguaranteed	0	129	438	557	548	652	619	523
of which: Bonds	0	0	10	10	5	0	51	76
Net financial flows								
Net inflows	**103**	**2,827**	**2,326**	**4,063**	**1,357**	**2,886**	**-416**	**2,191**
Net debt inflows	51	2,827	1,201	489	1,171	1,452	-2,272	173
Official creditors	268	241	1,332	861	204	-448	-696	376
of which: World Bank	0	68	188	126	27	-41	169	274
of which: IMF	81	-22	458	74	-268	-867	-755	-162
Private creditors	-217	2,586	-130	-372	968	1,900	-1,577	-203
Long-term	35	2,071	312	1,235	1,155	2,258	-1,404	-410
Bonds	0	0	0	1,000	1,585	3,141	1,237	162
Banks and other private	35	2,071	312	235	-430	-884	-2,641	-572
Short-term	-252	515	-442	-1,607	-188	-358	-173	207
Net equity inflows	52	..	1,125	3,574	186	1,434	1,857	2,018
Foreign direct investment	52	..	1,040	3,505	210	1,475	1,878	2,108
Portfolio equity	..	..	84	69	-24	-41	-22	-90
Major economic aggregates								
Gross national income (GNI)	6,540	25,929	38,569	45,412	39,335	43,643	42,429	34,679
Exports of goods, services & prim. income	..	..	13,167	16,217	15,587	19,332	20,032	18,094
Imports of goods, services & prim. income	..	..	20,302	25,560	24,103	26,330	26,655	23,558
Primary income on FDI	..	..	564	1,597	1,251	1,578	1,484	1,530
Personal transfers & comp. of employees	..	..	4,118	3,960	3,549	4,025	3,696	3,371
International reserves	392	5,628	12,715	14,877	13,585	14,803	11,372	10,727
Ratios								
External debt stocks to exports (%)	..	..	250.1	195.6	221.0	188.3	165.1	170.3
External debt stocks to GNI (%)	177.0	62.3	85.4	69.9	87.6	83.4	78.0	88.8
Debt service to exports (%)	..	..	32.7	32.1	38.7	43.7	41.5	23.6
Short-term to external debt stocks (%)	39.4	13.9	8.5	3.7	3.0	1.6	1.6	2.9
Multilateral to external debt stocks (%)	12.4	22.0	14.8	17.1	17.6	17.5	17.2	18.7
Reserves to external debt stocks (%)	3.4	34.8	38.6	46.9	39.4	40.7	34.4	34.8

Notes: Beginning 2006, the data for Serbia exclude Montenegro. Short-term debt before 2014 is World Bank staff estimates based on Central Bank data.

SIERRA LEONE

(US$ million, unless otherwise indicated)

	2000	2005	2010	2011	2012	2013	2014	2015
Summary external debt data								
External debt stocks	**1,248**	**1,805**	**931**	**1,050**	**1,126**	**1,396**	**1,238**	**1,378**
Long-term external debt	1,006	1,566	661	741	837	901	910	946
Public and publicly guaranteed	1,006	1,566	661	741	837	901	910	946
Official creditors	1,000	1,354	450	533	628	705	715	753
of which: IMF	196	217	266	274	274	281	303	391
Private creditors	5	213	211	208	210	195	195	193
of which: Bonds	0	0	0	0	0	0	0	0
Private nonguaranteed	..	..	..	..	..	..	..	..
of which: Bonds	..	..	..	..	..	..	..	..
Short-term external debt	46	21	4	35	14	214	25	41
interest arrears on long-term	39	11	0	0	0	0	1	0
Long-term external debt								
Disbursements	**77**	**51**	**66**	**95**	**106**	**89**	**52**	**80**
Public and publicly guaranteed	77	51	66	95	106	89	52	80
Official creditors	77	51	66	95	106	89	52	80
Private creditors	0	0	0	0	0	0	0	0
of which: Bonds	0	0	0	0	0	0	0	0
Private nonguaranteed	..	..	..	..	..	..	..	..
of which: Bonds	..	..	..	..	..	..	..	..
Principal repayments	**10**	**5**	**5**	**7**	**8**	**10**	**14**	**14**
Public and publicly guaranteed	10	5	5	7	8	10	14	14
Official creditors	10	5	5	7	8	10	14	14
Private creditors	0	0	0	0	0	0	0	0
of which: Bonds	0	0	0	0	0	0	0	0
Private nonguaranteed	..	..	..	..	..	..	..	..
of which: Bonds	..	..	..	..	..	..	..	..
Interest payments	**9**	**9**	**4**	**6**	**6**	**7**	**8**	**7**
Public and publicly guaranteed	9	9	4	6	6	7	8	7
Official creditors	9	9	4	6	6	7	8	7
Private creditors	0	0	0	0	0	0	0	0
of which: Bonds	0	0	0	0	0	0	0	0
Private nonguaranteed	..	..	..	..	..	..	..	..
of which: Bonds	..	..	..	..	..	..	..	..
Net financial flows								
Net inflows	**59**	**107**	**309**	**898**	**637**	**716**	**279**	**703**
Net debt inflows	57	54	83	128	77	285	-111	184
Official creditors	56	64	102	97	98	85	79	167
of which: World Bank	68	19	32	35	39	14	10	5
of which: IMF	-12	18	41	9	0	7	41	102
Private creditors	1	-10	-19	31	-21	200	-190	17
Long-term	..	..	..	..	..	..	..	..
Bonds	..	..	..	..	..	..	..	..
Banks and other private	..	..	..	..	..	..	..	..
Short-term	1	-10	-19	31	-21	200	-190	17
Net equity inflows	1	53	225	770	560	431	389	519
Foreign direct investment	1	53	225	770	553	422	389	519
Portfolio equity	..	..	0	0	7	9	..	..
Major economic aggregates								
Gross national income (GNI)	616	1,590	2,645	3,050	3,452	4,874	4,824	4,390
Exports of goods, services & prim. income	62	267	427	548	1,243	1,768	1,494	..
Imports of goods, services & prim. income	262	509	1,191	2,711	2,689	2,707	3,231	..
Primary income on FDI	2	41	46	219	180	378	374	..
Personal transfers & comp. of employees	7	2	44	59	65	70	62	66
International reserves	49	171	409	439	478	533	601	620
Ratios								
External debt stocks to exports (%)	1,998.3	675.5	218.3	191.8	90.6	78.9	82.9	..
External debt stocks to GNI (%)	202.6	113.5	35.2	34.4	32.6	28.6	25.7	31.4
Debt service to exports (%)	76.4	6.9	2.7	3.4	1.7	1.5	2.3	..
Short-term to external debt stocks (%)	3.7	1.2	0.4	3.3	1.2	15.3	2.0	3.0
Multilateral to external debt stocks (%)	46.1	47.9	39.9	39.6	43.2	39.6	45.6	42.9
Reserves to external debt stocks (%)	3.9	9.4	43.9	41.8	42.5	38.2	48.5	45.0

Notes: Short-term debt is based on data from the BIS.

SOLOMON ISLANDS

(US$ million, unless otherwise indicated)

	2000	2005	2010	2011	2012	2013	2014	2015
Summary external debt data								
External debt stocks	**156.2**	**167.4**	**230.8**	**257.5**	**228.1**	**204.0**	**187.3**	**207.5**
Long-term external debt	152.1	151.2	201.9	210.3	191.5	166.0	140.8	158.0
Public and publicly guaranteed	120.7	144.2	125.3	117.8	110.2	101.1	89.6	81.2
Official creditors	117.3	143.8	125.2	117.8	110.2	101.1	89.6	81.2
of which: IMF	0.9	0.9	24.9	34.4	34.6	34.9	31.8	27.7
Private creditors	3.4	0.4	0.1	0.0	0.0	0.0	0.0	0.0
of which: Bonds	0.0	0.0	0.0	0.0	0.0	0.0	0.0	0.0
Private nonguaranteed	31.5	7.0	76.6	92.4	81.3	64.9	51.1	76.8
of which: Bonds	..	..	..	..	..	..	..	..
Short-term external debt	3.2	15.3	4.0	12.9	2.0	3.0	14.8	21.7
interest arrears on long-term	1.8	12.3	4.0	8.9	0.0	0.0	0.0	0.0
Long-term external debt								
Disbursements	**3.4**	**5.7**	**36.8**	**27.3**	**2.2**	**5.5**	**13.4**	**34.6**
Public and publicly guaranteed	3.4	5.7	0.0	0.0	0.0	0.0	0.0	2.1
Official creditors	3.4	5.3	0.0	0.0	0.0	0.0	0.0	2.1
Private creditors	0.0	0.4	0.0	0.0	0.0	0.0	0.0	0.0
of which: Bonds	0.0	0.0	0.0	0.0	0.0	0.0	0.0	0.0
Private nonguaranteed	0.0	0.0	36.8	27.3	2.2	5.5	13.4	32.5
of which: Bonds	..	..	..	..	..	..	..	..
Principal repayments	**6.2**	**10.0**	**17.5**	**12.6**	**21.8**	**38.9**	**13.5**	**8.5**
Public and publicly guaranteed	2.7	5.8	8.6	6.6	6.5	6.4	6.5	5.4
Official creditors	2.7	3.2	8.4	6.5	6.5	6.4	6.5	5.4
Private creditors	0.0	2.6	0.2	0.1	0.0	0.0	0.0	0.0
of which: Bonds	0.0	0.0	0.0	0.0	0.0	0.0	0.0	0.0
Private nonguaranteed	3.5	4.2	8.9	6.0	15.3	32.5	7.0	3.2
of which: Bonds	..	..	..	..	..	..	..	..
Interest payments	**2.7**	**3.9**	**3.2**	**2.6**	**8.1**	**5.3**	**2.2**	**2.2**
Public and publicly guaranteed	0.8	1.7	1.7	1.7	1.5	1.4	1.4	1.1
Official creditors	0.8	1.7	1.7	1.7	1.5	1.4	1.4	1.1
Private creditors	0.0	0.0	0.0	0.0	0.0	0.0	0.0	0.0
of which: Bonds	0.0	0.0	0.0	0.0	0.0	0.0	0.0	0.0
Private nonguaranteed	1.9	2.3	1.5	0.9	6.5	3.9	0.8	1.1
of which: Bonds	..	..	..	..	..	..	..	..
Net financial flows								
Net inflows	**-2.4**	**-2.0**	**105.5**	**89.1**	**8.1**	**-63.2**	**11.8**	**32.1**
Net debt inflows	-4.4	-2.3	27.9	28.5	-21.3	-32.2	10.6	30.4
Official creditors	0.6	2.1	1.1	3.3	-6.3	-6.1	-7.6	-5.9
of which: World Bank	0.4	0.1	-1.2	-1.3	-1.2	-1.4	-1.6	0.6
of which: IMF	0.0	0.0	9.5	9.8	0.2	0.2	-1.1	-2.7
Private creditors	-5.0	-4.4	26.8	25.2	-15.1	-26.0	18.2	36.3
Long-term	-3.5	-6.4	27.8	21.2	-13.1	-27.0	6.4	29.3
Bonds	..	..	..	..	..	..	..	..
Banks and other private	-3.5	-6.4	27.8	21.2	-13.1	-27.0	6.4	29.3
Short-term	-1.5	2.0	-1.0	4.0	-2.0	1.0	11.8	7.0
Net equity inflows	2.0	0.3	77.6	60.6	29.5	-31.0	1.2	1.7
Foreign direct investment	2.0	0.3	77.6	60.6	29.5	-31.0	1.2	1.7
Portfolio equity	..	..	..	..	..	..	..	..
Major economic aggregates								
Gross national income (GNI)	435.5	415.5	496.5	672.5	931.4	1,051.4	1,099.6	1,153.9
Exports of goods, services & prim. income	128.8	154.9	334.8	566.1	652.3	604.8	613.4	577.6
Imports of goods, services & prim. income	176.4	250.1	610.9	712.8	728.0	740.1	743.5	696.1
Primary income on FDI	8.3	5.3	47.6	76.1	64.3	10.2	45.8	60.7
Personal transfers & comp. of employees	4.3	7.2	14.3	16.9	20.7	20.6	16.3	18.6
International reserves	32.0	94.8	265.8	412.3	469.5	491.5	466.9	494.1
Ratios								
External debt stocks to exports (%)	121.3	108.1	68.9	45.5	35.0	33.7	30.5	35.9
External debt stocks to GNI (%)	35.9	40.3	46.5	38.3	24.5	19.4	17.0	18.0
Debt service to exports (%)	7.1	9.1	6.2	2.7	4.6	7.3	2.8	2.4
Short-term to external debt stocks (%)	2.1	9.1	1.7	5.0	0.9	1.5	7.9	10.5
Multilateral to external debt stocks (%)	64.3	63.9	45.8	38.8	41.2	42.4	40.9	33.4
Reserves to external debt stocks (%)	20.5	56.7	115.2	160.1	205.8	241.0	249.3	238.2

SOMALIA

(US$ million, unless otherwise indicated)

	2000	2005	2010	2011	2012	2013	2014	2015
Summary external debt data								
External debt stocks	**2,579**	**2,770**	**3,045**	**3,053**	**3,055**	**3,056**	**2,953**	**2,892**
Long-term external debt	1,825	1,882	1,990	1,992	1,985	1,977	1,913	1,876
Public and publicly guaranteed	1,825	1,882	1,990	1,992	1,985	1,977	1,913	1,876
Official creditors	1,792	1,846	1,954	1,955	1,948	1,940	1,878	1,841
of which: IMF	164	180	244	243	243	243	229	219
Private creditors	33	35	37	36	36	37	35	34
of which: Bonds	0	0	0	0	0	0	0	0
Private nonguaranteed	..	..	..	..	..	..	..	..
of which: Bonds	..	..	..	..	..	..	..	..
Short-term external debt	591	709	811	818	827	835	811	797
interest arrears on long-term	569	709	811	818	827	835	811	797
Long-term external debt								
Disbursements	..	..	..	..	..	..	..	..
Public and publicly guaranteed	0	0	0	0	0	0	0	0
Official creditors	0	0	0	0	0	0	0	0
Private creditors	0	0	0	0	0	0	0	0
of which: Bonds	0	0	0	0	0	0	0	0
Private nonguaranteed	..	..	..	..	..	..	..	..
of which: Bonds	..	..	..	..	..	..	..	..
Principal repayments	..	..	..	..	..	..	..	..
Public and publicly guaranteed	0	0	0	0	0	0	0	0
Official creditors	0	0	0	0	0	0	0	0
Private creditors	0	0	0	0	0	0	0	0
of which: Bonds	0	0	0	0	0	0	0	0
Private nonguaranteed	..	..	..	..	..	..	..	..
of which: Bonds	..	..	..	..	..	..	..	..
Interest payments	..	..	..	..	..	..	..	..
Public and publicly guaranteed	0	0	0	0	0	0	0	0
Official creditors	0	0	0	0	0	0	0	0
Private creditors	0	0	0	0	0	0	0	0
of which: Bonds	0	0	0	0	0	0	0	0
Private nonguaranteed	..	..	..	..	..	..	..	..
of which: Bonds	..	..	..	..	..	..	..	..
Net financial flows								
Net inflows	**-7**	**24**	**112**	**102**	**107**	**446**	**434**	**516**
Net debt inflows	-7	..	..	..	..	..	..	..
Official creditors	..	..	..	..	..	..	..	..
of which: World Bank	..	..	..	..	..	..	..	..
of which: IMF	0	0	0	0	0	0	0	0
Private creditors	-7	..	..	..	..	..	..	..
Long-term	..	..	..	..	..	..	..	..
Bonds	..	..	..	..	..	..	..	..
Banks and other private	..	..	..	..	..	..	..	..
Short-term	-7	..	..	..	..	..	..	..
Net equity inflows	0	24	112	102	107	446	434	516
Foreign direct investment	0	24	112	102	107	446	434	516
Portfolio equity	..	..	..	..	..	..	..	..
Major economic aggregates								
Gross national income (GNI)	..	..	..	..	..	4,927	5,257	5,486
Exports of goods, services & prim. income	..	..	..	..	..	..	..	..
Imports of goods, services & prim. income	..	..	..	..	..	..	..	..
Primary income on FDI	..	..	..	..	..	..	..	..
Personal transfers & comp. of employees	..	..	..	..	..	..	..	..
International reserves	..	..	..	..	..	..	..	..
Ratios								
External debt stocks to exports (%)	..	..	..	..	..	..	..	..
External debt stocks to GNI (%)	..	..	..	..	..	62.0	56.2	52.7
Debt service to exports (%)	..	..	..	..	..	..	..	..
Short-term to external debt stocks (%)	22.9	25.6	26.6	26.8	27.1	27.3	27.5	27.6
Multilateral to external debt stocks (%)	27.5	27.3	26.3	26.2	26.1	26.0	25.9	25.7
Reserves to external debt stocks (%)	..	..	..	..	..	..	..	..

Notes: Long-term public and publicly guaranteed debt data are World Bank staff estimates based on the original terms of the loans.

SOUTH AFRICA

(US$ million, unless otherwise indicated)

	2000	2005	2010	2011	2012	2013	2014	2015
Summary external debt data								
External debt stocks	**25,435**	**44,737**	**108,392**	**116,929**	**144,959**	**139,790**	**141,103**	**137,887**
Long-term external debt	15,595	30,146	83,912	93,654	114,347	109,791	110,474	106,338
Public and publicly guaranteed	9,088	20,743	36,274	41,551	56,502	54,586	56,642	57,598
Official creditors	145	286	1,139	1,449	2,782	3,046	3,601	3,305
of which: IMF	287	315	2,750	2,741	2,744	2,750	2,587	2,474
Private creditors	8,943	20,457	35,135	40,102	53,720	51,540	53,040	54,293
of which: Bonds	4,749	12,242	32,329	38,548	53,133	51,242	52,522	52,409
Private nonguaranteed	6,507	9,403	47,638	52,103	57,845	55,205	53,832	48,740
of which: Bonds	1,110	3,196	8,786	12,638	14,069	12,152	10,366	10,309
Short-term external debt	9,553	14,276	21,730	20,534	27,868	27,249	28,042	29,075
interest arrears on long-term	0	0	0	0	0	0	0	0
Long-term external debt								
Disbursements	**3,611**	**2,678**	**7,001**	**9,995**	**7,842**	**8,944**	**8,518**	**15,465**
Public and publicly guaranteed	1,597	2,678	3,777	3,990	3,915	3,742	4,084	2,786
Official creditors	91	58	913	490	1,415	526	1,397	1,342
Private creditors	1,506	2,620	2,864	3,500	2,500	3,215	2,687	1,445
of which: Bonds	765	0	2,000	3,500	2,500	3,000	2,429	0
Private nonguaranteed	2,014	0	3,224	6,005	3,928	5,202	4,435	12,679
of which: Bonds	712	0	1,135	3,852	2,738	3,543	1,209	1,823
Principal repayments	**2,631**	**2,870**	**3,470**	**2,737**	**5,293**	**8,702**	**3,153**	**2,656**
Public and publicly guaranteed	1,649	2,870	1,678	1,520	2,674	5,503	1,048	191
Official creditors	0	27	40	42	37	25	22	120
Private creditors	1,649	2,844	1,638	1,478	2,638	5,478	1,027	71
of which: Bonds	306	1,091	0	104	1,670	4,972	1,000	0
Private nonguaranteed	982	0	1,792	1,217	2,618	3,199	2,104	2,465
of which: Bonds	0	0	834	0	1,307	2,083	2,104	203
Interest payments	**746**	**1,269**	**2,191**	**2,975**	**3,560**	**3,222**	**3,703**	**4,504**
Public and publicly guaranteed	549	1,058	1,573	2,061	2,612	2,352	2,409	2,943
Official creditors	1	12	20	40	62	70	131	219
Private creditors	548	1,046	1,553	2,021	2,550	2,282	2,278	2,724
of which: Bonds	278	771	1,488	1,968	2,475	2,278	2,277	2,720
Private nonguaranteed	196	212	618	914	948	869	1,294	1,561
of which: Bonds	27	212	460	664	776	602	968	869
Net financial flows								
Net inflows	**4,800**	**16,310**	**5,607**	**5,197**	**10,876**	**3,333**	**10,001**	**20,582**
Net debt inflows	-282	2,888	3,975	6,062	9,884	-377	6,159	13,842
Official creditors	91	31	873	448	1,378	502	1,375	1,221
of which: World Bank	3	8	363	199	494	284	1,270	1,123
of which: IMF	0	0	0	0	0	0	0	0
Private creditors	-373	2,857	3,102	5,614	8,506	-879	4,784	12,620
Long-term	889	-224	2,658	6,810	1,172	-260	3,991	11,587
Bonds	1,171	-1,091	2,301	7,248	2,261	-512	534	1,620
Banks and other private	-282	867	357	-438	-1,089	253	3,457	9,968
Short-term	-1,262	3,081	444	-1,196	7,334	-619	793	1,033
Net equity inflows	5,082	13,422	1,632	-865	992	3,710	3,842	6,741
Foreign direct investment	913	6,192	-4,194	2,903	1,671	2,699	1,292	-595
Portfolio equity	4,169	7,230	5,826	-3,769	-679	1,011	2,551	7,335
Major economic aggregates								
Gross national income (GNI)	133,188	252,831	367,345	405,947	386,627	356,448	340,516	304,931
Exports of goods, services & prim. income	39,507	72,730	112,387	132,170	123,784	119,856	117,102	104,802
Imports of goods, services & prim. income	38,771	78,292	115,601	139,516	140,298	138,299	132,559	115,800
Primary income on FDI	2,329	4,320	6,165	8,375	8,486	8,053	8,707	7,062
Personal transfers & comp. of employees	325	614	1,070	1,158	1,085	971	913	825
International reserves	6,083	18,579	38,175	42,595	43,995	44,864	44,267	41,620
Ratios								
External debt stocks to exports (%)	64.4	61.5	96.4	88.5	117.1	116.6	120.5	131.6
External debt stocks to GNI (%)	19.1	17.7	29.5	28.8	37.5	39.2	41.4	45.2
Debt service to exports (%)	9.9	6.4	5.6	4.8	7.9	10.6	6.7	7.7
Short-term to external debt stocks (%)	37.6	31.9	20.0	17.6	19.2	19.5	19.9	21.1
Multilateral to external debt stocks (%)	0.6	0.6	1.1	1.2	1.9	2.2	2.6	2.4
Reserves to external debt stocks (%)	23.9	41.5	35.2	36.4	30.4	32.1	31.4	30.2

Notes: Long-term public and publicly guaranteed and long-term private nonguaranteed debt data are World Bank staff estimates based on reports provided by the country.

SRI LANKA

(US$ million, unless otherwise indicated)

	2000	2005	2010	2011	2012	2013	2014	2015
Summary external debt data								
External debt stocks	**9,250**	**11,300**	**21,684**	**25,795**	**35,694**	**39,211**	**42,264**	**43,920**
Long-term external debt	8,312	10,045	17,349	19,894	26,157	29,771	33,118	35,092
Public and publicly guaranteed	7,945	9,658	16,430	18,682	22,954	25,428	25,825	27,448
Official creditors	6,934	8,983	13,613	14,807	15,894	16,637	17,026	17,215
of which: IMF	253	483	1,920	2,325	3,118	2,665	1,821	1,240
Private creditors	1,010	674	2,817	3,875	7,061	8,791	8,799	10,233
of which: Bonds	65	65	2,000	3,000	4,000	5,250	7,000	8,650
Private nonguaranteed	368	388	919	1,213	3,203	4,343	7,293	7,644
of which: Bonds	..	100	..	..	..	100	2,263	2,140
Short-term external debt	685	772	2,416	3,576	6,419	6,775	7,325	7,588
interest arrears on long-term	112	0	0	0	0	5	62	11
Long-term external debt								
Disbursements	**757**	**929**	**3,091**	**3,196**	**7,907**	**5,117**	**9,251**	**4,351**
Public and publicly guaranteed	587	818	2,994	2,751	5,952	3,932	4,090	3,756
Official creditors	348	670	1,810	1,613	2,145	2,065	2,025	1,358
Private creditors	240	149	1,183	1,138	3,807	1,868	2,065	2,399
of which: Bonds	0	0	1,000	1,000	1,500	1,250	1,750	2,150
Private nonguaranteed	169	111	97	445	1,955	1,185	5,161	595
of which: Bonds	..	0	..	..	..	100	2,163	0
Principal repayments	**453**	**246**	**727**	**818**	**1,377**	**921**	**4,909**	**1,962**
Public and publicly guaranteed	439	227	582	664	1,211	739	2,698	1,718
Official creditors	216	123	507	588	604	613	718	809
Private creditors	223	104	75	76	607	126	1,981	909
of which: Bonds	50	0	0	0	500	0	0	500
Private nonguaranteed	14	19	145	154	165	183	2,211	244
of which: Bonds	..	0	..	..	..	0	0	123
Interest payments	**213**	**106**	**616**	**448**	**567**	**635**	**705**	**702**
Public and publicly guaranteed	178	84	596	405	532	585	655	654
Official creditors	125	65	308	268	292	326	310	312
Private creditors	54	19	288	137	240	259	345	343
of which: Bonds	6	4	72	124	224	235	323	318
Private nonguaranteed	35	22	20	43	35	50	50	48
of which: Bonds	..	7	..	..	..	0	5	5
Net financial flows								
Net inflows	**175**	**595**	**1,013**	**4,040**	**10,792**	**4,728**	**4,762**	**2,566**
Net debt inflows	0	539	1,822	3,961	10,159	4,092	4,115	2,198
Official creditors	45	661	1,900	1,447	2,326	997	588	43
of which: World Bank	23	73	83	132	97	126	127	62
of which: IMF	-86	115	597	422	786	-455	-720	-506
Private creditors	-46	-122	-77	2,514	7,833	3,095	3,527	2,155
Long-term	172	137	1,060	1,353	4,990	2,744	3,035	1,840
Bonds	-50	0	1,000	1,000	1,000	1,350	3,913	1,527
Banks and other private	222	137	60	353	3,990	1,394	-878	314
Short-term	-218	-259	-1,138	1,160	2,843	351	493	314
Net equity inflows	175	57	-809	80	632	636	647	368
Foreign direct investment	175	272	240	251	360	410	469	426
Portfolio equity	..	-216	-1,049	-171	272	226	178	-58
Major economic aggregates								
Gross national income (GNI)	16,016	24,107	56,109	64,641	67,221	72,543	78,215	80,467
Exports of goods, services & prim. income	6,527	7,963	11,423	14,109	13,716	15,211	16,890	17,029
Imports of goods, services & prim. income	8,554	10,441	16,159	23,368	23,117	23,391	25,105	25,231
Primary income on FDI	109	115	303	385	449	737	670	811
Personal transfers & comp. of employees	1,154	1,976	4,123	5,153	6,000	6,422	7,036	7,000
International reserves	1,039	2,650	6,710	6,248	6,378	6,611	7,316	6,543
Ratios								
External debt stocks to exports (%)	141.7	141.9	189.8	182.8	260.2	257.8	250.2	257.9
External debt stocks to GNI (%)	57.8	46.9	38.6	39.9	53.1	54.1	54.0	54.6
Debt service to exports (%)	12.1	5.5	12.3	9.3	14.8	13.5	37.6	18.7
Short-term to external debt stocks (%)	7.4	6.8	11.1	13.9	18.0	17.3	17.3	17.3
Multilateral to external debt stocks (%)	36.9	40.3	28.1	24.6	18.6	17.6	16.2	15.7
Reserves to external debt stocks (%)	11.2	23.4	30.9	24.2	17.9	16.9	17.3	14.9

Notes: Short-term debt before 2009 is based on data from the BIS.

ST. LUCIA

(US$ million, unless otherwise indicated)

	2000	2005	2010	2011	2012	2013	2014	2015
Summary external debt data								
External debt stocks	**222.2**	**415.7**	**579.6**	**451.2**	**429.8**	**474.0**	**529.3**	**529.4**
Long-term external debt	153.5	238.6	321.3	310.1	342.9	358.2	371.4	417.1
Public and publicly guaranteed	153.5	238.6	321.3	310.1	342.9	358.2	371.4	417.1
Official creditors	120.7	164.6	258.0	258.7	249.5	246.5	249.6	256.9
of which: IMF	1.0	1.1	33.0	41.2	41.2	41.3	38.0	33.4
Private creditors	32.8	74.0	63.3	51.4	93.4	111.7	121.8	160.2
of which: Bonds	23.5	70.9	63.3	51.4	93.4	111.7	121.8	160.2
Private nonguaranteed	..	..	..	..	..	..	..	..
of which: Bonds	..	..	..	..	..	..	..	..
Short-term external debt	67.8	176.0	225.3	99.9	45.7	74.5	119.9	78.9
interest arrears on long-term	0.0	0.0	5.3	3.9	1.6	2.2	2.2	2.2
Long-term external debt								
Disbursements	**48.7**	**12.6**	**36.4**	**20.0**	**6.9**	**12.0**	**25.2**	**21.4**
Public and publicly guaranteed	48.7	12.6	36.4	20.0	6.9	12.0	25.2	21.4
Official creditors	16.8	12.6	36.4	20.0	6.9	12.0	25.2	19.4
Private creditors	31.9	0.0	0.0	0.0	0.0	0.0	0.0	2.0
of which: Bonds	23.5	0.0	0.0	0.0	0.0	0.0	0.0	2.0
Private nonguaranteed	..	..	..	..	..	..	..	..
of which: Bonds	..	..	..	..	..	..	..	..
Principal repayments	**20.9**	**14.2**	**29.9**	**31.3**	**28.2**	**20.5**	**16.8**	**45.6**
Public and publicly guaranteed	20.9	14.2	29.9	31.3	28.2	20.5	16.8	45.6
Official creditors	11.7	9.5	18.0	19.4	16.3	15.6	15.8	17.5
Private creditors	9.2	4.7	11.9	11.9	11.9	4.9	1.0	28.1
of which: Bonds	0.0	4.7	11.9	11.9	11.9	4.9	1.0	28.1
Private nonguaranteed	..	..	..	..	..	..	..	..
of which: Bonds	..	..	..	..	..	..	..	..
Interest payments	**6.4**	**12.8**	**10.6**	**11.3**	**14.4**	**13.6**	**16.4**	**21.9**
Public and publicly guaranteed	6.4	12.8	10.6	11.3	14.4	13.6	16.4	21.9
Official creditors	5.2	6.3	7.4	6.7	6.4	6.1	5.9	10.8
Private creditors	1.2	6.5	3.2	4.6	8.0	7.5	10.5	11.1
of which: Bonds	1.0	6.3	3.2	4.6	8.0	7.5	10.5	11.1
Private nonguaranteed	..	..	..	..	..	..	..	..
of which: Bonds	..	..	..	..	..	..	..	..
Net financial flows								
Net inflows	**58.2**	**140.7**	**212.5**	**-82.0**	**-27.9**	**72.2**	**146.0**	**26.9**
Net debt inflows	40.3	65.4	144.5	-126.8	-73.1	19.7	52.9	-68.2
Official creditors	5.1	3.1	18.4	9.1	-9.4	-3.5	8.5	-1.1
of which: World Bank	1.0	3.3	11.8	2.1	-2.6	6.7	2.6	0.0
of which: IMF	0.0	0.0	0.0	8.5	0.0	0.0	-0.9	-3.0
Private creditors	35.2	62.3	126.1	-135.9	-63.8	23.3	44.3	-67.1
Long-term	22.7	-4.7	-11.9	-11.9	-11.9	-4.9	-1.0	-26.1
Bonds	23.5	-4.7	-11.9	-11.9	-11.9	-4.9	-1.0	-26.1
Banks and other private	-0.8	0.0	..	..	..	..	..	..
Short-term	12.5	67.0	138.0	-124.0	-51.9	28.2	45.4	-40.9
Net equity inflows	17.9	75.3	67.9	44.8	45.2	52.4	93.1	95.0
Foreign direct investment	17.9	75.3	67.9	44.8	45.2	52.4	93.1	95.0
Portfolio equity	..	..	..	..	..	..	..	..
Major economic aggregates								
Gross national income (GNI)	739.6	874.2	1,209.9	1,270.2	1,275.8	1,308.4	1,378.8	1,414.4
Exports of goods, services & prim. income	380.6	533.0	626.6	589.1	621.7	631.7	650.0	680.4
Imports of goods, services & prim. income	494.2	675.5	844.7	852.3	811.7	739.3	783.7	728.2
Primary income on FDI	33.4	51.1	31.7	12.0	23.3	19.8	..	..
Personal transfers & comp. of employees	23.8	27.1	29.0	29.4	29.8	30.1	34.2	35.0
International reserves	78.8	116.4	206.3	213.4	232.0	192.2	257.7	317.5
Ratios								
External debt stocks to exports (%)	58.4	78.0	92.5	76.6	69.1	75.0	81.4	77.8
External debt stocks to GNI (%)	30.0	47.6	47.9	35.5	33.7	36.2	38.4	37.4
Debt service to exports (%)	7.9	6.0	7.4	7.6	7.0	5.7	5.7	10.6
Short-term to external debt stocks (%)	30.5	42.3	38.9	22.1	10.6	15.7	22.6	14.9
Multilateral to external debt stocks (%)	44.8	34.7	40.9	52.8	52.7	47.3	40.7	40.9
Reserves to external debt stocks (%)	35.5	28.0	35.6	47.3	54.0	40.6	48.7	60.0

Notes: Short-term debt is based on data from the BIS.

ST. VINCENT AND THE GRENADINES

(US$ million, unless otherwise indicated)

	2000	2005	2010	2011	2012	2013	2014	2015
Summary external debt data								
External debt stocks	**195.1**	**252.6**	**295.5**	**303.4**	**287.1**	**310.6**	**338.9**	**338.7**
Long-term external debt	163.3	247.8	277.5	280.4	264.1	287.5	311.7	313.6
Public and publicly guaranteed	163.3	247.8	277.5	280.4	264.1	287.5	311.7	313.6
Official creditors	104.8	114.8	228.8	242.6	238.7	270.0	294.6	302.9
of which: IMF	0.5	0.5	17.9	23.0	23.0	23.0	27.2	24.9
Private creditors	58.5	133.0	48.7	37.8	25.4	17.5	17.1	10.7
of which: Bonds	0.0	0.0	0.0	0.0	0.0	0.0	0.0	0.0
Private nonguaranteed	..	..	..	..	..	..	..	..
of which: Bonds	..	..	..	..	..	..	..	..
Short-term external debt	31.4	4.3	0.0	0.0	0.0	0.0	0.0	0.1
interest arrears on long-term	0.4	4.3	0.0	0.0	0.0	0.0	0.0	0.1
Long-term external debt								
Disbursements	**8.5**	**42.4**	**78.1**	**28.3**	**12.0**	**47.1**	**49.4**	**28.9**
Public and publicly guaranteed	8.5	42.4	78.1	28.3	12.0	47.1	49.4	28.9
Official creditors	8.5	12.4	78.1	28.3	12.0	46.2	41.4	28.9
Private creditors	0.0	30.0	0.0	0.0	0.0	1.0	8.0	0.0
of which: Bonds	0.0	0.0	0.0	0.0	0.0	0.0	0.0	0.0
Private nonguaranteed	..	..	..	..	..	..	..	..
of which: Bonds	..	..	..	..	..	..	..	..
Principal repayments	**6.1**	**15.5**	**26.5**	**25.2**	**28.4**	**24.8**	**22.9**	**25.4**
Public and publicly guaranteed	6.1	15.5	26.5	25.2	28.4	24.8	22.9	25.4
Official creditors	5.7	7.7	15.4	14.3	16.0	15.9	14.6	19.0
Private creditors	0.4	7.7	11.1	10.9	12.4	8.9	8.4	6.4
of which: Bonds	0.0	0.0	0.0	0.0	0.0	0.0	0.0	0.0
Private nonguaranteed	..	..	..	..	..	..	..	..
of which: Bonds	..	..	..	..	..	..	..	..
Interest payments	**5.1**	**8.2**	**10.0**	**10.1**	**8.4**	**8.1**	**7.7**	**7.7**
Public and publicly guaranteed	5.1	8.2	10.0	10.1	8.4	8.1	7.7	7.7
Official creditors	3.3	3.5	5.7	6.6	5.6	6.2	6.6	6.8
Private creditors	1.8	4.7	4.3	3.4	2.8	1.9	1.1	0.8
of which: Bonds	0.0	0.0	0.0	0.0	0.0	0.0	0.0	0.0
Private nonguaranteed	..	..	..	..	..	..	..	..
of which: Bonds	..	..	..	..	..	..	..	..
Net financial flows								
Net inflows	**13.3**	**50.6**	**114.7**	**82.9**	**71.8**	**111.9**	**142.0**	**123.2**
Net debt inflows	1.6	26.9	51.7	8.3	-16.5	22.4	32.2	2.5
Official creditors	2.8	4.6	62.8	19.2	-4.0	30.3	32.6	8.9
of which: World Bank	-0.1	3.0	3.1	2.0	0.3	3.7	2.1	0.2
of which: IMF	0.0	0.0	0.0	5.2	0.0	0.0	5.7	-1.0
Private creditors	-1.2	22.3	-11.1	-10.9	-12.4	-7.9	-0.4	-6.4
Long-term	-0.4	22.3	-11.1	-10.9	-12.4	-7.9	-0.4	-6.4
Bonds	..	..	..	..	..	..	..	..
Banks and other private	-0.4	22.3	-11.1	-10.9	-12.4	-7.9	-0.4	-6.4
Short-term	-0.8	0.0	0.0	0.0	0.0	0.0	0.0	0.0
Net equity inflows	11.8	23.7	63.1	74.6	88.3	89.5	109.8	120.7
Foreign direct investment	11.8	23.7	63.1	74.6	88.3	89.5	109.8	120.7
Portfolio equity	..	..	..	..	..	..	..	..
Major economic aggregates								
Gross national income (GNI)	377.1	521.1	668.9	663.2	689.1	720.7	729.7	749.1
Exports of goods, services & prim. income	182.6	208.9	195.9	192.3	202.4	208.6	199.9	198.8
Imports of goods, services & prim. income	222.8	329.2	414.1	399.1	420.1	443.1	426.4	399.3
Primary income on FDI	12.7	22.1	11.0	7.4	5.6	5.8	..	..
Personal transfers & comp. of employees	19.3	22.4	29.1	29.2	31.1	31.6	36.1	36.7
International reserves	55.2	69.5	112.7	89.6	111.0	135.1	157.4	166.0
Ratios								
External debt stocks to exports (%)	106.9	120.9	150.9	157.7	141.9	148.9	169.5	170.3
External debt stocks to GNI (%)	51.7	48.5	44.2	45.7	41.7	43.1	46.4	45.2
Debt service to exports (%)	7.2	11.3	18.6	18.4	18.2	15.8	15.6	17.2
Short-term to external debt stocks (%)	16.1	1.7	0.0	0.0	0.0	0.0	0.0	0.0
Multilateral to external debt stocks (%)	33.9	32.8	71.3	74.2	75.6	76.4	73.8	73.9
Reserves to external debt stocks (%)	28.3	27.5	38.1	29.5	38.7	43.5	46.4	49.0

Notes: Short-term debt data are excluded since BIS data include debt liabilities of offshore centers located in the country. BIS short-term debt data for 2011, 2012, 2013, 2014 and 2015 are $362 million, $422 million, $474 million, $1,223 million and $696 million respectively.

SUDAN

(US$ million, unless otherwise indicated)

	2000	2005	2010	2011	2012	2013	2014	2015
Summary external debt data								
External debt stocks	**16,076**	**17,563**	**22,286**	**21,148**	**21,796**	**22,472**	**21,762**	**21,406**
Long-term external debt	10,647	11,232	14,444	15,093	15,697	16,402	15,922	15,772
Public and publicly guaranteed	10,151	11,232	14,444	15,093	15,697	16,402	15,922	15,772
Official creditors	8,393	9,145	11,815	11,350	11,366	11,618	11,350	11,206
of which: IMF	693	593	664	651	645	639	591	557
Private creditors	1,758	2,087	2,629	3,743	4,331	4,785	4,572	4,566
of which: Bonds	0	0	0	0	0	0	0	0
Private nonguaranteed	496	..	..	..	..	..	..	..
of which: Bonds	..	..	..	..	..	..	..	..
Short-term external debt	4,736	5,738	7,179	5,404	5,455	5,431	5,250	5,077
interest arrears on long-term	4,474	5,377	6,772	4,891	5,090	5,182	5,103	4,974
Long-term external debt								
Disbursements	**861**	**387**	**935**	**793**	**319**	**422**	**283**	**543**
Public and publicly guaranteed	861	387	935	793	319	422	283	543
Official creditors	318	387	935	793	319	422	283	543
Private creditors	543	0	0	0	0	0	0	0
of which: Bonds	0	0	0	0	0	0	0	0
Private nonguaranteed	..	..	..	..	..	..	..	..
of which: Bonds	..	..	..	..	..	..	..	..
Principal repayments	**143**	**291**	**397**	**416**	**274**	**211**	**179**	**412**
Public and publicly guaranteed	143	291	397	416	274	211	179	412
Official creditors	143	291	397	416	274	211	179	412
Private creditors	0	0	0	0	0	0	0	0
of which: Bonds	0	0	0	0	0	0	0	0
Private nonguaranteed	..	..	..	..	..	..	..	..
of which: Bonds	..	..	..	..	..	..	..	..
Interest payments	**42**	**67**	**83**	**100**	**76**	**73**	**69**	**100**
Public and publicly guaranteed	42	67	83	100	76	73	69	100
Official creditors	42	67	83	100	76	73	69	100
Private creditors	0	0	0	0	0	0	0	0
of which: Bonds	0	0	0	0	0	0	0	0
Private nonguaranteed	..	..	..	..	..	..	..	..
of which: Bonds	..	..	..	..	..	..	..	..
Net financial flows								
Net inflows	**1,009**	**-519**	**2,854**	**2,220**	**2,203**	**1,776**	**1,245**	**1,817**
Net debt inflows	617	78	783	473	-110	88	-8	80
Official creditors	121	67	532	367	38	204	94	124
of which: World Bank	-4	-1	0	0	0	0	0	5
of which: IMF	-54	-28	-6	-11	-7	-7	-11	-8
Private creditors	496	11	251	106	-148	-116	-102	-44
Long-term	543	..	..	..	..	..	..	..
Bonds	..	..	..	..	..	..	..	..
Banks and other private	543	..	..	..	..	..	..	..
Short-term	-47	11	251	106	-148	-116	-102	-44
Net equity inflows	392	-597	2,071	1,747	2,314	1,688	1,254	1,737
Foreign direct investment	392	-676	2,064	1,734	2,311	1,688	1,251	1,737
Portfolio equity	..	78	7	13	2	0	2	..
Major economic aggregates								
Gross national income (GNI)	11,548	24,581	60,507	64,564	60,267	63,708	71,181	82,276
Exports of goods, services & prim. income	1,839	5,019	11,785	11,040	5,140	6,057	6,060	4,977
Imports of goods, services & prim. income	2,594	8,899	15,677	14,822	12,270	13,567	11,167	11,998
Primary income on FDI	..	699	2,393	2,299	424	1,144	722	430
Personal transfers & comp. of employees	641	704	1,456	824	596	620	507	151
International reserves	138	1,869	1,036	193	193	193	181	174
Ratios								
External debt stocks to exports (%)	874.3	349.9	189.1	191.6	424.1	371.0	359.1	430.1
External debt stocks to GNI (%)	139.2	71.5	36.8	32.8	36.2	35.3	30.6	26.0
Debt service to exports (%)	13.5	8.0	4.2	4.8	7.0	4.9	4.3	10.5
Short-term to external debt stocks (%)	29.5	32.7	32.2	25.6	25.0	24.2	24.1	23.7
Multilateral to external debt stocks (%)	12.2	14.7	15.0	16.5	15.9	15.9	16.0	15.7
Reserves to external debt stocks (%)	0.9	10.6	4.6	0.9	0.9	0.9	0.8	0.8

Notes: Long-term public and publicly guaranteed debt data exclude penalty interest. Short-term debt is based on data from the BIS.

SWAZILAND

(US$ million, unless otherwise indicated)

	2000	2005	2010	2011	2012	2013	2014	2015
Summary external debt data								
External debt stocks	**334.3**	**475.2**	**701.8**	**644.0**	**480.3**	**458.2**	**416.5**	**390.8**
Long-term external debt	262.9	370.0	396.7	372.9	334.6	310.8	283.5	272.9
Public and publicly guaranteed	262.9	370.0	396.7	372.9	334.6	310.8	283.5	272.9
Official creditors	243.1	338.6	370.1	351.7	314.9	295.2	269.8	262.8
of which: IMF	8.4	9.2	74.4	74.1	74.2	74.4	70.0	66.9
Private creditors	19.8	31.4	26.6	21.1	19.7	15.6	13.7	10.1
of which: Bonds	0.0	0.0	0.0	0.0	0.0	0.0	0.0	0.0
Private nonguaranteed	..	..	..	..	..	..	..	..
of which: Bonds	..	..	..	..	..	..	..	..
Short-term external debt	63.0	96.1	230.8	197.0	71.5	73.0	63.1	51.0
interest arrears on long-term	0.0	15.1	35.8	48.0	42.5	41.7	40.3	37.9
Long-term external debt								
Disbursements	**15.8**	**51.7**	**11.5**	**32.1**	**5.2**	**18.2**	**19.4**	**29.3**
Public and publicly guaranteed	15.8	51.7	11.5	32.1	5.2	18.2	19.4	29.3
Official creditors	15.8	51.1	11.5	32.1	5.2	18.2	19.4	29.3
Private creditors	0.0	0.6	0.0	0.0	0.0	0.0	0.0	0.0
of which: Bonds	0.0	0.0	0.0	0.0	0.0	0.0	0.0	0.0
Private nonguaranteed	..	..	..	..	..	..	..	..
of which: Bonds	..	..	..	..	..	..	..	..
Principal repayments	**12.4**	**18.8**	**29.3**	**28.0**	**35.5**	**20.6**	**27.7**	**18.7**
Public and publicly guaranteed	12.4	18.8	29.3	28.0	35.5	20.6	27.7	18.7
Official creditors	12.4	18.1	28.7	27.4	34.9	20.2	27.3	18.6
Private creditors	0.0	0.7	0.6	0.6	0.5	0.4	0.4	0.2
of which: Bonds	0.0	0.0	0.0	0.0	0.0	0.0	0.0	0.0
Private nonguaranteed	..	..	..	..	..	..	..	..
of which: Bonds	..	..	..	..	..	..	..	..
Interest payments	**16.1**	**14.7**	**13.5**	**14.4**	**15.7**	**10.2**	**11.7**	**9.5**
Public and publicly guaranteed	16.1	14.7	13.5	14.4	15.7	10.2	11.7	9.5
Official creditors	10.2	10.5	13.0	14.0	13.0	9.0	8.8	7.0
Private creditors	5.9	4.2	0.5	0.4	2.7	1.2	2.9	2.5
of which: Bonds	0.0	0.0	0.0	0.0	0.0	0.0	0.0	0.0
Private nonguaranteed	..	..	..	..	..	..	..	..
of which: Bonds	..	..	..	..	..	..	..	..
Net financial flows								
Net inflows	**57.6**	**70.9**	**217.3**	**8.4**	**-147.6**	**29.7**	**38.2**	**-120.0**
Net debt inflows	13.7	86.0	163.3	-41.9	-150.3	-0.1	-16.9	0.9
Official creditors	3.4	33.1	-17.1	4.7	-29.8	-1.9	-7.9	10.7
of which: World Bank	-0.4	-0.3	-5.5	-1.4	1.1	3.5	6.3	7.7
of which: IMF	0.0	0.0	0.0	0.0	0.0	0.0	0.0	0.0
Private creditors	10.2	52.9	180.4	-46.6	-120.5	1.8	-8.9	-9.8
Long-term	0.0	-0.1	-0.6	-0.6	-0.5	-0.4	-0.4	-0.2
Bonds	..	..	..	..	..	..	..	..
Banks and other private	..	-0.1	-0.6	-0.6	-0.5	-0.4	-0.4	-0.2
Short-term	10.2	53.0	181.0	-46.0	-120.0	2.3	-8.5	-9.6
Net equity inflows	43.9	-15.1	54.0	50.3	2.7	29.8	55.1	-120.9
Foreign direct investment	42.5	-15.8	49.3	50.3	2.7	29.8	55.1	-120.9
Portfolio equity	1.4	0.8	4.7	..	..	..	..	..
Major economic aggregates								
Gross national income (GNI)	1,558.7	2,762.4	3,301.6	4,707.4	4,611.5	4,201.4	4,194.2	3,874.1
Exports of goods, services & prim. income	1,375.0	2,075.9	2,275.3	2,397.6	2,368.2	2,280.8	2,334.6	2,144.2
Imports of goods, services & prim. income	1,521.4	2,276.0	3,063.4	3,265.8	3,188.6	2,948.9	2,971.7	2,416.9
Primary income on FDI	65.9	44.0	401.6	397.6	466.1	524.8	602.6	416.5
Personal transfers & comp. of employees	56.8	95.4	54.7	38.1	31.3	30.0	24.5	18.7
International reserves	351.8	243.9	756.3	600.5	741.0	762.5	690.8	548.0
Ratios								
External debt stocks to exports (%)	24.3	22.9	30.8	26.9	20.3	20.1	17.8	18.2
External debt stocks to GNI (%)	21.4	17.2	21.3	13.7	10.4	10.9	9.9	10.1
Debt service to exports (%)	2.2	1.8	2.0	1.9	2.2	1.4	1.7	1.3
Short-term to external debt stocks (%)	18.8	20.2	32.9	30.6	14.9	15.9	15.1	13.0
Multilateral to external debt stocks (%)	44.8	50.4	35.1	37.3	47.0	44.8	44.8	43.7
Reserves to external debt stocks (%)	105.2	51.3	107.8	93.2	154.3	166.4	165.8	140.2

Notes: Short-term debt is based on data from the BIS.

SYRIAN ARAB REPUBLIC

(US$ million, unless otherwise indicated)

	2000	2005	2010	2011	2012	2013	2014	2015
Summary external debt data								
External debt stocks	**22,236**	**5,594**	**5,275**	**4,979**	**4,747**	**4,765**	**4,608**	**4,420**
Long-term external debt	16,480	5,031	4,282	4,004	3,955	3,905	3,671	3,528
Public and publicly guaranteed	16,480	5,031	4,282	4,004	3,955	3,905	3,671	3,528
Official creditors	15,512	5,031	4,282	4,004	3,955	3,905	3,671	3,528
of which: IMF	48	52	430	429	429	430	404	387
Private creditors	968	0	0	0	0	0	0	0
of which: Bonds	0	0	0	0	0	0	0	0
Private nonguaranteed	..	..	..	..	..	..	..	..
of which: Bonds	..	..	..	..	..	..	..	..
Short-term external debt	5,708	511	562	546	364	430	532	504
interest arrears on long-term	2,388	198	221	222	321	406	461	479
Long-term external debt								
Disbursements	**18**	**189**	**286**	**222**	0	0	0	0
Public and publicly guaranteed	18	189	286	222	0	0	0	0
Official creditors	18	189	286	222	0	0	0	0
Private creditors	0	0	0	0	0	0	0	0
of which: Bonds	0	0	0	0	0	0	0	0
Private nonguaranteed	..	..	..	..	..	..	..	..
of which: Bonds	..	..	..	..	..	..	..	..
Principal repayments	**239**	**439**	**508**	**509**	0	0	0	0
Public and publicly guaranteed	239	439	508	509	0	0	0	0
Official creditors	224	428	508	509	0	0	0	0
Private creditors	16	11	0	0	0	0	0	0
of which: Bonds	0	0	0	0	0	0	0	0
Private nonguaranteed	..	..	..	..	..	..	..	..
of which: Bonds	..	..	..	..	..	..	..	..
Interest payments	**127**	**110**	**111**	**109**	0	0	0	0
Public and publicly guaranteed	127	110	111	109	0	0	0	0
Official creditors	126	110	111	109	0	0	0	0
Private creditors	1	0	0	0	0	0	0	0
of which: Bonds	0	0	0	0	0	0	0	0
Private nonguaranteed	..	..	..	..	..	..	..	..
of which: Bonds	..	..	..	..	..	..	..	..
Net financial flows								
Net inflows	**-556**	**143**	**1,039**	**500**	**-281**	**-19**	**47**	**-46**
Net debt inflows	-826	-357	-430	-304	-281	-19	47	-46
Official creditors	-206	-239	-221	-287	0	0	0	0
of which: World Bank	-16	-1	-1	-1	0	0	0	0
of which: IMF	0	0	0	0	0	0	0	0
Private creditors	-621	-118	-209	-17	-281	-19	47	-46
Long-term	-16	-11	..	..	..	..	..	..
Bonds	..	..	..	..	..	..	..	..
Banks and other private	-16	-11	..	..	..	..	..	..
Short-term	-605	-107	-209	-17	-281	-19	47	-46
Net equity inflows	270	500	1,469	804	..	..	..	..
Foreign direct investment	270	500	1,469	804	..	..	..	..
Portfolio equity	..	..	..	..	..	..	..	..
Major economic aggregates								
Gross national income (GNI)	18,446	27,980	..	..	..	..	..	..
Exports of goods, services & prim. income	7,190	11,907	19,919	..	..	..	..	..
Imports of goods, services & prim. income	6,614	12,359	21,235	..	..	..	..	..
Primary income on FDI	..	1,220	1,684	..	..	..	..	..
Personal transfers & comp. of employees	180	823	1,623	1,623	1,623	1,623	1,623	1,623
International reserves	..	17,347	19,465	..	..	..	..	..
Ratios								
External debt stocks to exports (%)	309.3	47.0	26.5	..	..	..	..	..
External debt stocks to GNI (%)	120.5	20.0	..	..	..	..	..	..
Debt service to exports (%)	6.8	4.8	3.1	..	..	..	..	..
Short-term to external debt stocks (%)	25.7	9.1	10.7	11.0	7.7	9.0	11.6	11.4
Multilateral to external debt stocks (%)	2.6	18.1	32.1	32.7	34.6	35.2	33.4	32.4
Reserves to external debt stocks (%)	0.0	310.1	369.0	0.0	0.0	0.0	0.0	0.0

Notes: Long-term public and publicly guaranteed debt data are World Bank staff estimates. Short-term debt is based on data from the BIS.

TAJIKISTAN

(US$ million, unless otherwise indicated)

	2000	2005	2010	2011	2012	2013	2014	2015
Summary external debt data								
External debt stocks	**1,141**	**1,121**	**3,562**	**3,924**	**4,621**	**4,868**	**5,178**	**5,100**
Long-term external debt	846	850	2,734	2,946	3,340	3,451	3,747	3,899
Public and publicly guaranteed	755	826	1,806	1,968	2,001	2,016	2,038	1,954
Official creditors	704	817	1,806	1,968	2,001	2,016	2,038	1,954
of which: IMF	218	244	227	246	287	287	266	244
Private creditors	51	8	0	0	0	0	0	0
of which: Bonds	0	0	0	0	0	0	0	0
Private nonguaranteed	91	24	927	979	1,339	1,435	1,709	1,945
of which: Bonds	..	..	..	..	..	..	..	..
Short-term external debt	77	27	601	731	994	1,130	1,165	957
interest arrears on long-term	45	2	0	0	16	1	1	0
Long-term external debt								
Disbursements	**37**	**108**	**924**	**723**	**556**	**431**	**665**	**702**
Public and publicly guaranteed	36	105	251	200	105	105	178	53
Official creditors	36	105	251	200	105	105	178	53
Private creditors	0	0	0	0	0	0	0	0
of which: Bonds	0	0	0	0	0	0	0	0
Private nonguaranteed	1	2	673	523	451	325	487	648
of which: Bonds	..	..	..	..	..	..	..	..
Principal repayments	**28**	**42**	**630**	**513**	**334**	**320**	**322**	**293**
Public and publicly guaranteed	15	37	37	34	74	93	108	103
Official creditors	15	37	37	34	74	93	108	103
Private creditors	0	0	0	0	0	0	0	0
of which: Bonds	0	0	0	0	0	0	0	0
Private nonguaranteed	12	5	593	479	261	227	213	190
of which: Bonds	..	..	..	..	..	..	..	..
Interest payments	**21**	**10**	**54**	**64**	**94**	**104**	**91**	**89**
Public and publicly guaranteed	7	9	23	28	30	30	31	30
Official creditors	4	9	23	28	30	30	31	30
Private creditors	4	0	0	0	0	0	0	0
of which: Bonds	0	0	0	0	0	0	0	0
Private nonguaranteed	14	1	31	36	63	74	60	59
of which: Bonds	..	..	..	..	..	..	..	..
Net financial flows								
Net inflows	**19**	**77**	**902**	**387**	**532**	**281**	**515**	**360**
Net debt inflows	-4	23	880	361	508	261	374	191
Official creditors	36	84	274	187	71	12	65	-61
of which: World Bank	23	35	11	-2	-3	-7	-7	-7
of which: IMF	16	15	60	21	40	..	-4	-11
Private creditors	-40	-61	606	174	437	249	309	252
Long-term	-11	-3	80	44	190	98	274	459
Bonds	..	..	..	..	..	..	..	..
Banks and other private	-11	-3	80	44	190	98	274	459
Short-term	-29	-58	527	130	247	151	35	-207
Net equity inflows	24	54	21	26	24	19	141	169
Foreign direct investment	24	54	15	26	24	19	139	169
Portfolio equity	..	..	7	0	-1	0	1	0
Major economic aggregates								
Gross national income (GNI)	824	2,234	5,563	6,483	7,581	8,456	11,420	9,380
Exports of goods, services & prim. income	..	1,264	2,249	2,955	3,528	3,733	3,186	2,564
Imports of goods, services & prim. income	..	1,733	3,064	4,205	5,097	5,252	4,309	3,532
Primary income on FDI	..	2	11	17	32	35	48	43
Personal transfers & comp. of employees	..	467	2,021	2,722	3,222	3,698	3,384	2,259
International reserves	93	168	324	289	298	461	177	64
Ratios								
External debt stocks to exports (%)	..	88.7	158.3	132.8	130.9	130.4	162.5	198.9
External debt stocks to GNI (%)	138.4	50.2	64.0	60.5	60.9	57.6	45.3	54.4
Debt service to exports (%)	..	5.8	30.9	20.0	12.5	11.8	13.7	16.8
Short-term to external debt stocks (%)	6.8	2.4	16.9	18.6	21.5	23.2	22.5	18.8
Multilateral to external debt stocks (%)	16.3	46.3	26.6	24.8	21.1	19.9	18.9	18.5
Reserves to external debt stocks (%)	8.1	15.0	9.1	7.4	6.4	9.5	3.4	1.3

Notes: Long-term private nonguaranteed debt data from 2013 are World Bank staff estimates based on reports provided by the country. Short-term debt before 2010 is based on data from the BIS. Data include MDRI debt relief.

TANZANIA

(US$ million, unless otherwise indicated)

	2000	2005	2010	2011	2012	2013	2014	2015
Summary external debt data								
External debt stocks	**7,186**	**8,400**	**8,893**	**10,013**	**11,588**	**13,141**	**14,352**	**15,049**
Long-term external debt	5,973	7,006	6,825	7,686	8,831	10,629	11,770	12,431
Public and publicly guaranteed	5,973	6,446	5,601	6,438	7,366	9,112	9,911	10,690
Official creditors	5,779	6,341	5,488	6,030	6,762	7,745	8,530	9,321
of which: IMF	364	387	647	643	641	753	682	592
Private creditors	194	105	113	408	604	1,367	1,381	1,369
of which: Bonds	0	0	0	0	0	0	0	0
Private nonguaranteed	0	560	1,224	1,248	1,465	1,517	1,859	1,741
of which: Bonds	..	..	..	..	..	..	..	..
Short-term external debt	849	1,006	1,421	1,684	2,117	1,759	1,900	2,026
interest arrears on long-term	647	615	908	989	1,054	1,108	1,122	1,114
Long-term external debt								
Disbursements	**211**	**466**	**1,254**	**1,179**	**978**	**2,011**	**1,579**	**1,448**
Public and publicly guaranteed	211	466	1,038	872	795	1,857	1,295	1,143
Official creditors	206	447	1,021	568	792	1,037	1,236	1,120
Private creditors	5	19	17	304	2	821	60	22
of which: Bonds	0	0	0	0	0	0	0	0
Private nonguaranteed	0	0	216	307	184	153	284	306
of which: Bonds	0	0	0	0	0	0	0	0
Principal repayments	**94**	**31**	**131**	**76**	**78**	**80**	**117**	**159**
Public and publicly guaranteed	94	31	52	33	35	60	53	59
Official creditors	77	31	35	26	27	28	27	41
Private creditors	17	0	17	7	7	32	27	18
of which: Bonds	0	0	0	0	0	0	0	0
Private nonguaranteed	0	0	79	44	43	19	64	100
of which: Bonds	..	..	..	..	..	..	..	..
Interest payments	**51**	**44**	**50**	**53**	**60**	**62**	**83**	**109**
Public and publicly guaranteed	51	42	32	39	43	58	76	99
Official creditors	49	42	31	36	39	45	52	68
Private creditors	2	0	2	3	4	13	24	30
of which: Bonds	0	0	0	0	0	0	0	0
Private nonguaranteed	0	2	17	14	17	3	7	10
of which: Bonds	..	..	..	..	..	..	..	..
Net financial flows								
Net inflows	**668**	**900**	**2,141**	**2,285**	**2,667**	**2,545**	**2,542**	**2,383**
Net debt inflows	205	459	1,100	1,283	1,265	1,629	1,562	1,362
Official creditors	172	378	1,016	540	762	1,119	1,181	1,019
of which: World Bank	129	261	650	258	535	697	614	582
of which: IMF	43	-38	30	-2	-3	110	-28	-61
Private creditors	33	81	84	743	503	510	380	343
Long-term	-12	19	137	561	135	923	253	210
Bonds	..	..	..	..	..	..	..	..
Banks and other private	-12	19	137	561	135	923	253	210
Short-term	44	62	-53	182	368	-412	127	133
Net equity inflows	463	441	1,041	1,002	1,403	916	980	1,021
Foreign direct investment	463	439	1,038	999	1,399	912	976	1,017
Portfolio equity	..	3	3	3	4	4	4	4
Major economic aggregates								
Gross national income (GNI)	10,056	16,575	31,078	33,619	38,510	43,922	47,512	44,134
Exports of goods, services & prim. income	1,411	3,053	6,530	7,582	8,807	8,590	8,836	9,566
Imports of goods, services & prim. income	2,230	4,641	9,792	12,866	13,383	14,353	14,331	13,363
Primary income on FDI	13	319	653	729	560	617	541	578
Personal transfers & comp. of employees	8	19	344	410	390	382	389	389
International reserves	974	2,049	3,905	3,726	4,052	4,674	4,390	4,073
Ratios								
External debt stocks to exports (%)	509.2	275.2	136.2	132.1	131.6	153.0	162.4	157.3
External debt stocks to GNI (%)	71.5	50.7	28.6	29.8	30.1	29.9	30.2	34.1
Debt service to exports (%)	11.9	4.4	2.9	1.9	1.8	1.8	2.7	3.6
Short-term to external debt stocks (%)	11.8	12.0	16.0	16.8	18.3	13.4	13.2	13.5
Multilateral to external debt stocks (%)	45.5	58.0	49.2	47.6	47.0	48.5	47.5	48.9
Reserves to external debt stocks (%)	13.6	24.4	43.9	37.2	35.0	35.6	30.6	27.1

Notes: Long-term public and publicly guaranteed debt data include debt liabilities of Zanzibar. Long-term private nonguaranteed debt data from 2004 to 2007 are World Bank staff estimates and from 2008 are reported by Central Bank. Short-term debt is based on data from the BIS. Data include the effects of HIPC and MDRI debt relief.

THAILAND

(US$ million, unless otherwise indicated)

	2000	2005	2010	2011	2012	2013	2014	2015
Summary external debt data								
External debt stocks	**79,830**	**58,467**	**106,358**	**109,943**	**134,257**	**137,353**	**135,292**	**129,654**
Long-term external debt	61,778	42,332	54,207	61,165	74,585	73,963	77,801	77,054
Public and publicly guaranteed	29,462	17,452	21,207	26,479	34,765	34,050	33,451	30,642
Official creditors	20,820	7,862	6,877	6,899	6,362	6,037	5,558	5,392
of which: IMF	3,172	121	1,494	1,490	1,491	1,494	1,406	1,345
Private creditors	8,643	9,590	14,329	19,580	28,403	28,013	27,893	25,251
of which: Bonds	2,630	3,836	8,004	12,894	21,894	21,854	21,754	19,200
Private nonguaranteed	32,316	24,880	33,000	34,687	39,820	39,913	44,350	46,412
of which: Bonds	8,414	4,685	4,265	3,618	6,040	5,575	9,720	6,688
Short-term external debt	14,880	16,014	50,657	47,288	58,181	61,896	56,085	51,255
interest arrears on long-term	0	0	2	5	2	0	0	0
Long-term external debt								
Disbursements	**4,031**	**17,083**	**16,838**	**17,452**	**29,509**	**19,846**	**19,437**	**20,191**
Public and publicly guaranteed	3,031	2,521	6,442	6,128	9,735	1,552	479	184
Official creditors	2,156	434	160	493	735	1,552	479	184
Private creditors	876	2,086	6,282	5,635	9,000	0	0	0
of which: Bonds	0	936	5,080	4,890	9,000	0	0	0
Private nonguaranteed	1,000	14,562	10,396	11,324	19,775	18,294	18,958	20,008
of which: Bonds	0	1,600	0	700	1,500	0	4,370	118
Principal repayments	**8,961**	**16,464**	**9,386**	**8,815**	**13,316**	**11,054**	**12,937**	**17,304**
Public and publicly guaranteed	3,026	2,709	803	1,197	757	1,211	454	1,154
Official creditors	1,666	2,321	534	779	619	871	348	343
Private creditors	1,361	388	269	418	137	340	106	811
of which: Bonds	174	172	150	0	0	40	100	724
Private nonguaranteed	5,935	13,755	8,582	7,618	12,560	9,842	12,483	16,149
of which: Bonds	1,044	908	460	180	550	465	625	1,350
Interest payments	**3,777**	**1,074**	**1,076**	**1,176**	**1,354**	**1,213**	**1,473**	**1,466**
Public and publicly guaranteed	1,578	437	231	263	410	333	364	358
Official creditors	1,008	234	113	114	112	80	75	70
Private creditors	569	202	118	149	298	253	288	288
of which: Bonds	193	135	56	88	255	213	251	252
Private nonguaranteed	2,199	637	845	913	944	880	1,109	1,109
of which: Bonds	476	286	234	311	339	353	429	428
Net financial flows								
Net inflows	**-9,363**	**18,388**	**42,533**	**7,440**	**37,980**	**19,511**	**4,093**	**-3,069**
Net debt inflows	-13,665	5,145	24,831	5,266	27,088	12,510	688	-1,942
Official creditors	292	-1,886	-374	-285	115	681	131	-160
of which: World Bank	272	-101	-5	-61	95	890	-7	-7
of which: IMF	-198	0	0	0	0	0	0	0
Private creditors	-13,958	7,031	25,205	5,552	26,972	11,829	557	-1,782
Long-term	-5,420	2,505	7,826	8,923	16,078	8,111	6,369	3,047
Bonds	-1,218	1,456	4,470	5,410	9,950	-505	3,645	-1,956
Banks and other private	-4,202	1,049	3,355	3,513	6,128	8,616	2,724	5,003
Short-term	-8,538	4,526	17,379	-3,371	10,895	3,718	-5,812	-4,830
Net equity inflows	4,302	13,243	17,702	2,174	10,892	7,002	3,404	-1,128
Foreign direct investment	3,402	6,993	15,305	2,151	10,808	10,295	9,216	7,842
Portfolio equity	900	6,250	2,398	23	85	-3,293	-5,811	-8,969
Major economic aggregates								
Gross national income (GNI)	123,900	180,829	325,891	362,470	381,197	396,751	382,492	368,807
Exports of goods, services & prim. income	85,997	131,740	232,906	269,589	285,514	292,768	289,580	280,743
Imports of goods, services & prim. income	77,269	143,582	227,536	271,096	299,595	308,240	283,209	255,284
Primary income on FDI	..	4,501	12,804	9,679	15,890	19,698	16,202	14,804
Personal transfers & comp. of employees	1,697	1,187	4,433	5,256	5,657	6,585	6,524	5,895
International reserves	32,016	50,691	167,530	167,389	173,328	161,328	151,253	151,266
Ratios								
External debt stocks to exports (%)	92.8	44.4	45.7	40.8	47.0	46.9	46.7	46.2
External debt stocks to GNI (%)	64.4	32.3	32.6	30.3	35.2	34.6	35.4	35.2
Debt service to exports (%)	16.3	13.7	4.7	3.9	5.4	4.4	5.2	6.9
Short-term to external debt stocks (%)	18.6	27.4	47.6	43.0	43.3	45.1	41.5	39.5
Multilateral to external debt stocks (%)	6.7	1.4	0.2	0.2	0.4	1.0	1.0	1.0
Reserves to external debt stocks (%)	40.1	86.7	157.5	152.3	129.1	117.5	111.8	116.7

TOGO

(US$ million, unless otherwise indicated)

	2000	2005	2010	2011	2012	2013	2014	2015
Summary external debt data								
External debt stocks	**1,446.0**	**1,686.9**	**1,278.3**	**622.1**	**746.8**	**896.0**	**987.1**	**1,056.1**
Long-term external debt	1,229.6	1,439.5	998.0	362.1	442.7	555.9	671.3	801.4
Public and publicly guaranteed	1,229.6	1,439.5	998.0	362.1	442.7	555.9	671.3	801.4
Official creditors	1,229.6	1,439.5	998.0	362.1	442.7	506.3	638.5	770.4
of which: IMF	83.8	29.7	241.5	254.2	254.5	253.2	226.6	200.6
Private creditors	0.0	0.0	0.0	0.0	0.0	49.6	32.8	31.0
of which: Bonds	0.0	0.0	0.0	0.0	0.0	0.0	0.0	0.0
Private nonguaranteed	..	..	..	..	..	..	..	..
of which: Bonds	..	..	..	..	..	..	..	..
Short-term external debt	132.5	217.7	38.9	5.8	49.6	86.9	89.2	54.1
interest arrears on long-term	62.6	166.7	9.9	2.8	3.6	2.9	1.2	1.4
Long-term external debt								
Disbursements	**24.4**	**9.9**	**82.8**	**28.9**	**126.6**	**183.7**	**176.0**	**187.6**
Public and publicly guaranteed	24.4	9.9	82.8	28.9	126.6	183.7	176.0	187.6
Official creditors	24.4	9.9	82.8	28.9	126.6	123.2	176.0	175.1
Private creditors	0.0	0.0	0.0	0.0	0.0	60.4	0.0	12.5
of which: Bonds	0.0	0.0	0.0	0.0	0.0	0.0	0.0	0.0
Private nonguaranteed	..	..	..	..	..	..	..	..
of which: Bonds	..	..	..	..	..	..	..	..
Principal repayments	**9.9**	**7.9**	**27.8**	**10.0**	**13.0**	**37.8**	**29.2**	**23.1**
Public and publicly guaranteed	9.9	7.9	27.8	10.0	13.0	37.8	29.2	23.1
Official creditors	9.9	7.9	27.8	10.0	13.0	25.7	17.6	12.2
Private creditors	0.0	0.0	0.0	0.0	0.0	12.1	11.6	10.9
of which: Bonds	0.0	0.0	0.0	0.0	0.0	0.0	0.0	0.0
Private nonguaranteed	..	..	..	..	..	..	..	..
of which: Bonds	..	..	..	..	..	..	..	..
Interest payments	**4.6**	**0.3**	**7.9**	**4.6**	**9.3**	**11.4**	**15.6**	**18.6**
Public and publicly guaranteed	4.6	0.3	7.9	4.6	9.3	11.4	15.6	18.6
Official creditors	4.6	0.3	7.9	4.6	9.3	11.4	15.6	18.1
Private creditors	0.0	0.0	0.0	0.0	0.0	0.0	0.0	0.6
of which: Bonds	0.0	0.0	0.0	0.0	0.0	0.0	0.0	0.0
Private nonguaranteed	..	..	..	..	..	..	..	..
of which: Bonds	..	..	..	..	..	..	..	..
Net financial flows								
Net inflows	**-6.8**	**86.1**	**193.2**	**51.4**	**266.0**	**261.3**	**245.9**	**165.6**
Net debt inflows	-44.3	15.8	110.7	6.8	156.7	182.1	138.6	112.9
Official creditors	5.1	-9.2	98.7	32.8	113.7	95.8	146.2	146.6
of which: World Bank	9.9	0.0	-22.0	0.0	13.7	0.0	14.9	4.2
of which: IMF	-9.4	-11.2	43.6	13.9	0.0	-1.8	-12.2	-16.2
Private creditors	-49.4	25.0	12.0	-26.0	43.0	86.3	-7.6	-33.7
Long-term	..	..	..	..	..	48.3	-11.6	1.6
Bonds	..	..	..	..	..	..	..	..
Banks and other private	..	..	..	..	..	48.3	-11.6	1.6
Short-term	-49.4	25.0	12.0	-26.0	43.0	38.0	4.0	-35.3
Net equity inflows	37.5	70.4	82.5	44.6	109.4	79.2	107.3	52.7
Foreign direct investment	31.4	54.4	78.0	44.6	109.4	79.2	107.3	52.7
Portfolio equity	6.1	16.0	4.5	0.0	..	..	..	..
Major economic aggregates								
Gross national income (GNI)	1,265.3	2,079.9	2,761.6	3,197.5	3,282.2	3,438.9	4,032.0	3,626.2
Exports of goods, services & prim. income	456.5	857.3	1,395.8	2,079.0	2,004.9	2,318.2	2,141.2	1,671.0
Imports of goods, services & prim. income	664.1	1,249.0	1,951.3	2,651.3	2,541.2	3,148.7	2,918.9	2,155.2
Primary income on FDI	17.2	47.2	67.0	120.2	180.4	179.9	191.6	..
Personal transfers & comp. of employees	34.2	192.5	336.6	244.1	344.8	397.4	427.3	397.4
International reserves	140.9	191.5	714.9	774.3	441.6	507.1	507.0	574.0
Ratios								
External debt stocks to exports (%)	316.7	196.8	91.6	29.9	37.2	38.7	46.1	63.2
External debt stocks to GNI (%)	114.3	81.1	46.3	19.5	22.8	26.1	24.5	29.1
Debt service to exports (%)	6.6	2.5	2.6	0.7	1.1	2.3	2.7	3.5
Short-term to external debt stocks (%)	9.2	12.9	3.0	0.9	6.6	9.7	9.0	5.1
Multilateral to external debt stocks (%)	53.0	52.1	66.1	32.7	26.5	27.4	28.8	30.9
Reserves to external debt stocks (%)	9.7	11.4	55.9	124.5	59.1	56.6	51.4	54.3

Notes: Short-term debt is based on data from the BIS. Data include the effects of Paris Club debt restructuring agreement and HIPC and MDRI debt relief.

TONGA

(US$ million, unless otherwise indicated)

	2000	2005	2010	2011	2012	2013	2014	2015
Summary external debt data								
External debt stocks	**74.0**	**89.0**	**153.7**	**190.6**	**197.4**	**199.1**	**193.5**	**173.4**
Long-term external debt	65.0	79.5	143.5	180.5	187.2	188.9	183.9	164.3
Public and publicly guaranteed	65.0	79.5	143.5	180.5	187.2	188.9	183.9	164.3
Official creditors	65.0	79.5	142.4	180.0	187.0	188.8	183.8	164.2
of which: IMF	8.6	9.4	10.1	10.1	10.1	10.1	9.5	9.1
Private creditors	0.0	0.0	1.1	0.4	0.3	0.2	0.1	0.1
of which: Bonds	0.0	0.0	0.0	0.0	0.0	0.0	0.0	0.0
Private nonguaranteed	..	..	..	..	..	..	..	..
of which: Bonds	..	..	..	..	..	..	..	..
Short-term external debt	0.4	0.1	0.0	0.0	0.0	0.0	0.0	0.0
interest arrears on long-term	0.2	0.1	0.0	0.0	0.0	0.0	0.0	0.0
Long-term external debt								
Disbursements	**5.4**	**4.5**	**40.9**	**36.9**	**9.9**	**1.3**	**5.1**	**2.2**
Public and publicly guaranteed	5.4	4.5	40.9	36.9	9.9	1.3	5.1	2.2
Official creditors	5.4	4.5	40.7	36.9	9.9	1.3	5.1	2.2
Private creditors	0.0	0.0	0.2	0.0	0.0	0.0	0.0	0.0
of which: Bonds	0.0	0.0	0.0	0.0	0.0	0.0	0.0	0.0
Private nonguaranteed	..	..	..	..	..	..	..	..
of which: Bonds	..	..	..	..	..	..	..	..
Principal repayments	**3.7**	**3.7**	**2.7**	**3.3**	**3.4**	**3.4**	**5.9**	**12.6**
Public and publicly guaranteed	3.7	3.7	2.7	3.3	3.4	3.4	5.9	12.6
Official creditors	2.4	3.7	2.6	3.3	3.3	3.3	5.9	12.5
Private creditors	1.3	0.0	0.1	0.0	0.2	0.1	0.0	0.0
of which: Bonds	0.0	0.0	0.0	0.0	0.0	0.0	0.0	0.0
Private nonguaranteed	..	..	..	..	..	..	..	..
of which: Bonds	..	..	..	..	..	..	..	..
Interest payments	**0.9**	**1.2**	**2.4**	**2.6**	**2.9**	**3.1**	**3.0**	**2.8**
Public and publicly guaranteed	0.9	1.2	2.4	2.6	2.9	3.1	3.0	2.8
Official creditors	0.8	1.2	2.3	2.6	2.9	3.1	3.0	2.8
Private creditors	0.1	0.0	0.1	0.0	0.0	0.0	0.0	0.0
of which: Bonds	0.0	0.0	0.0	0.0	0.0	0.0	0.0	0.0
Private nonguaranteed	..	..	..	..	..	..	..	..
of which: Bonds	..	..	..	..	..	..	..	..
Net financial flows								
Net inflows	**6.5**	**8.1**	**47.2**	**37.4**	**8.3**	**4.6**	**55.2**	**2.3**
Net debt inflows	1.7	0.9	38.2	33.6	6.5	-2.1	-0.8	-10.4
Official creditors	3.0	0.9	38.1	33.7	6.6	-2.0	-0.8	-10.4
of which: World Bank	-0.1	4.5	0.8	-0.2	-0.2	-0.3	4.6	1.7
of which: IMF	0.0	0.0	0.0	0.0	0.0	0.0	0.0	0.0
Private creditors	-1.3	..	0.1	0.0	-0.2	-0.1	0.0	0.0
Long-term	-1.3	..	0.1	0.0	-0.2	-0.1	0.0	0.0
Bonds	..	..	..	..	..	..	..	..
Banks and other private	-1.3	..	0.1	0.0	-0.2	-0.1	0.0	0.0
Short-term	0.0	0.0	0.0	0.0	0.0	0.0	0.0	0.0
Net equity inflows	4.8	7.2	9.0	3.7	1.8	6.7	56.0	12.6
Foreign direct investment	4.8	7.2	9.0	3.7	1.8	6.7	56.0	12.6
Portfolio equity	..	..	..	..	..	..	..	..
Major economic aggregates								
Gross national income (GNI)	191.0	258.7	381.7	454.7	469.2	443.8	439.0	..
Exports of goods, services & prim. income	..	59.0	68.4	99.5	112.9	112.2	72.9	76.1
Imports of goods, services & prim. income	..	156.8	238.3	291.3	286.0	293.1	220.3	209.5
Primary income on FDI	..	..	4.5	5.5	8.0	7.0	..	..
Personal transfers & comp. of employees	..	68.6	77.2	78.7	117.6	121.0	117.6	117.6
International reserves	24.6	46.9	104.5	143.3	152.4	155.5	158.8	156.1
Ratios								
External debt stocks to exports (%)	..	151.0	224.7	191.6	174.8	177.4	265.3	227.9
External debt stocks to GNI (%)	38.7	34.4	40.3	41.9	42.1	44.9	44.1	..
Debt service to exports (%)	..	8.8	7.4	5.9	5.6	5.8	12.3	20.2
Short-term to external debt stocks (%)	0.5	0.1	0.0	0.0	0.0	0.0	0.0	0.0
Multilateral to external debt stocks (%)	72.2	75.4	46.0	35.7	33.2	31.6	31.6	33.5
Reserves to external debt stocks (%)	33.3	52.6	68.0	75.2	77.2	78.1	82.1	90.0

Notes: Short-term debt is based on data from the BIS.

TUNISIA

(US$ million, unless otherwise indicated)

	2000	2005	2010	2011	2012	2013	2014	2015
Summary external debt data								
External debt stocks	**11,355**	**17,922**	**22,472**	**22,642**	**25,261**	**25,661**	**26,372**	**27,363**
Long-term external debt	9,688	14,738	17,073	17,274	18,613	18,517	17,990	19,021
Public and publicly guaranteed	8,888	12,997	14,671	14,931	16,569	16,879	16,475	17,839
Official creditors	6,093	8,417	10,220	11,295	12,500	13,336	12,682	13,128
of which: IMF	77	49	420	419	419	572	1,537	1,768
Private creditors	2,795	4,580	4,451	3,636	4,068	3,543	3,793	4,711
of which: Bonds	1,327	3,510	3,819	3,063	3,571	3,110	3,364	4,315
Private nonguaranteed	800	1,741	2,402	2,343	2,044	1,638	1,514	1,182
of which: Bonds	..	..	..	..	..	..	..	..
Short-term external debt	1,590	3,135	4,979	4,949	6,230	6,572	6,846	6,575
interest arrears on long-term	0	0	0	0	0	0	0	0
Long-term external debt								
Disbursements	**1,542**	**1,256**	**1,642**	**2,244**	**3,417**	**1,509**	**2,435**	**3,750**
Public and publicly guaranteed	1,242	1,126	1,545	2,157	3,361	1,489	2,435	3,750
Official creditors	709	843	1,507	2,131	2,047	1,255	1,803	2,686
Private creditors	533	283	39	26	1,314	234	632	1,064
of which: Bonds	0	249	0	0	1,298	225	500	1,000
Private nonguaranteed	300	130	97	87	56	20	0	0
of which: Bonds	..	..	..	..	..	..	..	..
Principal repayments	**1,296**	**1,187**	**1,617**	**1,905**	**1,899**	**1,800**	**1,314**	**1,669**
Public and publicly guaranteed	1,264	1,129	1,397	1,759	1,609	1,374	1,191	1,337
Official creditors	662	873	887	860	880	875	1,110	1,269
Private creditors	602	255	510	899	729	499	81	67
of which: Bonds	371	136	0	814	650	443	0	0
Private nonguaranteed	32	58	220	146	290	426	124	332
of which: Bonds	..	..	..	..	..	..	..	..
Interest payments	**489**	**686**	**670**	**678**	**610**	**572**	**454**	**463**
Public and publicly guaranteed	479	584	546	559	500	489	454	463
Official creditors	297	334	309	330	342	318	343	308
Private creditors	182	249	237	230	158	171	112	155
of which: Bonds	99	200	193	203	135	155	96	141
Private nonguaranteed	10	102	124	119	110	83	0	0
of which: Bonds	..	..	..	..	..	..	..	..
Net financial flows								
Net inflows	**996**	**587**	**1,482**	**704**	**4,342**	**1,353**	**3,541**	**3,229**
Net debt inflows	258	-141	169	310	2,797	203	2,442	2,110
Official creditors	7	-31	619	1,270	1,167	531	1,740	1,717
of which: World Bank	-17	-57	74	444	404	-127	170	510
of which: IMF	-40	..	..	..	..	151	1,047	301
Private creditors	251	-111	-451	-961	1,631	-328	702	393
Long-term	199	99	-594	-931	351	-670	428	664
Bonds	-371	113	0	-814	648	-218	500	1,000
Banks and other private	570	-13	-594	-117	-298	-452	-73	-336
Short-term	52	-210	144	-29	1,280	342	274	-271
Net equity inflows	738	728	1,313	395	1,545	1,151	1,099	1,118
Foreign direct investment	755	716	1,339	439	1,560	1,071	1,027	966
Portfolio equity	-18	12	-26	-44	-15	80	72	153
Major economic aggregates								
Gross national income (GNI)	20,525	30,636	41,984	43,650	43,140	44,194	45,911	41,734
Exports of goods, services & prim. income	8,653	14,884	22,556	22,950	22,600	22,513	22,103	17,930
Imports of goods, services & prim. income	10,299	16,495	26,595	28,235	28,471	28,642	28,759	23,718
Primary income on FDI	468	962	1,658	1,716	1,533	1,756	1,362	984
Personal transfers & comp. of employees	796	1,393	2,063	2,004	2,266	2,291	2,347	1,971
International reserves	1,811	4,437	9,459	7,454	8,357	7,287	7,235	..
Ratios								
External debt stocks to exports (%)	131.2	120.4	99.6	98.7	111.8	114.0	119.3	152.6
External debt stocks to GNI (%)	55.3	58.5	53.5	51.9	58.6	58.1	57.4	65.6
Debt service to exports (%)	22.1	13.7	10.4	11.5	11.5	11.8	8.7	12.9
Short-term to external debt stocks (%)	14.0	17.5	22.2	21.9	24.7	25.6	26.0	24.0
Multilateral to external debt stocks (%)	30.6	30.9	30.2	33.8	34.6	36.9	33.5	34.2
Reserves to external debt stocks (%)	15.9	24.8	42.1	32.9	33.1	28.4	27.4	..

Notes: Long-term private nonguaranteed debt data from 2008 are World Bank staff estimates based on reports provided by the country.

TURKEY

(US$ million, unless otherwise indicated)

	2000	2005	2010	2011	2012	2013	2014	2015
Summary external debt data								
External debt stocks	**116,799**	**173,649**	**300,526**	**305,016**	**336,739**	**389,221**	**400,874**	**397,923**
Long-term external debt	83,565	119,926	216,089	218,981	234,177	257,264	273,684	294,222
Public and publicly guaranteed	55,736	64,483	93,010	94,714	98,949	105,134	104,204	102,027
Official creditors	12,537	12,435	26,427	28,168	29,490	31,910	30,792	29,451
of which: IMF	4,323	14,807	7,277	4,521	2,510	1,650	1,552	1,485
Private creditors	43,200	52,048	66,583	66,546	69,459	73,224	73,412	72,575
of which: Bonds	20,392	29,409	45,774	47,020	52,446	58,427	62,694	64,163
Private nonguaranteed	27,828	55,443	123,080	124,267	135,228	152,130	169,480	192,196
of which: Bonds	1,784	4,025	6,202	4,003	11,835	20,885	28,781	29,137
Short-term external debt	28,912	38,916	77,160	81,513	100,051	130,307	125,638	102,216
interest arrears on long-term	0	0	0	0	0	0	0	0
Long-term external debt								
Disbursements	**22,959**	**41,260**	**48,617**	**54,302**	**64,551**	**77,973**	**75,006**	**37,296**
Public and publicly guaranteed	14,078	7,756	14,578	10,993	12,441	12,644	13,872	9,066
Official creditors	2,393	1,001	5,561	3,952	3,064	3,901	4,045	2,761
Private creditors	11,685	6,755	9,017	7,042	9,378	8,743	9,827	6,305
of which: Bonds	6,980	5,230	6,665	4,820	7,927	7,613	9,002	5,170
Private nonguaranteed	8,881	33,504	34,039	43,308	52,110	65,329	61,134	28,230
of which: Bonds	454	3,125	2,300	2,085	6,965	8,635	8,355	2,910
Principal repayments	**13,744**	**24,651**	**45,491**	**40,165**	**41,307**	**46,916**	**41,348**	**11,806**
Public and publicly guaranteed	6,268	7,958	6,015	6,511	5,672	5,070	7,011	6,453
Official creditors	1,745	1,653	1,788	1,714	1,739	1,796	2,019	1,802
Private creditors	4,523	6,305	4,227	4,797	3,933	3,274	4,992	4,651
of which: Bonds	1,858	3,886	2,575	3,285	2,274	1,500	3,037	2,750
Private nonguaranteed	7,476	16,693	39,476	33,654	35,635	41,846	34,337	5,353
of which: Bonds	..	1,150	420	523	404	1,965	915	2,394
Interest payments	**5,000**	**6,562**	**8,868**	**12,171**	**8,541**	**9,345**	**9,874**	**6,418**
Public and publicly guaranteed	3,467	4,637	4,691	4,759	4,752	4,507	4,549	4,368
Official creditors	659	596	488	580	611	536	544	472
Private creditors	2,808	4,041	4,203	4,180	4,141	3,972	4,004	3,897
of which: Bonds	1,479	2,838	3,368	3,433	3,507	3,443	3,624	3,641
Private nonguaranteed	1,533	1,925	4,177	7,412	3,789	4,837	5,325	2,050
of which: Bonds	126	338	228	385	266	813	1,158	1,472
Net financial flows								
Net inflows	**19,498**	**34,989**	**41,305**	**30,855**	**58,817**	**73,656**	**44,184**	**15,405**
Net debt inflows	18,027	19,345	29,122	15,682	39,779	60,455	28,989	2,069
Official creditors	4,020	-5,972	1,602	-569	-679	1,247	2,025	959
of which: World Bank	800	-300	2,088	964	759	451	78	-240
of which: IMF	3,372	-5,320	-2,171	-2,807	-2,004	-857	0	0
Private creditors	14,007	25,316	27,520	16,252	40,458	59,208	26,963	1,109
Long-term	8,567	17,261	-647	11,899	21,920	28,952	31,632	24,531
Bonds	5,576	3,319	5,970	3,098	12,214	12,783	13,405	2,936
Banks and other private	2,991	13,942	-6,617	8,801	9,706	16,169	18,227	21,595
Short-term	5,440	8,055	28,167	4,353	18,538	30,256	-4,669	-23,422
Net equity inflows	1,471	15,644	12,183	15,173	19,038	13,201	15,195	13,336
Foreign direct investment	982	9,975	8,715	16,158	12,762	12,359	12,636	15,731
Portfolio equity	489	5,669	3,468	-985	6,276	842	2,559	-2,395
Major economic aggregates								
Gross national income (GNI)	262,566	477,610	724,653	767,505	782,275	814,666	790,667	708,694
Exports of goods, services & prim. income	53,189	110,456	162,642	188,275	211,277	215,276	225,656	203,122
Imports of goods, services & prim. income	67,873	132,890	208,733	264,396	260,644	280,090	270,615	236,685
Primary income on FDI	279	1,051	2,871	2,937	2,646	3,662	2,328	3,396
Personal transfers & comp. of employees	4,560	1,368	1,819	1,883	1,881	1,901	1,739	1,395
International reserves	22,488	50,579	80,713	78,322	99,943	110,927	106,906	92,921
Ratios								
External debt stocks to exports (%)	219.6	157.2	184.8	162.0	159.4	180.8	177.6	195.9
External debt stocks to GNI (%)	44.5	36.4	41.5	39.7	43.0	47.8	50.7	56.1
Debt service to exports (%)	38.9	37.4	36.5	30.8	26.2	28.6	24.7	10.7
Short-term to external debt stocks (%)	24.8	22.4	25.7	26.7	29.7	33.5	31.3	25.7
Multilateral to external debt stocks (%)	4.9	4.4	6.6	7.0	6.9	6.7	6.3	6.1
Reserves to external debt stocks (%)	19.3	29.1	26.9	25.7	29.7	28.5	26.7	23.4

Notes: Long-term public and publicly guaranteed debt data include nonresident deposits made under the Dresdner Bank scheme, amounting to $1.1 billion at end-2015.

TURKMENISTAN

(US$ million, unless otherwise indicated)

	2000	2005	2010	2011	2012	2013	2014	2015
Summary external debt data								
External debt stocks	**2,627.0**	**1,152.8**	**529.1**	**454.3**	**503.9**	**506.9**	**411.2**	**402.9**
Long-term external debt	2,288.1	911.0	366.8	299.3	309.8	328.6	309.3	272.4
Public and publicly guaranteed	2,271.3	877.8	359.5	265.5	270.6	280.7	263.2	234.2
Official creditors	838.6	685.9	341.6	265.5	270.6	280.7	263.2	234.2
of which: IMF	91.0	99.8	107.5	107.2	107.3	107.5	101.2	96.7
Private creditors	1,432.7	192.0	17.8	0.0	0.0	0.0	0.0	0.0
of which: Bonds	0.0	0.0	0.0	0.0	0.0	0.0	0.0	0.0
Private nonguaranteed	16.7	33.1	7.4	33.8	39.2	47.8	46.0	38.1
of which: Bonds	..	..	..	..	..	..	..	..
Short-term external debt	248.0	142.0	54.8	47.8	86.8	70.8	0.8	33.8
interest arrears on long-term	5.0	5.0	0.8	0.8	0.8	0.8	0.8	0.8
Long-term external debt								
Disbursements	**430.1**	**89.0**	**25.5**	**44.4**	**54.7**	**58.0**	**43.3**	**22.3**
Public and publicly guaranteed	420.9	24.9	17.9	13.6	45.6	46.0	23.0	10.1
Official creditors	292.6	24.9	17.9	13.6	45.6	46.0	23.0	10.1
Private creditors	128.3	0.0	0.0	0.0	0.0	0.0	0.0	0.0
of which: Bonds	0.0	0.0	0.0	0.0	0.0	0.0	0.0	0.0
Private nonguaranteed	9.2	64.1	7.5	30.9	9.1	12.0	20.2	12.2
of which: Bonds	..	..	..	..	..	..	..	..
Principal repayments	**353.0**	**261.4**	**142.8**	**120.9**	**41.0**	**40.6**	**47.1**	**48.1**
Public and publicly guaranteed	347.4	189.1	129.8	118.4	37.1	35.3	33.4	30.7
Official creditors	44.0	112.6	96.7	100.0	37.1	35.3	33.4	30.7
Private creditors	303.4	76.5	33.1	18.4	0.0	0.0	0.0	0.0
of which: Bonds	0.0	0.0	0.0	0.0	0.0	0.0	0.0	0.0
Private nonguaranteed	5.5	72.3	13.0	2.5	3.9	5.3	13.7	17.3
of which: Bonds	..	..	..	..	..	..	..	..
Interest payments	**101.9**	**39.1**	**10.8**	**9.6**	**7.7**	**6.6**	**6.6**	**5.5**
Public and publicly guaranteed	101.2	37.3	10.3	9.0	7.1	6.2	6.0	4.6
Official creditors	27.8	23.9	9.6	8.7	7.1	6.2	6.0	4.6
Private creditors	73.4	13.4	0.8	0.3	0.0	0.0	0.0	0.0
of which: Bonds	0.0	0.0	0.0	0.0	0.0	0.0	0.0	0.0
Private nonguaranteed	0.7	1.8	0.4	0.6	0.6	0.4	0.6	0.9
of which: Bonds	..	..	..	..	..	..	..	..
Net financial flows								
Net inflows	**147.1**	**-52.2**	**3,485.0**	**3,307.6**	**3,182.3**	**3,733.6**	**4,096.3**	**4,266.0**
Net debt inflows	16.1	-470.4	-147.3	-83.5	52.6	1.4	-73.8	7.3
Official creditors	248.6	-87.7	-78.7	-86.4	8.5	10.7	-10.3	-20.6
of which: World Bank	19.6	-1.8	-1.4	-1.5	-1.6	-1.7	-1.8	-1.9
of which: IMF	0.0	0.0	0.0	0.0	0.0	0.0	0.0	0.0
Private creditors	-232.5	-382.7	-68.6	3.0	44.2	-9.3	-63.5	27.9
Long-term	-171.5	-84.7	-38.6	10.0	5.2	6.7	6.5	-5.1
Bonds	..	..	..	..	..	..	..	..
Banks and other private	-171.5	-84.7	-38.6	10.0	5.2	6.7	6.5	-5.1
Short-term	-61.1	-298.0	-30.0	-7.0	39.0	-16.0	-70.0	33.0
Net equity inflows	131.0	418.2	3,632.3	3,391.1	3,129.6	3,732.2	4,170.1	4,258.8
Foreign direct investment	131.0	418.2	3,632.3	3,391.1	3,129.6	3,732.2	4,170.1	4,258.8
Portfolio equity	..	..	..	..	..	..	..	..
Major economic aggregates								
Gross national income (GNI)	2,727.4	7,541.4	20,689.2	26,406.3	31,835.2	35,894.5	40,144.6	35,663.7
Exports of goods, services & prim. income	..	..	..	..	..	..	..	..
Imports of goods, services & prim. income	..	..	..	..	..	..	..	..
Primary income on FDI	..	..	..	..	..	..	..	..
Personal transfers & comp. of employees	..	..	35.0	34.0	37.0	40.0	29.8	..
International reserves	..	..	..	..	..	..	..	..
Ratios								
External debt stocks to exports (%)	..	..	..	..	..	..	..	..
External debt stocks to GNI (%)	96.3	15.3	2.6	1.7	1.6	1.4	1.0	1.1
Debt service to exports (%)	..	..	..	..	..	..	..	..
Short-term to external debt stocks (%)	9.4	12.3	10.4	10.5	17.2	14.0	0.2	8.4
Multilateral to external debt stocks (%)	1.8	3.5	2.7	2.5	8.6	15.5	22.7	24.3
Reserves to external debt stocks (%)	..	..	..	..	..	..	..	..

Notes: Long-term public and publicly guaranteed debt from 2010 are World Bank staff estimates. Long-term private nonguaranteed debt data (excluding bonds) only cover European Bank for Reconstruction and Development lending.

UGANDA

(US$ million, unless otherwise indicated)

	2000	2005	2010	2011	2012	2013	2014	2015
Summary external debt data								
External debt stocks	**3,535**	**4,461**	**2,975**	**3,263**	**3,776**	**4,804**	**4,998**	**5,756**
Long-term external debt	3,051	4,209	2,673	2,963	3,478	4,064	4,213	4,873
Public and publicly guaranteed	3,051	4,209	2,673	2,963	3,478	4,064	4,213	4,873
Official creditors	3,027	4,182	2,673	2,963	3,478	4,064	4,213	4,873
of which: IMF	354	173	275	273	272	270	252	240
Private creditors	24	27	0	0	0	0	0	0
of which: Bonds	4	0	0	0	0	0	0	0
Private nonguaranteed	..	..	..	..	..	..	..	..
of which: Bonds	..	..	..	..	..	..	..	..
Short-term external debt	129	79	26	26	26	469	533	643
interest arrears on long-term	58	29	26	26	26	27	26	26
Long-term external debt								
Disbursements	**219**	**228**	**486**	**335**	**559**	**630**	**463**	**883**
Public and publicly guaranteed	219	228	486	335	559	630	463	883
Official creditors	219	224	486	335	559	630	463	883
Private creditors	0	4	0	0	0	0	0	0
of which: Bonds	0	0	0	0	0	0	0	0
Private nonguaranteed	..	..	..	..	..	..	..	..
of which: Bonds	..	..	..	..	..	..	..	..
Principal repayments	**26**	**99**	**40**	**35**	**38**	**44**	**51**	**46**
Public and publicly guaranteed	26	99	40	35	38	44	51	46
Official creditors	25	98	40	35	38	44	51	46
Private creditors	1	1	0	0	0	0	0	0
of which: Bonds	0	0	0	0	0	0	0	0
Private nonguaranteed	..	..	..	..	..	..	..	..
of which: Bonds	..	..	..	..	..	..	..	..
Interest payments	**21**	**33**	**21**	**26**	**28**	**36**	**44**	**41**
Public and publicly guaranteed	21	33	21	26	28	36	44	41
Official creditors	20	32	21	26	28	36	44	41
Private creditors	0	0	0	0	0	0	0	0
of which: Bonds	0	0	0	0	0	0	0	0
Private nonguaranteed	..	..	..	..	..	..	..	..
of which: Bonds	..	..	..	..	..	..	..	..
Net financial flows								
Net inflows	**279**	**470**	**415**	**976**	**1,456**	**1,970**	**1,220**	**1,721**
Net debt inflows	177	89	237	298	520	1,027	474	946
Official creditors	184	95	447	298	520	584	410	836
of which: World Bank	187	112	323	171	187	351	165	214
of which: IMF	-10	-30	0	-2	-2	-2	-2	-1
Private creditors	-7	-7	-209	0	0	443	64	110
Long-term	-1	3	0	..	..	..	..	..
Bonds	..	..	..	..	..	..	..	..
Banks and other private	-1	3	0	..	..	..	..	..
Short-term	-6	-10	-209	0	0	443	64	110
Net equity inflows	102	381	177	679	936	943	746	775
Foreign direct investment	102	381	248	573	922	848	741	775
Portfolio equity	..	..	-70	106	14	95	5	0
Major economic aggregates								
Gross national income (GNI)	6,086	8,748	19,844	19,931	22,766	24,324	26,359	25,652
Exports of goods, services & prim. income	716	1,592	3,528	4,315	5,004	5,315	4,760	4,874
Imports of goods, services & prim. income	1,574	2,641	6,500	7,855	8,280	8,368	8,400	8,613
Primary income on FDI	19	202	183	262	252	344	347	686
Personal transfers & comp. of employees	238	322	771	816	913	941	888	1,049
International reserves	808	1,344	2,706	2,617	3,167	3,338	3,316	2,909
Ratios								
External debt stocks to exports (%)	493.6	280.3	84.3	75.6	75.5	90.4	105.0	118.1
External debt stocks to GNI (%)	58.1	51.0	15.0	16.4	16.6	19.8	19.0	22.4
Debt service to exports (%)	10.6	10.8	1.8	1.5	1.4	1.5	2.1	1.8
Short-term to external debt stocks (%)	3.7	1.8	0.9	0.8	0.7	9.8	10.7	11.2
Multilateral to external debt stocks (%)	74.5	88.1	81.2	83.0	80.5	74.2	73.0	67.5
Reserves to external debt stocks (%)	22.9	30.1	91.0	80.2	83.9	69.5	66.4	50.5

Notes: Data include the effects of HIPC and MDRI debt relief.

UKRAINE

(US$ million, unless otherwise indicated)

	2000	2005	2010	2011	2012	2013	2014	2015
Summary external debt data								
External debt stocks	**13,910**	**35,095**	**124,297**	**135,465**	**132,069**	**147,656**	**131,206**	**122,825**
Long-term external debt	9,683	19,973	80,771	86,527	84,524	105,643	100,910	90,401
Public and publicly guaranteed	8,142	10,443	25,097	25,368	27,051	32,303	34,849	34,731
Official creditors	5,005	5,123	14,731	12,528	11,797	11,656	13,483	13,371
of which: IMF	3,779	3,059	16,262	16,212	12,795	7,190	7,608	12,486
Private creditors	3,136	5,321	10,366	12,840	15,254	20,647	21,365	21,360
of which: Bonds	2,379	2,943	9,058	11,768	14,197	20,607	21,343	21,352
Private nonguaranteed	1,541	9,530	55,674	61,158	57,473	73,340	66,061	55,671
of which: Bonds	..	550	4,313	5,863	6,522	9,769	7,580	4,695
Short-term external debt	447	12,063	27,264	32,727	34,750	34,823	22,689	19,938
interest arrears on long-term	183	110	1,671	13	1,518	48	2,397	2,945
Long-term external debt								
Disbursements	**1,411**	**7,857**	**32,216**	**28,446**	**16,765**	**37,611**	**11,349**	**18,103**
Public and publicly guaranteed	183	1,415	7,944	3,352	4,163	11,566	4,699	14,927
Official creditors	151	567	4,259	600	560	3,116	3,699	1,624
Private creditors	32	847	3,685	2,753	3,603	8,450	1,000	13,302
of which: Bonds	0	747	3,685	2,750	3,600	8,450	1,000	13,302
Private nonguaranteed	1,228	6,442	24,272	25,094	12,602	26,046	6,650	3,176
of which: Bonds	..	450	0	1,550	0	3,975	0	0
Principal repayments	**2,121**	**4,055**	**22,866**	**23,215**	**21,114**	**26,430**	**10,591**	**24,563**
Public and publicly guaranteed	1,257	1,231	1,427	3,071	2,492	6,407	1,293	14,324
Official creditors	1,215	569	497	2,818	1,288	3,313	1,112	1,080
Private creditors	42	662	929	254	1,204	3,094	181	13,244
of which: Bonds	33	637	691	15	1,186	2,076	165	13,230
Private nonguaranteed	864	2,825	21,439	20,143	18,622	20,023	9,299	10,239
of which: Bonds	..	0	801	0	0	0	2,189	2,885
Interest payments	**574**	**1,033**	**3,527**	**4,318**	**4,472**	**5,315**	**5,159**	**4,072**
Public and publicly guaranteed	502	563	589	848	908	1,251	1,613	1,343
Official creditors	149	134	225	263	219	151	392	219
Private creditors	352	429	363	586	689	1,100	1,222	1,124
of which: Bonds	344	222	257	490	611	1,061	1,221	1,124
Private nonguaranteed	72	470	2,938	3,470	3,564	4,064	3,546	2,729
of which: Bonds	..	41	407	423	403	497	613	547
Net financial flows								
Net inflows	**-541**	**12,775**	**24,993**	**18,992**	**-480**	**11,995**	**-12,520**	**-319**
Net debt inflows	-1,282	5,200	19,153	12,352	-7,244	7,147	-12,841	-4,499
Official creditors	-1,662	-301	7,195	-2,218	-4,142	-5,775	3,471	5,804
of which: World Bank	88	316	-85	-26	37	92	1,387	891
of which: IMF	-598	-300	3,433	..	-3,413	-5,578	884	5,260
Private creditors	380	5,501	11,959	14,571	-3,103	12,921	-16,312	-10,304
Long-term	354	3,803	5,589	7,450	-3,621	11,378	-1,829	-7,005
Bonds	-33	561	2,193	4,285	2,414	10,349	-1,354	-2,812
Banks and other private	387	3,242	3,396	3,165	-6,035	1,029	-475	-4,192
Short-term	26	1,698	6,370	7,121	518	1,543	-14,483	-3,299
Net equity inflows	741	7,575	5,840	6,640	6,764	4,848	321	4,180
Foreign direct investment	595	7,493	5,550	6,121	6,248	3,668	712	4,003
Portfolio equity	146	82	290	519	516	1,180	-391	177
Major economic aggregates								
Gross national income (GNI)	30,320	85,157	134,410	159,364	172,813	178,236	130,247	89,423
Exports of goods, services & prim. income	18,640	43,384	70,341	89,137	93,598	89,486	70,939	52,160
Imports of goods, services & prim. income	18,007	43,695	76,332	103,078	110,909	108,153	77,076	54,977
Primary income on FDI	43	268	2,218	4,084	4,775	5,005	1,742	471
Personal transfers & comp. of employees	33	2,408	6,535	7,822	8,449	9,667	7,354	5,845
International reserves	1,353	18,988	33,327	30,409	22,656	18,776	6,622	12,368
Ratios								
External debt stocks to exports (%)	74.6	80.9	176.7	152.0	141.1	165.0	185.0	235.5
External debt stocks to GNI (%)	45.9	41.2	92.5	85.0	76.4	82.8	100.7	137.4
Debt service to exports (%)	20.1	13.6	38.4	31.8	31.3	42.3	27.8	58.3
Short-term to external debt stocks (%)	3.2	34.4	21.9	24.2	26.3	23.6	17.3	16.2
Multilateral to external debt stocks (%)	17.1	7.9	10.7	8.3	8.1	7.3	9.7	10.2
Reserves to external debt stocks (%)	9.7	54.1	26.8	22.4	17.2	12.7	5.0	10.1

UZBEKISTAN

(US$ million, unless otherwise indicated)

	2000	2005	2010	2011	2012	2013	2014	2015
Summary external debt data								
External debt stocks	**4,948**	**4,632**	**7,802**	**8,300**	**9,119**	**10,675**	**13,308**	**14,838**
Long-term external debt	4,232	4,168	7,154	7,666	8,108	9,857	12,432	13,813
Public and publicly guaranteed	3,766	3,626	3,423	3,756	3,983	4,379	5,568	6,498
Official creditors	2,117	2,451	3,197	3,529	3,821	4,254	5,382	6,243
of which: IMF	469	376	405	403	404	405	381	364
Private creditors	1,649	1,175	226	227	163	125	185	255
of which: Bonds	0	0	0	0	0	0	0	0
Private nonguaranteed	467	542	3,730	3,910	4,125	5,478	6,864	7,315
of which: Bonds	..	..	..	..	..	..	..	..
Short-term external debt	246	88	244	231	607	413	495	661
interest arrears on long-term	3	8	70	70	0	0	0	0
Long-term external debt								
Disbursements	**770**	**404**	**1,191**	**947**	**1,028**	**2,378**	**2,752**	**2,421**
Public and publicly guaranteed	713	262	455	603	587	780	999	1,301
Official creditors	409	200	440	528	577	770	883	1,184
Private creditors	304	62	15	75	10	10	116	116
of which: Bonds	0	0	0	0	0	0	0	0
Private nonguaranteed	57	142	736	344	441	1,598	1,753	1,121
of which: Bonds	..	..	..	..	..	..	..	..
Principal repayments	**589**	**620**	**493**	**460**	**516**	**528**	**674**	**959**
Public and publicly guaranteed	448	510	370	295	293	284	305	289
Official creditors	148	177	256	226	217	232	266	262
Private creditors	301	333	114	69	76	52	40	27
of which: Bonds	0	0	0	0	0	0	0	0
Private nonguaranteed	141	110	123	165	224	244	369	670
of which: Bonds	..	..	..	..	..	..	..	..
Interest payments	**207**	**140**	**118**	**158**	**173**	**163**	**206**	**300**
Public and publicly guaranteed	183	117	63	68	75	66	67	70
Official creditors	75	63	59	62	66	64	64	65
Private creditors	108	53	4	6	9	2	3	5
of which: Bonds	0	0	0	0	0	0	0	0
Private nonguaranteed	24	23	55	90	97	97	139	229
of which: Bonds	..	..	..	..	..	..	..	..
Net financial flows								
Net inflows	**-190**	**-122**	**2,298**	**2,109**	**1,521**	**2,285**	**2,786**	**2,696**
Net debt inflows	-264	-314	662	474	958	1,656	2,160	1,627
Official creditors	196	5	184	302	360	538	617	922
of which: World Bank	27	11	5	9	41	48	47	120
of which: IMF	-65	-18	0	0	0	0	0	0
Private creditors	-461	-318	478	172	598	1,118	1,543	705
Long-term	-81	-239	514	185	152	1,311	1,461	539
Bonds	..	..	..	..	..	..	..	..
Banks and other private	-81	-239	514	185	152	1,311	1,461	539
Short-term	-380	-79	-36	-13	446	-194	82	166
Net equity inflows	75	192	1,636	1,635	563	629	626	1,068
Foreign direct investment	75	192	1,636	1,635	563	629	626	1,068
Portfolio equity	..	..	..	..	..	..	..	..
Major economic aggregates								
Gross national income (GNI)	13,541	14,283	40,492	47,104	52,596	59,137	65,386	67,959
Exports of goods, services & prim. income	..	..	..	..	..	..	..	..
Imports of goods, services & prim. income	..	..	..	..	..	..	..	..
Primary income on FDI	..	..	..	..	..	..	..	..
Personal transfers & comp. of employees	..	..	2,845	4,262	5,668	6,633	5,588	..
International reserves	..	..	..	..	..	..	..	..
Ratios								
External debt stocks to exports (%)	..	..	..	..	..	..	..	..
External debt stocks to GNI (%)	36.5	32.4	19.3	17.6	17.3	18.1	20.4	21.8
Debt service to exports (%)	..	..	..	..	..	..	..	..
Short-term to external debt stocks (%)	5.0	1.9	3.1	2.8	6.7	3.9	3.7	4.5
Multilateral to external debt stocks (%)	9.2	17.2	15.5	15.9	18.8	20.6	19.0	21.2
Reserves to external debt stocks (%)	..	..	..	..	..	..	..	..

Notes: Short-term debt is based on data from the BIS.

VANUATU

(US$ million, unless otherwise indicated)

	2000	2005	2010	2011	2012	2013	2014	2015
Summary external debt data								
External debt stocks	**112.3**	**100.3**	**174.3**	**170.8**	**348.2**	**177.4**	**172.3**	**170.3**
Long-term external debt	73.1	71.9	99.3	98.8	92.2	84.3	76.7	74.2
Public and publicly guaranteed	73.1	71.9	99.3	98.8	92.2	84.3	76.7	74.2
Official creditors	73.1	71.9	99.3	98.8	92.2	84.3	76.7	74.2
of which: IMF	21.2	23.3	25.1	25.0	25.0	25.1	23.6	46.1
Private creditors	0.0	0.0	0.0	0.0	0.0	0.0	0.0	0.0
of which: Bonds	0.0	0.0	0.0	0.0	0.0	0.0	0.0	0.0
Private nonguaranteed	..	..	..	..	..	..	..	..
of which: Bonds	..	..	..	..	..	..	..	..
Short-term external debt	18.0	5.2	50.0	47.0	231.0	68.0	72.0	50.0
interest arrears on long-term	0.0	0.2	0.0	0.0	0.0	0.0	0.0	0.0
Long-term external debt								
Disbursements	**14.2**	**0.0**	**0.0**	**0.0**	**0.0**	**0.0**	**0.0**	**3.4**
Public and publicly guaranteed	14.2	0.0	0.0	0.0	0.0	0.0	0.0	3.4
Official creditors	14.2	0.0	0.0	0.0	0.0	0.0	0.0	3.4
Private creditors	0.0	0.0	0.0	0.0	0.0	0.0	0.0	0.0
of which: Bonds	0.0	0.0	0.0	0.0	0.0	0.0	0.0	0.0
Private nonguaranteed	..	..	..	..	..	..	..	..
of which: Bonds	..	..	..	..	..	..	..	..
Principal repayments	**0.9**	**1.1**	**3.6**	**3.4**	**3.8**	**3.7**	**3.5**	**3.0**
Public and publicly guaranteed	0.9	1.1	3.6	3.4	3.8	3.7	3.5	3.0
Official creditors	0.9	1.1	3.6	3.4	3.8	3.7	3.5	3.0
Private creditors	0.0	0.0	0.0	0.0	0.0	0.0	0.0	0.0
of which: Bonds	0.0	0.0	0.0	0.0	0.0	0.0	0.0	0.0
Private nonguaranteed	..	..	..	..	..	..	..	..
of which: Bonds	..	..	..	..	..	..	..	..
Interest payments	**0.6**	**0.7**	**1.4**	**1.3**	**1.2**	**1.4**	**1.3**	**1.2**
Public and publicly guaranteed	0.6	0.7	1.4	1.3	1.2	1.4	1.3	1.2
Official creditors	0.6	0.7	1.4	1.3	1.2	1.4	1.3	1.2
Private creditors	0.0	0.0	0.0	0.0	0.0	0.0	0.0	0.0
of which: Bonds	0.0	0.0	0.0	0.0	0.0	0.0	0.0	0.0
Private nonguaranteed	..	..	..	..	..	..	..	..
of which: Bonds	..	..	..	..	..	..	..	..
Net financial flows								
Net inflows	**48.6**	**-27.5**	**68.0**	**48.1**	**223.4**	**-142.1**	**22.7**	**31.3**
Net debt inflows	30.2	-41.1	17.4	-6.4	180.2	-166.7	0.5	2.2
Official creditors	13.4	-1.1	-3.6	-3.4	-3.8	-3.7	-3.5	24.2
of which: World Bank	-0.2	-0.3	-0.5	-0.6	-0.6	-0.6	-0.6	0.7
of which: IMF	0.0	0.0	0.0	0.0	0.0	0.0	0.0	23.8
Private creditors	16.9	-40.0	21.0	-3.0	184.0	-163.0	4.0	-22.0
Long-term	..	..	..	..	..	..	..	..
Bonds	..	..	..	..	..	..	..	..
Banks and other private	..	..	..	..	..	..	..	..
Short-term	16.9	-40.0	21.0	-3.0	184.0	-163.0	4.0	-22.0
Net equity inflows	18.4	13.5	50.6	54.5	43.1	24.5	22.2	29.1
Foreign direct investment	18.4	13.5	50.6	54.5	43.1	24.5	22.2	29.1
Portfolio equity	..	..	..	..	..	..	..	..
Major economic aggregates								
Gross national income (GNI)	259.0	369.0	675.7	768.8	734.1	797.0	815.2	..
Exports of goods, services & prim. income	175.7	204.6	363.0	393.0	393.7	424.5	433.5	358.2
Imports of goods, services & prim. income	178.8	258.6	427.4	466.5	479.5	450.4	445.8	516.4
Primary income on FDI	21.9	35.3	51.8	53.4	75.4	29.0	27.9	25.1
Personal transfers & comp. of employees	13.5	5.1	11.8	21.8	22.0	23.7	28.1	24.1
International reserves	38.9	67.2	161.4	173.8	182.2	179.2	184.0	269.2
Ratios								
External debt stocks to exports (%)	63.9	49.0	48.0	43.5	88.5	41.8	39.7	47.5
External debt stocks to GNI (%)	43.3	27.2	25.8	22.2	47.4	22.3	21.1	..
Debt service to exports (%)	1.6	1.6	1.6	1.5	2.1	1.4	1.3	1.4
Short-term to external debt stocks (%)	16.0	5.2	28.7	27.5	66.3	38.3	41.8	29.4
Multilateral to external debt stocks (%)	57.1	67.2	39.5	39.5	17.7	30.4	27.6	28.0
Reserves to external debt stocks (%)	34.7	67.0	92.6	101.8	52.3	101.0	106.8	158.1

Notes: Long-term public and publicly guaranteed debt data from 2010 are World Bank staff estimates. Short-term debt is based on data from the BIS.

VENEZUELA, REPÚBLICA BOLIVARIANA de

(US$ million, unless otherwise indicated)

	2000	2005	2010	2011	2012	2013	2014	2015
Summary external debt data								
External debt stocks	**42,753**	**45,357**	**101,766**	**118,172**	**130,630**	**132,346**	**135,748**	**123,666**
Long-term external debt	33,952	34,796	73,794	89,860	98,725	98,588	101,476	89,930
Public and publicly guaranteed	27,820	31,094	37,512	44,264	46,236	45,622	44,134	42,643
Official creditors	6,180	3,434	5,382	6,719	8,724	9,648	9,726	9,305
of which: IMF	616	453	3,917	3,905	3,909	3,917	3,685	3,524
Private creditors	21,640	27,660	32,130	37,546	37,511	35,974	34,408	33,339
of which: Bonds	16,217	24,401	30,620	36,627	36,624	35,097	33,586	32,280
Private nonguaranteed	6,132	3,702	36,282	45,596	52,489	52,966	57,342	47,286
of which: Bonds	3,880	3,670	8,067	6,942	12,110	12,626	17,080	2,300
Short-term external debt	8,186	10,108	24,055	24,407	27,996	29,841	30,587	30,212
interest arrears on long-term	59	5	..	..	..	..	..	..
Long-term external debt								
Disbursements	**2,343**	**7,252**	**4,729**	**9,266**	**2,661**	**1,579**	**1,234**	**1,706**
Public and publicly guaranteed	2,343	7,252	4,729	9,266	2,661	1,579	1,234	1,706
Official creditors	787	406	1,707	2,060	2,514	1,461	1,126	1,346
Private creditors	1,556	6,847	3,023	7,206	147	117	108	360
of which: Bonds	462	6,143	3,000	7,200	0	0	0	0
Private nonguaranteed	0	0	0	0	0	0	0	0
of which: Bonds	0	0	0	0	0	0	0	0
Principal repayments	**2,921**	**2,385**	**10,058**	**14,461**	**15,527**	**14,580**	**15,025**	**16,159**
Public and publicly guaranteed	2,265	1,698	885	2,516	690	2,213	2,618	2,309
Official creditors	613	739	479	726	504	529	1,013	1,043
Private creditors	1,652	959	406	1,790	186	1,684	1,605	1,266
of which: Bonds	1,119	226	119	1,186	0	1,540	1,498	1,193
Private nonguaranteed	655	687	9,174	11,946	14,837	12,367	12,407	13,849
of which: Bonds	0	0	659	0	2,365	0	0	0
Interest payments	**2,435**	**2,656**	**5,465**	**6,343**	**7,889**	**7,751**	**7,808**	**6,964**
Public and publicly guaranteed	1,867	2,308	2,789	3,119	4,002	3,948	3,976	3,769
Official creditors	343	204	177	205	207	229	382	411
Private creditors	1,524	2,103	2,612	2,914	3,795	3,718	3,594	3,358
of which: Bonds	1,298	1,840	2,503	2,812	3,613	3,615	3,457	3,272
Private nonguaranteed	568	349	2,676	3,224	3,888	3,803	3,831	3,195
of which: Bonds	304	296	708	582	1,213	1,055	1,111	166
Net financial flows								
Net inflows	**2,011**	**9,754**	**-1,981**	**-1,849**	**-6,630**	**-10,831**	**-11,709**	**-14,657**
Net debt inflows	-384	7,138	-2,108	-4,843	-9,277	-11,156	-13,045	-14,827
Official creditors	-333	-333	1,228	1,334	2,010	933	113	303
of which: World Bank	-158	-93	..	..	..	..	..	..
of which: IMF	-507	..	..	..	..	..	..	..
Private creditors	-52	7,471	-3,336	-6,177	-11,287	-12,089	-13,158	-15,130
Long-term	-752	5,200	-6,557	-6,529	-14,876	-13,934	-13,904	-14,755
Bonds	-657	5,916	2,222	6,014	-2,365	-1,540	-1,498	-1,193
Banks and other private	-95	-717	-8,779	-12,543	-12,510	-12,394	-12,406	-13,562
Short-term	700	2,271	3,221	352	3,589	1,845	746	-375
Net equity inflows	2,395	2,616	127	2,994	2,647	325	1,336	170
Foreign direct investment	2,969	2,588	117	2,988	2,681	896	1,287	165
Portfolio equity	-574	28	10	6	-34	-571	49	5
Major economic aggregates								
Gross national income (GNI)	115,760	143,311	387,498	309,358	371,238	359,549	..	..
Exports of goods, services & prim. income	37,760	61,208	70,481	97,678	101,810	93,188	78,398	39,675
Imports of goods, services & prim. income	25,737	35,699	63,996	80,535	98,221	87,366	74,582	59,824
Primary income on FDI	1,424	3,895	4,510	6,280	6,307	4,109	3,539	2,823
Personal transfers & comp. of employees	17	148	143	138	118	120	117	104
International reserves	13,088	23,919	13,137	9,930	9,900	6,038	7,457	6,324
Ratios								
External debt stocks to exports (%)	113.2	74.1	144.4	121.0	128.3	142.0	173.2	311.7
External debt stocks to GNI (%)	36.9	31.6	26.3	38.2	35.2	36.8	..	..
Debt service to exports (%)	16.9	8.7	22.9	22.1	23.7	24.8	30.2	60.4
Short-term to external debt stocks (%)	19.1	22.3	23.6	20.7	21.4	22.5	22.5	24.4
Multilateral to external debt stocks (%)	7.5	6.2	4.4	4.7	4.3	4.3	4.3	4.4
Reserves to external debt stocks (%)	30.6	52.7	12.9	8.4	7.6	4.6	5.5	5.1

Notes: Long-term private nonguaranteed debt data from 2004 are based on Central Bank data. Short-term debt is based on Central Bank data.

VIETNAM

(US$ million, unless otherwise indicated)

	2000	2005	2010	2011	2012	2013	2014	2015
Summary external debt data								
External debt stocks	**12,785**	**18,530**	**44,902**	**53,886**	**61,577**	**65,452**	**72,423**	**77,798**
Long-term external debt	11,584	16,219	37,444	42,612	48,746	52,801	58,366	65,374
Public and publicly guaranteed	11,584	16,219	32,764	36,750	39,940	42,940	44,807	46,335
Official creditors	8,680	14,259	27,435	31,077	33,465	34,770	35,905	37,732
of which: IMF	378	272	529	496	484	485	456	436
Private creditors	2,904	1,960	5,329	5,673	6,475	8,170	8,902	8,603
of which: Bonds	560	1,171	2,020	2,001	1,982	2,586	1,900	1,877
Private nonguaranteed	..	..	4,680	5,862	8,806	9,861	13,559	19,039
of which: Bonds	..	..	..	90	90	290	290	290
Short-term external debt	823	2,040	6,928	10,778	12,347	12,166	13,601	11,988
interest arrears on long-term	78	74	0	0	0	0	0	0
Long-term external debt								
Disbursements	**1,272**	**2,047**	**6,878**	**6,968**	**8,727**	**9,465**	**13,841**	**12,981**
Public and publicly guaranteed	1,272	2,047	5,593	4,751	5,958	7,033	7,524	4,456
Official creditors	1,176	1,261	3,675	4,001	4,711	4,821	5,379	4,020
Private creditors	96	786	1,918	750	1,247	2,212	2,145	436
of which: Bonds	0	750	1,000	0	0	627	0	0
Private nonguaranteed	..	..	1,285	2,217	2,769	2,433	6,316	8,525
of which: Bonds	..	..	..	90	0	200	0	0
Principal repayments	**937**	**480**	**1,048**	**3,082**	**3,276**	**3,274**	**5,307**	**4,922**
Public and publicly guaranteed	937	480	1,048	1,201	1,473	1,896	2,689	1,877
Official creditors	134	303	735	823	1,024	1,362	1,389	1,215
Private creditors	802	177	313	378	449	534	1,300	662
of which: Bonds	0	41	19	19	19	23	685	23
Private nonguaranteed	..	..	0	1,881	1,803	1,378	2,618	3,045
of which: Bonds	..	..	..	0	0	0	0	0
Interest payments	**298**	**318**	**707**	**902**	**1,012**	**1,074**	**1,238**	**1,538**
Public and publicly guaranteed	298	318	563	689	744	763	808	821
Official creditors	77	256	398	457	494	514	508	519
Private creditors	220	62	165	232	250	249	301	302
of which: Bonds	23	22	93	126	126	126	140	86
Private nonguaranteed	..	..	144	213	268	311	429	717
of which: Bonds	..	..	..	4	9	9	32	32
Net financial flows								
Net inflows	**1,670**	**3,164**	**17,424**	**14,708**	**15,214**	**13,483**	**17,897**	**16,892**
Net debt inflows	372	1,845	7,940	7,703	7,008	6,011	9,969	6,445
Official creditors	1,020	904	2,902	3,145	3,675	3,459	3,991	2,804
of which: World Bank	173	378	1,501	1,082	1,285	1,303	1,379	1,096
of which: IMF	-21	-54	-38	-33	-13	0	0	0
Private creditors	-648	941	5,038	4,557	3,333	2,552	5,978	3,641
Long-term	-706	609	2,889	707	1,764	2,733	4,543	5,254
Bonds	..	709	981	71	-19	803	-685	-23
Banks and other private	-706	-100	1,908	636	1,783	1,929	5,228	5,277
Short-term	58	332	2,149	3,850	1,569	-181	1,435	-1,613
Net equity inflows	1,298	1,319	9,484	7,005	8,206	7,472	7,928	10,447
Foreign direct investment	1,298	1,204	7,101	5,941	6,943	6,202	7,676	10,313
Portfolio equity	..	115	2,383	1,064	1,263	1,270	252	134
Major economic aggregates								
Gross national income (GNI)	33,194	56,575	111,513	129,698	149,569	163,885	177,110	182,855
Exports of goods, services & prim. income	17,481	36,987	80,153	106,180	124,609	143,024	161,510	173,711
Imports of goods, services & prim. income	18,107	40,927	92,314	114,629	123,392	144,756	161,758	180,540
Primary income on FDI	..	..	..	..	..	..	..	..
Personal transfers & comp. of employees	1,340	3,150	8,260	8,600	10,000	11,000	12,000	13,200
International reserves	3,417	9,051	12,467	13,539	25,573	25,893	34,189	28,250
Ratios								
External debt stocks to exports (%)	73.1	50.1	56.0	50.7	49.4	45.8	44.8	44.8
External debt stocks to GNI (%)	38.5	32.8	40.3	41.5	41.2	39.9	40.9	42.5
Debt service to exports (%)	7.5	2.6	2.3	3.9	3.6	3.2	4.2	3.8
Short-term to external debt stocks (%)	6.4	11.0	15.4	20.0	20.1	18.6	18.8	15.4
Multilateral to external debt stocks (%)	14.8	27.8	27.9	26.7	26.0	27.5	26.3	25.9
Reserves to external debt stocks (%)	26.7	48.8	27.8	25.1	41.5	39.6	47.2	36.3

Notes: Short-term debt is based on data from the BIS.

YEMEN, REPUBLIC OF

(US$ million, unless otherwise indicated)

	2000	2005	2010	2011	2012	2013	2014	2015
Summary external debt data								
External debt stocks	**5,152**	**5,478**	**6,493**	**6,418**	**7,718**	**7,570**	**7,818**	**7,287**
Long-term external debt	4,109	4,814	5,933	5,876	6,912	6,884	6,836	6,469
Public and publicly guaranteed	4,109	4,814	5,933	5,876	6,912	6,884	6,836	6,469
Official creditors	4,046	4,807	5,930	5,874	6,911	6,883	6,836	6,469
of which: IMF	355	333	436	410	504	505	546	522
Private creditors	63	7	3	2	1	1	0	0
of which: Bonds	0	0	0	0	0	0	0	0
Private nonguaranteed	..	..	..	..	..	..	..	..
of which: Bonds	..	..	..	..	..	..	..	..
Short-term external debt	689	330	124	131	302	181	437	296
interest arrears on long-term	27	94	124	131	140	147	153	160
Long-term external debt								
Disbursements	**137**	**265**	**287**	**101**	**1,251**	**203**	**439**	**60**
Public and publicly guaranteed	137	265	287	101	1,251	203	439	60
Official creditors	137	265	287	101	1,251	203	439	60
Private creditors	0	0	0	0	0	0	0	0
of which: Bonds	0	0	0	0	0	0	0	0
Private nonguaranteed	..	..	..	..	..	..	..	..
of which: Bonds	..	..	..	..	..	..	..	..
Principal repayments	**81**	**94**	**155**	**175**	**181**	**194**	**275**	**279**
Public and publicly guaranteed	81	94	155	175	181	194	275	279
Official creditors	81	94	154	174	180	193	274	279
Private creditors	0	0	1	1	1	1	1	0
of which: Bonds	0	0	0	0	0	0	0	0
Private nonguaranteed	..	..	..	..	..	..	..	..
of which: Bonds	..	..	..	..	..	..	..	..
Interest payments	**45**	**55**	**74**	**75**	**73**	**75**	**77**	**74**
Public and publicly guaranteed	45	55	74	75	73	75	77	74
Official creditors	45	55	74	74	73	75	77	74
Private creditors	0	0	0	0	0	0	0	0
of which: Bonds	0	0	0	0	0	0	0	0
Private nonguaranteed	..	..	..	..	..	..	..	..
of which: Bonds	..	..	..	..	..	..	..	..
Net financial flows								
Net inflows	**266**	**-136**	**-189**	**-55**	**1,355**	**-159**	**-1,299**	**-1,558**
Net debt inflows	260	166	-232	-99	1,325	-26	488	-367
Official creditors	-15	116	159	-98	1,164	103	238	-219
of which: World Bank	51	102	28	-40	-33	-37	-46	-51
of which: IMF	-71	-56	26	-25	93	93	74	0
Private creditors	275	51	-391	-1	161	-129	249	-148
Long-term	0	0	-1	-1	-1	-1	-1	0
Bonds	..	..	..	..	..	..	..	..
Banks and other private	0	0	-1	-1	-1	-1	-1	0
Short-term	275	51	-390	..	162	-128	250	-148
Net equity inflows	6	-302	43	44	30	-134	-1,787	-1,191
Foreign direct investment	6	-302	43	44	30	-134	-1,787	-1,191
Portfolio equity	..	..	..	..	..	..	..	..
Major economic aggregates								
Gross national income (GNI)	8,863	15,139	29,194	28,848	30,894	34,721	..	..
Exports of goods, services & prim. income	4,158	6,963	9,325	10,437	9,415	9,592	9,458	1,890
Imports of goods, services & prim. income	4,221	7,745	12,503	13,099	15,207	14,747	17,005	8,265
Primary income on FDI	855	1,603	1,510	2,025	1,145	1,352	1,392	204
Personal transfers & comp. of employees	1,288	1,283	1,526	1,404	3,351	3,343	3,351	3,351
International reserves	2,900	6,115	5,868	4,449	6,068	5,284	..	..
Ratios								
External debt stocks to exports (%)	123.9	78.7	69.6	61.5	82.0	78.9	82.7	385.6
External debt stocks to GNI (%)	58.1	36.2	22.2	22.2	25.0	21.8	..	..
Debt service to exports (%)	5.9	3.1	2.8	2.6	2.7	2.8	3.8	18.8
Short-term to external debt stocks (%)	13.4	6.0	1.9	2.0	3.9	2.4	5.6	4.1
Multilateral to external debt stocks (%)	32.5	40.5	50.6	50.6	43.4	45.0	44.2	43.6
Reserves to external debt stocks (%)	56.3	111.6	90.4	69.3	78.6	69.8	..	..

Notes: Short-term debt is based on data from the BIS.

ZAMBIA

(US$ million, unless otherwise indicated)

	2000	2005	2010	2011	2012	2013	2014	2015
Summary external debt data								
External debt stocks	**5,811**	**5,461**	**4,384**	**5,099**	**5,849**	**5,927**	**7,540**	**8,785**
Long-term external debt	4,508	4,538	2,085	3,401	3,864	4,028	5,660	7,259
Public and publicly guaranteed	4,444	3,942	1,290	1,884	3,101	3,266	4,659	6,375
Official creditors	4,412	3,646	1,257	1,776	2,266	2,453	3,651	4,185
of which: IMF	1,227	689	1,117	1,137	1,126	1,110	1,011	907
Private creditors	31	295	33	108	835	813	1,008	2,191
of which: Bonds	0	0	0	0	750	750	750	2,000
Private nonguaranteed	65	596	794	1,517	763	763	1,002	883
of which: Bonds	..	..	..	..	..	..	..	..
Short-term external debt	76	234	1,183	561	859	788	868	620
interest arrears on long-term	33	90	159	159	163	165	167	169
Long-term external debt								
Disbursements	**261**	**218**	**177**	**737**	**1,349**	**329**	**1,946**	**1,949**
Public and publicly guaranteed	251	114	150	644	1,316	296	1,565	1,949
Official creditors	251	114	150	553	566	296	1,347	699
Private creditors	0	0	0	91	750	0	218	1,250
of which: Bonds	0	0	0	0	750	0	0	1,250
Private nonguaranteed	10	105	27	93	33	33	380	0
of which: Bonds	..	..	..	..	..	..	..	..
Principal repayments	**98**	**136**	**86**	**139**	**143**	**190**	**231**	**225**
Public and publicly guaranteed	79	71	47	56	101	147	90	107
Official creditors	79	59	38	40	78	125	67	79
Private creditors	1	12	8	16	23	23	23	28
of which: Bonds	0	0	0	0	0	0	0	0
Private nonguaranteed	18	66	40	82	42	42	141	118
of which: Bonds	..	..	..	..	..	..	..	..
Interest payments	**80**	**58**	**29**	**48**	**57**	**98**	**110**	**204**
Public and publicly guaranteed	76	29	11	12	39	80	76	178
Official creditors	76	29	11	12	39	40	35	137
Private creditors	0	0	0	0	0	40	41	41
of which: Bonds	0	0	0	0	0	40	40	40
Private nonguaranteed	4	28	18	35	18	18	33	26
of which: Bonds	..	..	..	..	..	..	..	..
Net financial flows								
Net inflows	**263**	**422**	**2,178**	**967**	**1,456**	**424**	**2,490**	**1,723**
Net debt inflows	159	88	850	0	1,488	49	1,757	1,413
Official creditors	198	-8	167	537	476	154	1,245	559
of which: World Bank	198	76	30	65	72	65	76	61
of which: IMF	26	-63	55	24	-12	-18	-35	-61
Private creditors	-39	96	683	-537	1,012	-105	513	854
Long-term	-9	27	-21	85	718	-32	435	1,104
Bonds	..	..	..	..	750	0	0	1,250
Banks and other private	-9	27	-21	85	-32	-32	435	-146
Short-term	-30	69	704	-622	294	-73	78	-250
Net equity inflows	104	334	1,328	966	-32	375	733	309
Foreign direct investment	99	329	1,228	942	-25	370	727	309
Portfolio equity	6	5	101	25	-7	5	6	0
Major economic aggregates								
Gross national income (GNI)	3,445	7,700	18,903	22,304	25,170	27,292	26,227	20,135
Exports of goods, services & prim. income	891	2,842	8,063	9,430	10,521	11,607	11,077	8,232
Imports of goods, services & prim. income	1,567	3,181	6,969	8,715	9,603	12,170	11,762	9,226
Primary income on FDI	71	461	1,303	1,093	239	1,020	1,322	34
Personal transfers & comp. of employees	..	53	44	46	73	54	58	47
International reserves	245	560	2,094	2,324	3,042	2,684	3,078	2,968
Ratios								
External debt stocks to exports (%)	652.0	192.2	54.4	54.1	55.6	51.1	68.1	106.7
External debt stocks to GNI (%)	168.7	70.9	23.2	22.9	23.2	21.7	28.7	43.6
Debt service to exports (%)	21.2	10.0	1.9	2.3	2.2	2.8	3.6	6.2
Short-term to external debt stocks (%)	1.3	4.3	27.0	11.0	14.7	13.3	11.5	7.1
Multilateral to external debt stocks (%)	41.4	57.2	21.1	19.0	18.4	20.0	29.3	26.6
Reserves to external debt stocks (%)	4.2	10.3	47.8	45.6	52.0	45.3	40.8	33.8

Notes: Long-term private nonguaranteed data are World Bank staff estimates based on reports provided by the country. Short-term debt is based on data from the BIS. Data include the effects of HIPC and MDRI debt relief.

ZIMBABWE

(US$ million, unless otherwise indicated)

	2000	2005	2010	2011	2012	2013	2014	2015
Summary external debt data								
External debt stocks	**3,843**	**4,445**	**6,605**	**7,312**	**8,655**	**8,196**	**8,036**	**8,735**
Long-term external debt	2,981	3,209	4,260	4,724	5,715	4,953	4,935	5,481
Public and publicly guaranteed	2,776	3,177	3,664	3,820	3,884	3,951	3,708	3,567
Official creditors	2,439	2,771	3,230	3,389	3,447	3,506	3,295	3,178
of which: IMF	294	125	529	527	520	519	487	464
Private creditors	337	406	433	431	437	445	413	389
of which: Bonds	0	0	0	0	0	0	0	0
Private nonguaranteed	205	32	596	904	1,831	1,001	1,228	1,913
of which: Bonds	..	..	..	..	..	..	..	..
Short-term external debt	568	1,111	1,817	2,061	2,420	2,724	2,614	2,791
interest arrears on long-term	55	534	938	1,054	1,144	1,236	1,214	1,258
Long-term external debt								
Disbursements	**185**	**25**	**847**	**1,584**	**1,433**	**1,710**	**1,442**	**1,023**
Public and publicly guaranteed	139	24	4	186	70	58	74	82
Official creditors	125	16	4	181	70	58	73	82
Private creditors	15	8	0	5	0	0	1	0
of which: Bonds	0	0	0	0	0	0	0	0
Private nonguaranteed	46	0	843	1,398	1,363	1,652	1,368	941
of which: Bonds	..	..	..	..	..	..	..	..
Principal repayments	**211**	**45**	**337**	**1,096**	**440**	**327**	**323**	**358**
Public and publicly guaranteed	146	31	1	6	5	12	68	48
Official creditors	113	21	1	6	5	8	68	47
Private creditors	33	10	0	0	0	4	0	1
of which: Bonds	0	0	0	0	0	0	0	0
Private nonguaranteed	65	14	336	1,091	435	315	255	310
of which: Bonds	..	..	..	..	..	..	..	..
Interest payments	**81**	**7**	**31**	**43**	**273**	**133**	**122**	**183**
Public and publicly guaranteed	64	3	13	14	14	6	21	19
Official creditors	50	2	13	14	14	6	21	19
Private creditors	13	1	0	0	0	0	0	0
of which: Bonds	0	0	0	0	0	0	0	0
Private nonguaranteed	17	4	18	29	259	127	101	164
of which: Bonds	..	..	..	..	..	..	..	..
Net financial flows								
Net inflows	**-306**	**-77**	**832**	**1,003**	**1,653**	**1,993**	**1,573**	**1,217**
Net debt inflows	-329	-180	666	616	1,254	1,593	1,029	796
Official creditors	-58	-169	-1	175	57	48	2	33
of which: World Bank	-20	-2	0	0	0	0	-2	-7
of which: IMF	-70	-165	-4	0	-7	-2	-2	-2
Private creditors	-271	-11	667	441	1,196	1,545	1,026	763
Long-term	-37	-16	507	313	927	1,333	1,114	630
Bonds	..	..	..	..	..	..	..	..
Banks and other private	-37	-16	507	313	927	1,333	1,114	630
Short-term	-233	5	160	128	269	212	-88	133
Net equity inflows	23	103	166	387	400	400	545	421
Foreign direct investment	23	103	166	387	400	400	545	421
Portfolio equity	..	..	..	..	..	..	..	..
Major economic aggregates								
Gross national income (GNI)	6,329	5,481	8,877	10,055	11,429	12,456	13,081	13,150
Exports of goods, services & prim. income	..	..	3,652	5,096	4,648	4,391	4,282	4,212
Imports of goods, services & prim. income	..	..	6,594	9,528	8,683	8,895	8,531	7,873
Primary income on FDI	..	..	..	..	..	..	..	..
Personal transfers & comp. of employees	..	..	1,413	1,919	2,114	1,890	1,904	2,047
International reserves	193	97	732	659	574	474	363	418
Ratios								
External debt stocks to exports (%)	..	..	180.9	143.5	186.2	186.7	187.7	207.4
External debt stocks to GNI (%)	60.7	81.1	74.4	72.7	75.7	65.8	61.4	66.4
Debt service to exports (%)	..	..	10.5	22.6	15.9	11.0	10.9	13.4
Short-term to external debt stocks (%)	14.8	25.0	27.5	28.2	28.0	33.2	32.5	31.9
Multilateral to external debt stocks (%)	35.2	33.4	24.1	21.8	18.8	19.9	19.1	16.9
Reserves to external debt stocks (%)	5.0	2.2	11.1	9.0	6.6	5.8	4.5	4.8

Notes: Data from 2001 include late interest fee owed to Paris Club and Commercial Creditors. Short-term debt is based on data from the BIS.

APPENDIX
About the Data

Data Sources and Methodology

Data Sources

Debtor reporting system

The principal sources of information for the tables in *International Debt Statistics 2017* are reports to the World Bank through the World Bank's Debtor Reporting System (DRS) from member countries that have received either International Bank for Reconstruction and Development (IBRD) loans or International Development Association (IDA) credits. The DRS has its origin in the World Bank's need to monitor and assess the financial position of its borrowers. Since 1951, borrowers have been required to provide statistics on their public external debt and private sector debt that benefit from a public guarantee. In its design, consistency, and continuity of coverage, the DRS is a unique resource. Reporting countries submit detailed reports on the annual status, transactions, and terms of the long-term external debt of public agencies and that of private ones guaranteed by a public agency in the debtor country. The DRS maintains these records on a loan-by-loan basis. In 1973, coverage of the DRS was expanded to include private sector nonguaranteed borrowing, but for this category of debt, data are provided by borrowers in aggregate rather than loan by loan.

Data submitted to the DRS are processed in the World Bank External Debt (WBXD) system, along with additional information received from the files of the African Development Bank, the Asian Development Bank, the Inter-American Development Bank (IDB), the International Monetary Fund (IMF), institutions of the World Bank Group (IBRD and IDA), and the European Bank for Reconstruction and Development (EBRD). The WBXD is an internal system of the World Bank. Among its outputs is the International Debt Statistics (IDS) database, from which the tables in this publication and online database are produced.

Data on exports and imports (on a balance of payments basis), international reserves, current account balances, foreign direct investment (FDI) on equity, portfolio equity flows, and primary income of FDI are drawn mainly from the files of the IMF, supplemented by United Nations Conference on Trade and Development (UNCTAD) reports and country data. Balance of payments data are presented according to the sixth edition of the IMF's *Balance of Payments Manual* (BPM6). Official aid flows come from data collected and published by the Development Assistance Committee (DAC) of the Organisation for Economic Co-operation and Development (OECD). Short-term external debt data are as reported by debtor countries or are estimates based on the Bank for International Settlements (BIS) quarterly series of commercial banks' claims on low- and middle-income countries. For some countries, estimates were prepared by pooling creditor and debtor information. Data on the gross national income of most low- and middle-income countries are collected from national statistical organizations or central banks by visiting and resident World Bank missions.

Every effort has been made to ensure the accuracy and completeness of the external debt statistics. Coverage has been improved through the efforts of the reporting agencies and close collaboration between the Bank and our partners, Commonwealth Secretariat (COMSEC) and UNCTAD, which provide debt recording and reporting systems across the globe, as well as through the work of the World Bank missions, which visit member countries to gather data and to provide technical assistance on debt issues. Nevertheless, quality and coverage vary among debtors and may also vary for the same debtor from year to year. Data on long-term external debt reported by member countries are checked against, and supplemented by, data from several other sources. Among these sources are the statements and reports of several regional development banks, government lending agencies, and official government websites.

Quarterly external debt statistics

The Quarterly External Debt Statistics (QEDS) database, jointly developed by the World Bank and the IMF, brings together detailed external debt data of countries that subscribe to the IMF's Special Data Dissemination Standard (SDDS) and a selected number of countries that participate in the IMF's General Data Dissemination System (GDDS).

In October 2014, the World Bank, in collaboration with the IMF, launched the new QEDS database in line with the classifications and definitions of the 2013 *External Debt Statistics: Guide for Compilers and Users* (*2013 EDS Guide*) and sixth edition of the *Balance of Payments and International Investment Position Manual* (*BPM6*). The QEDS database reflects new concepts and definitions, classifications of external debt data, as well as expanded coverage that enhances the analytical use of the data. The database provides quarterly information on the stock of outstanding external debt, categorized by maturity as well as by borrowing entity and debt instrument. Reporting is voluntary but as of end 2015, 74 countries plus the Euro Area reported under the SDDS, and 47 countries reported under GDDS. The benefit of bringing together comparable external debt data is to facilitate macroeconomic analysis and cross-country data comparison.

The Quarterly External Debt Database, which is maintained by the World Bank, can be accessed via the Bank's website through the World Bank Open Data at www.databank.worldbank.org.

Quarterly public sector statistics debt

As part of the World Bank Open Data Initiative, in December 2010, the World Bank launched for the first time an online, quarterly, Public Sector Debt Statistics (PSDS) database (www.worldbank.org/qpsd), developed in partnership with the IMF, which allows researchers and policy makers to explore questions about recent developments in public sector debt. The PSDS database, with the endorsement of the Inter-Agency Task Force on Finance Statistics (TFFS), initially focused only on low- and middle-income, and emerging market countries; now in partnership with the OECD and Eurostat, the PSDS database has been expanded to include the advanced economies. The launch of the database is one of the recommendations in the G-20 Data Gaps Initiative.[1] The PSDS database facilitates timely dissemination in standard formats of external debt data. By bringing such data and metadata together in one central location, the database supports macroeconomic analysis and cross-country comparison.

The database is organized into five sets of tables on the following sectors: General government; o/w central government; o/w budgetary central government; nonfinancial public corporations; and financial public corporations. The database is structured by instruments, maturity, and by creditors as the presentation format articulated in table 4.3 in the *IMF Public Sector Debt Guide for compilers and users*. While central government is identified as having the most important key of macroeconomic analysis, the PSDS database provides data on other levels of public sector, valuation methods, and debt instruments, and clearly defined tiers of debt where appropriate for central, state, and local governments, as well as extra-budgetary agencies and funds.

As of end 2015, 78 countries participated in the Quarterly Public Sector Debt Database, which is maintained by the World Bank; it can be accessed through the Bank's website through the World Bank Open Data at www.databank.worldbank.org.

Methodology

Aggregations

Total debt stock and other aggregate measures are derived from the summation of loan-level data on stocks and flows after conversion to a common currency. Other tabulations are compiled using terms and conditions reported in the loan-level data, such as currency composition, cancellations, rescheduling of other liabilities into long-term public and publicly guaranteed external debt, and debt buybacks.

1. Please see http://www.imf.org/external/np/g20/pdf/102909.pdf. The Public Sector Debt Statistics database is recommendation number 18 in the Data Gaps Initiative Report.

Aggregates for regional and income groups are based on the World Bank's operational classifications, which may differ from common geographic usage or income groups used by other organizations. Country classifications of DRS reporting countries in 2015 are shown in country groups in the back of the publication. The same classification is used for all historical data shown in *International Debt Statistics* and the online tables and online database.

Currency conversion

Data on external obligations are normally reported to the World Bank in the currency of repayment and are converted into a common currency (U.S. dollars) using official exchange rates published by the IMF.

Commitments, disbursements, and debt service payments (flows) are converted to U.S. dollars at the annual average exchange rate for the year. Debt outstanding (disbursed and undisbursed) at the end of a given year (stock) is converted at the exchange rate in effect at the end of the relevant year. Consequently, year-to-year changes in debt outstanding and disbursed may not be equal to net flows (disbursements less principal repayments); similarly, changes in debt outstanding (including undisbursed debt) may not equal commitments less repayments. Discrepancies will be particularly significant when exchange rates have moved sharply during the year. Projected debt service is converted to U.S. dollars at rates in effect at the end of December 2015.

Beginning with 1991, all ruble debt owed to the former Soviet Union has been converted at a rate of US$1 = 0.6 ruble, except in cases where a bilateral agreement specifying a different conversion rate is in place. Adoption of this methodology does not constitute an endorsement by the World Bank staff of the appropriateness or validity of the exchange rate used. That matter must be resolved bilaterally between the Russian Federation and its debtor countries.

Starting with the 1988–89 edition of *World Debt Tables* (a predecessor of IDS), all data pertaining to IBRD loans from 1985 onward are recorded at their current market value. Starting with the 1991–92 edition, all data pertaining to Asian Development Bank loans from 1989 onward are recorded at their current market value. Starting with the 1998 edition, all data pertaining to African Development Bank and African Development Fund loans from 1997 onward are recorded at their current market value.

Debt stock and flow reconciliation

Because of currency conversions and the timing of transactions, there may be differences between the change in aggregate stocks from one period to the next and flows during the relevant period; changes in debt outstanding, including undisbursed amounts, will therefore differ from commitments less repayments.

Changes in the stock of debt from one period to the next can be attributed to five factors: the net flow of debt, the net change in interest arrears, the capitalization of interest, a reduction in debt resulting from debt forgiveness or other debt reduction mechanisms, and cross-currency valuation effects. Any residual difference in the change in stock not explained by one of those five factors may indicate inconsistencies in the reported data or specific phenomena prevailing in an individual country (for example, an incomplete historical series for all categories of debt). Starting in 1989, the IDS includes the debt stock reconciliation, but not all components are shown in the IDS print edition and online tables.

External debt restructuring

Starting in 1985, the WBXD includes information on the restructuring of debt by official creditors in the context of the Paris Club, restructuring by commercial creditors, debt swap operations, buybacks, and bond exchanges. It attempts to capture accurately the effect of debt restructuring on both external debt stocks and external debt flows, consistent with the terms on which the restructuring takes place. In the compilation and presentation of external debt data, a distinction is made between cash flows and imputed flows. According to this criterion, restructured service payments and the shift in liabilities from one financial instrument to another as a result of debt restructuring are considered to be imputed flows. Both cash flows and imputed flows are recorded separately in WBXD.

The imputed flows and stock changes associated with debt restructuring are included in the IDS tables and online database to complement the cash-basis transactions recorded in the main body of the data. Such data encompass information on the debt stock and debt flows restructured each year, the amount of principal forgiven (interest forgiven is shown as a memorandum item), and the amount of external debt stock reduced either by forgiveness or by a debt buyback operation. Changes in creditors and debtors that result from debt restructuring are also reflected. For example, when insured commercial credits are rescheduled, the creditor classification shifts from private to official (bilateral), reflecting the assumption of the assets by the official credit insurance agencies in the creditor country. The IDS data will show a reduction in the external debt owed to the original private creditors equal or similar to the amount of debt restructured and a corresponding increase in the debt owed to the new official creditor. Similarly on the debtor side, when a government accepts responsibility for the payment of restructured debt previously owed by a private enterprise, the relevant change in the debtor category will be reflected. Likewise, if short-term external debt is restructured into a long-term obligation, the stock of short-term external debt will decline and the stock of long-term external debt will rise by the amount of short-term debt restructured. In the event of a debt swap of long-term external debt (external debt to equity, external debt for nature, or external debt for development), the face value of the external debt swapped will be recorded as a decline in long-term external debt stock, but no flow transaction (principal repayment) will be recorded.

Projections of future disbursements and debt service payments

The WBXD system projects future disbursements and future debt service payments on the assumption that every existing loan commitment will be fully used and repaid in full.

Future disbursements

Disbursement projections are made using one of the following methods:

- *Specific schedules.* Debtor countries are requested to submit a schedule of future disbursements, if available, at the time each new loan is first reported.
- *Standard schedules.* In the absence of specific schedules, the WBXD system projects the future disbursement schedule according to the undisbursed balance of each loan at the end of the most recent reporting period.

These projected schedules are based on profiles derived from the disbursement pattern of comparable loans that fully disbursed. Thirty different profiles have been compiled corresponding to each category of creditor and, in the case of official creditors, for concessional and nonconcessional loans. Each profile is derived by applying regression analysis techniques to a body of data on actual disbursements for each fully disbursed loan in the WBXD database. The profiles are periodically updated to take into account the evolving pattern of disbursements observed for fully disbursed loans.

Future principal payments are generated by the WBXD system according to the repayment terms of each loan. Principal repayments (amortization) are based on the amount of the loan commitment. If the amortization schedule follows a set pattern (for example, equal semiannual payments), the WBXD system calculates repayments automatically using the loan commitment amount, the first and final payment dates, and the frequency of the payments. If future payments are irregular, the WBXD system requires a schedule.

Future interest payments are generated by the WBXD system according to the disbursed and outstanding balance of the loan at the beginning of the period. Using the interest rate specified in the loan contract, the first and final interest payment dates, and the frequency of payments, the WBXD system calculates the stream of future interest payments due. If interest payments are irregular, the WBXD system requires a schedule.

Future debt service payments are the sum of future principal and interest payments due on existing commitments, including the undisbursed portion. They do not include debt service payments that may become due as a result of new loans contracted in subsequent years, nor do they take into account the effect of any change to future debt service obligations resulting from actions such as prepayment or rescheduling or from cancellations that occurred after the most recent year-end data reported to the DRS.

Both projected disbursements and future debt service payments are converted into U.S. dollars using end-December 2015 exchange rates. Likewise, future interest payments on loans with a variable interest rate (for example, loans from commercial banks tied to the London Interbank Offered Rate [LIBOR]) are based on the interest rate prevailing at end-December 2015.

Treatment of arrears
The DRS collects information on arrears of both principal and interest. Principal in arrears is included in the amount of long-term external debt outstanding and is shown separately. Interest in arrears on long-term external debt and interest in arrears on the use of IMF credit are included as part of short-term external debt outstanding and are shown separately. Clearance of interest in arrears by repayment will be recorded as an interest payment in the relevant creditor category of the loan (or loans) on which the arrears were incurred, as a corresponding reduction in the level of short-term debt outstanding, and as a net reduction in interest arrears. Clearance of interest arrears through debt restructuring or forgiveness will be recorded as a reduction in the level of short-term debt outstanding and a net reduction in interest arrears. When interests are rescheduled, they will be capitalized: This change will be recorded as an increase in long-term debt outstanding equal to the amount of interest capitalized and the reduction in short-term debt outstanding noted previously.

External Debt and Its Components

This section describes the compilation of the major components of external debt included in the IDS tables and database and the relationship between them, as shown in figure A.1 on the next page. Information about general methods of compiling external debt data is discussed in the

Figure A.1. External Debt and Its Components

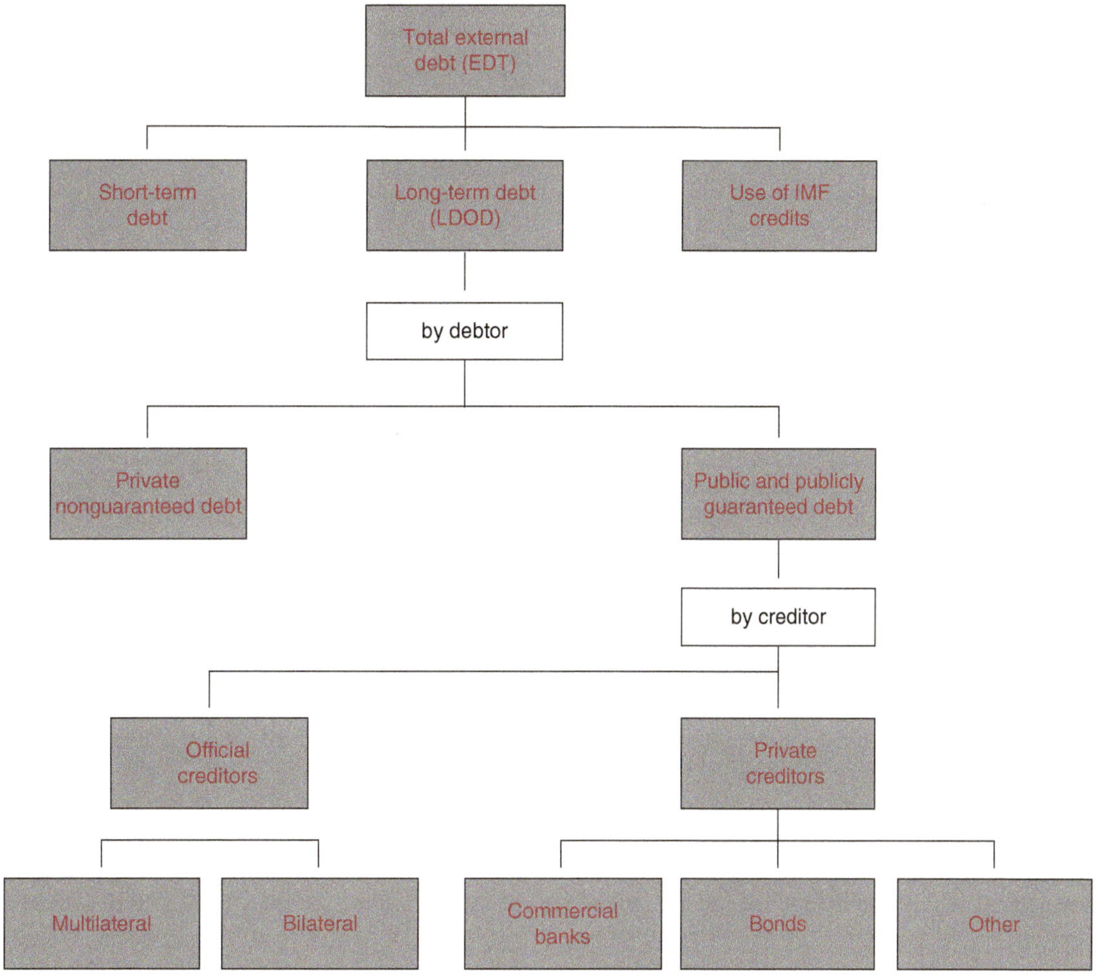

previous section titled "Methodology." For concise definitions, see the glossary.

Total external debt

Total external debt shown in the IDS is the sum of long-term external debt, short-term debt, and IMF credit. It represents the total debt owed to nonresident creditors and is repayable in both foreign and domestic currency.

Short-term debt

Short-term debt is defined as external debt with an original maturity of one year or less. The DRS requires debtor countries to report only on their long-term external debt. However, to gain a comprehensive picture of total external obligations, the World Bank encourages debtor countries to voluntarily provide information on their short-term external obligations.

By its nature, short-term external debt is difficult to monitor: Loan-by-loan registration is normally impractical, and monitoring systems typically rely on information requested periodically by the central bank from the banking sector. The World Bank regards the debtor country as the authoritative source of information on its short-term debt. Unless otherwise specified in the country tables, the data for short-term debt are derived from the data provided by the quarterly external debt statistics database (see QEDS). BIS data on international bank lending is the second source of the short-term debt. These data are reported on the basis of residual maturity, but an estimate of short-term external liabilities by original maturity can be derived by deducting from claims due in one year those that, 12 months earlier, had a maturity of between one and two years. However, not all commercial banks report to the BIS in a way that allows the full maturity distribution to be determined, and the BIS data include liabilities only to banks within the BIS reporting area. Consequently, the results should be interpreted with caution.

The flow of short-term debt may be derived from the change in claims (stock) data in the BIS quarterly series over consecutive periods, but valuation adjustments resulting from exchange rate movements will affect the calculations, as will prepayment and refinancing of long-term maturities falling due. When short-term external debt has been rescheduled, lags in reporting and differences in the treatment of the rescheduled external debt by debtors and creditors may result in double counting.

Interest in arrears on long-term external debt and interest in arrears on the use of IMF credit are added to short-term debt and are separately identified.

Use of IMF credit

Data related to the operations of the IMF are provided by the IMF Treasurer's Department. They are converted from special drawing rights (SDR) into dollars using end-of-period exchange rates for stocks and average-over-the-period exchange rates for flows. IMF trust fund operations under the Enhanced Structural Adjustment Facility, Extended Fund Facility, Poverty Reduction and Growth Facility, and Structural Adjustment Facility (Enhanced Structural Adjustment Facility in 1999) are presented together with all of the IMF's special facilities (buffer stock, supplemental reserve, compensatory and contingency facilities, oil facilities, and other facilities). SDR allocations are also included in this category. According to the BPM6, SDR allocations are recorded as the incurrence of a debt liability of the member receiving them (because of a requirement to repay the allocation in certain circumstances, and also because interest accrues). This debt item was introduced for the first time in IDS 2013 with historical data starting in 1999.

Long-term debt

Long-term debt has an original maturity of more than one year. It comprises the obligations of both public and private debtors. Private nonguaranteed debt comprises the external obligations of private debtors that are not guaranteed for repayment by a public entity in the debtor country.

Public and publicly guaranteed debt comprises the external obligations of public debtors and has two components: (a) public debt, which is borrowing by the national government or agency, by a political subdivision or agency, or by autonomous public bodies, and (b) publicly guaranteed debt, which is borrowing by a private agency that is guaranteed for repayment by a public entity.

Private nonguaranteed debt

The DRS reporting requirements were expanded in 1973 to include long-term private nonguaranteed debt. Data are reported annually on an aggregate basis and include, for the reporting year, the total amount of disbursed and outstanding debt; the amount of disbursements, principal repayments, and interest payments; the principal and interest rescheduled; and the projected principal and interest payments for future years. The aggregate data are usually reported in U.S. dollars, and no information on the underlying currency composition is given.

DRS reporting countries recognize the importance of monitoring borrowing by their private sector, particularly when it constitutes a significant portion of total external debt, but many countries acknowledge the difficulty of this process. Detailed data are available only when countries have registration requirements for private nonguaranteed debt in place, most commonly in connection with exchange controls. When formal registration of private nonguaranteed debt is not mandatory, compilers must rely on balance of payments data and financial surveys.

The data on private nonguaranteed debt in this publication is as reported or as estimated for countries where this type of external debt is known to be significant. The estimation of private nonguaranteed debt is based on the national data on quarterly external debt statistics (QEDS) or IMF data. Flows are derived from the change in stock over consecutive periods and are adjusted for the effects of exchange rate movements (assuming the currency composition mirrors that of public and publicly guaranteed debt) and for any known debt restructuring. Principal repayments are estimated on the basis of the average maturity observed for loans to private sector borrowers in countries reporting to the DRS and on the basis of the stock of debt outstanding. Interest payments are estimated on the basis of the stock of debt outstanding and interest rates prevailing in international capital markets.

Balance of payments data provide a useful guideline in the estimation process: private nonguaranteed external debt may be derived as a residual between net long-term external borrowing recorded in the balance of payments and net long-term public and publicly guaranteed external debt reported to the DRS.

Public and publicly guaranteed debt

Data related to public and publicly guaranteed debt are reported to the DRS on a loan-by-loan basis. The data provide annual information on the disbursed and outstanding balance and the undisbursed balance of each loan, the cumulative disbursements, the principal and interest paid and principal and interest restructured in the reporting year, and the stock of any outstanding payment's arrears of principal and interest. Detailed information on the terms and conditions of each loan is also reported. Public debt and publicly guaranteed debt are shown as a single line in this publication and then further disaggregated by creditor type and, in the case of private creditors, by type of credit instrument.

Official creditors

Official creditors include multilateral and bilateral lenders. In general, official creditors provide loans (and, in some cases, provide grants) to public bodies, although in some cases they may lend to other entities with a public guarantee.

Multilateral creditors are international financial institutions such as the World Bank, regional development banks, and other multilateral and intergovernmental agencies whose lending is administered on a multilateral basis. Funds administered by an international financial organization on behalf of a single donor government constitute bilateral loans (or grants). For lending by a number of multilateral creditors, the data presented in this publication are taken from the creditors' records. Such creditors include the African Development Bank, the Asian Development Bank, the IDB, IBRD, and IDA. (IBRD and IDA are institutions of the World Bank.)

Bilateral creditors are governments and their agencies, including central banks, aid agencies, official export credit agencies, and autonomous agencies such as the U.S. Department of Agriculture or the Federal Home Loan Bank. Member countries of the OECD Development Assistance Committee (DAC) and some other countries also report information on loans extended bilaterally or officially guaranteed to the Creditor Reporting System of the OECD.

Private creditors

Private creditors include commercial banks, bondholders, and other private creditors. This line includes only publicly guaranteed creditors. Nonguaranteed private creditors are shown separately.

Bonds include publicly issued or privately placed bonds.

Commercial bank loans are loans from private banks and other private financial institutions.

Credits of other private creditors include credits from manufacturers, exporters, and other suppliers of goods, plus bank credits covered by a guarantee of an export credit agency. This line is included in the online database but is not shown in the published tables. It can be obtained as the difference between (a) credits of total private creditors and (b) bonds and commercial bank loans.

Sources of the Macroeconomic Indicators

The macroeconomic data are prepared by The World Bank from a variety of sources. Data on Personal Transfers and Compensation of Employees are prepared by World Bank staff based on IMF balance of payments statistics. Data on foreign direct investments and current account balance are prepared by World Bank staff based on IMF balance of payments statistics and UNCTAD publication. Other macroeconomic data are from IMF balance of payments statistics.

Data on exports of goods, services, and primary income are based on countries' balance of payments statistics for the following countries:

Benin (2015)
Burkina Faso (2015)
Cambodia (2015)
Comoros (from 2013)
Côte d'Ivoire (from 2014)
Dominica (from 2014)
Grenada (from 2014)
Guinea (from 2014)
Guinea-Bissau (2014)
Iran, Islamic Rep. (from 2011)
Kenya (2015)
Madagascar (2014)
Mali (2015)
Niger (from 2014)
Samoa (2015)
Senegal (2015)
St. Lucia (from 2014)
St. Vincent, and the Grenadines (from 2014)
Togo (2015)
Tonga (from 2014)

Data on imports of goods, services, and primary income are based on countries' balance of payments statistics for the following countries:

Benin (2015)
Burkina Faso (2015)
Cambodia (2015)
Comoros (from 2013)
Côte d'Ivoire (from 2014)
Dominica (from 2014)
Grenada (from 2014)
Guinea (from 2014)
Guinea-Bissau (2014)
Iran, Islamic Rep. (from 2011)
Kenya (2015)
Madagascar (2014)
Mali (2015)
Niger (from 2014)
Samoa (2015)
Senegal (2015)
St. Lucia (from 2014)
St. Vincent, and the Grenadines (from 2014)
Togo (2015)
Tonga (from 2014)

Data on current account balance are based on countries' balance of payments statistics for the following countries:

Benin (2015)
Burkina Faso (2015)
Cambodia (2015)
Central African Republic (from 2005)
Chad (from 2005)
Comoros (from 2013)
Côte d'Ivoire (from 2014)
Dominica (from 2014)
Ethiopia (2015)
Grenada (from 2014)
Guinea (from 2014)
Guinea-Bissau (from 2014)
Iran, Islamic Rep. (from 2010)
Kenya (2015)
Mali (2015)
Mauritania (2007–2011)
Samoa (2015)
Senegal (2015)
St. Lucia (from 2014)
St. Vincent and the Grenadines (from 2014)
Togo (2015)
Tonga (from 2014)
Zimbabwe (from 2009)

Data on personal transfers and compensation of employees are based on countries' balance of payments statistics for the following countries:

Dominica (from 2014)
Gambia, The (from 2013)
Grenada (from 2014)
Iran (from 2011)
Mali (2014)
St. Lucia (from 2014)
St. Vincent and the Grenadines (from 2014)

Data on portfolio equity are based on countries' balance of payments statistics for the following countries:

Ghana (2011)
Guatemala (from 2008)
Honduras (from 2009)
India (2015)
Kenya (2015)
Kosovo (from 2014)
Mali (2014)
Mozambique (from 2010)
Niger (from 2013)
Nigeria (2015)
Papua New Guinea (2015)
Sierra Leone (from 2012)

Data on foreign direct investment are based on countries' balance of payments statistics for the following countries:

Burundi (from 2014)
Cambodia (2015)
Dominica (from 2014)
Grenada (from 2014)
India (2015)
Jamaica (2012-14)
Kazakhstan (2014)
Malaysia (from 2010)
Mongolia (2014)
Niger (2014)
Nigeria (2015)
Papua New Guinea (2015)
Samoa (2014)
St. Lucia (from 2014)
St. Vincent and the Grenadines (from 2014)
Solomon Islands (2014)
Tanzania (2014)
Uganda (2014)
Vietnam (2014)

Country Groups

Regional Groups

East Asia and Pacific

Cambodia (A)
China (P)
Fiji (A)
Indonesia (A)
Lao PDR (A)
Malaysia (E)
Mongolia (A)
Myanmar (E)
Papua New Guinea (A)
Philippines (A)
Samoa (A)
Solomon Islands (A)
Thailand (A)
Tonga (A)
Vanuatu (E)
Vietnam (A)

Europe and Central Asia

Albania (A)
Armenia (A)
Azerbaijan (A)
Belarus (A)
Bosnia and Herzegovina[a] (A)
Bulgaria (A)
Georgia (A)
Kazakhstan (A)
Kosovo (A)
Kyrgyz Republic (A)
Macedonia, FYR (A)
Moldova (A)
Montenegro (A)
Romania (A)
Russian Federation (P)
Serbia[a,b] (A)
Tajikistan (A)
Turkey (A)
Turkmenistan (E)
Ukraine (A)
Uzbekistan (A)

Latin America and the Caribbean

Argentina (A)
Belize (A)
Bolivia (A)
Brazil (A)
Colombia (A)
Costa Rica (A)
Dominica (A)
Dominican Republic (A)
Ecuador (A)
El Salvador (A)
Grenada (A)
Guatemala (A)
Guyana (A)
Haiti (A)
Honduras (A)
Jamaica (A)
Mexico (A)
Nicaragua (A)
Panama (A)
Paraguay (A)
Peru (A)
St. Lucia (A)
St. Vincent and the Grenadines (A)
Venezuela, RB (A)

Middle East and North Africa

Algeria (A)
Djibouti (A)
Egypt, Arab Rep. (A)
Iran, Islamic Rep. (A)
Jordan (A)
Lebanon (A)
Morocco (A)
Syrian Arab Republic (E)
Tunisia (A)
Yemen, Rep. (A)

South Asia

Afghanistan (A)
Bangladesh (A)
Bhutan (A)
India (A)
Maldives (A)
Nepal (A)
Pakistan (A)
Sri Lanka (A)

Sub-Saharan Africa

Angola (A)
Benin (A)
Botswana (A)
Burkina Faso (A)
Burundi (A)
Cabo Verde (A)
Cameroon (A)
Central African Republic (A)
Chad (A)
Comoros (A)
Congo, Dem. Rep. (P)
Congo, Rep. (A)
Côte d'Ivoire (A)
Eritrea (E)
Ethiopia (A)
Gabon (A)
Gambia, The (A)
Ghana (A)
Guinea (A)
Guinea-Bissau (A)
Kenya (A)
Lesotho (A)
Liberia (A)
Madagascar (A)
Malawi (A)
Mali (A)
Mauritania (A)
Mauritius (A)
Mozambique (A)
Niger (A)
Nigeria (E)
Rwanda (A)
São Tomé and Príncipe (A)
Senegal (A)
Sierra Leone (A)
Somalia (E)
South Africa (P)
Sudan[c] (P)
Swaziland (A)
Tanzania (A)
Togo (A)
Uganda (A)
Zambia (A)
Zimbabwe (A)

Note: Letters in parenthesis indicate DRS reporters' status: (A) as reported, (P) preliminary, and (E) estimated. The status "as reported" indicates that the country was fully current in its reporting under the DRS and that World Bank staff are satisfied that the reported data give an adequate and fair representation of the country's total public debt. "Preliminary" data are based on reported or collected information, but because of incompleteness or other reasons, an element of staff estimation is included. "Estimated" data indicate that countries are not current in their reporting and that a significant element of staff estimation has been necessary in producing the data tables.

a. For Bosnia and Herzegovina, total debt before 1999, excluding IBRD and IMF obligations and short-term debt, is included under Serbia.
b. Data prior to 2006 include Montenegro.
c. Data include South Sudan.

Income Groups

Low-income countries

Afghanistan
Benin
Burkina Faso
Burundi
Central African Republic
Chad
Comoros
Congo, Dem. Rep.
Eritrea
Ethiopia
Gambia, The
Guinea
Guinea-Bissau
Haiti
Liberia
Madagascar
Malawi
Mali
Mozambique
Nepal
Niger
Rwanda
Sierra Leone
Senegal
Somalia
Tanzania
Togo
Uganda
Zimbabwe

Middle-income countries

Albania
Algeria
Angola
Argentina
Armenia
Azerbaijan
Bangladesh
Belarus
Belize
Bhutan
Bolivia
Bosnia and Herzegovina
Botswana
Brazil
Bulgaria
Cabo Verde
Cambodia
Cameroon
China
Colombia
Congo, Rep.
Costa Rica
Côte d'Ivoire
Djibouti
Dominica
Dominican Republic
Ecuador
Egypt, Arab Rep.
El Salvador
Fiji
Gabon
Georgia
Ghana
Grenada
Guatemala
Guyana
Honduras
India
Indonesia
Iran, Islamic Rep.
Jamaica
Jordan
Kazakhstan
Kenya
Kosovo
Kyrgyz Republic
Lao PDR
Lebanon
Lesotho
Macedonia, FYR
Malaysia
Maldives
Mauritania
Mauritius
Mexico
Moldova
Mongolia
Montenegro
Morocco
Myanmar
Nicaragua
Nigeria
Pakistan
Panama
Papua New Guinea
Paraguay
Peru
Philippines
Romania
Russian Federation
Samoa
São Tomé and Príncipe
Serbia
Solomon Islands
South Africa
Sri Lanka
St. Lucia
St. Vincent and the Grenadines
Sudan
Swaziland
Syrian Arab Republic
Tajikistan
Thailand
Tonga
Tunisia
Turkey
Turkmenistan
Ukraine
Uzbekistan
Vanuatu
Venezuela, RB
Vietnam
Yemen, Rep.
Zambia

Note: Low-income countries are those with a GNI per capita of $1,025 or less in 2015. Middle-income countries are those with a GNI per capita of more than $1,026 but less than $12,475. Italicized countries are IDA-only countries as of July 1, 2016; IDA-only excludes blend and IBRD countries.

Glossary

Debt Reporting System (DRS)

Average terms of new commitments provide information on the interest rate, maturity, and grace period of new commitments on public and publicly guaranteed external debt contracted with public and private creditors. Averages are weighted by the amounts of the loans.

Bilateral official creditors are official agencies that make loans on behalf of one government to another government or to public (and, in some cases, private) borrowers in another country.

Bonds are debt instruments issued by public and publicly guaranteed or private debtors with durations of one year or longer. Bonds usually give the holder the unconditional right to fixed money income or contractually determined, variable money income.

Commercial banks are private banks that provide loans and other financial services.

Commitments of public and publicly guaranteed debt constitute the total amount of new long-term loans to public sector borrowers or borrowers with a public sector guarantee extended by official and private lenders and for which contracts were signed in the year specified.

Concessional debt conveys information about the borrower's receipt of aid from official lenders at concessional terms as defined by the DAC, that is, loans with an original grant element of 25 percent or more. Loans from major regional development banks—African Development Bank, Asian Development Bank, and the Inter-American Development Bank—and from the World Bank are classified as concessional according to each institution's classification and not according to the DAC definition, as was the practice in earlier reports.

Contractual obligations on outstanding long-term external debt are the anticipated debt service payments on long-term external debt contracted up to December 31 of the reporting year.

Currency composition of public and publicly guaranteed debt provides information on the share of loans outstanding and disbursed by currency of repayment. For major multilateral creditors, the currency composition of the relevant unit of account is also taken into account. The principal currencies in which the external debt of low- and middle-income countries is contracted (the euro, Japanese yen, U.S. dollar, SDR, and all other currencies) are separately identified. Beginning in 2001, debt denominated in the currencies of the members in the Euro Area is included under the euro rather than the national currencies that previously prevailed.

Current account balance shows the difference between the sum of exports and income receivable and the sum of imports and income payable (exports and imports refer to both goods and services, while income refers to both primary and secondary income).

Debt buyback is the repurchase by a debtor of its own debt, either at a discount price or at par value. In the event of a buyback of long-term debt, the face value of the debt bought back will be recorded as a decline in stock outstanding of long-term debt, and the cash amount received by creditors will be recorded as a principal repayment. For example, if a country buys back long-term external debt of face value B at a price P, then long-term external debt will decline by B, and principal repayment will increase by P. The difference between the price at which the debt was bought back and the face value is recorded as a debt stock write-off (the related transactions are not separately identified in the International Debt Statistics [IDS] publication but are available in the online database).

Debt forgiveness grants include both debts canceled by agreement between debtor and creditor and reductions in the net present value of official nonconcessional loans resulting from concessional rescheduling or refinancing. Data are recorded on a disbursement basis and include debt forgiveness from bilateral and multilateral creditors.

Debt outstanding and disbursed is the value at year's end of long-term external debt owed by public and publicly guaranteed debtors and private nonguaranteed debtors.

Debt restructurings are revisions to debt service obligations agreed on by creditors and debtors. Such agreements change the amount and timing of future principal and interest payments.

Debt service to exports is the ratio of the sum of principal repayments and interest paid on total long-term debt (public and publicly guaranteed debt and private nonguaranteed debt) to the value of exports of goods and services and receipts of primary income from abroad.

Debt stock-flow reconciliation shows the indicators that affect the change in debt stocks from one period to the next.

Disbursements are drawings during the year specified on loan commitments contracted by the borrower.

Exports of goods, services, and primary income constitute the total value of exports of goods and services, receipts of compensation of nonresident workers, and investment income from abroad.

External debt flows are debt-related transactions during the year specified. They include disbursements, principal repayments, and interest payments.

External debt stocks comprise public and publicly guaranteed long-term external debt, private nonguaranteed long-term external debt, use of IMF credit, and short-term external debt, including interest arrears on long-term debt. The relation between external debt stock and its components is illustrated on page 163 (figure A.1).

External debt stocks to exports is the ratio of outstanding external debt to the value of exports of goods and services and receipts of primary income from abroad.

External debt stocks to GNI is the ratio of outstanding external debt to gross national income.

Foreign direct investment refers to direct investment equity flows in the reporting economy. It is the sum of equity capital, reinvestment earnings, and other capital. Direct investment is a category of cross-border investment associated with a resident in one economy having control or a significant degree of influence on the management of an enterprise that is resident in another economy. Ownership of 10 percent or more of the ordinary shares or voting stock is the criterion for determining the existence of a direct investment relationship.

Grace period is the time between the date on which a loan is committed and the date on which the first principal payment is due. The information presented in International Debt Statistics is the average grace period on all public and publicly guaranteed debt committed during the specified period.

Grants are legally binding commitments that obligate a specific value of funds available for disbursement for which there is no payment requirement. They include debt forgiveness grants and grants from bilateral and multilateral agencies (such as the International Development Association).

Gross national income (GNI) is the sum of value added by all resident producers, plus any product taxes (less subsidies) not included in the valuation of output, plus net receipts of primary income compensation of employees and property income from abroad. Yearly average exchange rates are used to convert GNI from local currency to U.S. dollars.

Heavily Indebted Poor Country (HIPC) Initiative is a program of the World Bank and the International Monetary Fund (IMF) to provide debt relief to qualifying countries with unsustainable debt burdens.

Imports of goods, services, and primary income constitute the total value of goods and services imported and income payable to nonresidents. Interest arrears on long-term debt are interest payments due but not paid, shown on a cumulative basis.

Interest arrears are due and payable immediately and are therefore regarded as short-term obligations. Thus, an increase in interest arrears on long-term debt will be recorded as an increase in short-term debt. Interest in arrears on the use of IMF credit is also considered to be part of short-term external debt.

Interest payments are the amounts of interest paid in foreign currency, goods, or services in the year specified.

Interest rate is the interest rate applicable to a loan commitment as specified in the loan contract. The information presented in International Debt Statistics is the average interest on all public and publicly guaranteed debt committed during the specified period.

International Bank for Reconstruction and Development (IBRD) is a multilateral official creditor. IBRD is the nonconcessional lending arm of the World Bank Group.

International Development Association (IDA) is a multilateral official creditor. It is the concessional financing arm of the World Bank Group. IDA also provides grant financing to qualified borrowers.

IMF charges are the amounts of interest paid in foreign currency in the year specified for transactions with the IMF.

IMF purchases are the total drawings on the general resources account of the IMF during the year specified, excluding drawings in the reserve tranche.

IMF repurchases are the amounts of principal (amortization) paid in foreign currency in the year specified for transactions with the IMF.

International reserves constitute the sum of a country's monetary authority's holdings of special drawing rights, its reserve position in the IMF, its holdings of foreign exchange, and its holdings of gold (valued at year-end London prices).

Long-term external debt is debt that has an original or extended maturity of more than one year and that is owed to nonresidents by residents of an economy and is repayable in foreign currency, goods, or services.

Long-term private sector debt is long-term debt owed by the private sector, whether publicly guaranteed or not.

Long-term public sector debt is long-term external debt owed by the public sector.

Maturity is the date on which the final principal repayment on a loan is due. It is the sum of the grace and repayment periods. The information presented in International Debt Statistics is the average maturity on all public and publicly guaranteed debt committed during the specified period.

Multilateral Debt Relief Initiative (MDRI) is a program of the World Bank, the IMF, the Inter-American Development Bank, and the African Development Bank that provides additional debt relief to countries that have completed the HIPC process.

Multilateral official creditors are official agencies owned or governed by more than one country that provide loan financing. They include international financial institutions such as the World Bank, regional development banks, and other intergovernmental agencies.

Multilateral to external debt stocks is the ratio of the stock of debt owed to multilateral creditors to total external debt.

Net flows on external debt are disbursements on long-term external debt and IMF purchases minus principal repayments on long-term external debt and IMF repurchases. Up to 1984, this calculation included only long-term external debt and IMF flows. Since 1985, the calculation includes the change in stock of short-term debt (excluding interest arrears on long-term external debt).

Official creditors are governments or other bilateral public entities, such as export-import agencies, development agencies, and multilateral financial institutions, such as the World Bank and regional development banks.

Personal transfers and compensation of employees is the sum of personal transfers and compensation of employees. Personal transfers consist of all current transfers in cash or in kind made or received by resident households to or from nonresident households. Personal transfers thus include all current transfers between resident and nonresident individuals. Compensation of employees refers to the income of border, seasonal, and other short-term workers who are employed in an economy where they are not resident and of residents employed by nonresident entities.

Portfolio equity is the category of international investment that covers investment in equity securities. Equity securities include shares, stocks, participation, or similar documents (such as American Depositary Receipts) that usually denote ownership of equity.

Present value of debt outstanding is the nominal value of all future debt service obligations on existing debt discounted at prevailing market rates of interest. The interest rates used in this calculation are the Commercial Interest Reference Rates (CIRR) for each relevant currency compiled and published by the Organisation for Economic Co-operation and Development.

Primary income on FDI are payments of direct investment income (debit side), which consist of income on equity (dividends, branch profits, and reinvested earnings) and income on the intercompany debt (interest).

Principal arrears on long-term debt are principal repayments due but not paid on long-term external debt, shown on a cumulative basis.

Principal repayments are the amounts of principal (amortization) paid in foreign currency, goods, or services in the year specified with respect to long-term external debt.

Private creditors are bondholders, commercial banks, and other trade-related lenders.

Private nonguaranteed debt is debt owed by private sector borrowers to external creditors on loans that do not benefit from a public sector guarantee by the debtor country.

Public and publicly guaranteed debt outstanding and disbursed is the value of debt at year's end of public sector borrowers, or borrowers with a public sector guarantee, owed to official and private lenders.

Public and publicly guaranteed external debt comprises public debt (an external obligation of a public debtor, such as the national government or agency, a political subdivision or agency, or an autonomous public body) and publicly guaranteed external debt (an external obligation of a private debtor that is guaranteed for repayment by a public entity).

Public debt is an external obligation of a public debtor, including the national government, a political subdivision (or an agency of either), and autonomous public bodies.

Publicly guaranteed debt is an external obligation of a private debtor that is guaranteed for repayment by a public entity.

Reserves to external debt stocks is the ratio of international reserves to outstanding external debt.

Reserves to imports (months) is the ratio of international reserves to the value of imports of goods, services, and primary income in the year shown and is expressed in months:

$$\frac{\text{Reserves}}{\text{Imports/12}}$$

Short-term external debt has an original maturity of one year or less. Available data permit no distinction among public, publicly guaranteed, and private nonguaranteed short-term external debt.

Short-term to external debt stock ratio is the ratio of short-term external debt to total outstanding external debt.

Special Drawing Rights (SDRs) refer to an international reserve asset that was created by the IMF in 1969 to supplement its member countries' official reserves. The value of SDRs is based on a basket of four key international currencies: the U.S. dollar, the pound sterling, the Japanese yen, and the euro. In addition to playing a role as a supplementary reserve asset, SDRs serve as the unit of account for the IMF and some other international organizations.

Technical cooperation grants include (a) free-standing technical cooperation grants, which are intended to finance the transfer of technical and managerial skills or of technology for the purpose of building up general national capacity without reference to any specific investment projects, and (b) investment-related technical cooperation grants, which are aimed at strengthening the capacity to execute specific investment projects.

Total amount forgiven is the total amount of principal and interest due, principal and interest in arrears, and debt stock forgiven in the year specified.

Total amount rescheduled is the total amount of external debt rescheduled, including principal and interest due, principal and interest in arrears, charges, penalties, and debt stock in the year specified.

Total change in external debt stocks is the difference in the external debt stock between two consecutive years.

Use of IMF credit denotes members' drawings on the IMF other than amounts drawn against the country's reserve tranche position. Use of IMF credit includes purchases and drawings under Stand-By, Extended, Structural Adjustment, Enhanced Structural Adjustment, and Systemic Transformation Facility Arrangements as well as trust fund loans. SDR allocations are also included in this category.

Quarterly Debt Statistics

Central bank sector is identical to the definition of that subsector in the 2008 System of National Accounts (SNA). The central bank is the financial institution (or institutions) that exercises control over key aspects of the financial system. It carries out such activities as issuing currency, managing international reserves, transacting with the IMF, and providing credit to deposit-taking corporations.

Central government subsector consists of the institutional unit(s) of the central government plus those nonmarket Nonprofit institutions that are controlled by the central government. The political authority of the central government extends over the entire territory of the country.

Currency and deposits consist of notes and coins and deposits (both transferable and other). Notes and coins represent claims of a fixed nominal value usually on a central bank or government; commemorative coins are excluded. Deposits include all claims that are (a) on the central bank, deposit-taking corporations other than the central bank, and, in some cases, other institutional units; and (b) represented by evidence of deposit.

Debt liabilities owed by residents to residents of the same economy are classified as *domestic debt*, and debt liabilities owed by residents to nonresidents are classified as *external debt*. The definition of residence follows the current international standards (the System of National Accounts 2008 [2008 SNA] and the *Balance of Payments and International Investment Position Manual*, Sixth Edition [BPM6]).

Debt securities are negotiable financial instruments serving as evidence of a debt. The security normally specifies a schedule for interest payments and principal repayments. Examples of debt securities are bills, bonds, and debentures, including bonds that are convertible into shares, commercial paper, negotiable certificates of deposit, loans that have become negotiable from one holder to another, nonparticipating preferred stocks or shares, asset-backed securities and collateralized debt obligations, banker's acceptances, and similar instruments normally traded in the financial markets.

Deposit-taking corporations, except the central bank sector is identical with the corresponding subsector in the 2008 SNA. It includes commercial banks, institutions such as savings banks, savings and loan associations, credit unions or cooperatives, traveler's check companies, and specialized banks or other financial institutions if they take deposits or issue close substitutes for deposits Post office savings banks or other government-controlled savings banks are also included if they are institutional units separate from the government. Deposit-taking corporations that engage exclusively (or almost exclusively) with nonresidents, often called offshore banks or offshore banking units, are included in the deposit-taking corporations sector, but they may be excluded from the money-issuing sector because their liabilities are not included in broad money.

General government sector is identical with the definition of that sector in the 2008 SNA. The government units of a country consist of those authorities and their agencies that are units established by political processes and exercise legislative, judicial, and executive authority over other institutional units within a given territorial area. General government agencies that are residents of an economy include all departments, establishments, and bodies located in the economic territory of an economy's central, state, and local governments and all embassies, consulates, military establishments, and other entities, which are located elsewhere, of an economy's general government.

Insurance, pension, and standardized guarantee schemes comprise (a) nonlife insurance technical reserves, (b) life insurance and annuity entitlements, (c) pension entitlements, claims of pension funds on pension managers, and entitlements to nonpension funds, and (d) provisions for calls under standardized guarantees.

Loans include those financial assets created through the direct lending of funds by a creditor (lender) to a debtor (borrower) through an arrangement in which the lender either receives no security evidencing the transactions or receives a nonnegotiable document or instrument.

Other accounts receivable/payable covers items other than equity; currency and deposits; loans; insurance, pension, and standardized guarantee schemes; trade credit and advances; and SDRs.

Other sectors comprises other financial corporations (i.e., other than deposit-taking corporations), nonfinancial corporations, and households and nonprofit institutions serving households (NPISHs) subsectors.

SDR allocations are recorded as the incurrence of a debt liability of the member receiving them (because of a requirement to repay the allocation in certain circumstances, and also because of interest accrues).

Trade credit and advances consist of liabilities arising from the direct extension of credit by suppliers for transactions in goods and services, and advance payments by buyers for goods and services and for work in progress (or to be undertaken).